"The glory fades not and the grief is past."

Printed and bound by Antony Rowe Ltd, Eastbourne

OUR HEROES

Containing

THE PHOTOGRAPHS

WITH BIOGRAPHICAL NOTES

OF

Officers of Irish Regiments

AND OF

Irish Officers of British Regiments

WHO HAVE FALLEN IN ACTION,
OR
WHO HAVE BEEN MENTIONED FOR
DISTINGUISHED CONDUCT,
FROM AUGUST, 1914, TO JULY, 1916.

Together with a brief Military History of the chief events of the War in which Irish Regiments were engaged.

Originally printed and published in 1916

This Edition Reprinted by
LONDON STAMP EXCHANGE LTD
5 BUCKINGHAM STREET . STRAND
LONDON . WC2N 6BS
Telephone 01 - 839 4684
The Military Book & Medal Specialist
ISBN 0948130 11 3

THE RETREAT FROM MONS.

THE FIRST PERIOD OF THE GREAT WAR.

INTRODUCTORY REMARKS.

The time has not yet come when it will be possible to write a complete or even a reasonably accurate history of the Great War, and the purpose of the present sketch is merely to trace in a general way the progress of the operations in which our Irish Regiments took so glorious a part. Roughly speaking, and without claiming any gifts of prophecy, the war divides itself into two periods; the first, with which alone we are dealing now, the great defensive in which, with inferior numbers and inferior equipment, the Allies bore the brunt and broke the force of the German attack. In the second, which was initiated on 1st July 1916, the Allies after two years of ceaseless organization of man-power and munition-power have definitely gained the upper hand and wrested from the enemy the power to attack. To that great offensive, the progress and events of which are still on the lap of the gods, and to its end in victory we hope to devote a second volume of "Our Heroes."

The causes of the Great War are by no means obscure as we view them in the light of the events of the war. We see a great military Power in Central Europe, the greatest the world had ever seen, organised entirely on a military basis, constantly increasing and perfecting its military forces, and at the same time building up a mighty fleet. We see that Power constantly increasing in wealth from their industrial organisation, and at the same time full of a growing impatience with what they regard as undue restrictions on their expansion imposed by nations whom they regarded as inferior to and far less deserving than themselves. We see the other nations of Europe, alarmed by preparations the object of which, viz. world-power, neither the Kaiser nor the Philosophers and Professors who spoke for the ruling class in Germany, took the trouble to conceal, or even to veil in euphemistic language, gradually drawing together in a defensive alliance. Looking back now we can see that there could be only one end to such a situation. Germany must strike or all her vast preparation will go for naught.

An excuse was easily found. On the 29th of June, in Sarajevo, in Bosnia, the Crown Prince and Princess of Austria had been barbarously murdered by a Bosnian fanatic. A month later Austria presented certain drastic demands to the Servian Government with regard partly to reparation for the murder of the Archduke, and partly with regard to safeguards for the future. On the advice of Russia, the Servian Government accepted all the Austrian demands in full with the exception of two, which involved obviously a violation of the national independence of Servia, but offering to refer the two rejected demands to the Hague Convention. The Austrian Ambassador immediately announced that nothing short of a complete acceptance would satisfy his Government, and the same evening demanded his passport and left Belgrade.

Then, while the drums for Armageddon were beating in almost every country in Europe, began that six days of intense and feverish diplomatic activity on the part of the British Cabinet. With an almost pathetic belief in the good faith and the honest intentions of Germany, they exhausted all the resources of diplomacy. It was, of course, all in vain. Germany had determined that the day had come, and the most she would give Sir Edward Grey was a vague and insulting promise that if England stood aside the independence of Belgium would be respected *after the war*, and that France would be let off with the loss of all her colonies.

Events now moved fast. On August 1st Germany declared war on Russia, a declaration which involved automatically a state of war with France. On August 4th the Germans demanded a free passage through Belgium, which was categorically refused. On the same day German troops crossed the frontier at Gemminict, and immediately the British Ambassador at Berlin was instructed to demand his passport and return home. The great war had begun.

On the night of the 7th August the first transports conveying the British Expeditionary Force sailed. The Aldershot Division was the first to go, and within ten days the whole Force, amounting to 150,000 or 160 000 men, had been landed in France. This was the amount of military aid which it was understood had been promised France in case of an unprovoked attack by Germany. Of course, it very soon became evident that this Force was entirely inadequate and that the British Empire would have to throw into the struggle every ounce of its resources both in men and in money and in the production of the munitions of war. But it was not until much later that the nation and the Cabinet came to realise this.

In the first Expeditionary Force the following Irish Regiments were included:—

1st Irish Guards.
1st Royal Irish Fusiliers.
2nd Royal Dublin Fusiliers.
2nd Royal Munster Fusiliers.
2nd Inniskilling Fusiliers.
2nd Connaught Rangers.
2nd Royal Irish Regiment.
2nd Royal Irish Rifles.
5th (Royal Irish) Lancers.
4th (Royal Irish) Dragoon Guards.
6th (Inniskilling) Dragoons.
The North Irish Horse.
The South Irish Horse.

The British Force was immediately hurried to the Belgian Frontier, and on Saturday, August 22nd, was disposed on a line from Condé on the west, through the town of Mons, to Binche on the east. Here they were attacked on the Sunday afternoon by General von Kluck with an overwhelming superiority of force. Not only that, but it soon became apparent that both their flanks were unprotected. The British were on the extreme left of the Allied line, and of course their left was at all times liable to be outflanked by a superior force, but in addition, Sir John French was informed at 5 o'clock on Sunday that the French on his right had been defeated at Charleroi, that the Germans had crossed the Sambre, and that the 5th French Army was falling back. To prevent a great disaster there was evidently nothing for it but an immediate retreat. How the retreat was conducted cannot be described better than in the official despatch of Sir John French:—

"In view of the possibility of my being driven from the Mons position, I had previously ordered a position in rear to be reconnoitred. This position rested on the fortress of Maubeuge on the right and extended west to Jenlain, south-east of Valenciennes, on the left. The position was reported difficult to hold, because standing crops and buildings made the siting of trenches very difficult and limited the field of fire in many important localities. It nevertheless afforded a few good artillery positions.

"When the news of the retirement of the French and the heavy German threatening on my front reached me, I endeavoured to confirm it by aeroplane reconnaissance; and as a result of this I determined to effect a retirement to the Maubeuge position at daybreak on the 24th.

"A certain amount of fighting continued along the whole line throughout the night, and at daybreak on the 24th the 2nd Division from the neighbourhood of Harmignies made a powerful demonstration as if to retake Binche. This was supported by the artillery of both the 1st and 2nd Divisions, whilst the 1st Division took up a supporting position in the neighbourhood of Peissant. Under cover of this demonstration the Second Corps retired on the line Dour-Quarouble-Frameries. The 3rd Division on the right of the Corps suffered considerable loss in this operation from the enemy, who had retaken Mons.

"The Second Corps halted on this line, where they partially entrenched themselves, enabling Sir Douglas Haigh with the First Corps gradually to withdraw to the new position; and he effected this without much further loss, reaching the line Bavai-Maubeuge about 7 p.m. Towards midday the enemy appeared to be directing his principal effort against our left.

"I had previously ordered General Allenby with the Cavalry to act vigorously in advance of my left front and endeavour to take the pressure off.

"About 7.30 a.m. General Allenby received a message from Sir Charles Fergusson, commanding 5th Division, saying that he was very hard pressed and in urgent need of support. On receipt of this message General Allenby drew in the Cavalry and endeavoured to bring direct support to the 5th Division.

"During the course of this operation General De Lisle, of the 2nd Cavalry Brigade, thought he saw a good opportunity to paralyse the further advance of the enemy's infantry by making a mounted attack on his flank. He formed up and advanced for this purpose, but was held up by wire about 500 yards from his objective, and the 9th Lancers and 18th Hussars suffered severely in the retirement of the Brigade.

"The 19th Infantry Brigade, which had been guarding the Line of Communications, was brought up by rail to Valenciennes on the 22nd and 23rd. On the morning of the 24th they were moved out to a position south of Quarouble to support the left flank of the Second Corps.

"With the assistance of the Cavalry Sir Horace Smith-Dorrien was enabled to effect his retreat to a new position; although, having

FIELD-MARSHAL THE RIGHT HON. EARL ROBERTS OF KANDAHAR, V.C., K.G., K.P., G.C.B., O.M., G.C.S.I., G.C.I.E., COLONEL OF THE IRISH GUARDS.

two corps of the enemy on his front and one threatening his flank, he suffered great losses in doing so.

"At nightfall the position was occupied by the Second Corps to the west of Bavai, the First Corps to the right. The right was protected by the fortress of Maubeuge, the left by the 19th Brigade in position between Jenlain and Bry, and the Cavalry on the outer flank.

"The French were still retiring, and I had no support except such as was afforded by the Fortress of Maubeuge; and the determined attempts of the enemy to get round my left flank assured me that it was his intention to hem me against that place and surround me. I felt that not a moment must be lost in retiring to another position.

"I had every reason to believe that the enemy's forces were somewhat exhausted, and I knew that they had suffered heavy losses. I hoped, therefore, that his pursuit would not be too vigorous to prevent me effecting my object.

"The operation, however, was full of danger and difficulty, not only owing to the very superior force in my front, but also to the exhaustion of the troops.

"The retirement was recommenced in the early morning of the 25th to a position in the neighbourhood of Le Cateau, and rearguards were ordered to be clear of the Maubeuge-Bavia-Eth Road by 5.30 a.m.

"Two Cavalry Brigades, with the Divisional Cavalry of the Second Corps, covered the movement of the Second Corps. The remainder of the Cavalry Division, with the 19th Brigade, the whole under the command of General Allenby, covered the west flank.

"The 4th Division commenced its detrainment at Le Cateau on Sunday, the 23rd, and by the morning of the 25th eleven battalions and a Brigade of Artillery with Divisional Staff were available for service.

"I ordered General Snow to move out to take up a position with his right south of Solesmes, his left resting on the Cambrai-Le Cateau Road south of La Chaprie. In this position the Division rendered great help to the effective retirement of the Second and First Corps to the new position.

"Although the troops had been ordered to occupy the Cambrai-Le Cateau-Landrecies position, and the ground had, during the 25th, been partially prepared and entrenched, I had grave doubts—owing to the information I received as to the accumulating strength of the enemy against me—as to the wisdom of standing there to fight.

"Having regard to the continued retirement of the French on my right, my exposed left flank, the tendency of the enemy's western corps (II.) to envelop me, and, more than all, the exhausted condition of the troops, I determined to make a great effort to continue the retreat till I could put some substantial obstacle, such as the Somme or the Oise, between my troops and the enemy, and afford the former some opportunity of rest and reorganisation. Orders were, therefore, sent to the Corps Commanders to continue their retreat as soon as they possibly could towards the general line Vermand-St. Quentin-Ribemont.

"The cavalry, under General Allenby, were ordered to cover the retirement.

"Throughout the 25th and far into the evening, the First Corps continued its march on Landrecies, following the road along the eastern border of the Forêt de Mormal, and arrived at Landrecies about 10 o'clock. I had intended that the Corps should come further west so as to fill up the gap between Le Cateau and Landrecies, but the men were exhausted and could not get further in without rest.

"The enemy, however, would not allow them this rest, and about 9.30 p.m. a report was received that the 4th Guards Brigade in Landrecies was heavily attacked by troops of the 9th German Army Corps, who were coming through the forest on the north of the town. This brigade fought most gallantly, and caused the enemy to suffer tremendous loss in issuing from the forest into the narrow streets of the town. This loss has been estimated from reliable sources at from 700 to 1,000. At the same time information reached me from Sir Douglas Haig that his 1st Division was also heavily engaged south and east of Maroilles. I sent urgent messages to the Commander of the two French Reserve Divisions on my right to come up to the assistance of the First Corps, which they eventually did. Partly owing to this assistance, but mainly to the skilful manner in which Sir Douglas Haig extricated his Corps from an exceptionally difficult position in the darkness of the night, they were able at dawn to resume their march south towards Wassigny on Guise.

"By about 6 p.m. the Second Corps had got into position with their right on Le Cateau, their left in the neighbourhood of Caudry, and the line of defence was continued thence by the 4th Division towards Seranvillers, the left being thrown back.

"During the fighting on the 24th and 25th the Cavalry became a good deal scattered, but by the early morning of the 26th General Allenby had succeeded in concentrating two brigades to the south of Cambrai.

"The 4th Division was placed under the orders of the General Officer Commanding the Second Army Corps.

"On the 24th the French Cavalry Corps, consisting of three divisions, under General Sordêt, had been in billets north of Avesnes. On my way back from Bavai, which was my 'Poste de Commandement' during the fighting of the 23rd and 24th, I visited General Sordêt, and earnestly requested his co-operation and support. He promised to obtain sanction from his Army Commander to act on my left flank, but said that his horses were too tired to move before the next day. Although he rendered me valuable assistance later on in the course of the retirement, he was unable for the reasons given to afford me any support on the most critical day of all, viz., the 26th.

"At daybreak it became apparent that the enemy was throwing the bulk of his strength against the left of the position occupied by the Second Corps and the 4th Division.

"At this time the guns of four German Army Corps were in position against them, and Sir Horace Smith-Dorrien reported to me that he judged it impossible to continue his retirement at daybreak (as ordered) in face of such an attack.

"I sent him orders to use his utmost endeavours to break off the action and retire at the earliest possible moment, as it was impossible for me to send him any support, the First Corps being at the moment incapable of movement.

"The French Cavalry Corps, under General Sordêt, was coming up on our left rear early in the morning, and I sent an urgent message to him to do his utmost to come up and support the retirement of my left flank; but owing to the fatigue of his horses he found himself unable to intervene in any way.

"There had been no time to entrench the position properly, but the troops showed a magnificent front to the terrible fire which confronted them.

"The Artillery, although outmatched by at least four to one, made a splendid fight, and inflicted heavy losses on their opponents.

"At length it became apparent that, if complete annihilation was to be avoided, a retirement must be attempted; and the order was given to commence it about 3.30 p.m. The movement was covered with the most devoted intrepidity and determination by the Artillery, which had itself suffered heavily, and the fine work done by the Cavalry in the further retreat from the position assisted materially in the final completion of this most difficult and dangerous operation.

"Fortunately the enemy had himself suffered too heavily to engage in an energetic pursuit.

"I cannot close the brief account of this glorious stand of the British troops without putting on record my deep appreciation of the valuable services rendered by General Sir Horace Smith-Dorrien.

"I say without hesitation that the saving of the left wing of the Army under my command on the morning of the 26th August could never have been accomplished unless a commander of rare and unusual coolness, intrepidity, and determination had been present to personally conduct the operation.

"The retreat was continued far into the night of the 26th and through the 27th and 28th, on which date the troops halted on the line Noyon-Chauny-La Fère, having then thrown off the weight of the enemy's pursuit.

"The Cavalry, under General Allenby, were ordered to cover the retirement."

Of course it should be noted that a General's despatch, although the best and only reliable description of military operations which can be given until the end of the war, is necessarily incomplete. It narrates events entirely from the military point of view, and gives us little of the human interest in that terrible four days of retreat. For glimpses of the actual conditions of this heroic fight, in which a small army, exhausted with fighting and marching, without sleep, without food, turning desperately at bay from time to time, as at Landrecies, Le Cateau, Etreux, and taking a heavy toll of the pursuing Germans, and finally baffling every attempt of the enemy to get anything like a definite decision, we must turn to some of the accounts written by officers and men describing what they had seen.

"I got my baptism of fire on Sunday night, August 23rd," writes a private in the 1st Battalion of the Irish Guards. "I will never forget that day. The fighting was awful. You would have thought the earth was going to open its mouth and swallow us. When we got to Mons we thought we were going to get tea. We got our fill, not of tea, but of shells and bullets. We acted as advance party for the Guards Brigade. I understand that we were originally intended only to act as supports, with the Coldstreams as the advance party, but as the Irish Guards had practically no battle honours on their colours, our C.O. got the C.O. of the Coldstreams to reverse things so that we became the advance section. We were fighting on into the next morning, when we got the order to retire. . . . ."

"The Royal Irish Regiment had been surprised and fearfully cut up," writes a private of the Gordons, "and so, too, had the Middlesex, and it was found impossible for our B and C companies to reinforce them. We (D company) were 1½ miles away, and were ordered to proceed to No. 2 and relieve the Royal Irish as much as possible. We crept from our trenches and crossed to the other side of the road, where we had the benefit of a ditch and the road camber as cover. We made most excellent progress until 150 yards from No. 1. At that distance there was a small white house, flush with the road standing in a clearance. Our young sub. was leading and safely crossed the front of the house. Immediately the Germans opened a hellish cyclone of shrapnel at the house. They could not see us, but I guess they knew the reason why troops would or might pass that house. However, we were to relieve the R.I.'s, and, astounding as it may seem, we passed that house and I was the only one to be hit. Even yet I am amazed at our luck.

"By this time dusk had set in, four villages were on fire, and the Germans had been, and were, shelling the hospitals. We managed to get into the R.I.'s trench and beat off a very faint-hearted Uhlan attack on us. About 9 p.m. came our orders to retire. What a pitiful handful we were against that host, and yet we held the flower of the German Army at bay all day! We picked up a dead officer of ours and retreated all night. At 2 p.m. we halted, and at 4 a.m. (Monday) we started retiring again."

The gallant stand of the Munsters, who were cut off and surrounded, is described by Capt. Leboeuf, of the French Army.

"I was close to the Munster Fusiliers," he says, "when they got cut up. They had been falling back steadily when orders came that they were to hold their ground to cover the retreat of the main army. The colonel in command simply nodded his head when he got the orders, and he passed them on to the men as though he were giving orders to a waiter at a hotel. The men received the orders in the same unconcerned way, and started to make trenches for themselves. While some were digging, others were firing at the enemy. They could see the Germans closing in all round, and knew that there was no retreat. What they didn't know was that a dispatch rider with orders to continue the retreat, now that the main army was safe, had been shot down. They never showed the slightest sign of worry, but kept fighting on till they had exhausted their ammunition. For a time they kept going with the remains of the pouches of the wounded, but soon that ceased, and then the end came.

"It was a glorious end, and the Germans were forced to pay a tribute to the fine fight the men had made."

Captain Jervis, of the Munsters, thus describes the death of Major Charrier:

"The regiment was left behind, and for several hours fell back fighting, under the personal direction of Major Charrier, who, although well aware of the impossible nature of his task, issued his orders and made all arrangements with all the precision which made him so well known in Aldershot. Eventually the Germans worked round to the rear and cut us off completely, the key of our position being a loopholed house. The major personally led two charges in a magnificent attempt to capture this. In the first of these he was wounded, but insisted upon still retaining command and cheering us on. Shortly afterwards he was wounded again, but even this did not keep him from what he considered his duty. He heroically continued the direction of the action till after sunset, six hours' intermittent fighting. Mr. Gower came up to make a report to him, and found him near one of our guns which had been put out of action. In reply to Mr. Gower he said: 'All right, we will line the hedge; follow me!' Still leading and setting an example to all, he was shot a third time, and mortally. He fell in the road. Yesterday we sent out a party of our men to collect and bury the dead, and they found Paul Charrier lying as he had fallen, head towards the enemy."

How the Munsters came to be cut off is told by Mrs. Victor Rickard, the widow of Colonel Rickard, in her little book, "The Story of the Munsters":—

"To the meadow near the bridge where the Munsters were collected an orderly carrying a dispatch came up at about three o'clock in the afternoon. The time of the dispatch was not marked upon the message, which was to order the Munsters to retire 'at once.' The orderly who carried the message had, he said, been chased by the enemy, and after lying hidden for a time under the nearest cover, believed that it was not possible for him to bring the message through to Major Charrier. Upon this incident the tragedy of the whole day turned. Time had been lost, time too precious ever to regain; the exclusive supremacy is nearly always a question of minutes."

"There was terrible fighting at Landrecies," said Private Quigley. "The Coldstreams bore the brunt of that; we acted as supports. A lot of us were in our bare feet at the time the Germans attacked us. . . ."

"Fierce fighting," wrote Private Mullaney. "We were caught like rats in a trap . . . we didn't know which side to turn, as we seemed to be surrounded on all sides by Germans. I don't know how we got out of it alive. . . . We got equipped the best way we could, and set to barricading the streets outside. We pulled out carts, doors, shutters, and dug the pavements out to block the thoroughfare. We set two Maxims in position, and let the Germans come up in their masses to within twenty yards of us. Then we let them have it right and left, until they could not advance on account of the heaps of their own dead."

In Compiegne the German cavalry got an opportunity to charge the Irish Guards, who were holding the edge of a wood. A Guardsman who was present describes the fight as follows:—

"When the shock came, it seemed terrific, for the Irishmen didn't recoil in the least, but flung themselves right across the path of the German horsemen. Those far off could hear the crack of the rifles and see the German horses impaled on the bayonets of the front rank of the Guardsmen; then the whole force of infantry and cavalry were mixed up in one confused heap, like so many pieces from a jigsaw puzzle. Shells from the British and German batteries kept dropping close to the tangled mass of fighting men, and then the German horsemen got clear and took to flight as fast as their horses could carry them. Some had no horses, and they were bayoneted where they stood."

"The Irish Guards at ——, well! I would never have believed that discipline would have enabled one man to do what this C.O. (Colonel Morris) did. Got the men up from lining one of the sides in the woods—cursed them into heaps for firing high and wasting ammunition, and then got them down to it again, and all in a thick wood where one could only see thirty to forty yards straight; with Germans, from the sound of their firearms and bugles, only 100 to 150 yards away, and an absolute hail of bullets. Gad! It was a fine performance, and they gave the Germans hell, and then some!"

FIELD MARSHAL VISCOUNT FRENCH, G.C.B., G.C.V.O., K.C.M.G.

THE BATTLE OF THE MARNE.

"On Saturday, September 5th, I met the French Commander-in-Chief at his request, and he informed me of his intention to take the offensive forthwith, as he considered conditions were very favourable to success.

"General Joffre announced to me his intention of wheeling up the left flank of the 6th Army, pivoting on the Marne and directing it to move on the Ourcq; cross and attack the flank of the 1st German Army, which was then moving in a south-easterly direction east of that river.

"He requested me to effect a change of front to my right—my left resting on the Marne and my right on the 5th Army—to fill the gap between that army and the 6th. I was then to advance against the enemy in my front and join in the general offensive movement.

"These combined movements practically commenced on Sunday, September 6th, at sunrise; and on that day it may be said that a great battle opened on a front extending from Ermenonville, which was just in front of the left flank of the 6th French Army, through Lizy on the Marne, Mauperthuis, which was about the British centre, Courtecon, which was the left of the 5th French Army, to Esternay and Charleville, the left of the 9th Army under General Foch, and so along the front of the 9th, 4th, and 3rd French Armies to a point north of the fortress of Verdun.

"This battle, in so far as the 6th French Army, the British Army, the 5th French Army and the 9th French Army were concerned, may be said to have concluded on the evening of September 10th, by which time the Germans had been driven back to the line Soissons-Reims, with a loss of thousands of prisoners, many guns, and enormous masses of transport.

"About the 3rd September the enemy appears to have changed his plans and to have determined to stop his advance South direct upon Paris; for on the 4th September air reconnaissances showed that his main columns were moving in a south-easterly direction generally east of a line drawn through Nanteuil and Lizy on the Ourcq.

"I should conceive it to have been about noon on the 6th September, after the British Forces had changed their front to the right and occupied the line Jouy-Le Chatel-Faremoutiers-Villeneuve Le Comte, and the advance of the 6th French Army north of the Marne towards the Ourcq became apparent, that the enemy realised the powerful threat that was being made against the flank of his columns moving south-east and began the great retreat which opened the battle above referred to.

"On the 7th September both the 5th and 6th French Armies were heavily engaged on our flank. The 2nd and 4th Reserve German Corps on the Ourcq vigorously opposed the advance of the French towards that river, but did not prevent the 6th Army from gaining some headway, the Germans themselves suffering serious losses. The French 5th Army threw the enemy back to the line of the Petit Morin river after inflicting severe losses upon them, especially about Montceaux, which was carried at the point of the bayonet.

"The enemy retreated before our advance, covered by his 2nd and 9th and Guard Cavalry Divisions, which suffered severely.

"Our Cavalry acted with great vigour, especially General De Lisle's Brigade with the 9th Lancers and 18th Hussars.

"On the 8th September the enemy continued his retreat northward, and our Army was successfully engaged during the day with strong rearguards of all arms on the Petit Morin River, thereby materially assisting the progress of the French Armies on our right and left, against whom the enemy was making his greatest efforts. On both sides the enemy was thrown back with very heavy loss. The First Army Corps encountered stubborn resistance at La Trétoire (north of Rebais). The enemy occupied a strong position with infantry and guns on the northern bank of the Petit Morin River; they were dislodged with considerable loss. Several machine guns and many prisoners were captured, and upwards of two hundred German dead were left on the ground

"The forcing of the Petit Morin at this point was much assisted by the Cavalry and the 1st Division, which crossed higher up the stream.

"On the 9th September the First and Second Army Corps forced the passage of the Marne and advanced some miles to the north of it. The Third Corps encountered considerable opposition, as the bridge at La Ferté was destroyed and the enemy held the town on the opposite bank in some strength, and thence persistently obstructed the construction of a bridge; so the passage was not effected until after nightfall.

"During the day's pursuit the enemy suffered heavy loss in killed and wounded, some hundreds of prisoners fell into our hands, and a battery of eight machine guns was captured by the 2nd Division.

"The advance was resumed at daybreak on the 10th up to the line of the Ourcq, opposed by strong rearguards of all arms. The 1st and 2nd Corps, assisted by the Cavalry Division on the right, the 3rd and 5th Cavalry Brigades on the left, drove the enemy northwards. Thirteen guns, seven machine guns, about 2,000 prisoners, and quantities of transport fell into our hands. The enemy left many dead on the field. On this day the French 5th and 6th Armies had little opposition.

"As the 1st and 2nd German Armies were now in full retreat, this evening marks the end of the battle which practically commenced on the morning of the 6th instant; and it is at this point in the operations that I am concluding the present dispatch.

"Although I deeply regret to have had to report heavy losses in killed and wounded throughout these operations, I do not think they have been excessive in view of the magnitude of the great fight, the outlines of which I have only been able very briefly to describe, and the demoralisation and loss in killed and wounded which are known to have been caused to the enemy by the vigour and severity of the pursuit.

"In concluding this dispatch I must call your Lordship's special attention to the fact that from Sunday, August 23rd, up to the present date (September 17th), from Mons back almost to the Seine, and from the Seine to the Aisne, the Army under my command has been ceaselessly engaged without one single day's halt or rest of any kind.

"In this manner the Battle of the Aisne commenced.

"The Aisne Valley runs generally East and West, and consists of a flat-bottomed depression of width varying from half a mile to two miles, down which the river follows a winding course to the West at some points near the southern slopes of the valley and at others near the northern. The high ground both on the north and south of the river is approximately 400 feet above the bottom of the valley and is very similar in character, as are both slopes of the valley itself, which are broken into numerous rounded spurs and re-entrants. The most prominent of the former are the Chivre spur on the right bank and Sermoise spur on the left. Near the latter place the general plateau on the south is divided by a subsidiary valley of much the same character, down which the small River Vesle flows to the main stream near Sermoise. The slopes of the plateau overlooking the Aisne on the north and south are of varying steepness, and are covered with numerous patches of wood, which also stretch upwards and backwards over the edge on to the top of the high ground. There are several villages and small towns dotted about in the valley itself and along its sides, the chief of which is the town of Soissons.

"The Aisne is a sluggish stream of some 170 feet in breadth, but, being 15 feet deep in the centre, it is unfordable. Between Soissons on the west and Villers on the east (the part of the river attacked and secured by the British Forces) there are eleven road bridges across it. On the north bank a narrow-gauge railway runs from Soissons to Vailly, where it crosses the river and continues eastward along the south bank. From Soissons to Sermoise a double line of railway runs along the south

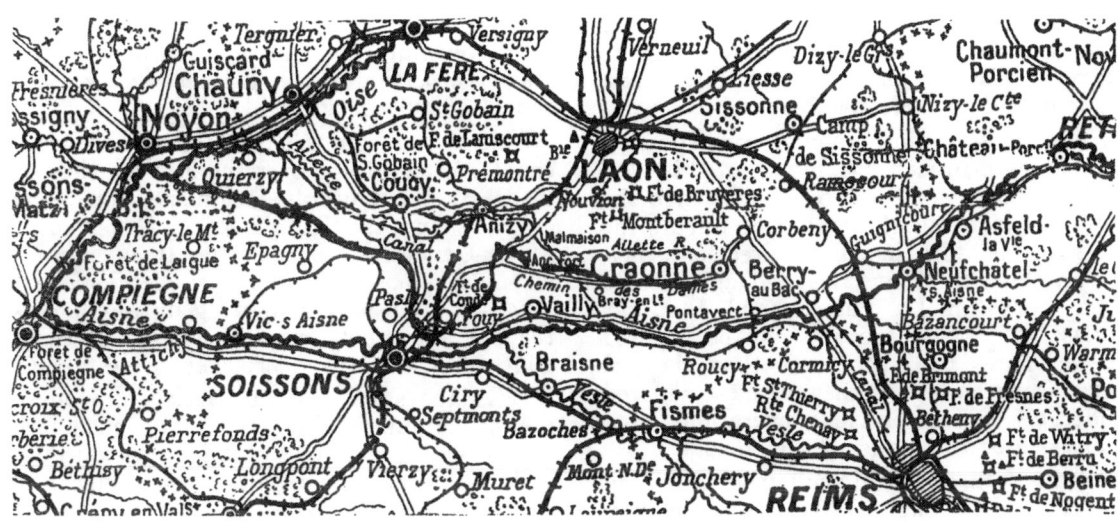

bank, turning at the latter place up the Vesle Valley towards Bazoches.

"The position held by the enemy is a very strong one, either for a delaying action or for a defensive battle. One of its chief military characteristics is that from the high ground on neither side can the top of the plateau on the other side be seen except for small stretches. This is chiefly due to the woods on the edges of the slopes. Another important point is that all the bridges are under either direct or high-angle artillery fire.

"The tract of country above described, which lies north of the Aisne, is well adapted to concealment, and was so skilfully turned to account by the enemy as to render it impossible to judge the real nature of his opposition to our passage of the river, or to accurately gauge his strength; but I have every reason to conclude that strong rearguards of at least three army corps were holding the passages on the early morning of the 13th."

It was on these slopes of the plateau north of the Aisne that the Germans took up their first entrenched position, and it may be said that what is known as the Battle of the Aisne was our first experience of the trench warfare, which from that onward became universal in all the sectors of the Western front. The features of the Aisne operations was the seizure by the First Army Corps, under Sir Douglas Haig, of the advanced position extending from Chemin-de-Dames on the right through Chivy, to Le Cour de Soupir, with the 1st Cavalry Brigade extending to the Chavonne-Soissons road. These positions were successfully held through the whole of the three weeks' fighting, and it was this alone which enabled us to successfully hold our positions on the north bank of the river.

OPERATIONS IN ARTOIS, AND PICARDY, ARMENTIERES—YPRES.

Early in October, for many reasons, it was decided that the British Expeditionary Force should be relieved by a French force on the Aisne and be transferred to a sector nearer their base of supplies. The British force were now on the left flank of the French, while the Belgian Army, on the left flank of the British, were in no condition, after the hard fighting it had undergone, to oppose the evident design of the enemy to outflank the Allies in the north. Sir John French had therefore to take dangerous risks by extending his force on a front longer than their numbers warranted.

"From the best information at my disposal," writes Sir John French, "I judged at this time that the considerable reinforcements which the enemy had undoubtedly brought up during the 16th, 17th and 18th had been directed principally on the line of the Lys and against the Second Corps at La Bassée; and that Sir Douglas Haig would probably not be opposed north of Ypres by much more than the 3rd Reserve Corps, which I knew to have suffered considerably in its previous operations, and perhaps one or two Landwehr Divisions.

"I fully realised the difficult task which lay before us, and the onerous rôle which the British Army was called upon to fulfil.

"That success has been attained, and all the enemy's desperate attempts to break through our line frustrated, is due entirely to the marvellous fighting power and the indomitable courage and tenacity of officers, non-commissioned officers and men.

"No more arduous task has ever been assigned to British soldiers; and in all their splendid history there is no instance of their having answered so magnificently to the desperate calls which of necessity were made upon them.

"Having given these orders to Sir Douglas Haig, I enjoined a defensive rôle upon the Second and Third and Cavalry Corps, in view of the superiority of force which had accumulated in their front. As regards the Fourth Corps, I directed Sir Henry Rawlinson to endeavour to conform generally to the movements of the First Corps.

"It now became clear to me that the utmost we could do to ward off any attempts of the enemy to turn our flank to the North, or to break in from the eastward was to maintain our present very extended front, and to hold fast our positions until French reinforcements could arrive from the South.

"During the 22nd the necessity of sending support to the Fourth Corps on his right somewhat hampered the General Officer Commanding the First Corps; but a series of attacks all along his front had been driven back during the day with heavy loss to the enemy. Late in the evening the enemy succeeded in penetrating a portion of the line held by the Cameron Highlanders north of Pilkem.

"At 6 a.m. on the morning of the 23rd a counter attack to recover the lost trenches was made by the Queen's Regiment, the Northamptons and the King's Royal Rifles, under Major-General Bulfin. The attack was very strongly opposed and the bayonet had to be used. After severe fighting during most of the day the attack was brilliantly successful, and over six hundred prisoners were taken.

"On the same day an attack was made on the 3rd Infantry Brigade. The enemy advanced with great determination, but with little skill, and consequently the loss inflicted on him was exceedingly heavy; some fifteen hundred dead were seen in the neighbourhood of Langemarck. Correspondence found subsequently on a captured German officer stated that the effectives of this attacking Corps were reduced to 25 per cent. in the course of the day's fighting.

"Sir Douglas Haig describes the position at this period as serious, the Germans being in possession of Zandvoorde Ridge.

"Subsequent investigation showed that the enemy had been reinforced at this point by the whole German Active Fifteenth Corps.

"The General Officer Commanding First Corps ordered the line Gheluvelt to the corner of the canal to be held at all costs. When this line was taken up the 2nd Brigade was ordered to concentrate in rear of the 1st Division and the 4th Brigade line. One battalion was placed in reserve in the woods one mile south of Hooge.

"Further precautions were taken at night to protect this flank, and the Ninth French Corps sent three battalions and one Cavalry Brigade to assist.

"The First Corps' Communications through Ypres were threatened by the advance of the Germans towards the canal; so orders were issued for every effort to be made to secure the line then held, and, when this had been thoroughly done, to resume the offensive.

peror himself considered the success of this attack to be one of vital importance to the successful issue of the war.

"Perhaps the most important and decisive attack (except that of the Prussian Guard on 15th November) made against the First Corps

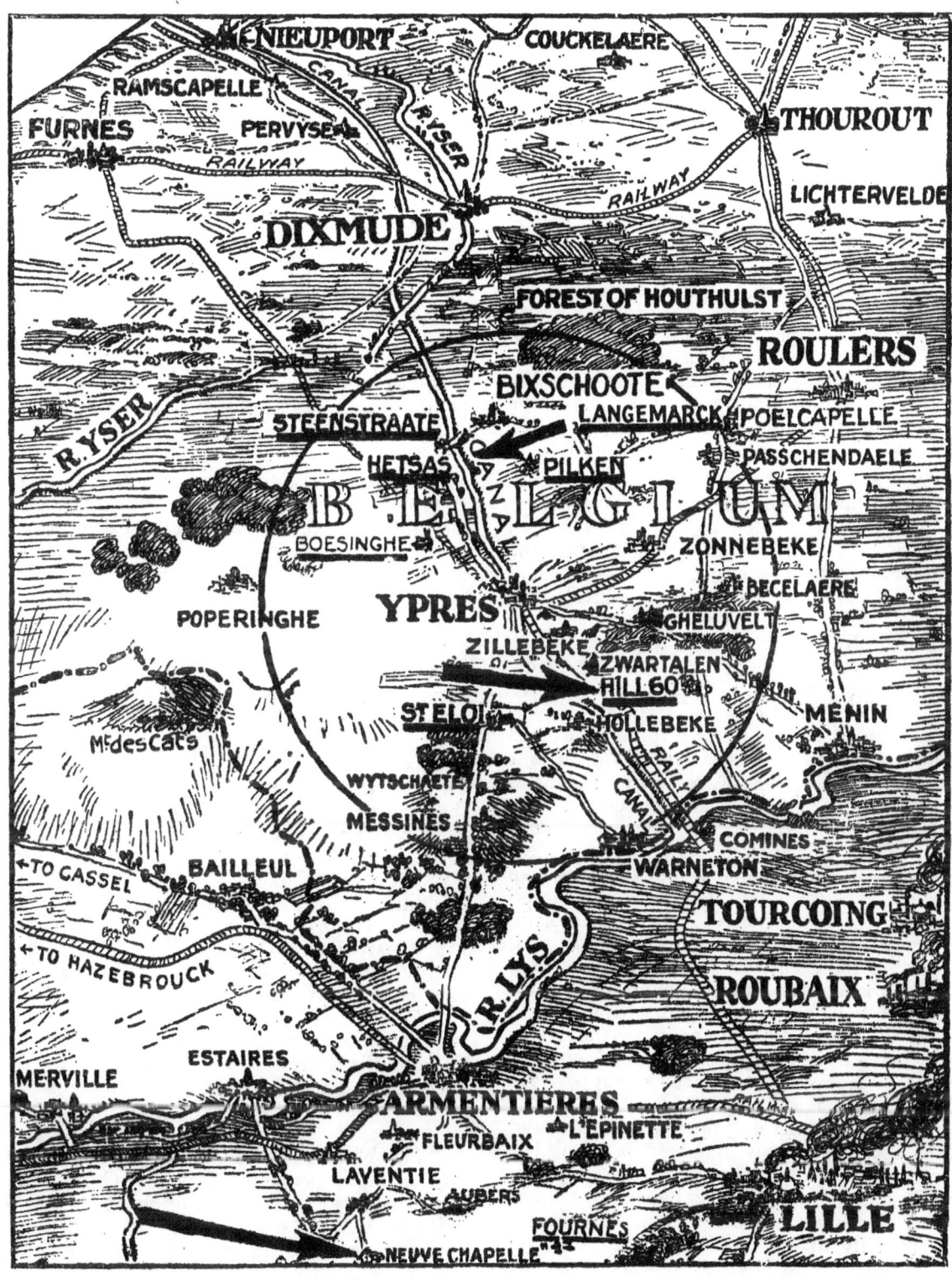

"An order taken from a prisoner who had been captured on this day purported to emanate from the German General, Von Beimling, and said that the Fifteenth German Corps, together with the 2nd Bavarian and Thirteenth Corps, were entrusted with the task of breaking through the line to Ypres; and that the Em-

during the whole of its arduous experiences in the neighbourhood of Ypres took place on the 31st October.

"After several attacks and counter attacks during the course of the morning along the Menin-Ypres road, south-east of Gheluvelt, an attack against that place developed in great force, and the line of the First Division was broken. On the south the 7th Division and General Bulfin's detachment were being heavily shelled. The retirement of the 1st Division exposed the left of the 7th Division, and owing to this the Royal Scots Fusiliers, who remained in the trenches, were cut off and surrounded. A strong infantry attack was developed against the right of the 7th Division at 1.30 p.m.

"The 1st Division rallied on the line of the woods east of the bend of the road, the German advance by the road being checked by enfilade fire from the north.

"The attack against the right of the 7th Division forced the 22nd Brigade to retire, thus exposing the left of the 2nd Brigade. The General Officer Commanding the 7th Division used his reserve, already posted on his flank, to restore the line; but, in the meantime, the 2nd Brigade, finding their left flank exposed, had been forced to withdraw. The right of the 7th Division thus advanced as the left of the 2nd Brigade went back, with the result that the right of the 7th Division was exposed, but managed to hold on to its old trenches till nightfall.

"Meantime, on the Menin road, a counter-attack delivered by the left of the 1st Division and the right of the 2nd Division against the right flank of the German line was completely successful, and by 2.30 p.m. Gheluvelt had been retaken with the bayonet, the 2nd Worcestershire Regiment being to the fore in this, admirably supported by the 42nd Brigade, Royal Field Artillery. The left of the 7th Division, profiting by their capture of Gheluvelt, advanced almost to its original line; and connection between the 1st and 7th Divisions was re-established. The recapture of Gheluvelt released the 6th Cavalry Brigade, till then held in support of the 1st Division. Two regiments of this brigade were sent at once to clear the woods to the south-east, and close the gap in the line between the 7th Division and 2nd Brigade. They advanced with much dash, partly mounted and partly dismounted; and, surprising the enemy in the woods, succeeded in killing large numbers and materially helped to restore the line. About 5 p.m. the French Cavalry Brigade also came up to the cross-roads just east of Hooge, and at once sent forward a dismounted detachment to support our 7th Cavalry Brigade.

"Throughout the day the extreme right and left of the First Corps' line held fast, the left being only slightly engaged, while the right was heavily shelled and subjected to slight infantry attacks. In the evening the enemy were steadily driven back from the woods on the front of the 7th Division and 2nd Brigade; and by 10 p.m. the line as held in the morning had practically been re-occupied.

"During the night touch was restored between the right of the 7th Division and left of the 2nd Brigade, and the Cavalry were withdrawn into reserve, the services of the French Cavalry being dispensed with.

"About the 10th instant, after several units of these Corps had been completely shattered in futile attacks, a division of the Prussian Guard, which had been operating in the neighbourhood of Arras, was moved up to this area with great speed and secrecy. Documents found on dead officers prove that the Guard had received the Emperor's special commands to break through and succeed where their comrades of the line had failed.

"They took a leading part in the vigorous attacks made against the centre on the 11th and 12th; but, like their comrades, were repulsed with enormous loss.

"Throughout this trying period Sir Douglas Haig, ably assisted by his Divisional and Brigade Commanders, held the line with marvellous tenacity and undaunted courage.

"Words fail me to express the admiration I feel for their conduct, or my sense of the incalculable services they rendered. I venture to predict that their deeds during these days of stress and trial will furnish some of the most brilliant chapters which will be found in the military history of our time.

"The First Corps was brilliantly supported by the 3rd Cavalry Division under General Byng. Sir Douglas Haig has constantly brought this officer's eminent services to my notice. His troops were repeatedly called upon to restore the situation at critical points, and to fill gaps in the line caused by the tremendous losses which occurred.

"Both Corps and Cavalry Division Commanders particularly bring to my notice the name of Brigadier-General Kavanagh, Commanding the 7th Cavalry Brigade, not only for his skill but his personal bravery and dash. This was particularly noticeable when the 7th Cavalry Brigade was brought up to support the French troops when the latter were driven back near the village of Klein Zillebeke on the night of the 7th November. On this occasion I regret to say Colonel Gordon Wilson, Commanding the Royal Horse Guards, and Major the Hon. Hugh Dawnay, Commanding the 2nd Life Guards, were killed.

"In these two officers the Army has lost valuable cavalry leaders.

"Another officer whose name was particularly mentioned to me was that of Brigadier-General FitzClarence, V.C., Commanding the 1st Guards Brigade. He was, unfortunately, killed in the night attack of the 11th November.

"The First Corps Commander informs me that on many occasions Brigadier-General the Earl of Cavan, Commanding the 4th Guards Brigade, was conspicuous for the skill, coolness and courage with which he led his troops, and for the successful manner in which he dealt with many critical situations.

"I have more than once during this campaign brought forward the name of Major-General Bulfin to Your Lordship's notice. Up to the evening of the 2nd November, when he was somewhat severely wounded, his services continued to be of great value."

"During the early days of December certain indications along the whole front of the Allied Line induced the French Commanders and myself to believe that the enemy had withdrawn considerable forces from the Western Theatre.

"Arrangements were made with the Commander of the 8th French Army for an attack to be commenced on the morning of December 14th.

"Operations began at 7 a.m. by a combined heavy artillery bombardment by the two French and the 2nd British Corps.

"The British objectives were the Petit Bois and the Maedelsteed Spur, lying respectively to the west and south-west of the village of Wytschaete.

"At 7.45 a.m. the Royal Scots, with great dash, rushed forward and attacked the former, while the Gordon Highlanders attacked the latter place.

"The Royal Scots, in face of a terrible machine-gun and rifle fire, carried the German trench on the west edge of the Petit Bois, capturing two machine-guns and 53 prisoners, including one officer.

"The Gordon Highlanders, with great gallantry, advanced up the Maedelsteed Spur, forcing the enemy to evacuate their front trench. They were, however, losing heavily, and found themselves unable to get any further. At nightfall they were obliged to fall back to their original position.

"Although not successful, the operation was most creditable to the fighting spirit of the Gordon Highlanders, most ably commanded by Major A. W. F. Baird, D.S.O.

"As the 32nd French Division on the left had been unable to make any progress, the further advance of our infantry into the Wytschaete Wood was not practicable.

"Possession of the western edge of the Petit Bois was, however, retained.

"The ground was devoid of cover and so water-logged that a rapid advance was impossible, the men sinking deep in the mud at every step they took.

"The casualties during the day were about 17 officers and 407 other ranks. The losses of the enemy were very considerable, large numbers of dead being found in the Petit Bois and also in the communicating trenches in front of the Gordon Highlanders, in one of which a hundred were counted by a night patrol.

"On this day the artillery of the 4th Division, 3rd Corps, was used in support of the attack, under orders of the General Officer Commanding 2nd Corps.

"The remainder of the 3rd Corps made demonstrations against the enemy with a view to preventing him from detaching troops to the area of operations of the 2nd Corps.

"From the 15th to the 17th December the offensive operations which were commenced on the 14th were continued, but were confined chiefly to artillery bombardment.

"The infantry advance against Wytschaete Wood was not practicable until the French on our left could make some progress to afford protection to that flank.

"On the 17th it was agreed that the plan of attack as arranged should be modified; but I was requested to continue demonstrations along my line in order to assist and support certain French operations which were being conducted elsewhere.

"From daylight on the 20th December the enemy commenced a heavy fire from artillery and trench mortars on the whole front of the Indian Corps. This was followed by infantry attacks, which were in especial force against Givenchy, and between that place and La Quinque Rue.

"At about 10 a.m. the enemy succeeded in driving back the Sirhind Brigade, and capturing a considerable part of Givenchy, but the 57th Rifles and 9th Bhopals, north of the canal, and the Connaught Rangers, south of it, stood firm.

"The 15th Sikhs of the Divisional Reserve were already supporting the Sirhind Brigade. On the news of the retirement of the latter being received, the 47th Sikhs were also sent up to reinforce General Brunker. The 1st Manchester Regiment, 4th Suffolk Regiment, and two battalions of French Territorials under General Carnegy were ordered to launch a vigorous counter-attack from Pont Fixe through Givenchy to retake by a flank attack the trenches lost by the Sirhind Brigade.

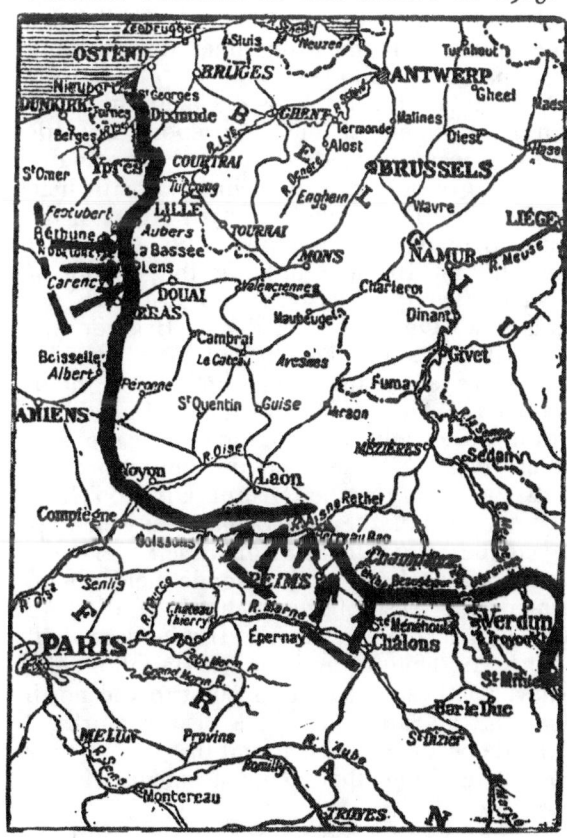

GENERAL POSITION IN THE SPRING OF 1915.

"Orders were sent to General Carnegy to divert his attack on Givenchy Village, and to re-establish the situation there,

"A battalion of the 58th French Division was sent to Annequin in support.

"About 5 p.m. a gallant attack by the 1st Manchester Regiment and one company of the 4th Suffolk Regiment had captured Givenchy, and had cleared the enemy out of the two lines of trenches to the North-East. To the east of the village the 9th Bhopal Infantry and 57th Rifles had maintained their positions, but the enemy were still in possession of our trenches to the north of the village.

"General Macbean, with the Secunderabad Cavalry Brigade, 2nd Battalion, 8th Gurkha Rifles, and the 47th Sikhs, was sent up to support General Brunker, who at 2 p.m. directed General Macbean to move to a position of readiness in the second line trenches from Maris northward, and to counter-attack vigorously if opportunity offered.

"Some considerable delay appears to have occurred, and it was not until 1 a.m. on the 21st that the 47th Sikhs and the 7th Dragoon Guards, under the command of Lieutenant-Colonel H. A. Lempriere, D.S.O., of the latter regiment, were launched in counter-attack.

"They reached the enemy's trenches, but were driven out by enfilade fire, their gallant Commander being killed.

"The main attack by the remainder of General Macbean's force, with the remnants of Lieutenant-Colonel Lempriere's detachment (which had again been rallied) was finally pushed in at about 4.30 a.m., and also failed.

"At 1 p.m. on the 22nd Sir Douglas Haig took over command from Sir James Willcocks. The situation in the front line was then approximately as follows:—

"South of the La Bassée Canal the Connaught Rangers of the Ferozepore Brigade had not been attacked. North of the canal a short length of our original line was still held by the 9th Bhopals and the 57th Rifles of the same Brigade. Connecting with the latter was the 1st Brigade holding the village of Givenchy and its eastern and northern approaches. On the left of the 1st Brigade was the 3rd Brigade. Touch had been lost between the left of the former and the right of the latter. The 3rd Brigade held a line along, and in places advanced to, the east of the Festubert Road. Its left was in communication with the right of the Meerut Division line, where troops of the 2nd Brigade had just relieved the 1st Seaforth Highlanders. To the north, units of the 2nd Brigade held an indented line west of the orchard, connecting with half of the 2nd Royal Highlanders, half of the 41st Dogras, and the 1st Battalion, 9th Gurkha Rifles. From this point to the north the 6th Jats and the whole of the Garhwal Brigade occupied the original line which they had held from the commencement of the operations.

"The relief of most units of the southern sector was effected on the night of 22nd December. The Meerut Division remained under the orders of the 1st Corps, and was not completely withdrawn until the 27th December.

"In the evening the position at Givenchy was practically re-established, and the 3rd Brigade had re-occupied the old line of trenches.

"During the 23rd the enemy's activities ceased, and the whole position was restored to very much its original condition.

"5. At 7.30 a.m. on the 25th January the enemy began to shell Bethune, and at 8 a.m. a strong hostile infantry attack developed south of the canal, preceded by a heavy bombardment of artillery, minenwerfers, and, possibly, the explosion of mines, though the latter is doubtful.

"The British line south of the canal formed a pronounced salient from the canal on the left, thence running forward toward the railway triangle and back to the main La Bassée—Bethune Road, where it joined the French. This line was occupied by half a battalion of the Scots Guards, and half a battalion of the Coldstream Guards, of the 1st Infantry Brigade. The trenches in the salient were blown in almost at once; and the enemy's attack penetrated this line. Our troops retired to a partially prepared second line, running approximately due north and south from the canal to the road, some 500 yards west of the railway triangle. This second line had been strengthened by the construction of a keep half way between the canal and the road. Here the other two half battalions of the above-mentioned regiments were in support.

"These supports held up the enemy who, however, managed to establish himself in the brick stacks and some communication trenches between the keep, the road, and the canal—and even beyond the west of the keep on either side of it.

"The counter-attack was delayed in order to synchronise with a counter-attack north of the canal which was arranged for 1 p.m.

"At 1 p.m. these troops moved forward, their flanks making good progress near the road and the canal, but their centre being held up. The 2nd Royal Sussex Regiment was then sent forward, late in the afternoon, to reinforce. The result was that the Germans were driven back far enough to enable a somewhat broken line to be taken up, running from the culvert on the railway, almost due south to the keep, and thence south-east to the main road.

"The French left near the road had also been attacked and driven back a little, but not to so great an extent as the British right. Consequently, the French left was in advance of the British right and exposed to a possible flank attack from the north.

"The Germans did not, however, persevere further in their attack.

"The above-mentioned line was strengthened during the night; and the 1st Guards Brigade, which had suffered severely, was withdrawn into reserve, and replaced by the 2nd Infantry Brigade.

"While this was taking place another, and equally severe attack was delivered north of the canal against the village of Givenchy.

"At 8.15 a.m., after a heavy artillery bombardment with high explosive shells, the enemy's infantry advanced under the effective fire of our artillery, which, however, was hampered by the constant interruption of telephonic communication between the observers and batteries. Neverthleess, our artillery fire, combined with that of the infantry in the fire trenches, had the effect of driving the enemy from his original direction of advance, with the result that his troops crowded together on the north-east corner of the village and broke through into the centre of the village as far as the keep, which had been previously put in a state of defence. The Germans had lost heavily, and a well-timed local counter-attack delivered by the reserves of the 2nd Welsh Regiment and 1st South Wales Borderers,

"7. On the 1st February a fine piece of work was carried out by the 4th Brigade in the neighbourhood of Cuinchy.

"Some of the 2nd Coldstream Guards were driven from their trenches at 2.30 a.m., but made a stand some twenty yards east of them in a position which they held till morning.

"A counter-attack, launched at 3.15 a.m. by one company of the Irish Guards and half a company of the 2nd Coldstream Guards, proved unsuccessful, owing to heavy rifle fire from the east and south.

"At 10.5 a.m., acting under orders of the 1st Division, a heavy bombardment was opened on the lost ground for ten minutes; and this was followed immediately by an assault by about 50 men of the 2nd Coldstream Guards with bayonets, led by Captain A. Leigh Bennett, followed by 30 men of the Irish Guards, led by Second Lieutenant F. F. Graham, also with bayonets. These were fol-

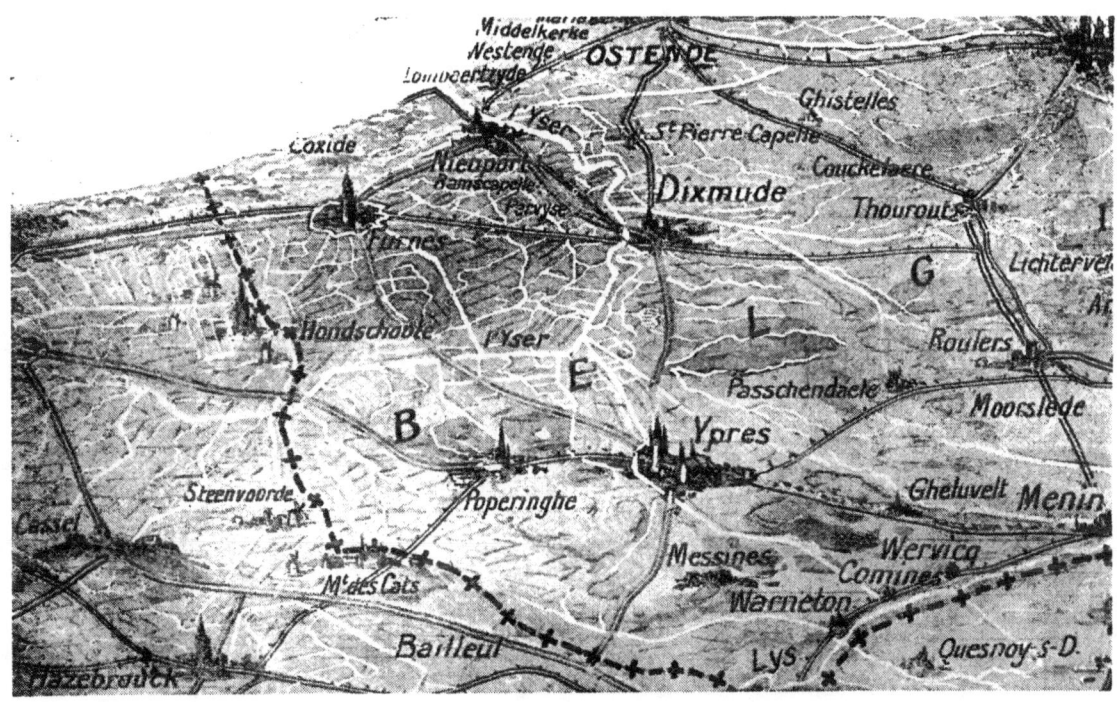

and by a company of the 1st Royal Highlanders (lent by the 1st Brigade as a working party—this company was at work on the keep at the time), was completely successful, with the result that, after about an hour's street fighting, all who had broken into the village were either captured or killed; and the original line round the village was re-established by noon.

"South of the village, however, and close to the canal, the right of the 2nd Royal Munster Fusiliers fell back in conformity with the troops south of the canal; but after dark that regiment moved forward and occupied the old line.

"During the course of the attack on Givenchy the enemy made five assaults on the salient at the north-east of the village about French Farm, but was repulsed every time with heavy loss.

lowed by a party of Royal Engineers with sand bags and wire.

"All the ground which had been lost was brilliantly retaken; the 2nd Coldstream Guards also taking another German trench and capturing two machine guns.

"Thirty-two prisoners fell into our hands.

"The General Officer Commanding 1st Division describes the preparation by the artillery as 'splendid, the high explosive shells dropping in the exact spot with absolute precision.'

"In forwarding his report on this engagement, the General Officer Commanding First Army writes as follows:—

"'Special credit is due—

"'(i) To Major-General Haking, Commanding 1st Division, for the prompt manner in which he arranged this counter-attack and for the general plan of action, which was crowned with success.

"'(ii) To the General Officer Commanding the 4th Brigade (Lord Cavan) for the thorough manner in which he carried out the orders of the General Officer Commanding the Division.

"'(iii) To the regimental officers, non-commissioned officers and men of the 2nd Coldstream Guards and Irish Guards, who, with indomitable pluck, stormed two sets of barricades, captured three German trenches, two machine guns, and killed or made prisoners many of the enemy.'

"The event of chief interest and importance which has taken place is the victory achieved over the enemy at the Battle of Neuve Chapelle, which was fought on the 10th, 11th, and 12th of March. The main attack was delivered by troops of the First Army under the command of General Sir Douglas Haig, supported by a large force of Heavy Artillery, a Division of Cavalry, and some Infantry of the general reserve.

"Secondary and holding attacks and demonstrations were made along the front of the Second Army under the direction of its Commander, General Sir Horace Smith-Dorrien.

"Whilst the success attained was due to the magnificent bearing and indomitable courage displayed by the troops of the 4th and Indian Corps, I consider that the able and skilful dispositions which were made by the General Officer Commanding First Army contributed largely to the defeat of the enemy and to the capture of his position. The energy and vigour with which General Sir Douglas Haig handled his command show him to be a leader of great ability and power.

"Another action of considerable importance was brought about by a surprise attack of the Germans made on the 14th March against the 27th Division holding the trenches east of St. Eloi. A large force of artillery was concentrated in this area under cover of mist, and a heavy volume of fire was suddenly brought to bear on the trenches at 5 p.m. This artillery attack was accompanied by two mine explosions; and, in the confusion caused by these and the suddenness of the attack, the position of St. Eloi was captured and held for some hours by the enemy.

"Well directed and vigorous counter attacks, in which the troops of the 5th Army Corps showed great bravery and determination, restored the situation by the evening of the 15th.

"A more detailed account of these operations will appear in subsequent pages of this despatch.

"On the 6th February a brilliant action by troops of the 1st Corps materially improved our position in the area south of the La Bassée Canal. During the previous night parties of Irish Guards and of the 3rd Battalion Coldstream Guards had succeeded in gaining ground whence converging fire could be directed on the flanks and rear of certain 'brickstacks' occupied by the Germans, which had been for some time a source of considerable annoyance.

"At 2 p.m. the affair commenced with a severe bombardment of the 'brickstacks' and the enemy trenches. A brisk attack by the 3rd Coldstream Guards and Irish Guards from our trenches west of the 'brickstacks' followed, and was supported by fire from the flanking positions which had been seized the previous night by the same regiments. The attack succeeded, the 'brickstacks' were occupied without difficulty, and a line established north and south through a point about forty yards east of the 'brickstacks.'

"Chiefly owing to these causes, the 5th Corps, up to the beginning of March, was constantly engaged in counter-attacks to retake trenches and ground which had been lost.

"In their difficult and arduous task, however, the troops displayed the utmost gallantry and devotion; and it is most creditable to the skill and energy of their leaders that I am able to report how well they have surmounted all their difficulties, that the ground first taken over by them is still intact, and held with little greater loss than is incurred by troops in all other parts of the line.

"On the 14th February the 82nd Brigade of the 27th Division was driven from its trenches east of St. Eloi; but by 7 a.m. on the 15th all these trenches had been recaptured, fifteen prisoners taken, and sixty German dead counted in front of the trenches. Similarly in the 28th Division trenches were lost by the 85th Brigade and retaken the following night.

"During the month of February the enemy made several attempts to get through all along the line, but he was invariably repulsed with loss. A particularly vigorous attempt was made on the 17th February against the trenches held by the Indian Corps, but it was brilliantly repulsed.

"On February 28th a successful minor attack was made on the enemy's trenches near St. Eloi by small parties of the Princess Patricia's Canadian Light Infantry. The attack was divided into three small groups, the whole under the command of Lieutenant Crabbe: No. 1 Group under Lieutenant Papineau, No. 2 Group under Sergeant Patterson, and No. 3 Group under Company Sergeant-Major Lloyd.

"The head of the party got within fifteen or twenty yards of the German trench and charged; it was dark at the time (about 5.15 a.m.).

"The time passed by the Cavalry in the French trenches was, on the whole, quiet and uneventful, but there are one or two incidents calling for remark.

"At about 1.45 a.m. on 16th February, a half-hearted attack was made against the right of the line held by the 2nd Cavalry Division, but it was easily repulsed by rifle fire, and the enemy left several dead in front of the trenches. The attack was delivered against the second and third trenches from the right of the line of this Division.

"At 6 a.m. on the 21st the enemy blew up one of the 2nd Cavalry Division trenches, held by the 16th Lancers, and some adjoining French trenches. The enemy occupied forty yards of our trench and tried to advance, but were stopped. An immediate counter-attack by the supporting squadron was stopped by machine-gun fire. The line was established opposite the gap, and a counter-attack by two squadrons and one company of French reserve was ordered. At 5.30 p.m. 2nd Cavalry Division reported that the counter-attack did not succeed in retaking the trench blown in, but that a new line had been established forty yards in rear of it, and that there was no further activity on the part of the enemy. At 10 p.m. the situation was unchanged.

"About the end of February many vital considerations induced me to believe that a vigorous offensive movement by the Forces under my command should be planned and carried out at the earliest possible moment.

"Amongst the more important reasons which convinced me of this necessity were:— The general aspect of the Allied situation throughout Europe, and particularly the marked success of the Russian Army in repelling the violent onslaughts of Marshal Von Hindenburg; the apparent weakening of the enemy in my front, and the necessity for assisting our Russian Allies to the utmost by holding as many hostile troops as possible in the Western Theatre; the efforts to this end which were being made by the French Forces at Arras and Champagne; and, perhaps the most weighty consideration of all, the need of fostering the offensive spirit in the troops under my command after the trying and possibly enervating experiences which they had gone through of a severe winter in the trenches.

"In a former despatch I commented upon the difficulties and drawbacks which the winter weather in this climate imposes upon a vigorous offensive. Early in March these difficulties became greatly lessened by the drying up of the country and by spells of brighter weather.

"As mentioned above, the main attack was carried out by units of the First Army, supported by troops of the Second Army and the general reserve.

"The object of the main attack was to be the capture of the village of Neuve Chapelle and the enemy's position at that point, and the establishment of our line as far forward as possible to the east of that place.

"The object, nature and scope of the attack, and instructions for the conduct of the operation were communicated by me to Sir Douglas Haig in a secret memorandum dated 19th February.

"The main topographical feature of this part of the theatre is a marked ridge which runs south-west from a point two miles south-west of Lille to the village of Fournes, whence two spurs run out, one due west to a height known as Haut Pommereau, the other following the line of the main road to Illies.

"The buildings of the village of Neuve Chapelle run along the Rue du Bois-Fauquisart Road. There is a triangle of roads just north of the village. This area consists of a few big houses, with walls, gardens, orchards, etc., and here, with the aid of numerous machine-guns, the enemy had established a strong post which flanked the approaches to the village.

"The Bois du Biez, which lies roughly south-east of the village of Neuve Chapelle, influenced the course of this operation.

"Full instructions as to assisting and supporting the attack were issued to the Second Army.

"The battle opened at 7.30 a.m. on the 10th March by a powerful artillery bombardment of the enemy's position at Neuve Chapelle. The artillery bombardment had been well prepared and was most effective, except on the extreme northern portion of the front of attack.

"At 8.5 a.m. the 23rd (left) and 25th (right) Brigades of the 8th Division assaulted the German trenches on the north-west of the village.

"At the same hour the Garhwal Brigade of the Meerut Division, which occupied the position to the south of Neuve Chapelle, assaulted the German trenches in its front.

"The Garhwal Brigade and the 25th Brigade carried the enemy's lines of entrenchments where the wire entanglements had been almost entirely swept away by our shrapnel fire. The 23rd Brigade, however, on the north-east, was held up by the wire entanglements, which were not sufficiently cut.

"At 8.5 a.m. the artillery turned on to Neuve Chapelle, and at 8.35 a.m. the advance of the infantry was continued.

"The 25th and Garhwal Brigades pushed on eastward and north-eastward respectively, and succeeded in getting a footing in the village. The 23rd Brigade was still held up in front of the enemy's wire entanglements, and could not progress. Heavy losses were suffered, especially in the Middlesex Regiment and the Scottish Rifles. The progress, however, of the 25th Brigade into Neuve Chapelle immediately to the south of the 23rd Brigade had the effect of turning the southern flank of the enemy's defences in front of the 23rd Brigade.

"This fact, combined with powerful artillery support, enabled the 23rd Brigade to get forward between 10 and 11 a.m., and by 11 a.m. the whole of the village of Neuve Chapelle and the roads leading northward and south-westward from the eastern end of that village were in our hands.

"During this time our artillery completely cut off the village and the surrounding country from any German reinforcements which could be thrown into the fight to restore the situation by means of a curtain of shrapnel fire Prisoners subsequently reported that all attempts at reinforcing the front line were checked.

"Steps were at once taken to consolidate the position won.

"Considerable delay occurred after the capture of the Neuve Chapelle position. The infantry was greatly disorganised by the violent nature of the attack and by its passage through the enemy's trenches and the buildings of the village. It was necessary to get units to some extent together before pushing on. The telephonic communication being cut by the enemy's fire rendered communication between front and rear most difficult. The fact of the left of the 23rd Brigade having been held up had kept back the 8th Division, and had involved a portion of the 25th Brigade in fighting to the north out of its proper direction of advance. All this required adjustment. An orchard held by the enemy north of Neuve Chapelle also threatened the flank of an advance towards the Aubers Ridge.

"I am of opinion that this delay would not have occurred had the clearly expressed order of the General Officer Commanding First Army been more carefully observed.

"The difficulties above enumerated might have been overcome at an earlier period of the day if the General Officer Commanding 4th Corps had been able to bring his reserve brigades more speedily into action.

"As it was, the further advance did not commence before 3.30 p.m.

"The 21st Brigade was able to form up in the open on the left without a shot being fired at it, thus showing that at the time the enemy's resistance had been paralysed. The Brigade pushed forward in the direction of Moulin Du Pietre.

"At first it made good progress, but was subsequently held up by the machine-gun fire from the houses and from a defended work in the line of the German entrenchments opposite the right of the 22nd Brigade.

"Further to the south the 24th Brigade, which had been directed on Pietre, was similarly held up by machine-guns in the houses and trenches at the road junction six hundred yards north-west of Pietre.

"The 25th Brigade, on the right of the 24th, was also held up by machine-guns from a bridge held by the Germans, over the River Des Layes, which is situated to the north-west of the Bois Du Biez.

"Whilst two Brigades of the Meerut Division were establishing themselves on the new line, the Dehra Dun Brigade, supported by the Jullundur Brigade of the Lahore Division, moved to the attack of the Bois Du Biez, but were held up on the line of the River Des Layes by the German post at the bridge which enfiladed them and brought them to a standstill.

"The defended bridge over the River Des Layes and its neighbourhood immediately assumed considerable importance. Whilst artillery fire was brought to bear, as far as circumstances would permit, on this point, Sir Douglas Haig directed the 1st Corps to despatch one or more battalions of the 1st Brigade in support of the troops attacking the bridge. Three battalions were thus sent to Richebourg St. Vaast. Darkness coming on, and the enemy having brought up reinforcements, no further progress could be made, and the Indian Corps and 4th Corps proceeded to consolidate the position they had gained.

"Whilst the operations which I have thus briefly recorded were going on, the 1st Corps in accordance with orders, delivered an attack in the morning from Givenchy, simultaneously with that against Neuve Chapelle; but as the enemy's wire was insufficiently cut, very little progress could be made, and the troops at this point did little more than hold fast the Germans in front of them.

"On the following day, March 11th, the attack was renewed by the 4th and Indian Corps, but it was soon seen that a further advance would be impossible until the artillery had dealt effectively with the various houses and defended localities which held up the troops along the entire front. Efforts were made to direct the artillery fire accordingly; but owing to the weather conditions, which did not permit of aerial observation, and the fact that nearly all the telephonic communications between the artillery observers and their batteries had been cut, it was impossible to do so with sufficient accuracy. Even when our troops which were pressing forward occupied a house here and there, it was not possible to stop our artillery fire, and the infantry had to be withdrawn.

"The two principal points which barred the advance were the same as on the preceding day—namely, the enemy's position about Moulin de Pietre and at the bridge over the River Des Layes.

"On the 12th March the same unfavourable conditions as regards weather prevailed, and hampered artillery action.

"Operations on this day were chiefly remarkable for the violent counter-attacks, supported by artillery, which were delivered by the Germans, and the ease with which they were repulsed.

"As most of the objects for which the operations had been undertaken had been attained and as there were reasons why I considered it inadvisable to continue the attack at that time, I directed Sir Douglas Haig on the night of the 12th to hold and consolidate the ground which had been gained by the 4th and Indian Corps, and to suspend further offensive operations for the present.

"The losses during these three days' fighting were, I regret to say, very severe, numbering:—

- "190 officers and 2,337 other ranks, killed.
- "359 officers and 8,174 other ranks, wounded.
- "23 officers and 1,728 other ranks, missing.

But the results attained were, in my opinion, wide and far-reaching.

"The enemy left several thousand dead on the battlefield which were seen and counted; and we have positive information that upwards of 12,000 wounded were removed to the north-east and east by train.

"Thirty officers and 1,657 other ranks of the enemy were captured.

"The action at St. Eloi commenced at 5 p.m. on the 14th March by a very heavy cannonade which was directed against our trenches in front of St. Eloi, the village itself and the approaches to it. There is a large mound lying to the south-east of the village. When the artillery attack was at its height a mine was exploded under this mound and a strong hostile infantry attack was immediately launched against the trenches and the mound.

"Our artillery opened fire at once, as well as our infantry, and inflicted considerable losses on the enemy during their advance; but, chiefly owing to the explosion of the mine and the surprise of the overwhelming artillery attack, the enemy's infantry had penetrated the first line of trenches at some points. As a consequence the garrisons of other works which had successfully resisted the assault were enfiladed and forced to retire just before it turned dark.

"A counter attack was at once organised by the General Officer Commanding 82nd Brigade, under the orders of the General Officer Commanding 27th Division, who brought up a reserve brigade to support it.

"The attack was launched at 2 a.m., and the 82nd Brigade succeeded in recapturing the portion of the village of St. Eloi which was in the hands of the enemy and a portion of the trenches east of it. At 3 a.m. the 80th Brigade in support took more trenches to the east and west of the village.

"The counter attack, which was well carried out under difficult conditions, resulted in the recapture of all lost ground of material importance.

"It is satisfactory to be able to record that, though the troops occupying the first line of trenches were at first overwhelmed, they afterwards behaved very gallantly in the counter-attack for the recovery of the lost ground; and the following units earned and received the special commendation of the Army Commander:—The 2nd Royal Irish Fusiliers, the 2nd Duke of Cornwall's Light Infantry, the 1st Leinster Regiment, the 4th Rifle Brigade, and the Princess Patricia's Canadian Light Infantry.

"A vigorous attack made by the enemy on the 17th to recapture these trenches was repulsed with great loss.

"Throughout the period under review night enterprises by smaller or larger patrols, which were led with consummate skill and daring, have been very active along the whole line.

"A moral superiority has thus been established, and valuable information has been collected.

"I cannot speak too highly of the invincible courage and the remarkable resource displayed by these patrols.

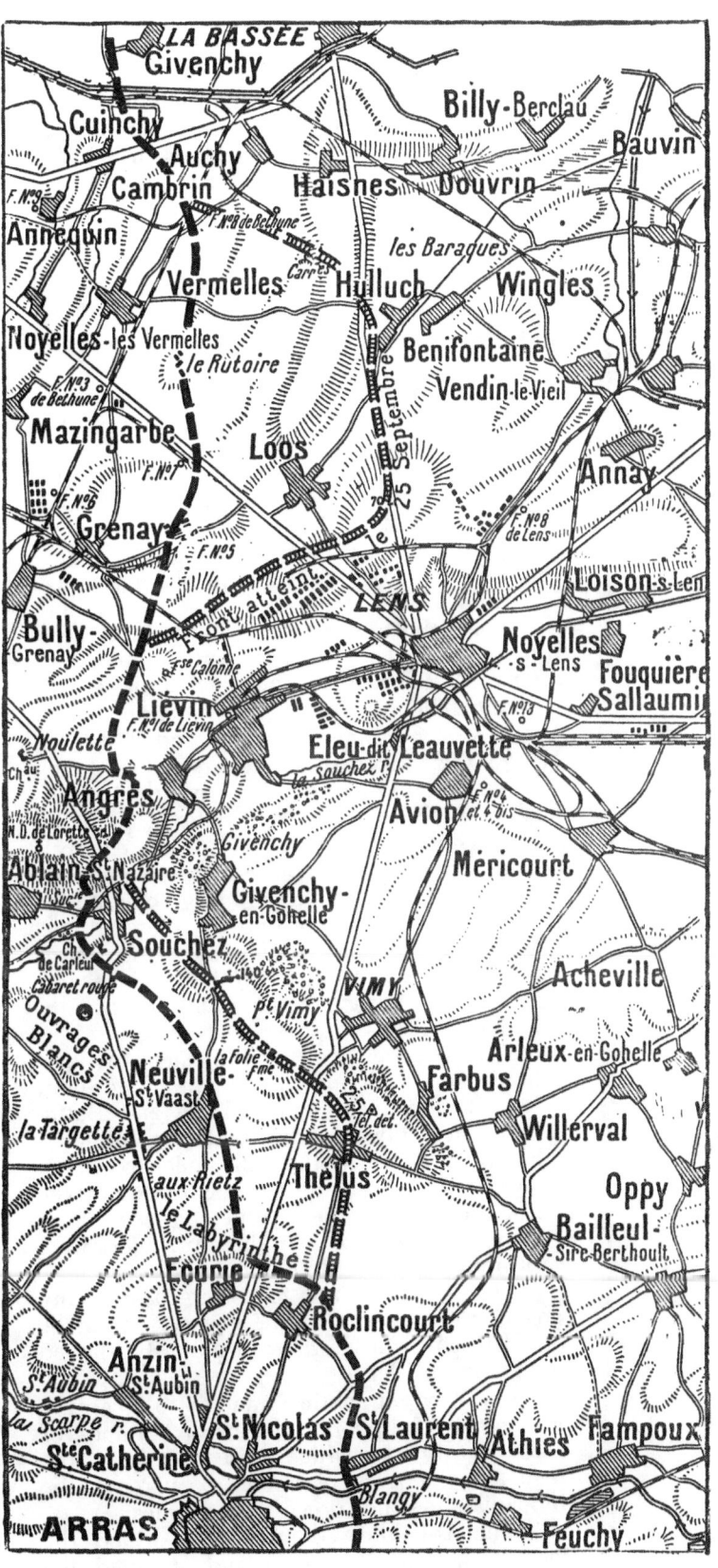

"In the North the town and district of Ypres have once more in this campaign been successfully defended against vigorous and sustained attacks made by large forces of the enemy, and supported by a mass of heavy and field artillery, which, not only in number, but also in weight and calibre, is superior to any concentration of guns which has previously assailed that part of the line.

"In the South a vigorous offensive has again been taken by the troops of the First Army, in the course of which a large area of entrenched and fortified ground has been captured from the enemy, whilst valuable support has been afforded to the attack which our Allies have carried on with such marked success against the enemy's positions to the east of Arras and Lens.

"On the night of Saturday, April 17th, a commanding hill which afforded the enemy excellent artillery observation toward the West and North-West was successfully mined and captured.

"This hill, known as Hill 60, lies opposite the northern extremity of the line held by the 2nd Corps.

"The operation was planned and the mining commenced by Major-General Bulfin before the ground was handed over to the troops under Lieutenant-General Sir Charles Fergusson, under whose supervision the operation was carried out.

"The mines were successfully fired at 7 p.m. on the 17th instant, and immediately afterwards the hill was attacked and gained, without difficulty, by the 1st Battalion, Royal West Kent Regiment, and the 2nd Battalion, King's Own Scottish Borderers. The attack was well supported by the Divisional Artillery, assisted by French and Belgian batteries.

"During the night several of the enemy's counter-attacks were repulsed with heavy loss, and fierce hand-to-hand fighting took place; but on the early morning of the 18th the enemy succeeded in forcing back the troops holding the right of the hill to the reverse slope, where, however, they hung on throughout the day.

"On the evening of the 18th these two battalions were relieved by the 2nd Battalion, West Riding Regiment and the 2nd Battalion, King's Own Yorkshire Light Infantry, who again stormed the hill under cover of heavy artillery fire, and the enemy was driven off at the point of the bayonet.

"In this operation fifty-three prisoners were captured, including four officers.

"On the 20th and following days many unsuccessful attacks by the enemy were made on Hill 60, which was continuously shelled by heavy artillery.

"On May 1st another attempt to recapture Hill 60 was supported by great volumes of asphyxiating gas, which caused nearly all the men along a front of about 400 yards to be immediately struck down by its fumes.

"The splendid courage with which the leaders rallied their men and subdued the natural tendency to panic (which is inevitable on such occasions), combined with the prompt intervention of supports, once more drove the enemy back.

"A second and more severe 'gas' attack, under much more favourable weather conditions, enabled the enemy to recapture this position on May 5th.

"The enemy owes his success in this last attack entirely to the use of asphyxiating gas. It was only a few days later that the means, which have since proved so effective, of counteracting this method of making war were put into practice. Had it been otherwise, the enemy's attack on May 5th would most certainly have shared the fate of all the many previous attempts he had made.

"Following a heavy bombardment, the enemy attacked the French Division at about 5 p.m., using asphyxiating gases for the first time. Aircraft reported that at about 5 p.m. thick yellow smoke had been seen issuing from the German trenches between Langemarck and Bixschoote. The French reported that two simultaneous attacks had been made east of the Ypres-Staden Railway, in which these asphyxiating gases had been employed.

"What follows almost defies description. The effect of these poisonous gases was so virulent as to render the whole of the line held by the French Division mentioned above practically incapable of any action at all. It was at first impossible for anyone to realise what had actually happened. The smoke and flames hid everything from sight, and hundreds of men were thrown into a comatose or dying condition, and within an hour the whole position had to be abandoned, together with about 50 guns.

"I wish particularly to repudiate any idea of attaching the least blame to the French Division for this unfortunate incident.

"After all the examples our gallant Allies have shown of dogged and tenacious courage in the many trying situations in which they have been placed throughout the course of this campaign, it is quite superfluous for me to dwell on this aspect of the incident, and I would only express my firm conviction that, if any troops in the world had been able to hold their trenches in the face of such a treacherous and altogether unexpected onslaught, the French Division would have stood firm.

"The left flank of the Canadian Division was thus left dangerously exposed to serious attack in flank, and there appeared to be a prospect of their being overwhelmed and of a successful attempt by the Germans to cut off the British troops occupying the salient to the East.

"In the course of these two or three days many circumstances combined to render the situation east of the Ypres Canal very critical and most difficult to deal with.

"The confusion caused by the sudden retirement of the French Division, and the necessity for closing up the gap and checking the enemy's advance at all costs, led to a mixing up of units and a sudden shifting of the areas of command, which was quite unavoidable. Fresh units, as they came up from the

South, had to be pushed into the firing line in an area swept by artillery fire, which, owing to the capture of the French guns, we were unable to keep down.

"All this led to very heavy casualties; and I wish to place on record the deep admiration which I feel for the resource and presence of mind evinced by the leaders actually on the spot.

"During the whole of this time the town of Ypres and all the roads to the East and West were uninterruptedly subjected to a violent artillery fire, but in spite of this the supply of both food and ammunition was maintained throughout with order and efficiency.

"During the afternoon of the 25th many German prisoners were taken, including some officers. The hand-to-hand fighting was very severe, and the enemy suffered heavy loss.

"Up to the morning of the 8th the enemy made attacks at short intervals, covered by gas, on all parts of the line to the east of Ypres, but was everywhere driven back with heavy loss.

"Throughout the whole period since the first break of the line on the night of April 22nd all the troops in this area had been constantly subjected to violent artillery bombardment from a large mass of guns with an unlimited supply of ammunition. It proved impossible whilst under so vastly superior fire of artillery to dig efficient trenches, or to properly reorganise the line, after the confusion and demoralisation caused by the first great gas surprise and the subsequent almost daily gas attacks. Nor was it until after this date (May 8th) that effective preventatives had been devised and provided. In these circumstances a violent bombardment of nearly the whole of the 5th Corps front broke out at 7 a.m. on the morning of the 8th, which gradually concentrated on the front of the Division between north and south of Frezenberg. This fire completely obliterated the trenches and caused enormous losses.

"The artillery bombardment was shortly followed by a heavy infantry attack, before which our line had to give way.

"I relate what happened in Sir Herbert Plumer's own words:—

"'A counter attack was launched at 3.30 p.m. by the 1st York and Lancaster Regiment, 3rd Middlesex Regiment, 2nd East Surrey Regiment, 2nd Royal Dublin Fusiliers, and the 1st Royal Warwickshire Regiment. The counter-attack reached Frezenberg, but was eventually driven back and held up on a line running about north and south through Verlorenhoek, despite repeated efforts to advance. The 12th London Regiment on the left succeeded at great cost in reaching the original trench line, and did considerable execution with their machine gun.

"'After a comparatively quiet night and morning (10th-11th) the hostile artillery fire was concentrated on the trenches of the 2nd Cameron Highlanders and 1st Argyll and Sutherland Highlanders at a slightly more northern point than on the previous day. The Germans attacked in force and gained a footing in part of the trenches, but were promptly ejected by a supporting company of the 9th Royal Scots. After a second short artillery bombardment the Germans again attacked about 4.15 p.m., but were again repulsed by rifle and machine-gun fire. A third bombardment followed and this time the Germans succeeded in gaining a trench—or rather what was left of it—a local counter-attack failing. However, during the night the enemy were again driven out. The trench by this time being practically non-existent, the garrison found it untenable under the very heavy shell fire the enemy brought to bear upon it, and the trench was evacuated. Twice more did the German snipers creep back into it, and twice more they were ejected. Finally, a retrenchment was made, cutting off the salient which had been contested throughout the day. It was won owing solely to the superior weight and number of the enemy's guns, but both our infantry and our artillery took a very heavy toll of the enemy, and the ground lost has proved of little use to the enemy.

"'On the night of the 12th-13th the line was re-organised, the centre Division retiring into Army Reserve to rest, and their places being taken in the trenches by the two Cavalry Divisions; the Artillery and Engineers of the Centre Division forming with them what was known as the "Cavalry Force" under the command of General De Lisle.'

"On the early morning of the 24th a violent outburst of gas against nearly the whole front was followed by heavy shell fire, and the most determined attack was delivered against our position east of Ypres.

"The hour the attack commenced was 2.45 a.m. A large proportion of the men were asleep, and the attack was too sudden to give them time to put on their respirators.

"The 2nd Royal Irish and the 9th Argyll and Sutherland Highlanders, overcome by gas fumes, were driven out of a farm held in front of the left Division, and this the enemy proceeded to hold and fortify.

"All attempts to retake this farm during the day failed, and during the night of the 24th-25th the General Officer Commanding the left Division decided to take up a new line which, although slightly in rear of the old one, he considered to be a much better position. This operation was successfully carried out.

"Throughout the day the whole line was subjected to one of the most violent artillery attacks which it had ever undergone; and the 5th Corps and the Cavalry Divisions engaged had to fight hard to maintain their positions. On the following day, however, the line was consolidated, joining the right of the French at the same place as before, and passing through Wieltje (which was strongly fortified) in a southerly direction on to Hooge, where the Cavalry have since strongly occupied the chateau, and pushed our line further east.

"The state of the weather on the morning of the 18th much hindered an effective artillery bombardment, and further attacks had, consequently, to be postponed.

"Infantry attacks were made throughout the line in the course of the afternoon and evening; but, although not very much progress was made, the line was advanced to the La Quinque Rue-Bethune Road before nightfall.

"On the 19th May the 7th and 2nd Divisions were drawn out of the line to rest. The 7th Division was relieved by the Canadian Division and the 2nd Division by the 51st (Highland) Division.

"Sir Douglas Haig placed the Canadian and 51st Divisions, together with the artillery of the 2nd and 7th Divisions, under the command of Lieutenant-General Alderson, whom he directed to conduct the operations which had hitherto been carried on by the General Officer Commanding First Corps; and he directed the 7th Division to remain in Army Reserve.

"During the night of the 19th-20th a small post of the enemy in front of La Quinque Rue was captured.

"During the night of the 20th-21st the Canadian Division brilliantly carried on the excellent progress made by the 7th Division by seizing several of the enemy's trenches and pushing forward their whole line several hundred yards. A number of prisoners and some machine-guns were captured.

"On the 22nd instant the 51st (Highland) Division was attached to the Indian Corps, and the General Officer Commanding the Indian Corps took charge of the operations at La Quinque Rue, Lieutenant-General Alderson with the Canadians conducting the operations to the north of that place.

"On this day the Canadian Division extended their line slightly to the right and repulsed three very severe hostile counter-attacks.

"On the 24th and 25th May the 47th Division (2nd London Territorials) succeeded in taking some more of the enemy's trenches and making good the ground gained to the east and north.

"I had now reason to consider that the battle, which was commenced by the First Army on the 9th May and renewed on the 16th, having attained for the moment the immediate object I had in view, should not be further actively proceeded with; and I gave orders to Sir Douglas Haig to curtail his artillery attack and to strengthen and consolidate the ground he had won.

"In the battle of Festubert above described the enemy was driven from a position which was strongly entrenched and fortified, and ground was won on a front of four miles to an average depth of 600 yards.

"The enemy is known to have suffered very heavy losses, and in the course of the battle 785 prisoners and 10 machine guns were captured. A number of machine guns were also destroyed by our fire."

SECOND BATTLE OF YPRES.

"On 2nd June the enemy made a final offensive in the Ypres salient with the object of gaining our trenches and position at Hooge. The attack was most determined and was preceded by a severe bombardment. A gallant defence was made by troops of the 3rd Cavalry Division and 1st Indian Cavalry Division, and our position was maintained throughout.

"During the first weeks of June the front of the Second Army was extended to the North as far as the village of Boesinghe.

"After the conclusion of the Battle of Festubert the troops of the First Army were engaged in several minor operations.

"By an attack delivered on the evening of 15th June after a prolonged bombardment the 1st Canadian Brigade obtained possession of the German front line trenches north-east of Givenchy, but were unable to retain them owing to their flanks being too much exposed.

"On 16th June an attack was carried out by the 5th Corps on the Bellewaarde Ridge, east of Ypres.

"The enemy's front line was captured, many of his dead and wounded being found in the trenches.

"The troops, pressing forward, gained ground as far East as the Bellewaarde Lake, but found themselves unable to maintain this advanced position. They were, however, successful in securing and consolidating the ground won during the first part of the attack, on a front of a thousand yards, including the advanced portion of the enemy's salient north of the Ypres-Menin Road.

"During this action the fire of the artillery was most effective, the prisoners testifying to its destructiveness and accuracy. It also prevented the delivery of counter attacks, which were paralysed at the outset.

"Over two hundred prisoners were taken, besides some machine-guns, trench material and gas apparatus.

"Holding attacks by the neighbouring 2nd and 6th Corps were successful in helping the main attack, whilst the 36th French Corps co-operated very usefully with artillery fire on Pilkem.

"Near Hill 60 the 15th Infantry Brigade made four bombing attacks, gaining and occupying about fifty yards of trench.

"On 6th July a small attack was made by the 11th Infantry Brigade on a German salient between Boesinghe and Ypres, which resulted in the capture of a frontage of about 500 yards of trench and a number of prisoners.

"From the 10th to the 12th July the enemy made attempts, after heavy shelling, to recapture the lost portion of their line; but our artillery, assisted by that of the French on our left, prevented any serious assault from being delivered. Minor attacks were constant, but were easily repulsed by the garrison of our trenches.

"On 19th July an enemy's redoubt at the western end of the Hooge defences was successfully mined and destroyed, and a small portion of the enemy's trenches was captured.

"Since my last despatch a new device has been adopted by the enemy for driving burning liquid into our trenches with a strong jet.

"Thus supported, an attack was made on the trenches of the Second Army at Hooge, on the Menin Road, early on 30th July. Most of the infantry occupying these trenches were driven back, but their retirement was due far more to the surprise and temporary confusion caused by the burning liquid than to the actual damage inflicted.

"Gallant endeavours were made by repeated counter attacks to recapture the lost section of trenches. These, however, proving unsuccessful and costly, a new line of trenches was consolidated a short distance further back.

"Attacks made by the enemy at the same time west of Bellewaarde Lake were repulsed.

"On 9th August these losses were brilliantly regained, owing to a successful attack carried out by the 6th Division. This attack was very well executed and resulted in the recapture, with small casualties, not only of the whole of the lost trenches, but, in addition, of four hundred yards of German trench north of the Menin Road.

"At the end of this engagement it was estimated that between four and five hundred German dead were lying on the battlefield.

"In fulfilment of the rôle assigned to it in these operations the Army under my command attacked the enemy on the morning of the 25th September.

"The main attack was delivered by the 1st and 4th Corps between the La Bassée Canal on the north and a point of the enemy's line opposite the village of Grenay on the south.

"At the same time a secondary attack, designed with the object of distracting the enemy's attention and holding his troops to their ground, was made by the 5th Corps on Bellewaarde Farm, situated to the east of Ypres. Subsidiary attacks with similar objects were delivered by the 3rd and Indian Corps north of the La Bassée Canal and along the whole front of the Second Army.

"These attacks started at daybreak and were at first successful all along the line. Later in the day the enemy brought up strong reserves, and after hard fighting and variable fortunes the troops engaged in this part of the line re-occupied their original trenches at nightfall. They succeeded admirably, however, in fulfilling the rôle allotted to them, and in holding large numbers of the enemy away from the main attack.

"The general plan of the main attack on the 25th September was as follows :—

"In co-operation with an offensive movement by the 10th French Army on our right, the 1st and 4th Corps were to attack the enemy from a point opposite the little mining village of Grenay on the south to the La Bassée Canal on the north. The Vermelles-Hulluch Road was to be the dividing line between the two Corps, the 4th Corps delivering the right attack, the 1st Corps the left.

"In view of the great length of line along which the British troops were operating it was necessary to keep a strong reserve in my own hand. The 11th Corps, consisting of the Guards, the 21st and the 24th Divisions, were detailed for this purpose.

"From the Vermelles-Hulluch Road southward the advantage of height is on the enemy's side as far as the Bethune-Lens Road. There the two lines of trenches cross a spur in which the rise culminates, and thence the command lies on the side of the British trenches.

"Due east of the intersection of spur and trenches, and a short mile away, stands Loos. Less than a mile further south-east is Hill 70, which is the summit of the gentle rise in the ground.

"Other notable tactical points in our front were :—

"'*Fosse 8*'" (a thousand yards south of Auchy), which is a coal mine with a high and strongly defended slag heap.

"'*The Hohenzollern Redoubt.*'—A strong work thrust out nearly five hundred yards in front of the German lines and close to our own. It is connected with their front line by three communication trenches abutting into the defences of Fosse 8.

"*Cité St. Elie.*—A strongly defended mining village lying fifteen hundred yards south of Haisnes.

"'*The Quarries.*'—Lying half way to the German trenches west of Cité St. Elie.

"*Hulluch.*—A village strung out along a small stream, lying less than half a mile southeast of Cité St. Elie and 3,000 yards northeast of Loos.

"The attacks of the 1st and 4th Corps were delivered at 6.30 a.m. and were successful all along the line, except just south of the La Bassée Canal.

"The enemy met the advance by wild infantry fire of slight intensity, but his artillery fire was accurate and caused considerable casualties.

"The 47th Division on the right of the 4th Corps rapidly swung its left forward and occupied the southern outskirts of Loos and a big double slag heap opposite Grenay, known as the Double Crassier. Thence it pushed on, and, by taking possession of the cemetery, the enclosures and chalk pits south of Loos, succeeded in forming a strong defensive flank.

"The 1st Division, attacking on the left of the 15th, was unable at first to make any headway with its right brigade.

"The brigade on its left (the 1st) was, however, able to get forward and penetrated into the outskirts of the village of Hulluch, capturing some gun positions on the way.

"The inability of the right of this division to get forward had, however, caused sufficient delay to enable the enemy to collect local reserves behind the strong second line.

"The assault of the 7th Division succeeded at once, and in a very short time they had reached the western edge of the Quarries, Cité St. Elie and even the village of Haisnes, the tendancy of the action having been to draw the troops northward.

"On the right of the 9th Division the 26th Brigade secured Fosse 8 after heavy fighting, and the 28th Brigade captured the front line of the German trenches east of Vermelles railway. At the latter point the fighting was extremely severe; and this brigade, suffering considerable losses, was driven back to its own trenches.

"At nightfall, after a heavy day's fighting and numerous German counter attacks, the line was, roughly, as follows:—

"From the Double Crassier, south of Loos, by the western part of Hill 70, to the western exit of Hulluch; thence by the Quarries and western end of Cité St. Elie, east of Fosse 8, back to our original line.

"The situation at the Quarries was readjusted by an attack of the 7th Division on the afternoon of September 26th; and on that evening very heavy attacks delivered by the enemy were repulsed with severe loss.

"On the 4th Corps front attacks on Hulluch and on the redoubt on the east side of Hill 70 were put in operation, but were anticipated by the enemy organising a very strong offensive from that direction. These attacks drove in the advanced troops of the 21st and 24th Divisions, which were then moving forward to attack.

"Soon after dawn on the 27th it became apparent that the brigade holding Fosse 8 was unable to maintain its position, and eventually it was slowly forced back until at length our front at this point coincided with the eastern portion of the Hohenzollern Redoubt.

"In the afternoon of this day the Guards Division, which had taken over part of the line to the north of the 4th Corps, almost restored our former line, bringing it up parallel to and slightly west of the Lens-La Bassée Road.

"This Division made a very brilliant and successful attack on Hill 70 in the afternoon. They drove the Germans off the top of the hill, but could not take the redoubt, which is on the north-east slopes below the crest. They also took the Chalk Pit which lies north of Puits 14, and all the adjacent woods, but were unable to maintain themselves in the Puits itself, which was most effectively commanded by well-posted machine-guns.

"The 47th Division on the right of the Guards captured a wood further to the south and repulsed a severe hostile counter attack.

"During the 29th and 30th September and the first days of October fighting was almost continuous along the northern part of the new line, particularly about the Hohenzollern Redoubt and neighbouring trenches, to which the enemy evidently attached great value. His attacks, however, invariably broke down with very heavy loss under the accurate fire of our infantry and artillery.

"The Germans succeeded in gaining some ground in and about the Hohenzollern Redoubt but they paid heavily for it in the losses they suffered.

"Our troops all along the front were busily engaged in consolidating and strengthening the ground won, and the efficient and thorough manner in which this work was carried out reflects the greatest credit upon all ranks. Every precaution was made to deal with the counter attack which was inevitable.

"During these operations the weather has been most unfavourable, and the troops have had to fight in rain and mud and often in darkness. Even these adverse circumstances have in no way affected the magnificent spirit continually displayed alike by officers and men. In the Casualty Clearing and Dressing Stations, of which I visited a great number during the course of the action, I found nothing but the most cheery optimism among the wounded.

"On the afternoon of 8th October our expectations in regard to a counter attack were fulfilled. The enemy directed a violent and intense attack all along the line from Fosse 8 on the north to the right of the French 9th Corps on the south. The attack was delivered by some twenty-eight battalions in first line, with larger forces in support, and was prepared by a very heavy bombardment from all parts of the enemy's front.

"At all parts of the line except two the Germans were repulsed with tremendous loss, and it is computed on reliable authority that they left some eight to nine thousand dead lying on the battlefield in front of the British and French trenches.

"The position assaulted and carried with so much brilliancy and dash by the 1st and 4th Corps on 25th September was an exceptionally strong one. It extended along a distance of some 6,500 yards, consisted of a double line, which included works of considerable strength, and was a network of trenches and bomb-proof shelters. Some of the dug-outs and shelters formed veritable caves thirty feet below the ground, with almost impenetrable head cover. The enemy had expended months of labour upon perfecting these defences.

"The total number of prisoners captured during these operations amounted to 57 officers and 3,000 other ranks. Material which fell into our hands included 26 field-guns, 40 machine-guns and 3 minenwerfer.

"I deeply regret the heavy casualties which were incurred in this battle, but in view of the great strength of the position, the stubborn defence of the enemy and the powerful artillery by which he was supported, I do not think they were excessive. I am happy to be able to add that the proportion of slightly wounded is relatively very large indeed."

THE GALLIPOLI EXPEDITION.

No operation of the Great War has been more widely discussed than the expedition to Gallipoli which had for its ostensible object the opening of the Straits of the Dardanelles, nor is any likely to be the subject of greater controversy when in the light of more detailed knowledge the history of this great struggle comes to be written. Nor is it matter for surprise that this should be so. The preliminary attempt, in violation of all the accepted lessons of warfare, to attempt the reduction of land forts by naval power alone, the subsequent landing of an army under circumstances in which no student of the art of war would have dared to predict success and few to prophesy anything but failure, the magnificent tenacity and heroism of the troops, the dramatic failure of the enterprise within sight of the promised land, and lastly the unheard-of manœuvre of re-embarking a great army practically without casualties in the immediate presence of a powerful and vigilant enemy : those deeds severally and conjointly serve to make the operation unique and unprecedented in the history of warfare.

It is not in controversy that the expedition to Gallipoli was a minor or subsidiary operation. That is to say, it was not in itself an operation the success or failure of which would *per se* achieve such decisive results as would force either side to give in and be willing to accept terms of peace from its opponent. It is obvious that all subsidiary movements are only justifiable if they tend to further the major plan of campaign. Should they tend in any way to hamper the main operations which are in progress in that locality or those localities where it is intended to force a decision, subsidiary expeditions are not only futile but actually mischievous. Practically all legitimate military enterprises which do not actually form part of the main operations are in the nature of a counter-stroke, and in order to appreciate the struggle for the Dardanelles it is essential to understand what is meant by a counter-stroke, what it actually aims at and what principles govern the selection of its objective. We may define a counter-stroke as a movement made by a belligerent who has lost the initiative for the purpose of relieving the pressure at a vital point. Primarily its aim is no more than

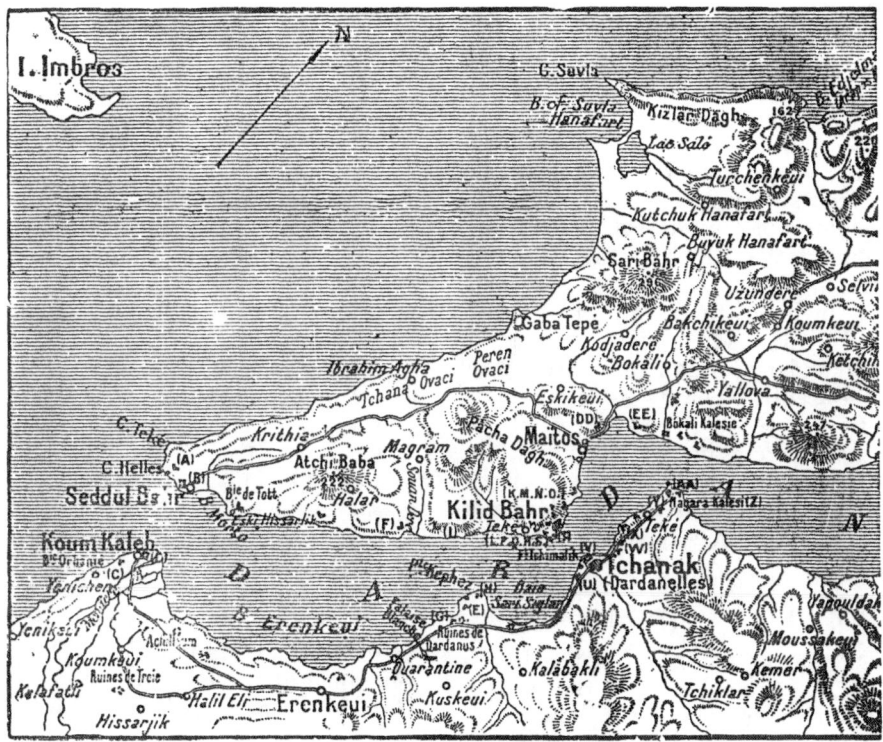

that and no less, but it will be understood that, like all military movements it must have an immediate objective, and the choice of that objective is the crux of the operation. A counter-stroke is not necessarily a minor operation.

In the light of these principles let us consider the Gallipoli expedition, which divides itself naturally into two main phases, the attack by naval power alone and the combined naval and military effort.

We may dismiss at once the idea that has been put forth from many sources that the then First Lord of the Admiralty, having conceived a rash and hare-brained scheme, ordered the Naval authorities to open the Dardanelles much as he might have ordered his butler to open a tin of sardines. As a matter of fact, we know that some of the experts consulted must have approved of the idea, but this by no means implies that even they were of opinion that success was certain.

The ostensible object of the expedition was the opening of the Straits of the Dardanelles with a view to admitting supplies of munitions to Russia and of facilitating the export of large stores of grain and so reducing the high prices of food in the Allied countries. It was also hoped that the movement would draw off and employ considerable Turkish forces that might otherwise be employed against Russia in the Caucasus or in Egypt against the Suez Canal, a communication vital to the Allied operations. But the main immediate object was political. At that time many neutral nations who are now particpants in the conflict had not made up their mind as to which cause they would espouse though it was obvious that they must be expected to come in at some time and the advent of any of them would mean a great accession of force to one side or the other. Turkey had already joined the Central Powers, but had done so at the bidding of a faction in league with Germany. A large proportion of the nation, if not the majority, was not in favour of the course adopted and a bombardment of Constantinople might lead to a revolution in favour of the Allies of the Entente. Italy had great interests in the Balkans and was evidently inclined to favour the Allied cause, while Bulgaria, Greece and Rumania, though largely under German influence, were not bound to the Central Powers by inclination. If the expedition succeeded, the effect would be stupendous and entirely in our favour, while even the anticipation of possible success might keep large forces from the arms of the German Coalition if it did not throw them into those of the Entente.

THE LANDING AT SEDD-EL-BAHR.

In the *Westminster Gazette* Colonel Josiah Wedgwood, M.P., thus described the gallant charge of the Irish troops at the landing at Sedd-el-Bahr:—

It was the Munsters that charged first with a sprig of shamrock on their caps, then the Dublins, the Worcesters, the Hampshires. Lying on the beach, on the rocks, on the lighters, they cried on the Mother of God. Even when I looked ashore I saw five Munsters. They at some moment had got ashore. They had been told off to cut the wire entanglements. They had left the shelter of the bank, charged fifteen yards to the wire, and there lay in a row at two yards' interval. One could hardly believe them dead. All the time great shells kept hitting the shivering ship and doing slaughter in the packed holds. These shells were fired from Asia, but it was the Maxims and pom-poms on Sedd-el-Bahr and on the amphitheatre that kept our heads down below the bulwarks and boilerplate. There now was Midshipman Drury swimming to the lighter which had broken loose, with a line in his mouth and a wound in his head. If ever a boy deserved his V.C. that lad did. And there was the captain of the *River Clyde*, now no longer a ship to be stuck to, but a part for ever of Gallipoli, alone with a boat by the spit of rock trying to lift in the wounded under fire. All these things I saw as in a dream as I moved from casemate to casemate watching to see the Turks wearing an "election smile," and trying to pretend in an even voice to men who had never seen death, that this was the best of all possible worlds. Columns of smoke rose from the castle and town of Sedd-el-Bahr as the great shells from the fleet passed over our heads and burst, and in every lull we hear the wounded. I looked at the Commander on the spit of rock trying to lift in the wounded, and every splash by his side meant a bullet. The Colonel, the second in command, was shot through the head on the bridge. One of my men came to me. "May I go over and help to get in those wounded?" "Why?" I said, and I remembered the story of Stephen Cranes of the man who went across the shell-swept field to get a drink because he was "dared to" by his companions. "I can't stand hearing them crying." He went with the second lot, and another of my men had been before him, and he had dived in without leave, being a single-taxer from Glasgow. He was shot through the stomach, but lives. The Turks could easily have killed all those who went to the wounded. They did not fire on them sometimes for ten minutes, and then a burst of fire would come. Then and afterwards I found them extraordinarily merciful as compared with the Germans in Flanders.

At twelve I had given up all hope. One gun on the ridge and we should be smashed to pieces. At one o'clock I got 20,000 more rounds from the fleet, and the Lancashires were appearing over the ridge to the left from "Lancashire Landing." We saw fifteen men in a window in the castle on the right by the water. They signalled that they were all that remained of the Dublins who had landed at the Camber at Sedd-el-Bahr.

Work of the "Elizabeth."

At three o'clock we got 150 men alive to the shore, and great chunks were flying out of the old castle as the "15" shells from the *Elizabeth* plastered the ten-foot walls. We watched our men working to the right and up into the castle ruins. One watched them through the fire zone and held one's breath and pressed the button of the Maxim. Then night came, but a house in Sedd-el-Bahr was burning brightly, and there was a full moon. We disembarked at once.

All around the wounded cried for help and shelter against the bullets, but there was no room on boats or gangways for anything but the men to come to shore. For three hours I stood at the end of the rocks up to my waist in water, my legs jammed between dead men, and helped men from the last boat to the rocks. Every man who landed that night jumped on to the backs of dead men to the most horrible accompaniment in the world. It was then that I first learnt the shout of "Allah," for the Turks charged. All night long the battle raged on shore. Everyone was firing at they did not know what. Our men went up the hill through the Turks, and the Turks came down through ours, down to the beach over and past each other. They went sometimes not seeing, sometimes glad to pass on in the darkness. One party of our men were found by daylight at the top of the gully on the left, in touch with the Lancashires. It is not necessary to burn your boats to ensure the courage of desperation. It is as good to have your ships firmly aground. The Paladins of that night's fighting knew this and knew what was their position. You must remember that for two nights no one had slept, and then another day dawned. We were firmly ashore at "Lancashire Landing" and at Du Toits battery to the north-east, and the Australians were dug in at Anzac. An end had to be made of V Beach.

The whole fleet collected, and all the morning blew the ridge and castle and town to pieces; and all the time that wonderful infantry went forward up the hill and through the ruined town. The troops that went in that attack had already lost half their strength. The officers that led up those narrow streets, dodging first through gateways, across the openings, and beckoning when safe for their men to come on, were nearly all killed. Dead beat before one o'clock, before the final rush they hesitated. Then our last Colonel, a staff man, Colonel Doughty Wylie, ran ashore with a cane, ran right up the hill; ran through the last handful of men sheltering under the crest; took them with that rush into the trench, and fell with a bullet through his head. But the Turks ran, and the ridge was ours. I had to take the Maxim guns up, skirting the village. If you have never felt afraid, try crawling up a gutter, crawling over dead men, with every wall and corner hiding a marksman trying to kill you. We got the guns into position, and then cleared the village, peering into dark rooms and broken courts in the growing twilight. Everywhere were our dead Munsters and Dublins—some horribly mutilated and burnt. No wounded had survived. Two German officers were found and killed. These fiends, it appeared, had instigated the things done to those dying Irishmen; and we never afterwards found similar Turkish atrocities. The Turks are the finest and best fighters in the world—save only the Canadians and Australians. Of that 29th Division that landed on V Beach, and was finally exterminated within the fortnight that followed the landing, one knows not how to write. On and on, by day and night, ever getting fewer and fewer, they pushed forward till the ground was sown with them. They had never been in action before. They had come from all the corners of the world—from Burma and Pretoria, from the Himalayas and Bermudas—and they all rest in Gallipoli; and may God rest their souls! There was once a division, of which much has been written, that charged over the Fa Al Hill of Al Buera, but their losses were nothing like these. Henderson taught us that Sharpsburg, where one-third of all the Federals and Confederates were left on the field was, for the numbers engaged, the bloodiest battle in history. Sharpsburg was a joy-ride compared with Sedd-el-Bahr; so by this one knows that the men of our race in the past have left bigger men behind them—bigger, at least, in soul and in the spirit of sacrifice.

"DUBLIN HILL."

In a graphic description in *New Ireland*, Mr. Michael M'Donagh thus describes one memorable incident in this long campaign of honour and bravery:—

"There is some dispute, I understand, between the Dublins and Inniskillings as to which regiment the men first in the Turkish trenches belonged. But does it really matter? There is no doubt that the Dublins get the credit for the feat. The battalion was specially complimented by Headquarters for their heroism and endurance. And well they deserved it. What a baptism of fire it was for those inexperienced Irish lads! And what a confirmation of suffering. Over ten hours of continuous open fighting against machine guns and artillery, and on a day of scorching heat! 'We have gained a great name for the capture, and for the splendid regiment which I have the honour to command,' says Colonel Downing. The General of the Division, Sir Bryan Mahon, said he had never seen better work by infantry.

"It recalls a famous episode of the Indian Mutiny. At the siege of Lucknow the bridge of Char Bagh, by which the relieving force had to advance, was raked front and flanks by Indian guns. 'Who is to carry the bridge?' asked Outram. 'My Blue Caps' (the pet name of the 1st Dublin Fusiliers) said Havelock. And they did. With the same irresistible dash, the 6th and 7th Dublins carried Chocolate Hill; in recognition of their feat the hill is now generally known as 'Dublin Hill.'

"AFTER THE BATTLE.

"But there is another side to war, and mournful and tragic though it be, it must not be ignored, even now that the victory has been won. At the last phase of the fight the hills and ravines were flooded with crimson and purple and yellow, as the sun, in regal splendour, went down into the western sea. Those vivid colours were appropriate to the scene—the raging hearts of the opposing forces of men engaged in a death-grapple, the bitter humiliation of the defeated, and the glory of the victor's triumph. Then the night fell and the darkness was softly lit by a multitude of stars in a cloudless and almost blue sky. It seemed to speak most soothingly to the exhausted men of peace, silence, tranquility, and the lapping coolness of running streams."

The Bravery of the Inniskillings.

The Press Association's special correspondent with the British Forces in Macedonia wrote:—

"I have conversed with several of the wounded who took part in the recent fighting on our front. Their narratives confirm what I have already telegraphed in regard to the remarkable pluck and powers of endurance displayed by our men, and although the engagement resulted in our retirement, the enemy was made to appreciate the qualities of the foe to whom he is now opposed, and will probably feel no encouragement to press our flanks too closely. As it was, all the conditions were in his favour. Not only were we outnumbered by about ten to one, but the enemy was abundantly provided with field, mountain, and machine guns. Moreover, as already explained, the mist concealed his movements and enabled him to get quite close to our position unseen.

"Our most advanced position was known as Rocky Bay. The Bulgarian attack began at three o'clock on Monday morning with a tremendous hail of lead poured upon our trenches, which also suffered from whirling fragments of stone, Bulgarian high-explosive shells splintering the rocks and sending fragments in all directions, thus greatly intensifying the effect of their fire. Their infantry then advanced to the attack in massed formation, and were punished severely by our fire. But the scarcity of our guns did not permit us to take a proper toll of his exposed ranks. Our men emptied their magazines, firing rapidly into the advancing crush, and then tried to stem the tide with the bayonet; but they were overborne by sheer weight of numbers, and the position was lost. Nevertheless, the casualties suffered by the Bulgarians made them very cautious about approaching our second line, and having the range to an inch, they plastered our trenches with shrapnel and high-explosive shells.

"It was soon recognised that the position was untenable owing to the weight of the fire the enemy were able to bring to bear, and our troops fell back to their third line of defence. Two companies of the Inniskillings, however, held on to the ridge known as Kevis Crest, and kept the Bulgarians practically the whole morning, although they were backed only by rifle fire. Hardly a man escaped, but their stand impressed and delayed the Bulgars, thus giving us much-needed time to complete our defensive dispositions on our third line, where the Bulgarians were finally held up.

"When these operations are regarded in their proper light—that is to say, as rearguard actions—the splendid work put in by our men can be appreciated, and the fact that the Bulgarians remained in possession of our first and second lines loses its significance."

Connaught Rangers' Brilliant Work.

The following account appeared in the *Daily Mail* of the work in Gallipoli of what is described as "one of the youngest battalions of the Connaught Rangers":—

"On August 20th the battalion was marched towards the left of the position held by the Indian Brigade. From here the next day the Rangers issued out to attack and capture the Kabak Kuzu wells and the Turkish trenches in the neighbourhood. It did not take them long. The men poured out from a gap in the line, shook out to four paces interval, and, with a cheer, carried all before them, bayonetting all the Turks in the trenches, capturing some ground on the Kalajik Aghala. All that night the position was consolidated, and in the morning it was still held by the Rangers. The next day we were thanked by three general officers, and congratulated on the magnificent charge. On August 27th the Rangers were called on to capture another trench on the Kalajik Aghala in conjunction with the Australians. The attack was begun in gallant fashion, but it was stern work. The regiment gained the end of their trench at last, but the troops on their right were held up by a machine gun, and holding on until few survived, they were forced to give way about midnight, as a large force of Turks had broken in by a communication trench. The battalion was again congratulated on its gallantry by three different general officers, of whom one wired to the Commanding Officer as follows:—'Heartiest congratulations from the New Zealand and Australian Division on your brilliant achievement this evening, which is a fitting sequel to the capture of Kabak Kuzu wells, and will go down to history among the finest feats of your distinguished regiment. Personally, as an Irishman who has served in two Irish regiments, it gives me the greatest pride and pleasure that the regiment should have performed such gallant deeds under my command. Stick to what you have got, and consolidate.'"

The 10th Division at the Dardanelles.

The following graphic account of the fighting at the Dardanelles by the 10th Division was written by an officer and a Connaught-man:—

". . . I am somewhere in Turkey—at least they tell me it is Turkey; it might be one of the summer resorts for the inhabitants of Hades—and have been having a rough time. The casualty lists from here since August 1st will convey more to your mind than pages of a letter from me. We met with a terrible hot reception when we arrived here to force a new landing. Shot and shell rained on us from the shore, and aeroplanes dropped bombs all round us. The oldest soldier amongst us that day said he had seen war in all its horrors, but he had never even dreamt of anything so terrible as that landing. Our naval guns did splendid work that day. After a continuous duel lasting from about 4 a.m. till far into the afternoon our big guns triumphed and the Turk had to push back. During all these dreadful hours we were pouring into small boats and wading for the shore. It was dangerous work, and many a poor fellow left the ship's side but never reached the beach, and then—up that shingly beach strewn with dead and dying, dashing through a hail of lead and steel, whilst the thunder of the guns and the bursting of the shrapnel turned the place into a real inferno. Well, thank God, I lived through it all, but all the poor Irish boys who found a grave on the shore—we were all Irish —the like never was on earth! If Irish soldiers never fired another shot their doings in this country since they landed would be sufficient to earn for them a fame equal to, if not greater, than their ancestors won in the past. English, Scotch and Colonial all unite in their praise. 'The Irish are great,' you hear on all sides. Truly they are great to fight and greater still to die. I have looked upon poor Catholic soldiers dying here on the battlefield and have felt prouder than ever I felt before, proud of being a Catholic and proud of being an Irishman."

How the Connaught Rangers Fought.

Private John Grimes, son of Mr. John Grimes, Arran Street, Ballina, writing after the great Irish charge subsequent to the landing of the Irish Division at Suvla Bay, states:—

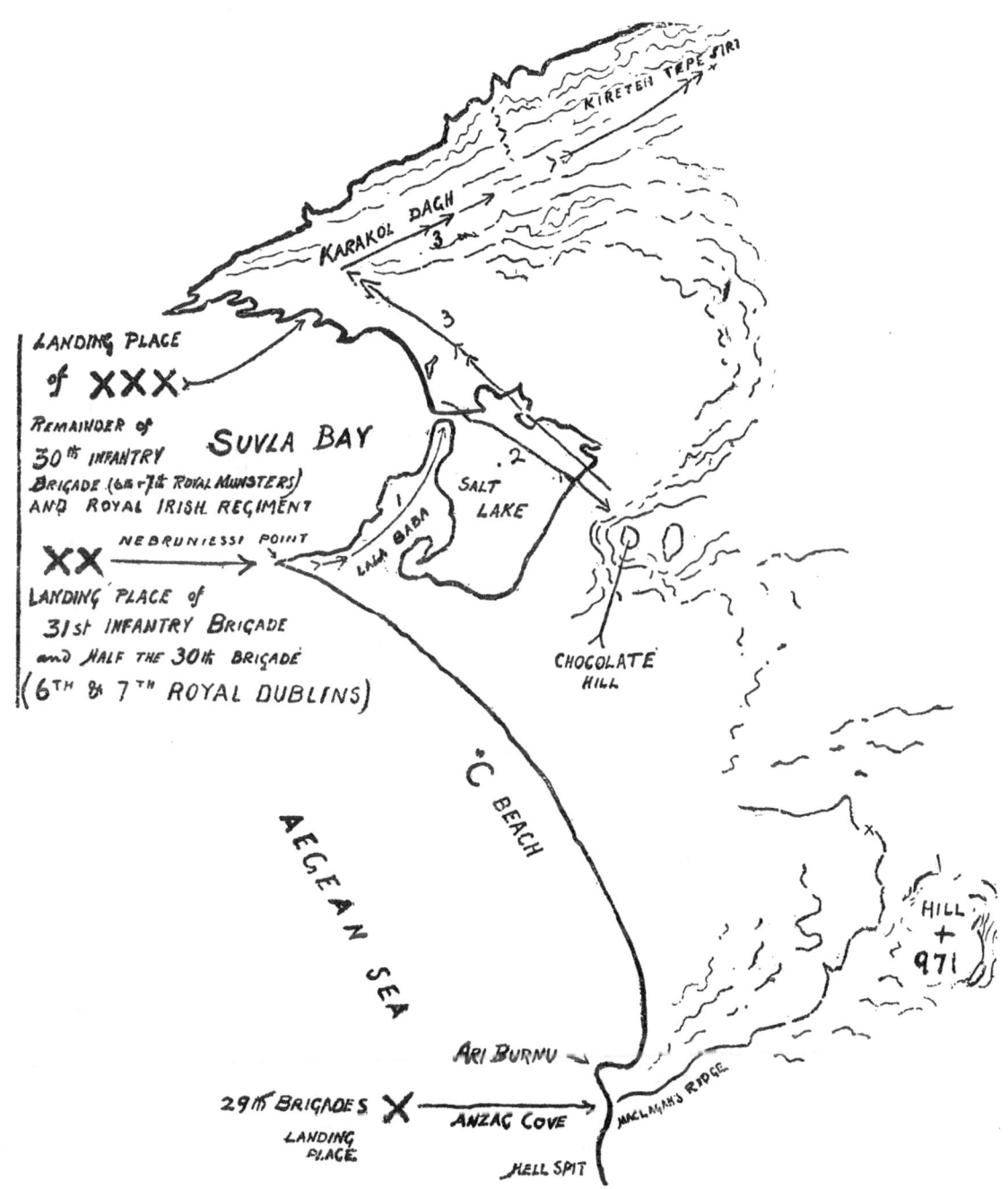

"None of the Connaughts will ever forget the evening of the 21st August. General Godley got the regiment to fall in at 2 p.m., and told us there were five lines of trenches and two spring wells to be taken. Three regiments took them previously, but lost them almost the next hour. He told us it was only the dash of the Irish troops with naked steel that could capture them, and no troops were more fitted than the Rangers to be selected for so dangerous an honour. At 3 o'clock, p.m., we fixed bayonets, and at 4.15 o'clock—an interval which looked like twelve hours—the flag of the Connaughts waved over both the trenches and the wells, though the Turks and Germans fought like devils and got within five yards of our trenches. The Rangers fought like demons, and repulsed the beggars every time, and when all was over we proudly held the trenches and wells. One of our generals said it was one of the finest feats yet performed on the Peninsula. We lost heavily in the terrible charge, but we avenged their deaths in the blood of many a Turk. I got two slight wounds, but took no notice of them. When we charged it was simply hell. The great guns of a dozen warships belched forth, and about ten other batteries of artillery covered our advance. In a few moments the whole mountain side was one sheet of flame. So you can see the Turks had a frightful time, and they will never forget the Ballina boys if the war lasted for five years more"

The 31st Infantry Brigade was composed of the 5th and 6th Royal Inniskilling Fusiliers and the 5th and 6th Royal Irish Fusiliers. They, together with half the 30th Brigade—namely, the 6th and 7th Royal Dublin Fusiliers, landed at Nebruniessi Point, marked "XX" on the map. They were heavily shelled in the steam tenders which took them ashore. Napoleon's soldier carried the famous marshal's baton in his knapsack. Many of our poor fellows did not know the value of the water-bottle which they slung so carelessly over their shoulders. It does not require an effort of the imagination to picture some of them, in their happy-go-lucky vein, landing with their water-bottles half filled. Be that as it may, very soon not a man of them was ignorant of its value. Before the morrow's sun had set, liquid gold, drop for drop, would not have purchased the contents of the water-bottle, were such exchange possible. The scorching August heat and the incessant fighting on the burning sands, which in these early days mainly formed the floor of our operating area, produced a very agony of thirst—so much so that the pain even of the most distressing wounds gave way to the pain of thirst, and the piteous cry of the wounded was often heard: "Water! Water!"

Taking Chocolate Hill.

The line of advance of all brigades was dominated by the Turkish guns in position on the hills, which formed a semi-circle whose extremities ran into the sea. From extremity to extremity measured about eight miles; from the sea line to the centre of the hills about five. The air was fragrant with thyme. The surface generally presented a flat appearance. Its only growth, with the exception of corn very sparingly sown, was a prickly shrub, mostly of the holly type in miniature, bearing something resembling the acorn. The coast gave little or no cover. Within this enclosed area the 10th Division operated. After disembarkation, the Royal Dublins, Inniskillings, and Irish Fusiliers marched over the bare promontory to Lala Baba (route marked "1" on the map) under heavy shrapnel fire. They right-turned sharply and faced the immediate objective—the hill called by the Turks Yilghin Burnu; by us Chocolate Hill, from its burnt appearance after shell fire. In extended order they advanced up the Salt Lake—route marked "2" on the map. At this season the Salt Lake is fairly dry under foot. Its surface glistens with the salt crystals deposited thereon. There was no cover—not a rock, not a shrub—and the advance was right under the enemy guns. It was such as to put the mettle of the bravest troops to the test. As the shrapnel burst over them, comrades fell on every side, but the ranks never wavered for a moment. A veteran officer of many campaigns remarked to me: "These boys are wonderful; they march under shell fire like seasoned troops. Why, they were as calm as if on parade at the Curragh." Chocolate Hill went down that Saturday evening of the landing before the fierce onslaught of the Dublins. Thus blooded, with the 31st Brigade they occupied the hill due south and did not pause till they reached the slopes of Burnt Hill, officially known as Hill W, if my memory serves me right. For military reasons they fell back on Chocolate Hill and dug themselves in. This position they held in the face of great opposition till Friday morning, August 13th, when, after incessant fighting and toil, which knew no sleep, they marched over route marked "3" on the map to rejoin the other half of the 30th Brigade.

The Munsters.

This second half of the 30th Brigade was made up of two battalions, the 6th and 7th Royal Munster Fusiliers. They landed at Suvla Bay, at point marked "XXX" on the map. A few hours later in Suvla Bay the Pioneer Regiment, that is the Royal Irish Regiment, under the command of Lord Granard, also landed. These three regiments formed the entire command of General Mahon during those early days. The artillery of the Brigade went to Cairo. To return to the Munster landing: A German aeroplane hovered like a bird of prey over the lighters, treating them to bombs, which fell harmlessly into the sea. As the lighters crunched upon the sand, about 25 yards from the water line, everyone was congratulating his neighbour on the calm passage. The men jumped into the sea, and, wading ashore, fell in, to find, just as they left the beach, that the Turks had sown contact mines in profusion, first one and then another, and yet another terrific explosion sending poor fellows to their doom. As yet without experience in the workings of explosives, all of us thought it was shell fire, and that the aeroplane had given range. Disembarkation from the lighter ceased. Everyone remained at his post awaiting the finishing stroke from the Turkish guns. After a brief delay, which seemed an eternity, word of command was given to continue the disembarkation. It was carried out in the most orderly way. These raw levies of the previous autumn formed up as cooly as if they were on their native sod. Fighting started straight off. They fought their way along the hill, Karakol Dagh, against an enemy in a very strong natural position, and by Friday evening they had a bivouac ready for their old comrades in arms, the 6th and 7th Dublin Fusiliers, between the heights of Karakol Dagh and the Gulf of Saros. The Inniskillings and Irish Fusiliers arrived, to the best of my belief, the previous day. I witnessed these regiments drag their weary limbs over the ridge of Karakol Dagh. The drawn face and haggard look told of that dreadful week, into which more privation and suffering had been compressed than fall to the lot of most men in a lifetime. Their faces were begrimed with smoke and sweat. The clay of the trenches showed on their hands and through the unshaven beard and close-cropped head, for water was still too scarce for washing purposes. How many inquiries were made about the water supply! How many comments on the virtues of water, which would have gladdened the heart of a total abstinence advocate. Never did eiderdown prove as soft as mother earth, when they sank down upon it, exhausted, to sweet oblivion of their cares, and, perchance to dream of their "Little Grey Home in the West." Whatever about their dreams, their first waking moments were for it. On all manner of odd writing desks, biscuit boxes, knapsacks, haversacks, butt end of rifles, rocks, letters were written. One poor mother just at this time got a letter from her son with a bullet wound through it. A comrade wrote a letter explanatory. After her boy had finished his letter to her, he put it into his breast-pocket. A bullet pierced it and his heart! A human document this, in the inhuman thing called war! It was a comfort to that poor mother that her lad's last thoughts on earth were for her, and I have no doubt he also told her, and it lit up the gloom of the home that he had been to confession. It will bring solid comfort to the bereaved ones to know that during this campaign in Gallipoli, those who fell confessed and received Holy Communion on the day they fell, or certainly a few days previously.

ALPHABETICAL INDEX

A.

Name	Page
ABBOTT, G. D., LT., Conn. Rangers	42
ABERCROMBIE, A. W., LT.-COL., Conn. Rangers	172
ADAMS, S. A., ENG.-LT., R.N.	222
ADCOCK, ST. JOHN, MAJOR, Leinster Regt.	84
ALEXANDER, H. C., LT. HON., 5th Lancers	48
ALEXANDER, H. R. G., LT. HON., D.S.O., Irish Guards	16
ALLANSON, C., COL., D.S.O., Gurkha Rifles	168
ALLENBY, E. H. H., MAJOR-GEN.	76
ALLGOOD, B., CAPT., R.I.R.	36
ALLISON, B. J., CORPORAL, Canadian E.F.	166
ANDERSON, A. J. R., LT., R.I. Regt.	36
ANDERSON, P. M. R., LT., R.I.R.	60
ANDERSON, M. K., LT., R.I. Regt.	84
ANDREWS, R. H., 2ND LT., R.E.	154
ANNESLEY, A., CAPT. HON., 10th Hussars	50
ANNESLEY, THE EARL, R.F.C.	12
APLIN, R. S., 2ND LT., R. Innis. Fus.	4
APPLEYARD, W. D., PRIVATE, R.D.F.	128
APTHORP, S. E., CAPT., D.S.O., Ind. Army	196
ARMSTRONG, G. C., 2ND LT., Coldstream Guards	176
ARMSTRONG, J. N., CAPT., R.A.M.C.	144
ARMSTRONG, W. M., CAPT., 10th Hussars	30
ARMSTRONG, M. R. L., LT., R.E.	204
ARNOTT, J., CAPT., 15th Hussars	166
ATKINSON, J. B., CAPT., R.I.F.	172
AUCHINLECK, D. G. H., CAPT., R. Innis. Fus.	24

B.

Name	Page
BADHAM, F. M., LT., R.N.V.R.	218
BADHAM, L. C., LT., Ind. Corps	212
BAILE, R. C., LT., R.E.	140
BAILEY, C. F. L., LT., R.D.F.	216
BALDWIN, O. G. DE COURCY, CAPT., R.M.F.	182
BALL, C. F., PRIVATE, R.D.F.	158
BALL, W. O. W., LT., R.A.M.C.	24
BANTOCK, A. T., 2ND LT., R. Fus.	192
BANNING, P. S., LT., R.M.F.	28
BARKER, W. H., CAPT., R.G.A.	192
BARNES, F. P., LT.-COL., A.S.C.	186
BARRETT, C. W., CAPT., R.F.C.	236
BARRETT, J., SURG., R.N.	92
BARRETT, P. G., CAPT., R.M.F.	10
BARTON, B. J. B., MAJOR, D.S.O., Duke of Wellington's Regt.	100
BARTON, C. G., LT., R. Innis. Fus.	190
BARTON, F. H., CAPT., Gurkha Rifles	28
BATE, A. F., 2ND LT., R.D.F.	60
BATE, A. L. F., COL., A.M.S., C.M.G.	228
BATTERSBY, A. W., LT., Conn. Rangers	90
BAYLISS, H. V., CAPT., Surrey Regt.	200
BEASLEY, J. J., 2ND LT., R.I. Fus.	132
BEATTY, D., ADMIRAL, C.B., D.S.O.	54
BEATTY, W. D., LT.-COL., R.F.C.	200
BECHER, H. O. D., CAPT., Cameronians	64
BEECH, R. A. J., LT., 16th Lancers	66
BELL, C. F. J., PRIVATE, R.D.F.	158
BELL, R. L., 2ND LT., R.D.F.	94
BELLINGHAM, R. C. N., CAPT., R.F.A.	74
BENNETT, F. E., 2ND LT., R.M.F.	120
BENNETT, G. R., 2ND LT., Conn. Rangers	150
BENNETT, J. W., LT., R.M.F.	144
BENISON, R. B., LT., Conn. Rangers	28
BENT, A. M., LT.-COL., C.M.G., R.M.F.	110
BENTLEY, G. M., CAPT., Northamptonshire Regt.	44
BERESFORD, G. DE LA P., LT., R.E.	168
BERNARD, H. C., COL., R.I.R.	230
BERNARD, R., LT., R.D.F.	230
BERNERS, H. H., CAPT., Irish Guards	10
BERRY, E. F., CAPT., 9th Gurkhas	218
BIBLE, G. R., LT., Sussex Regt.	238
BICKERSTAFFE-DREW, RT. REV. MGR., K.H.S.	38
BIGGS, C., PRIVATE, Canadian Scottish	230
BINGHAM, D. C., LT., Coldstream Guards	26
BIRD, E. B., MAJOR, R.A.M.C.	110
BIRD, W. D. B., LT.-COL., D.S.O., R.I.R.	38
BIRMINGHAM, W. A., 2ND LT., R.I. Fus.	150
BLACK, C. J. F., LT., R.M.L.I.	88
BLACKER, C. F., LT., Conn. Rangers	20
BLAKE, A. J. W., CAPT., Conn. Rangers	140
BLAKE, V. C. J., CAPT., Irish Guards	182
BLAQUIERE, J. DE, LT. HON., Scottish Rifles	68
BLOOD, B., CAPT., 4th Hussars	198
BOHILL, J., LT., R.I.R.	182
BANNISTER, G. E., MAJOR, R.F.A	8
BOND, R. H., LT., Royal Rifle Corps	12
BOND, R. E., MAJOR, 4th Rajputs	64
BOOTH, C. R., LT., Gordon Highlanders	210
BOOTH, E. B., MAJOR, R.A.M.C.	164
BOR, T. H., LT., R.N.R.	218
BORROWES, K. H., MIDSHIPMAN, R.N.	222
BORROWES, W., LT., R.N.	78
BOTHWELL, G., CORPORAL, K.R.R.	184
BOURKE, A. W., LT., R.I. Fus.	94
BOURKE, B. W., CAPT., R.D.F.	118
BOURKE, E. G. W., CAPT., K.R.R.	96
BOWEN-COLTHURST, R. M'G., Leinster Regt.	74
BOYCE, W. W., CAPT., R.A.M.C.	110
BOYD, G. F., CAPT., D.S.O., Leinster Regt.	16
BOYD, H. A., LT., R. Inniskilling Fus.	40
BOYD, W., SERGT., R.I.R.	38
BRABAZON, E. W., CAPT. HON., Coldstream Guards	90
BRADSTREET, G., LT., R.E.	174
BRENNAN, J. H., CAPT., Royal Welsh Fus.	24
BRIDGE, W. P., PRIVATE, R.D.F.	126
BROADWOOD, M. F., LT., West Kent Regt.	22
BROOKE, G., LT., Irish Guards	4
BROOKE, J. A., CAPT., V.C., Gordon Highlanders	57, 138
BROUN, McBRYDE, R. C., LT., R.D.F.	178
BROWN, F. G., CAPT., 101st Grenadiers (Ind. A.)	34
BROWN, H. W., LT., R.I. Reg.	50
BROWN, T. F., LT., Manchester Regt.	86
BROWNE, B. S., LT., R.A.M.C.	136
BROWNE, J. C., LT.-COL., D.S.O., A.S.C.	218
BROWNE, M. H. D. HON., CAPT., Coldstream Guards	142
BROWNE, W. T. R., MAJOR, A.S.C.	206
BRUCE, H. B., CAPT., Norfolk Regt.	62
BUCHANAN, J. H., LT., R.I. Fus.	74
BUCHANAN, R. B., Royal Scots Fus.	88
BULFIN, E. S., MAJOR-GEN., C.B.	30
BURGES, W. A., LT., R.I.R.	78
BURGESS, R. B., CAPT., R.E.	178
BURGH, H. G. DE, LT., M.C., R.F.A.	164
BURGH, T. DE, LT., 31st Lancers	38
BURKE, H. J., LT., South Staffs. Regt.	142
BURKE, J. E., LT., Conn. Rangers	150
BURNS-LINDOW, MAJOR, South I. Horse	110
BURROWES, G. W., LT., R.M.F.	114
BUTLER, O'BRIEN C., CAPT., R.A.M.C., R.I. Lancers	44
BUTLER, L. P., MAJOR HON., Irish Guards	54
BUTLER, P. R., CAPT., R.I. Regt.	76
BUTLER, P. R., CAPT.	180
BYRNE, J., CORPORAL, R.F.C.	204
BYRNE, R. C., LT., R.D.F.	184

C.

Name	Page
CAGNEY, P., DR., R.A.M.C.	186
CAMPBELL, H., LT., R.E.	212
CAMPBELL, J., PRIVATE, R.E.	212
CAMPBELL, MACD., LT., Lancs. Fus.	224
CAMPBELL, T. C., LT., R.E.	142
CARBERY, M. B. C., CAPT., R.I.F.	20
CARDEN, D. A., LT.-COL., Seaforth Highlanders	94
CARGIN, N., LT., N. Staffs Regt.	204
CARRETTE, A. E., LT., R.D.F.	216
CARRY, C. B., PRIVATE, R.H.A.	52
CARUTH, J. G., 2ND LT., R.I.R.	146

	PAGE
CASEMENT, F., CAPT., R.A.M.C.	214
CASEMENT, R. J., LT., 1st Canadians	214
CAULFIELD, J. C., LT., Manchester Regt.	42
CAVAN, EARL OF, BRIG.-GEN., M.V.O., D.S.O.	48
CHALMERS, W. A., LT., Ind. Army	210
CHARRIER, P. A., MAJOR, R.M.F.	18
CHENEVIX-TRENCH, F. M., MAJOR, R.F.A.	10
CHICHESTER, A. G. DE V., LT.-COL., Ind. Army	200
CHRISTIE, A. C., LT., Liverpool Regt.	172
CHRISTIE, J. H., CAPT., R.I.R.	96
CHUTE, C. F. T., LT., R.M.F.	22
CLARK, J., LT.-COL., C.B., Argyle and Suth. Highlanders	113
CLARK, J. L., LT.-COMM., D.S.O., R.N.	214
CLARKE, J., CAPT., R.A.M.C.	138
CLARKE, N. P., CAPT., R.D.F.	66
CLESHAM, T. H., LT., Manchester Regt.	238
CLIBBORN, J. B., LT., Canadian Rifles	194
COATES, G. W., LT., R.F.A.	66
COATES, MONTGOMERY B., LT., Rifle Brigade	144
CODDINGTON, H. J., CAPT., Durham Lt. Inf.	114
COLE-HAMILTON, A. R., COL., East Lancs. Regt.	118
COLHOUN, W. A., CAPT., R.I.F.	208
COLLEN, W. S., LT., R. Innis. Fus.	118
COLLES, A. G., CAPT., R.D.F.	74
COLLINS, N. H., LT., R. Innis. Fus.	206
COLLINS, T. R., STAFF-SERGT., Royal Scots	58
COMBE, S. B., LT., Nth. I. Horse	72
COMYN, L., LT.-COL., D.S.O.	200
CONNELLAN, P. M., MAJOR, Hamps. Regt.	28
CONROY, B., LT., R.D.F.	102
CONSIDINE, C. D., LT., R.D.F.	84
CONSIDINE, J. W., MAJOR, R.M.F.	142
CONWAY, E. P., MAJOR, R.M.F.	114
CONYERS, C., MAJOR, R.I.F.	92
CONYNGHAM, C. A. E., SURG.-CAPT., R.A.M.C.	12
COOKE, C. E., LT., R.I.F.	82
COOKE, E. R., CAPT., R.I.F.	216
CORBALLY, L., CAPT., R.F.A.	176
CORKEY, J. W., CAPT., R.A.M.C.	228
CORRY, C. B., GUNNER., R.H.A.	52
CORRY, T., SERGT., Irish Guards	212
CORSCADDEN, F. T., LT., R.I.R.	240
COSGRAVE, W., CORPORAL, V.C.	108
COSTELLO, G. P., LT., R.E.	118
COULTER, W. H., LT., R.I. Lancers	64
COURTENAY, M. H., LT.-COL., R.G.A.	198
COX, ST. JOHN A., LT.-COL., R.I. Regt.	54
CRAMER, L'ESTRANGE G., LT., R.M.F.	146
CRAWFORD, E., LT., R. Innis. Fus.	82
CRAWFORD, G. S., LT.-COL., R.A.M.C.	212
CREAGH, G. W., COL., C.M.G.	98
CREAGH, J., PRIVATE, S.A.M.R.	236
CREAGH, L., CAPT., Manchester Regt.	46
CREAN, T., MAJOR, V.C., R.A.M.C.	214
CRICHTON, MAJOR VISCOUNT, D.S.O., Royal Horse Guards	2
CRICHTON, H. F., MAJOR, Irish Guards	18
CROCKETT, C. L., LT., R. Innis. Fus.	206
CROFTON, H. L., CAPT., R. Innis. Fus.	84
CROFTON, LT.-COL. LORD, Northumberland Fus.	226
CROOKSHANK, A. C., PRIVATE, R.D.F.	158
CROZIER, B. B., MAJOR, R.F.A.	110
CROZIER, H. C., CAPT., R.D.F.	100
CROZIER, J. C. B., 2ND LT., R.M.F.	26
CRUICKSHANK, P., CAPT., R. Innis. Fus.	234
CRUISE, H. R., CAPT., King's African Rifles	218
CULLINAN, R. H., CAPT., R.M.F.	116
CUMMINS, H. J., LT., Gurkha Rifles	122
CURLEY, F., LT., R.E.	148
CUSACK, R. E., LT., R.D.F.	64
CUTHELL, A. H., MAJOR, West Yorks Regt.	124

D.

	PAGE
DALTON, C., LT.-COL., R.A.M.C.	22
DALY, J., SERGT.-MAJOR, R. Innis. Fus.	184

	PAGE
DANE, J. A., CAPT., R.F.A.	168
DARLEY, A. T., COMM., R.N.	26
DARLING, C. H. W., LT., R.I.R.	170
DARLING, W. C. F., LT., R.I.R.	148
DAVIDSON, J. S., CAPT., R.I.R.	236
DAVIES, N. J., LT., R.D.F.	218
DAVIS, C. L., CAPT., A.S.C.	38
DAVIS, H. O., CAPT., R.I.R.	24
DAVIS, R. C., LT., Manchester Regt.	180
DAVOREN, V. A., LT., Suffolk Regt.	140
DAY, FRANCIS I., MAJOR, R.M.F.	70
DAY, M. C., 2ND LT., Indian Army	10
DEANE, E. C., CAPT., R.A.M.C.	150
DEASE, M., LT., V.C., Royal Fus.	26, 57
DEANE, T. A. D., LT., R.M.L.I.	124
DELANEY, J., LANCE-CORPORAL, R.I. Regt.	52
DELMEGE, J. O'GRADY, LT., R.I. Dragoons	94
DENNIS, W. E., LT., R.H.A.	76
DEWAR, R. J., TROOPER, R.S.G.	212
DICKSON, W. T., CAPT., R.I.R.	240
DILL, J. R., LT., Ind. Army	96
DILL, R. F., CAPT., D.S.O., Ind. Army	58
DOBBIN, G. F., LT., R.I. Fus.	114
DOBBS, C. E. S., LT., A.S.C.	132
DOBBS, G. E. B., CAPT., R.E.	48
DONAGHEY, J., PRIVATE, R. Innis. Fus.	164
DONALDSON, D. H., LT., London Regt.	192
DOONER, A. E. C. F., LT., R.W. Fus.	104
DORAN, B. J. C., BRIG.-GEN., C.B.	54
DORMAN, E. C., CAPT., R.M.F.	120
DORMAN, T. R. H., LT., R.M.F.	234
DOWNING, G., LT.-COL., R.D.F.	188
DOWNING, H. G. O., LT., R.I. Regt.	162
DOWSE, C. E., LANCE-CORPORAL, R.D.F.	128
DOWSE, J. C. A., CAPT., M.C., R.A.M.C.	164
DOUGLASS, R. ST. J. BLACKER, Irish Guards	72
DOYLE, J. J., LT., R.D.F.	130
DRENNAN, J. S., LT., R.F.A.	164
DRURY, W. S., LT., R.D.F.	180
DUFF, L. G., CAPT., Gordon Highlanders	10
DUFFIN, S. B., CAPT., R. Innis. Fus.	137
DUGGAN, F. J., CAPT., R.F.A.	218
DUGGAN, CAPT. G. G., R. Innis. Fus.	122
DUGGAN, J. R., LT., R.I. Regt.	122
DUNN, J. V., CAPT., R.M.F.	120
DUNLOP, J. G. M., 2ND LT., R.D.F.	4
DURAND, F. W., CAPT., R.M.F.	62
DYMOCK, R. T. V., Shrops. Lt. Inf.	152

E.

	PAGE
EAGAR, W. G., CAPT., R.M.F.	118
EAGER, E. F., SERGT., R.I. Regt.	164
EASTWOOD, W., MAJOR, R.E.	118
EDGAR, H., LT., Durham Lt. Inf.	198
ELDRED, J. S., 2ND LT., R.I.R.	44
ELLIOTT, T. C. M., PRIVATE, R.D.F.	128
ELLIS, J. G. ST. J., 2ND LT., R.E.	154
ELLIS, W. F., LT., R. Innis. Fus.	204
ESMONDE, J. H. G., MIDSHIPMAN, R.N.	222
EWART, C. F. K., CAPT., R.I.R.	224

F.

	PAGE
FAIRNBAIRN, A. H., LT., R.I. Regt.	112
FEARN, C. F., LT., R. Innis. Fus.	104
FENTON, G. R., LT., Conn. Rangers	10
FERGUSSON, D., LT., Cameron Highlanders	192
FERNIE, N., LANCE-CORPORAL, R.I. Regt.	52
FERRAR, W. H., CAPT., Royal Welsh Regt.	6
FETHERSTONHAUGH, E., MAJOR, R.D.F.	72
FIELDING, T. E., MAJOR, D.S.O., R.A.M.C.	100
FIGGIS, N. J., LT., Leinster Regt.	114
FINEGAN, H. M., CAPT., King's Liverpool Regt.	90
FINLAY, R. A., LT., R.D.F.	84
FINLAY, G. G., LT., R.I. Regt.	242

Name	Page
Finn, Rev. F., R.D.F.	102
Fisher, H. D., Lt., Shrops. Lt. Inf.	240
Fitzclarence, C., Brig.-Gen., V.C., Irish Guards	68
Fitzgerald, D., Major Lord, Irish Guards	180
Fitzgerald, G. H., Capt., 4th Dragoon Guards	22
Fitzgerald, R. B., Lt., Durham Lt. Inf.	168
Fitzgibbon, M. J., Capt., R.D.F.	126
Fitzgibbon, R. A., Lt., Ind. Army	62
Fitzmaurice, J. G., Lt., R.M.F.	186
Fitzpatrick, G. R., Capt., Welsh Regt.	44
Fitzpatrick, T. W., Lt., R.I. Regt.	52
Fleming, A. F., Staff-Surg., R.N.	168
Fleming, F. C. A., M.C., R.A.M.C.	226
Fleming, G. M. M., Lt., R.A.M.C.	86
Fletcher, J. H., Capt., M.C., R.A.M.C.	188
Foot, W., Capt., M.C., Coldstream Guards	162
Forbes, J. D., Lt., Lancs. Fus.	152
Ford, K. G. H., Lt., Cheshire Regt.	174
Ford, R. D., 2nd Lt., R.I. Regt.	68
Fottrell, B. J., Lt., R.I. Regt.	66
Fowler, G. G., Lt., Royal Rifle Corps	144
Fox, V., Lt., 8th Inf. Brigade	170
Fraser, J., Lt., Conn. Rangers	60
Fraser, W., Lt., Black Watch	176
Freeman, F. P., Lt., R.A.M.C.	98
French, C. A., Capt., R.I. Regt.	84
French, V. D., Lt., Shrops. Lt. Inf.	102
Frend, W. G., Capt., Sherwood Foresters	8
Frizelle, E. S., Lt., Lancs. Fus.	116
Furnell, C. H. M., Capt., Canadian Scottish	230

G.

Name	Page
Gaitskeel, C. E., Lt., G. Leinster Regt.	40
Gallagher, W. A., Capt., East Lancs.	68
Gamble, R. M. B., Lt., Liverpool Regt.	102
Garstin, W. F. C., Major, R.I.F.	113
Gartside-Tipping, Lt.-Comm., R.N.	154
Gates, A., Capt., M.C., Sth. Lancs. Regt.	190
Gaussen, D., Capt., Highland Lt. Inf.	84
Geary, R., Lt., Surrey Rifles	194
Gerrard, H. V., Lt., Border Regt.	6
Gethin, R., Lt., R.M.F.	180
Gibbons, C. B., Lt., R.I. Regt.	20
Giles, V. M., Lt., R.I.R.	236
Gill, Father Rev., S.J., R.I.R.	110
Gilliat, G. P., Lt., Warwick Regt.	24
Gilliland, W., Lt., R. Innis. Fus.	124
Gilliland, V. K., Capt., R.I.R.	96
Gloster, H. C., Lt., Gordon Highlanders	94
Good, W., Lt., R.M.F.	154
Goodbody, O., Lt., R.E.	152
Goodbody, H. E., Capt., Leinster Regt.	90
Goodman, H., Capt., R.I.R.	62
Goold-Adams, J., Capt., Leinster Regt.	88
Gordon, de La Hay, Capt., M.C., Ind. Army	190
Gordon, E., Lt., Ind. Army	172
Gore, A. St. George, Capt., Ind. Army	86
Gore, G. R., 2nd Lt., Sussex Regt.	50
Gore-Langton, M. V., Capt., Irish Guards	152
Gort, Viscount, Capt., M.V.O., Gren. Guards	14
Gough, E. J. F., Capt., Irish Guards	70
Gough, J. B., Lt., R.H.A.	18
Gough, J. E., Brig.-Gen., V.C., C.M.G.	64
Gough, H. W., Hon. Lt., Irish Guards	16
Gray, Robert, Major, R.I. Fus.	28
Green, H., Lt., Ind. Army	116
Greer, J., Lt., M.C., Irish Guards	166
Griffiths, Capt., R.I.R.	232
Griffith, W., Lt., Leinster Regt.	122
Grimshaw, C., Major, R.D.F.	74
Grimshaw, E., Lt.-Col., R.D.F.	192
Grubb, D., Lt., R. Innis. Fus.	122
Grubb, L. L. E., 2nd Lt., Yorks Lt. Inf.	50
Grubb, W. B., Lt.-Comm., R.N.	34
Guernsey, Capt., Lord, Irish Guards	6
Guinness, Rev., P. W.	48
Gunning, D., Lt., R.I.F.	242
Gwynn, Rev. J., S.J., Irish Guards	154

H.

Name	Page
Hack, C. E., Capt., Conn. Rangers	40
Hackett, B. J., Capt., M.C., R.A.M.C.	166
Hackett, H. R. S., Lt., R.I. Fus.	156
Hall, G. P., Lt., Highland Lt. Inf.	4
Hall, J. R. Fitzgibbon, Lt., R.D.F.	92
Hall, R. S., Sergt.-Major, R.D.F.	2
Hamilton, A. D. P., Lt., R.N.	222
Hamilton, A. J., Capt. Lord, Irish Guards	26
Hamilton, E., Capt., R.D.F.	184
Hamilton, E. G., Major, D.S.O., Conn. Rangers	232
Hamilton, H., Sergt.-Major, K.R.R.	184
Hamilton, R. V., Lt., R.I.R.	242
Hamilton-Stubber, Capt., Life Guards	164
Hanafin, P. J., Lt.-Col., D.S.O., R.A.M.C.	200
Hanly, J. M. B., Lt., R.N.	236
Hare, H. V., Capt., Durham Lt. Inf.	34
Harper, E. M., Lt., R.M.F.	116
Harpur, J. H. de La, M.C., Lt., R.I.R.	168
Harrison, W. C., Lt.-Comm., R.N.	42
Harvey, E. G., Capt., Wilts Regt.	90
Hastings, G. H., Capt., Middlesex Regt.	192
Hatch, W. L. R., Lt., R.I. Fus.	70
Haughton, T. G., Lt., R.I.R.	232
Hawarden, Lt. Viscount R. Cornwallis, Coldstream Guards	6
Hawkes, J. C., Lt., R.A.M.C.	130
Hawkes, M. W., Capt., R.M.F.	136
Hay, A. V., Capt. Lord, Irish Guards	6
Hay, J. L., Lt., Northumberland F.	238
Head, H. d'Esterre, Lt., R.D.F.	104
Healy, G. R., Lt., R.M.F.	198
Healy, J. L., Lt., R.I.R.	236
Heffernan, W. P., Lt., R.I. Regt.	90
Henderson, E. L. Hume, Capt., R.M.F.	102
Henley, A. M., Lt.-Col., D.S.O., R.I. Lancers	238
Henry, E., Sergt., R.I.R.	54
Henry, J., Private, Irish Guards	214
Herbert-Stepney, H. A., Major, Irish Guards	42
Heuston, F., Capt., R. Montreal Regt.	216
Heuston, F. G., Lt., R.I. Fus.	216
Hewitt, A. R., Capt. Hon., Surrey Regt.	30
Hewson, F. B., Lt., York and Lancs. Regt.	232
Hickman Poole, H., Capt., R.D.F.	126
Hill, F. T., Major, York and Lancs. Regt.	138
Hind, E. W. G., Lt., R.I.R.	224
Hodge, H. B., Lce.-Corporal, Canadian Rifles	180
Hodge, S., Private, Canadian Rifles	180
Hodges, H. B., Lt., Yorks Lt. Inf.	84
Hodges, J. F., Lt., M.C., R.I. Fus.	100
Hollwey, J. B., Lt., M.C., R.F.A.	136
Holmes, C. C., Lt., Lincs. Regt.	14
Holmes, W. J., Sergt.-Major, Irish Guards	196
Holmpatrick, Lord, Lt., 16th Lancers	48
Holroyd-Smyth, C. E., Capt., M.C., Dragoon Guards	200
Homan, H. L., Capt., Middlesex Regt.	66
Hope, W. E., Lt., Irish Guards	42
Horan, H. E., Lt.	2
Horne, C. M., Capt., R.I.R.	192
Horsfall, A. M., Lt., R.M.F.	178
Howard, S. W., Capt., D.S.O., Conn. Rangers	212
Howley, J. J., Major, Lincs. Regt.	78
Hudson-Kinahan, C. B., Lt., African Rifles	178
Hudson-Kinahan, D., Lt., Irish Guards	204
Hughes, Lt., Sussex Regt.	40
Hughes, C. J., Lt., Conn. Rangers	232
Hume, A. S. V., Major, Scots. Horse	152
Hume-Kelly, G., Capt., Nth. Staffs. Regt.	34
Humfrey, W. K., Lt., Lancs. Fus.	72
Humphreys, G. G. P., Major, Ind. Army	36
Hunt, A. L., Capt., R.N.R.	170
Hunter, J. S. K., Lt., R.F.A.	234

		PAGE
I.		
IRVINE, C. E. S., LT., Rhodesian Rifles		140

J.		
JACKSON, J. L., CAPT., M.C., R.F.C.		186
JACOB, A. L. H., LT., London I. Rifles		152
JAMESON, A. G., LT.-COMM., R.N.		6
JAMESON, H. G., LT., R.E.		118
JARVIS, E. H., MAJOR, D.S.O., R. Innis. Fus.		204
JEFFERSON, V., PRIVATE, R.D.F.		158
JENINGS, G. C., LT., Shrops. Lt. Inf.		18
JENKINSON, J. W., CAPT., R.D.F.		82
JOHN, S. S., LT., M.C., Cheshire Regt.		156
JOHNS, B. D., CAPT., R. Welsh Fus.		194
JOHNSON, D. G., CAPT., D.S.O., S.W. Borderers		58
JOHNSON, M. T., LT., S.W. Borderers		64
JOHNSON, R. D., MAJOR, R.D.F.		86
JOHNSON, T. W. G., LT., M.C., Conn. Rangers		136
JOHNSTON, C. M., CAPT., R.I.F.		236
JOHNSTON, H. A., LT., R.F.C.		180
JOHNSTON, J. C., CAPT., R.I. Fus.		120
JONES, C. D., SERGT., R.I. Fus.		38
JONES, F. G., COL., R. Innis. Fus.		90
JONES, K. W., CAPT., E. Kent Regt.		132
JORDAN, P. J., LT., R. Innis. Fus.		138
JOURDAIN, H. F. N., LT.-COL., C.M.G., Conn. Rangers		200
JOY, C. B., LT., Cheshire Regt.		182
JOY, C. P., LT., R.I.R.		88
JOY, J. C. B., CAPT., Devon Regt.		174
JOYNT, N. L., CAPT., M.C., R.A.M.C.		226
JUDD, F. G. K., LT., R.D.F.		92
JULER, G. C., LT., R.I. Lancers		8
JULIAN, E. L., LT., R.D.F.		128

K.		
KAVANAGH, J. J., CAPT., Conn. Rangers		100
KAVANAGH-MCMURROUGH, C. T., BRIG.-GEN., C.B., M.V.O.		76
KEANE, J. CAPT. SIR, D.S.O., R.F.A.		166
KEATING, H. S., LT., Irish Guards		70
KEELING, G. B., LT., R.I.M.		218
KELLER, C., PRIVATE, R.D.F.		158
KELLY, C. P., LT., R.A.M.C.		231
KELLY, H. A., CAPT., R.E.		8
KELLY, J., CORPORAL, R.D.F.		158
KENNEDY, J. P., CAPT., Scots Rifles		64
KENNEY, STACPOOLE C., LT., Shrop. Lt. Inf.		216
KENNY, W., PRIVATE, V.C.		57
KERR, F., LT., R.I. Regt.		238
KERR-RAIT, R. S., CAPT., Ind. Army		163
KERR-RAIT, S. C., CAPT., R.F.A.		102
KERR-RAIT, W. C., CAPT., D.S.O., R.F.A.		102
KIDD, G. M., CAPT., M.C., R.I. Fus.		186
KIGGELL, LT., R.E.		186
KING, C. S., LT., R.M.F.		86
KING, R. A. F. S., LT., R.D.F.		194
KING-HARMAN, E., CAPT., Irish Guards		94
KINKEAD, R. C. G., CAPT., R.A.M.C.		82
KINSMAN, C. H., LT., King's L. Regt.		240
KITCHENER, FIELD-MARSHAL, EARL, OF KHARTOUM		221
KNIGHT, A. A. A., LT., R.M.F.		16
KNOX, H., CAPT., Manchester Regt.		38
KYLE, L., LT., R.E.		178

L.		
LAKIN, M. L., CAPT., 11th Hussars		98
LALOR, W. J. A., CAPT., M.C., Canadian Inf.		196
LAMBART, R., LT., D.S.O.		48
LAMBERT, C. H., LT., A.V.C.		116
LA NAUZE, W., LT., R.I.R.		96
LANE-JOYNT, A. W., LT., Dorset Regt.		210
LARGE, H. E., CAPT., Rifle Brigade		144
LA TOUCHE, DIGGES, A., LT., R.I.R.		148
LA TOUCHE, DIGGES, REV. DR., Australian I.F.		148
LAUGHLIN, A., LANCE-CORPORAL, R.I.R.		188
LAVERY, J. P., LT., M.C., R.G.A.		204
LAW, F. C., LT., R.M.		162
LAW PAKENHAM, T., LT., Irish Guards		154
LAW, W. J., MAJOR, Lancs. Fus.		176
LEADER, F. W. M., CAPT., Conn. Rangers		28
LEAHY, M. P., CAPT., R.A.M.C.		46
LECKY, A., LT., Leinster Regt.		6
LECKY, GAGE J., MAJOR, A.S.C.		76
LECKY, J. R. F., CAPT., R. Fus.		146
LEFROY, B. P., LT.-COL., D.S.O., Warwick Regt.		142
LEISCHING, W. H., LT., R.I.F.		54
LELAND, J. H. F., LT., R. Innis. Fus.		124
LENNOX, A., LT., R.I.F.		192
LENTAIGNE, V. A., 2ND LT., Conn. Rangers		10
LEONARD, F. P. M., LT., R. Innis. Fus.		206
LESLIE, N. J. B., CAPT., Rifle Brigade		26
LETTS, B. C., LT., R.A.M.C.		194
LEVINGE, SIR R. W., BART., 1st Life Guards		22
LEVIS, J. H. B., LT., R.I.R.		118
LEWIN, A. C., BRIG.-GEN., D.S.O., Conn. Rangers		156
LITTLE, J. W., LANCE-CORPORAL, R.D.F.		158
LLOYD, C. H., CAPT., M.C., R.F.A.		168
LLOYD, E. R., CAPT., R. Innis. Fus.		72
LLOYD, G., PRIVATE, Winnipeg Lt. Inf.		146
LOCHRIN, M. J., CAPT., R.A.M.C.		22
LONGFIELD, J. P., CAPT., Norfolk Regt.		146
LUARD, C. E., MAJOR, D.S.O., Norfolk Regt.		210
LUSHINGTON-TULLOCH, G. DE M., LT., Conn. Rangers		34
LYNCH, F. W., LT., Conn. Rangers		96
LYNCH, J. E., CAPT., York Regt.		148
LYONS, W. T., CAPT., R. Welsh Fus.		210
LYNDON, G. E. B., LT., M.C., R. Inns. Fus.		186

M.		
MACAULEY, W. J., CAPT., A.V.D.		30
MACAUSLAND, O. B., LT., R.I.R.		92
MACCABE, R., LT., London Regt.		178
MACCARTHY, W. J., LT.-COL., R.F.A.		2
MACDERMOT, H. M., LT., R.I. Fus.		112
MACDERMOT, R. W., LT., R.I.R.		174
MACDONALD, C., PRIVATE, R.D.F.		128
MACDONNELL, F. W., MAJOR, W. Yorks. Regt.		174
MACDOWEL, B. G., Conn. Rangers		145
MACGARRY, W. F. C., R.D.F.		130
MACKAY, C. L., LT., Worcs. Regt.		88
MACKAY, J., LT., Gordon Highlanders		170
MACLAUGHLIN, J., LT., R.D.F.		148
MACLAUGHLIN, J. N., CAPT., R.A.M.C.		196
MACLEAR, B., CAPT., R.D.F.		94
MACNAGHTEN, C. M., LT.-COL., C.M.G., Aus. I.F.		200
MACNAMARA, C. C., LT.-COL., R.I.R.		242
MADDEN, G. H. C., COL., Irish Guards		170
MADDICK, H., CAPT., R.I. Lancers		156
MAFFETT, H. T., CAPT., Leinster Regt.		22
MAHONY, F. H., CAPT., Cheshire Regt.		20
MAHONY, M. J., MAJOR, R.A.M.C.		196
MALLINS, C. O'C., 2ND LT., Conn. Rangers		12
MARRABLE, F. A., SERGT., R.D.F.		126
MARTIN, C. J., 2ND LT., A.S.C.		14
MARTYR, J. F., CAPT., R.I.R.		122
MASSEREENE AND FERRARD, MAJOR VISCOUNT, D.S.O.		16
MASTER, C. L., CAPT.		20

	PAGE
MATHIESON, K. R., LT., Irish Guards	24
MATTHEWS, D., LT., Conn. Rangers	234
MATTHEWS, W. F. A., PRIVATE, R.D.F.	158
MAUDE, F. S., BRIG.-GEN., C.M.G., D.S.O.	54
MAWHINNEY, R. J. W., LT.-COL., C.B., R.A.M.C.	224
MAXWELL, A., LT.-COL.	240
MAXWELL, R. S., LT., Black Watch	34
McALISTER, G. M. S., LT., Northumberland Fus.	214
McAULEY, B., CAPT., Border Regt.	116
McCALL, R. A., LT., Cheshire Regt.	138
McCALMONT, D., CAPT.	228
McCARTHY, H. L., CAPT., M.C., R.A.M.C.	166
McCLEAR, P., LT.-COL., R.D.F.	20
McCLELLAN, A. J., LT., R.I.R.	232
McCLENAGHAN, A. B. P., LT., Wilts. Regt.	82
McCOMBIE, L. H. B., CAPT., Uganda V.R.	154
McCONNELL, R. W., LT., Lancs. Regt.	210
McCONNELL, W. C., LT., R.I.R.	238
McCORMAC, H., LT., R. Innis. Fus.	112
McCORMICK, J. A. R., LT., R.N.V.R.	102
McCORMICK, J. G., LT., Worcs. Regt.	82
McCORMICK, J. H. G., CAPT., Warwick Regt.	82
McDONAGH, P., 2ND LT., Royal West Kent	36
McENROY, P., SERGT., Irish Guards	46
McENTIRE, J. T., CAPT., R.A.M.C.	2
McGONIGAL, R. W., LT., M.C., R.G.A.	166
McGRATH, J. J., PRIVATE, R.D.F.	128
McGRATH, N. G. S., LT., Dragoon Guards	36
McLAUGHLIN, A. M., LT., R.I.R.	94
M'LAUGHLIN, A., LT., R.I.R.	174
McMAHON, N. R., BRIG.-GEN., D.S.O.	52
McMAHON, P. S., LT., R.M.F.	176
McMULLEN, A. P., LT., R.N.	234
McNAMARA, V., LT., R.E.	170
McNICOL, R., CORPORAL, R.D.F.	190
MEEKE, REV. H.,	2
MELLOR, W., CAPT., R.I. Regt.	10
MEREDITH, W. J., LT., R.M.F.	78
MILLAR, E. C., SERGT., R.D.F.	126
MILLER, F. W. J. M., LT., Grenadier Guards	10
MILLER, J., CAPT., R. Welsh Fus.	112
MILLER, J. E. B., LT., R.I.R.	90
MILLER, I. F., LT., R. Inniskilling Fus.	48
MILTON, E. T., CAPT., Northumberland Fus.	146
MITCHELL, A. G., LT., R.I.R.	208
MITCHELL, H. M., LT., M.C., R.M.F.	226
MITCHELL, J., LT., M.C., R.F.A.	214
MOFFATT, J. R., CAPT., Leinster Regt.	66
MOLONEY, B. W., CAPT., Lancs. Regt.	68
MONCK, C. H. S., CAPT. THE HON., Coldstream Guards	40
MONTGOMERIE, W. G., CAPT., Leinster Regt.	60
MONTGOMERY, A., 2ND LT., Conn. Rangers	36
MONTGOMERY, A. A., COL., R.H.A.	2
MONTGOMERY, A. S., LT., R. Innis. Fus.	242
MONTGOMERY, R. T., LT., R.I. Fus.	240
MOON, G. B., SURG., R.N.	222
MOORE, D. W., LT., M.G.C.	224
MOORE, G. A., LT.-COL., C.M.G., R.A.M.C.	190
MOORHEAD, A. H., SURG.-COL., I.M.S.	180
MORAN, G. C., LT., R.D.F.	92
MORGAN, J. J. L., LT., R. Innis. Fus.	142
MORRIS, G. H., LT.-COL., HON., Irish Guards	44
MORROGH, F. M. D., LT., R.M.F.	86
MORROW, R., PRIVATE, V.C., R.I. Fus.	108
MORTON, W. J. E., LT., R.I.R.	172
MOWBRAY, J. S., CAPT., Black Watch	140
MOYNA, E. G. J., CAPT., Scots Fus.	152
MULHOLLAND, A. E. S., CAPT. HON.	18
MURDOCH, T. J. C., LT., Manchester Regt.	194
MURPHY, C. F., LT., Ox. and Bucks Lt. Inf.	18
MURPHY, J. N. H., LT., R.D.F.	120
MURRAY, C., PRIVATE, R.D.F.	126
MURRAY, H., LANCE-CORPORAL, R.I.R.	52
MURRAY, P. M., LT., SHERWOOD Foresters	46
MURRAY, R. N., CAPT., R. Innis. Fus.	240
MUSGRAVE, T., LT., Irish Guards	60
MYLNE, E. G., CAPT., Irish Guards	96

N.

	PAGE
NAGLE, G., CAPT., Sussex Regt.	208
NAIRNE, FITZMAURICE, G. E. F. MAJOR LORD, 1st Dragoons	26
NAPIER, LENNOX W. MAJOR SIR, S. Wales Borderers	130
NASH, E. R., CAPT., 16th Lancers	64
NASH, L. C., LT., K.R.R.	148
NEALE, A. H., LT., Ind. Army	198
NEILAN, G. A., LT., R.D.F.	216
NEILL, J. D., LT., R.I.R.	242
NEILL, R. L., LT., R.I.R.	90
NELIS, J. E. T., LT., R. Innis. Fus.	112
NELSON, C., CAPT., Ind. Army	138
NELSON, D., CAPT., V.C., R.F.A.	98
NESBITT, W. C., LT., R.D.F.	144
NEVILLE, V. T., CAPT., Dragoon Guards	92
NEWELL, C. E., LT., R. Innis. Fus.	208
NEWLAND, A. E., MAJOR, D.S.O., R.F.A.	162
NEWPORT, C. J., CAPT., R.I.R.	190
NEWTON-KING, A. R., LT., R.I.R.	68
NICHOLSON, O. H. L., CAPT., D.S.O.	38
NIXON, LT.-COL., D.S.O., Lancs. Regt.	226
NIXON, R. J., CAPT., M.C., R.A.	226
NIXON, G. F., LT., R.A.	78
NIXON, R. H., PRIVATE, M.C., R.E.	188
NOLAN, M. E., LT., R.E.	154
NOLAN, R. H., CAPT., R.A.M.C.	8
NORTHLAND, LORD, CAPT., Coldstream Guards	74
NORWAY, F. H., LT., Duke of C.'s Lt. Inf.	112
NUGENT, G. W., R.I.R.	132
NUGENT, W. A., CAPT. HON., King's Hussars	54

O.

	PAGE
OAKES, H. K., CAPT., Canadian Rifles	174
O'BRIEN, J. F., LT., R.M.F.	44
O'BRIEN, H. C. H., CAPT., R.M.F.	198
O'BRIEN, T. K., CAPT., Conn. Rangers	230
O'BRIEN-BUTLER, C. P., CAPT., R.A.M.C.	26
O'CALLAGHAN, G., CAPT., R.I. Regt.	88
O'CARROLL, F. B., LT., R.D.F.	132
O'CONNOR, M., LT.-COL., R.A.M.C.	178
O'CONNOR, R. D., CAPT., R.A.M.C.	24
ODLUM, W. H., MAJOR, I.M.S.	100
O'DONEL, G. O'D. F. T., CAPT., M.C., Royal Fus.	58
O'DONNELL, T. J., COL., D.S.O.	46
O'DONOVAN, M. H., LT., R.M.F.	224
O'DUFFY, K. E., LT., R.M.F.	120
O'DWYER, R. M., LT., R.F.A.	152
O'GOWAN, R., MAJOR-GEN., Scots. Rifles	196
O'HARA, D., CAPT., D.S.O., R.D.F.	124
O'KEEFFE, J. J., CAPT., A.S.C.	48
O'KEEFFE, M. W., SURG.-GEN., R.A.M.C.	98
O'KELLY, H. K., LT., D.S.O.	98
O'LEARY, M., SERGT., V.C.	57
O'LONE, R. J., CAPT., R.I.R.	170
O'NEIL, A. E. CAPT. HON., M.P., 2nd Life Guards	4
O'REILLY, C. J., CAPT., M.C., R.A.M.C.	168
ORMSBY, G. J. A., MAJOR, R.A.M.C.	58
ORR, R. C., CAPT., Somerset Lt. Inf.	42
ORR, W. L., LT., R.I.R.	146
O'SULLIVAN, A. M., CAPT., R.I.R.	92
O'SULLIVAN, REV. D.	233
O'SULLIVAN, G. R., CAPT., V.C., R. Innis. Fus.	108
OTWAY, H. F., LT., M.C., Leinster Regt.	100
OULTON, W. P., LT., M.C., R.D.F.	162
OZANNE, E. G., CAPT., R. Fus.	172

P.

	PAGE
PACK-BERESFORD, C. G., MAJOR, West Kent Regt.	12
PAGE-LESCHELLES, G., CAPT., R.D.F.	114
PALMER, C., CAPT., Shrops. Lt. Inf.	192

	PAGE
PALMER, I. M., LT., M.C., R.N.	136
PALMER, L. S. N., CAPT., R.D.F.	188
PALMER, R. L., CAPT., R.H.A.	136
PANTER, G. W., LT., R.F.C.	212
PANTER-DOWNES, E. M., BREVET-MAJOR	44
PANTON, H. S. C., CAPT., R.I.F.	188
PARKER, A., LT.-COL., R.I. Lancers	46
PARKER, R. G., MAJOR, Lancs. Regt.	2
PARKER, R. E., LT., R.H.A.	24
PARR, S. J., LT., M.C., R. Dragoons	226
PATRICK, R. M. F., CAPT., M.C., Ind. Army	190
PATTERSON, N. J., LT., R.F.A.	163
PAUL, W., PRIVATE, R.D.F.	128
PEACOCK, W. J., MAJOR, D.S.O., R. Innis. Fus.	228
PEEL, T. A., LT., R.A.M.C.	130
PENROSE, R. F., LT.-COMM., R.N.	4
PERSSE, D. E., CAPT., R.D.F.	60
PERY-KNOX-GORE, A. F., CAPT., A.S.C	14
PHIBBS, W. G., MAJOR, R.I. Fus.	18
PHILBY, D. D., LT., R.D.F.	50
PHILLIPS, B., COL., R. Welsh Fus.	146
PHILLIPS, E. G. D. M., LT., R.I.R.	78
PHILLIPS, T. M., CAPT., R.A.M.C.	12
PHILLIPS, T. McC., CAPT., R.A.M.C.	78
PIGOTT, E. J. K. P., LT., R.I.R.	104
PIKE, M., CAPT., R.F.C.	124
PIKE, R. N., CAPT., W. African F.	146
PIM, H. M., LT., M.C., Ind. Army	214
POE, C. V. L., CAPT., R. Rifle Corps	70
PONSONBY, G. M., CAPT., R. Innis. Fus.	62
PONSONBY, M. MAJOR HON., M.V.O., Gren. Guards	150
PORTER, J. G., CAPT., D.S.O., 9th Lancers	168
PRESSLEY, J. S., LT., Yorks Lt. Inf.	194
PRESTON, A. J. D., CAPT., R.D.F.	122
PRICE, E. D., LT., R.I.R.	218
PRITTIE, F. R. D., CAPT. HON., Rifle Brigade	30
PROCTOR, C. B., CAPT., R. Innis. Fus.	234
PROUDFOOT, R. W., LT., Black Watch	198
PURCELL, R. J. H., LT., King's Royal Rifles	14

Q.

	PAGE
QUIN, F. E., PRIVATE, Canadian F.	132
QUINN, E., CORPORAL, R.F.A.	180
QUINLAN, L., LT., R. Innis. Fus.	206

R.

	PAGE
RADCLIFFE, H. T., CAPT., Leinster Regt.	72
RAMSAY, A. L., LT., R.I.R.	208
RAMSAY, N., LT., Dragoon Guards	4
RAYMOND, A. A., LT., R.I.R.	124
REA, V. T. T., LT., R.I.R.	10
READ, A. M., CAPT., V.C., Northhampshire Regt.	150
READE, J. H. L., LT., Manchester Regt.	34
REEVES, V. C. M., MAJOR, Dorset Yeomanry	198
REID, B., LT., R.D.F.	230
RENNIE, G. J., CAPT., S. African Force	210
RENNY-TAILYOUR, F. T., LT., R.E.	8
REVELL, R. A., CAPT., Essex Regt.	88
REYNOLDS, T. J., CAPT., R.I.R.	12
RICE-SPRING, R., BRIG.-GEN., C.B., R.E.	16
RICHARDS, F. G., MAJOR, R.A.M.C.	86
RICHARDS, W. R., CAPT., R.D.F.	116
RICHARDSON, D. C. H., LT., 12th Lancers	2
RICHARDSON, E., PRIVATE, 17th Lancers	46
RICHARDSON, J. H. K., LT., R.H.A.	76
RICHARDSON, W. T., LT., R.I.R.	238
RICHEY, J. E., LT., M.C., R.E.	228
RIDINGS, C., CAPT., D.S.O., R. Innis. Fus.	100
RILLY, J., CAPT., M.C., R. Innis. Fus.	228
ROBERTS, A. G. M., LT., R. Innis. Fus.	74
ROBERTS, CORPORAL, R.I. Lancers	46
ROBERTS, T. D'E., LT.-COL., R.F.A.	96

	PAGE
ROBERTSON, E. J. M., LT., R.F.A.	176
ROBERTSON, F., CAPT., R. Fus.	104
ROBINSON, E. W., LT., R.I. Lancers	18
ROBINSON, F. R., LT., Sth. Staffs. Regt.	4
ROBINSON, G. ST. G., CAPT., Northamptonshire Regt.	54
ROBINSON, H. S., CORPORAL, 5th Buffs	212
ROBINSON, R. W., CAPT., R. Innis. Fus.	124
ROCHE, REV. F. C.	170
ROCHE, H. A., CAPT., R.M.F.	70
ROCHE, T., MAJOR, Wilts. Regt.	28
ROCHFORT, G. A. B., LT., Scots. Guards	108
ROE, S. G., CAPT., R. Innis. Fus.	24
ROGERS, F. L., LT., R.F.A.	176
ROGERS, G. M., LT., R.I.R.	242
ROGERS, M. C., LT., R.E.	84
RONAYNE, J. A., LT., R.M.F.	142
ROOKE, G., MAJOR, Ind. Army	82
ROONEY, G. C., MAJOR, R.N.	222
ROSE-CLELAND, A. M., LT., R.D.F.	240
ROSS, G. C. C., STAFF-SURG., R.N.	12
ROSS, K., LT., R.I.R.	234
ROSS, M., LT., R.I.R.	140
ROSS, R. J., COL., Middlesex Regt.	30
ROUPELL, G. R. P., LT., V.C., Surrey Regt.	98
RUSHTON, F. H. L., LT., R.I. Regt.	22
RUTTLEDGE, J. F., CAPT., M.C., W. Yorks. Regt.	224
RYAN, C. E., CAPT., M.C., R.F.A.	184
RYAN, D. G. J., CAPT., D.S.O., Ind. Army	184
RYAN, G. J., MAJOR, D.S.O., R.M.F.	182
RYAN, J. H. A., CAPT., K. Liverpool Regt.	156

S.

	PAGE
SADLIER-JACKSON, L. W. DE VERE, CAPT., D.S.O., 9th Lancers	30
SAKER, R., MAJOR, Conn. Rangers	86
SALTER, J. W., LT., R.I.R.	236
SAMPSON, F. C., MAJOR, D.S.O., R.A.M.C.	196
SAMUELS, A. M. O'B., 2ND LT., R.I.F.	6
SARGAISON, W. H., LT., Conn. Rangers	176
SARSFIELD, W. S., MAJOR, Conn. Rangers	50
SCHUTE, J. H., LT., R.I.F.	132
SEWELL, H. S., LT.-COL., D.S.O., 4th Dragoon Guards	166
SHANNON, C. R., CAPT., R.E.	174
SHAW, R., LT., Cheshire Regt.	182
SHELTON, E. W., PVTE., Columbian Contingent	206
SHERIDAN, R. B., LT., R.D.F.	230
SHERLOCK, D., MAJOR, R.A.	196
SHERLOCK, E., CAPT., M.C., R.F.A.	162
SHERLOCK, G. L. E., CAPT., 3rd Hussars	22
SHERLOCK, H. B., CAPT., M.C., R.A.M.C.	184
SHIELDS, H. J. S., LT., R.A.M.C.	28
SHORTT, V. D., CAPT., Northampton Regt.	148
SIMMS, H. R., LT., R.N.	206
SIMMS, CAPT., M.V.O., R.M.F.	20
SMALL, H. A., LT., Liverpool Regt.	242
SMALL, R. G. D., CAPT., Leinster Regt.	30
SMILEY, S. T., SUB.-LT., R.N.	210
SMITH, E. H. S., LT., R.E.	172
SMITH, G., CAPT., Gordon Highlanders	104
SMITH, H. S., LT.-COL., D.S.O., Leicester Regt.	152
SMITHWICK, J. A., CAPT., R.I. Regt.	156
SMITH, R. J., CAPT., Lancs. Fus.	206
SMYTH, I. J., LT., R. Innis. Fus.	138
SMYTH, J., CAPT., Fancs. Fus.	118
SNELL, P. S., LT., R.I.F.	112
SOADY, G. P., PRIVATE, Canadian Force	72
SOMERS, J., SERGT., V.C., R. Innis. Fus.	108
SOMERVILLE, R. N., LT., R.E.	142
STACK, E. H. B., CAPT., Ind. Army	36
STACPOOLE, G. E. G., LT., R.I. Regt.	70
STACPOOLE, R. DE, LT., Conn. Rangers	40
STANTON, R., 2ND LT., R.D.F.	144
STANUELL, C. M., 2ND LT., Durham Lt. Inf.	8

STAPLETON, J. H., M.C.	228
STEPNEY, H., MAJOR, Irish Guards	42
STEVENSON, W. H., LT., R. Innis. Fus.	240
STEWART, G., CAPT., Coldstream Guards	42
STEWART, H., CAPT., R.A.M.C.	14
STEWART, J. A., LT., R.M.F.	172
STEWART, J. M., LT., Irish Guards	68
ST. GEORGE, A. BLIGH, LT., Life Guards	26
STOKAE, J. C., LT., Manchester Regt.	172
STOKES, H. D., LT., King's Own Regt.	74
STRITCH, S., CAPT., Conn. Rangers	194
STUART, C. G., LT., R.N.	188
STUART, J., LT., VISCOUNT, R. Scots Fus.	142
STYLES, F. E., LT., R.M.F.	70
SULIVAN, P. H., 2ND LT., R.M.F.	28
SUPPLE, E. J. C., Duke of Wellington's Regt.	116
SUTTON, R. W., CAPT., R.D.F.	156
SYMES, T. A., PRIVATE, R.D.F.	128

T.

TABATEAU, A. E., FLEET-PAYMASTER, R.N.	176
TAILYOUR, G. H. F., MAJOR, R.H.A.	52
TALBOT, A. D., CAPT., Lancs. Fus.	114
TAYLOR, C. L., SERGT., Sth. I. Horse	188
TAYLOR, E. F., LT.-COL., A.S.C.	14
TAYLOR, H. M., MAJOR, R.I. Fus.	116
TEELING, A. N. A. J. DE L., Norfolk Regt.	20
THOMAS-O'DONEL, G. O'D. F., CAPT., R. Fus.	58
THOMPSON, F. P., LT. Hampshire Regt.	230
THOMSON, E. P., MAJOR, R.M.F.	40
THUNDER, S. H. J., LT.-COL., Northamptonshire Regt.	200
TIDMARSH, D. M., LT., M.C., R.F.C.	228
TIERNEY, T., WT.-OFFICER, R.N.	156
TIMONEY, T. E., PRIVATE, R.D.F.	158
TIPPET, C. H., MAJOR, R.D.F.	126
TISDALL, C. A., MAJOR, Irish Guards	62
TISDALL, C. H., LT., West Kent Regt.	198
TOBIN, R. P., CAPT., R.D.F.	126
TOOMEY, A. R., LT., Leinster Regt.	122
TOTTENHAM, A. H., LT., R. Innis. Fus.	232
TOTTENHAM, E. L., LT., N. Lancs. Regt.	232
TOTTENHAM, D. F. C. L., LT., R.N.	222
TRAILL, H. E. O'B., MAJOR, R.A.	110
TRAILL, W. S., MAJOR, D.S.O., R.E.	184
TRAVERS, H. M., CAPT., R.M.F.	36
TRAVERS, R. S. V., LT., R.M.F.	130
TRIMBLE, A. E. C., LT., R. Innis. Fus.	227
TRIMBLE, M. D., LT., R. Innis. Fus.	216
TURNER, R., LT., M.C., R.D.F.	228
TYNDALL, J. C., R.D.F.	60
TYRRELL, W., LT., R.A.M.C.	76

U.

UNIACKE, R. F., COL., R. Innis. Fus.	88
USHER, I. W., LT., R.I. Regt.	224
USSHER, B., CAPT., Leinster Regt.	104
USSHER, S., CAPT., Ind. Army	104

V.

VALENTINE, R. L., LT., R.D.F.	206
VANCE, C. R. G., LT., Cheshire Regt.	64
VANCE, P. H. G. I., SUB-LT., R.N.	222
VANDELEUR, W. M. C., CAPT., Essex Regt.	18
VANRENEN, A. S., COL., R. Innis. Fus.	122
VERNON, C. E. G., CAPT., R. Innis. Fus.	120
VERNON, H. F., SUB-LT., R.N.	222
VERSCHOYLE, F. S., LT., R.E.	88
VINCENT, A. B. L., LT., Dragoon Guards	164
VŒUX DES, H. C., LT., R.M.F.	96

W.

WALDRON, F. F., CAPT., R.F.C.	14
WALKER, C. A. L., LT., R. Innis. Fus.	238
WALKER, C. E., CAPT., R.A.	136
WALKER, J. M., LT.-COMM., R.N.	208
WALKER, T. K., LT., Irish Guards	204
WALLACE, K. M., LT., R.I.F.	204
WALLACE, Q., CAPT., M.C., R.A.M.C.	162
WALLER, H. W. L., CAPT., R.A.	132
WALLIS, B. H., LT., M.C., Ind. Army	190
WALSH, A. C. M., 2ND LT., R.H.A.	68
WALSH, P. J., LT.-SURG., R.A.M.C.	140
WALSHE, E. J. C., LT., Leinster Regt.	78
WALSHE, R. H., CAPT., M.C., R.H.A.	186
WARMINGTON, A. E., CAPT., R.I. Regt.	208
WARNOCK, H. A. H., LT., R.I.F.	140
WARNOCK, R., LT., M.C., R. Scots Fus.	226
WARREN, P. T., LT., R.A.M.C.	114
WATSON, J., LT., R.E.	14
WEATHERILL, E. T., LT., R.D.F.	126
WELDON, H. W. C., LT., R.I.F.	208
WELDRICK, G. J., LT., R.N.R.	86
WELLESLEY, R., CAPT., LORD, Grenadier Guards	8
WEST, R. ANNESLEY, LT., Nth. I. Horse	38
WESTON, A. H., BRIG.-GEN., D.S.O.	52
WHEELER, C. P., CAPT., R. Berks. Regt.	138
WHEELER, G. M., MAJOR, V.C., I.E.F.	194
WHEELER, S. G. DE C., CAPT., R.D.F.	76
WHELAN, J. P., CAPT., R.I.R.	40
WHITFIELD, A. N., LT., R.I.R.	20
WHITE, E. S., WARRANT OFFICER, R.N.	186
WHITE, J. M., LT., A.V.C.	210
WHITE, T., LT., N. Lancs. Regt.	242
WHITE, W. H., MAJOR, R.I. Regt.	120
WHITFORD, M., LT., R.I.R.	234
WHITSITT, J. R., LT., R. Innis. F.	130
WHITTY, J. L., LT., Leinster Regt.	110
WICKHAM, A. T. C., LT., Conn. Rangers	4
WILLIAMS, C. B., CAPT., R.I.R.	132
WILLIAMS, DE COURCY, 2ND LT., Middlesex Regt.	34
WILLINGTON, J. V. Y., LT., Leinster Regt.	120
WILSON, C. H., CADET, R.N.	40
WILSON, H. H., MAJOR-GEN., D.S.O.	48
WILSON, H. W., CAPT., E. Yorks Regt.	154
WISELEY, F. J., LT., R.A.M.C.	138
WOODS, J., MAJOR, I.M.S.	92
WOOD-MARTIN, F. W., CAPT., Suffolk Regt.	94
WOODROFFE, R. L., LT., Irish Guards	44
WOOKEY, M., LT., R.I. Regt.	74
WORDSWORTH, J. L., LT., R.I. Lancers	44
WORKMAN, E., LT., M.C.	182
WORTHINGTON, N. T., LT., Lancs. Regt.	178
WYLIE, A. W., LT., Lincs. Regt.	72
WYNTER, C. D., CAPT., Irish Guards	170
WYNYARD, D., CAPT., Surrey Regt.	82

Y.

YATE, C. A. L., MAJOR, Yorks. Lt. Inf.	16
YOUNG, C. R., LT., R.A.M.C.	6
YOUNG, G. N. P., LT., Leinster Regt.	58
YOUNG, R. A., LT., R.M.F.	68
YOUNG, S. V., 2ND LT., R.E.	150

OUR HEROES

MENTIONED IN DESPATCHES.

Company Sergeant=Major Robert S. Hall entered the 1st Battalion Royal Dublin Fusiliers in 1894, and served with the Battalion all through the South African campaign, receiving the Queen's Medal with 5 clasps and the King's Medal with 2 clasps. He afterwards served in Malta, Crete and Egypt, and was eventually transferred to the 2nd Battalion, with which he is now at the front. He has been mentioned in Sir John French's despatches, and the French Government have awarded him the Medaille Militaire for distinguished service in the field.

✧ ✧ ✧

The Rev. Hugh Meeke, M.A., Presbyterian Chaplain, mentioned in Sir John French's despatches. He is the son of the Rev. James Meeke, B.A., Kingsmills, Co. Armagh. During his service Mr. Meeke has acted as Military Chaplain in Dublin, Tientsin (China), and Aldershot. He was in the retreat from Mons, and is at present with the troops near Ypres.

✧ ✧ ✧

Lieutenant Henry E. Horan, who has been awarded the Distinguished Service Cross.

✧ ✧ ✧

Major R. G. Parker, King's Own Lancaster Regiment, who has been mentioned in Sir John French's despatches, is the son of Mr. R. G. Parker, J.P., of Ballyvalley, Killaloe, Co. Clare. He served in the South African War, being present at nearly all the important engagements during the campaign. He was mentioned in despatches twice, and received the Queen's Medal with 6 clasps and the King's Medal with 2 clasps.

✧ ✧ ✧

Colonel Archie A. Montgomery, R.H.A., entered the service in November, 1891; was gazetted Lieutenant in 1894 and Captain in 1900, and obtained his majority in June, 1909. He served in the South African War, taking part in numerous engagements during the campaign. He was mentioned in despatches in September, 1901, received the Queen's Medal with 4 clasps and the King's Medal with 2 clasps. Since December, 1910, he has been serving on the General Staff. He has been mentioned in Sir John French's despatches.

✧ ✧ ✧

Major Viscount Crichton, M.V.O., D.S.O., of the Royal Horse Guards, who has been mentioned in Sir John French's despatches, is the eldest son of the Earl of Erne, K.P., and is extra Equerry to King George V., having previously acted as A.D.C. to His Majesty when, as Duke of Cornwall and York, he made his celebrated tour of the Colonies in 1901. He passed from the Royal Military College at Sandhurst into the Royal Horse Guards, and served in the South African campaign, acting as A.D.C. to Major-General Brocklehurst, being mentioned in despatches, and receiving the Queen's Medal with 5 clasps and the D.S.O. In 1903 he married Lady Mary Grosvenor, daughter of the first Duke of Westminster.

✧ ✧ ✧

Lieutenant Derek C. H. Richardson, 12th Royal Lancers, mentioned in despatches of October 19th, is the only son of Mr. Charles H. Richardson, J.P., Cedarhurst, Co. Down. He was educated at Eton and Sandhurst, and entered the army in 1907. He accompanied his Regiment to the front in August, and has been in the midst of the fighting ever since. He took part in the brilliant charge made by his Regiment on August 28th, and again on October 31st, when the 12th Lancers drove the Germans out of a small town at the point of the bayonet—an exploit which gained for them unlimited praise from Sir John French.

✧ ✧ ✧

Captain James T. McEntire, R.A.M.C., mentioned in despatches. He is the eldest son of the late Mr. Alexander Knox McEntire, B.L., Merrion Square, Dublin. He was educated at St. Andrew's College, Dublin, and Trinity College, obtaining his commission in the R.A.M.C. in 1903 and his Captaincy in 1907. He left for the front on August 18th, and has been mentioned in despatches, and has been awarded the Cross of the Legion of Honour by the French Government for gallantry and conspicuous service in the field.

✧ ✧ ✧

Lieutenant George O'Donel F. Thomas O'Donel, 4th Battalion Royal Fusiliers. He is mentioned in despatches, and is the only son of Mr. and Mrs. Thomas O'Donel, of Newport House, Newport, Co. Mayo, and grand-nephew of the late Sir George C. O'Donel, Bart. He was educated at Cheltenham College, and entered the Royal Donegal Artillery Militia as Lieutenant, from which regiment he was gazetted to the Royal Fusiliers, in which he is now serving. He was married last week at Kensington to Violet, only daughter of Mr. George Claude Braddell, of Newlands, Ferns, Co. Wexford. He is a keen sportsman, and when stationed in Mullingar was well known in the hunting field.

✧ ✧ ✧

Lieutenant=Col. Morgan John MacCarthy, 32nd Brigade, Royal Field Artillery, who was mentioned in Sir John French's first despatches, served with distinction through the South African War. He was at the defence of Ladysmith, and in the operations in Natal, and in the Transvaal, and was mentioned in despatches in September, 1901. He received the Queen's Medal with four clasps.

1. SERGT.-MAJOR R. S. HALL, 1st Royal Dublin Fusiliers.
2. REV. HUGH MEEKE, M.A., Chaplain.
3. LIEUT. HENRY E. HORAN.
4. MAJOR R. G. PARKER, King's Own Lancaster Regiment.
5. COLONEL ARCHIE A. MONTGOMERY, Royal Horse Artillery.
6. MAJOR VISCOUNT CRICHTON, M.V.O., D.S.O., Royal Horse Guards.
7. LIEUT. DEREK C. H. RICHARDSON, 12th Royal Lancers.
8. CAPT. JAMES T. McENTIRE, Royal Army Medical Corps.
9. LT. GEORGE F. T. O'DONEL, 4th Royal Fusiliers.

Supplement to Irish Life, December 4th, 1914.

DIED FOR THEIR COUNTRY.

2nd Lieutenant John Gunning Moore Dunlop, Royal Dublin Fusiliers, who was killed in action while directing part of the firing line at Clarg. He was third son of the late Mr. Archibald Dunlop, M.D., of Holywood, Co. Down. He received his commission from Cambridge University in September, 1910, and was gazetted to the Special Reserve of Officers, Royal Dublin Fusiliers, in June, 1911.

✧ ✧ ✧

Lieutenant Commander R. F. Penrose, of Waterford, who went down with the battleship "Bulwark" in the disaster at Sheerness.

✧ ✧ ✧

Lieutenant Gerald Percy Hall, Highland Light Infantry, who was killed in action on the 17th November. He was the second son of Mr. and Mrs. R. Hall, of Glenmervyn, Glanmire, Co. Cork. He was only 19 years of age.

✧ ✧ ✧

Captain the Hon. Arthur Edward Bruce O'Neill, M.P., 2nd Life Guards, who was killed in action on November 6th, was the elder son of Lord O'Neill, 2nd Baron, and entered the Army in 1897, obtaining his Captaincy five years later. He served in the South African War, 1899-1900, and was present at the relief of Kimberley, and in the operations at Paardeberg and Dreitfontein. He also saw service south of the Orange River and at Colesberg. He received the Queen's Medal with three clasps. In January, 1910, he was elected unopposed Unionist Member for the Mid-Antrim division, and continued to represent that constituency until the time of his death. In 1902 he married Lady Annabel Crewe-Milnes, eldest daughter of the Marquis of Crewe.

✧ ✧ ✧

2nd Lieutenant R. S. Aplin, Royal Inniskilling Fusiliers, killed in action. He was born in 1892, and joined the 4th Battalion of the Royal Inniskilling Fusiliers in 1913, and left for the front in September.

✧ ✧ ✧

Lieutenant A. T. C. Wickham, Connaught Rangers, killed in action. Gazetted to the 4th Battalion of the Connaught Rangers in October, 1907. He was the son of Mr. and Mrs. Wickham, of the Manor, Holcombe, near Bath.

✧ ✧ ✧

Lieutenant F. R. Robinson, South Staffordshire Regiment, who was killed in action on the 27th October, was the youngest son of the late Mr. St. George C. W. Robinson and Mrs. Robinson, Woodville, Sligo, and nephew of Sir Edward Carson. He was educated at Malvern College, and receiving his commission shortly before the declaration of war, he accompanied the first British Expeditionary Force which landed in France, and he took part in nearly all the important engagements of the campaign up to the time of his death.

✧ ✧ ✧

Lieutenant George Brooke, of the Irish Guards, who died from wounds received while with the Expeditionary Forces in France, was the eldest son of Sir George Brooke, Bart., of Summerton, Castleknock, Co. Dublin. Mr. Brooke saw service in the South African War and received the Queen's Medal with three clasps. He was formerly Gentleman-in-Waiting to Lord Cadogan, Lord Lieutenant of Ireland, and married in 1907, Nina, only daughter of Lord Arthur William Hill. Mr. Brooke was in his 38th year, and rejoined his old regiment at the beginning of the present war. During his period of retirement he lived at Ballyfad House, Inch, Co. Wexford, and though fond of hunting, his chief recreations were shooting and the breaking of gundogs.

✧ ✧ ✧

Lieutenant Norman Ramsay, 4th Dragoon Guards, killed in action in France, November 4th. Lieut. Ramsay was born in April, 1880, and was the second son of the late Captain John Ramsay, R.E., and Mrs. Ramsay. He was related to and named after Norman Ramsay, who distinguished himself at Fuentes d'Onoro, in 1811, during the Peninsular War. Lieut. Ramsay was educated at Cheltenham College, and entered Cooper's Hill in 1898. Taking a direct commission in the Royal Field Artillery, in January, 1900, he served in South Africa from February, 1901, to the end of the war, being mentioned in despatches. He retired from the Army at the end of 1903, but volunteered for service at the beginning of the present war, and in September received a commission in the 4th Dragoon Guards and sailed for France on October 18th.

✧ ✧ ✧

Lieutenant Gerrard Ferrers Nixon, R.F.A., who was killed in action on October 25th, was gazetted 2nd Lieutenant, December, 1910, and obtained his promotion as 1st Lieutenant three years later. He was the youngest son of Major-General Nixon, D.L., of Clone, Ballyragget, Co. Kilkenny.

1. 2nd LIEUT. JOHN GUNNING MOORE DUNLOP, Royal Dublin Fusiliers.
2. 2nd LIEUT. R. S. APLIN, Royal Inniskilling Fusiliers.
3. LIEUT. COMMANDER R. F. PENROSE, H.M.S. "Bulwark."
4. LIEUT. GERALD PERCY HALL, Highland Light Infantry.
5. CAPTAIN THE HON. ARTHUR EDWARD BRUCE O'NEIL, M.P., 2nd Life Guards.
6. LIEUT. A. T. C. WICKHAM, Connaught Rangers.
7. LIEUT. F. R. ROBINSON, South Staffordshire Regiment.
8. LIEUT. GEORGE BROOKE, Irish Guards.
9. LIEUT. NORMAN RAMSAY, 4th Dragoon Guards.

DIED FOR THEIR COUNTRY.

2nd Lieutenant Arthur M. O'B. Samuels, Royal Irish Fusiliers, was killed in action in France on October the 13th. He was the son of the late Lieut.-Col. Wm. Frederick Samuels and Mrs. Samuels, Kingstown. He was attached to the South Irish Horse, and later to the Inniskilling Fusiliers. He was gazetted to the Special Reserve of the Royal Irish Fusiliers, and was commissioned to the first Battalion on the outbreak of the war, and accompanied the regiment to the front.

◇ ◇ ◇

Lieutenant=Commander Arthur George Jameson, R.N., commanding Submarine D2, who met his death by being washed overboard on November 23rd. He was the third son of Mr. Robert W. Jameson, of Campfield House, Dundrum, Co. Dublin. He entered the Navy in 1898, and became a Lieutenant in July, 1905, and two months later joined the Forth to specialise in submarine duties, and after having the command of the B. class he was made Captain of "C2" in 1908-1910. During 1911 he was Lieutenant on the H.M.S. "Neptune," Sir Francis Bridgeman's Flagship in the Home Fleet, and was one of the officers who qualified for War Staff Duties in the first batch appointed for that purpose in April, 1912. On passing out at the end of that year he served on the H.M.S. "Antrim" for War Staff Duties in the 3rd Cruiser Squadron, and returned to the submarine branch of the service in March of this year.

◇ ◇ ◇

Lieutenant Averell Lecky, 2nd Battalion Prince of Wales' Leinster Regiment, was killed in action near Armentieres on October 20th. He was the second son of Lieut.-Col. John Page Lecky, late 75th Regiment, now residing in Guernsey, and grandson of the late Mr. Hugh Lecky, of Beardville, Co. Antrim. He joined the service in December, 1908, and was gazetted first Lieutenant in October, 1910.

◇ ◇ ◇

Captain Lord Arthur Vincent Hay, Irish Guards, killed in action. Second son of the late 10th Marquis of Tweedale. He was born in 1886, and in 1911 he married Menda, daughter of the late Mr. Ambrose Ralli, and was heir presumptive to his brother the 11th Marquis of Tweedale.

◇ ◇ ◇

Captain Walter Hughes Ferrar, 2nd Battalion Royal Welsh Regiment, was killed in action on November 2nd. He was the youngest son of the late Mr. A. M. Ferrar, D.L., of Torwood, Belfast. Captain Ferrar entered the Army in 1897, and obtained his Company in 1904. He served in the South African War in 1900-2, being employed with the Mounted Infantry. He was present at the relief of Ladysmith and took part in various actions, including those at Paardeberg, Vet River, Zand River, and Diamond Hill. From May to November, 1900, he was serving in the Orange River Colony and was in action at Wittebergen and at Witpoort. He was in the operations in Cape Colony and in the Orange River Colony, and was in several actions in the Transvaal during the spring of 1902. He obtained the Queen's Medal with five clasps and the King's Medal with two clasps.

◇ ◇ ◇

Captain Lord Guernsey, Irish Guards, killed in action, was the eldest son of the 8th Earl of Aylesford. He was born in June, 1883. After serving for a time in the Irish Guards he retired and was attached as Captain to the Warwickshire Yeomanry, but he rejoined his regiment on the outbreak of hostilities. In 1905 he acted as A.D.C. to the Governor of Gibraltar, and in June, 1907, he married the Hon. Gladys Cecil Fellowes, 2nd daughter of Lord De Ramsey.

◇ ◇ ◇

Lieut. Charles Robert Young, R.A.M.C., who died of wounds received at the battle of the Aisne, was the son of Dr. B. Poyntz Young, of Sandymount Road, Dublin. He was 4th officer of SS. "Bray Head," of Belfast, previous to joining the Expeditionary Force. He was only 23 years of age.

◇ ◇ ◇

Lieutenant Harry Vernon Gerrard, Border Regiment, was killed in action on November 2nd. He was the fourth son of the late Mr. Thomas Gerrard, Crown Solicitor, and Mrs. Gerrard, of 5 Appian Way, Leeson Park, Dublin. He first joined the 4th Battalion of the Royal Munster Fusiliers, and was subsequently attached to the Army Service Corps. He was gazetted to the 2nd Battalion of the Royal Garrison Regiment on its formation, and served as Adjutant of the Battalion at Malta and in South Africa. When the regiment was subsequently disbanded, he was appointed to the 2nd Batt. of the Border Regiment. Being seconded, he served in the Southern Nigerian Regiment (West African Field Force), but rejoining the Border Regiment on the outbreak of hostilities he proceeded with it to the front. He was promoted to Captain's rank on the 30th October, and three days later he was killed in action near Ypres.

◇ ◇ ◇

Lieutenant Robert Cornwallis, Viscount Hawarden, Coldstream Guards, killed in action. He was the only son of the 5th Viscount Hawarden, and entered the service in February, 1911, and obtained his promotion as first Lieutenant in September, 1913. He succeeded his father in 1908, and bears the title of Baron de Montalt in Ireland and also a Baronetcy created in 1705.

1. 2nd LIEUT. ARTHUR M. O'B. SAMUELS, Royal Irish Fusiliers.
2. LIEUT.-COMM. ARTHUR G. JAMESON, R.N., Submarine D2.
3. LIEUT. AVERELL LECKY, 2nd Prince of Wales Leinster Regiment.
4. CAPTAIN LORD ARTHUR VINCENT HAY, Irish Guards.
5. CAPT. WALTER HUGHES FERRAR, 2nd Royal Welsh Regiment.
6. CAPT. LORD GUERNSEY, Irish Guards.
7. LIEUT. CHARLES R. YOUNG, Royal Army Medical Corps.
8. LIEUT. HARRY VERNON GERRARD, Border Regiment.
9. LIEUT. ROBERT CORNWALLIS, VISCOUNT HAWARDEN, Coldstream Guards.

DIED FOR THEIR COUNTRY.

Lieutenant George Crickett Juler, 5th Royal Irish Lancers, entered the service February 8th, 1908, and was promoted 1st Lieutenant, March, 1909, he was well-known in Dublin, where the regiment was stationed for a considerable time at Marlborough Barracks, and left with them in August for the front, where he was killed in action.

✧ ✧ ✧

Captain Lord Richard Wellesley, Grenadier Guards, killed in action. He was the second son of the fourth Duke of Wellington. He entered the Army as 2nd Lieutenant in May, 1900, was promoted Lieutenant in January, 1904, and obtained his Captaincy in June, 1908. He served in South Africa during the war from 1899 to 1901. He took part in the operations in the Orange Free State, being slightly wounded at Paardeberg, was also in action at Poplar Grove, Karee Siding, Houtnek, Vet River and Zand River. He was in action in the Transvaal near Johannesberg and Pretoria, and was again in the Transvaal from July to November, 1900, being in action at Belfast. He received the Queen's Medal with four clasps and the King's Medal with two clasps. In 1908 he married Louise Nesta Pamela, only daughter of Sir Maurice Fitzgerald, Knight of Kerry.

✧ ✧ ✧

2nd Lieutenant Charles Martin Stanuell, Durham Light Infantry, killed in action. He was gazetted from the Royal Military College in January, 1914. When at school at Cheltenham and also at Sandhurst he was regarded as a brilliant Rugby three-quarter, he played against Woolwich for two years, and last November was reckoned as a very important addition to his side. When Woolwich and Sandhurst combined and met the Army at Queen's Club in December, Captain Rainsford-Hannay marked young Stanuell as a very promising player for future army teams.

✧ ✧ ✧

Capt. Harry Holdsworth Kelly, F.R.G.S., Royal Engineers, who was killed in action on October 24th, was the youngest son of Lieut. H. H. Kelly, of Montrose House, Southsea, and grandson of the late Mr. John Collum, of Bellevue, Co. Fermanagh. Captain Kelly was educated at Rugby School, and entered the Army in 1889. He served with the Egyptian Army from 1903 to 1913, he was Resident Engineer for the construction of the town and harbour of Port Sudan and received the 4th class of Osmani for his services in connection with this work. For the last five years of his service in Egypt he was Inspector of Roads and Communications, and was awarded the Sudan Medal in 1911. He acted as Intelligence Officer in the expedition against the Beir and Annauk tribes in 1912, also as Chief Commissioner of the Sudan Ugunda Boundary Commission receiving the 3rd class Osmani. He also had the third class Mejidieh. In the years 1907, 1911 and 1913 he spent his leave in exploring Abyssinia, and when the present war broke out he accompanied the expeditionary forces in the 38th Field Company Royal Engineers.

✧ ✧ ✧

Major George Emil Bolster, R.F.A., who was killed in an engagement near Ypres was the eldest son of the late Surgeon-Major T. G. Bolster, A.M.S., and nephew of Deputy-Inspector General George Bolster, R.N, of Springville, Kanturk, Co. Cork. He entered the service in November, 1895, was promoted in 1898, obtained his captaincy in 1901, and his majority in 1912. While making a reconnaissance he and his escort of only three men, were shot by the Germans. Major Bolster was a well-known sportsman and freqently hunted with the Duhallow and Kildare Hounds.

✧ ✧ ✧

Captain William Reginald Frend, 2nd Battalion, Sherwood Foresters. Entered the service in 1898, was made Lieutenant in 1900 and Captain in September, 1904. He served in the South African War, taking part in the operations in the Orange Free State, including the actions at Houtnek, Vet River and Zand River, also in the Transvaal and Cape Colony, South of the Orange River and was again fighting in the Transvaal in the summer of 1901 and the spring of 1902. He obtained the Queen's Medal with three clasps and the King's Medal with two. He was appointed Adjutant of his Regiment in December, 1912.

✧ ✧ ✧

Lieutenant Henry Frederick Thornton Renny=Tailyour, Royal Engineers, gazetted in December, 1912. He was son of Colonel H. Renny-Tailyour, of Shrewsbury House, Merrion, Co. Dublin.

✧ ✧ ✧

Captain Raymond H. Nolan, Royal Army Medical Corps, was gazetted Lieut. in January, 1909, and promoted Captain in July, 1912. He was married a little over a year ago to the eldest daughter of the Master of the Rolls and Mrs. O'Connor.

✧ ✧ ✧

Lieutenant John Fraser, Connaught Rangers, who died of wounds received in the Battle of the Aisne, was the eldest son of Mr. J. Fraser, of Riversdale, Boyle, Co. Roscommon, he joined the Connaught Rangers in January, 1905, and after three years' service in India, he was employed with the King's African Rifles (6th Battalion) in the operations in Somaliland from 1908 to 1910, for which he obtained the Medal with clasps. From July, 1909 to January, 1913, he acted as A.D.C. to the Governor and Commander-in-Chief in Uganda. He was a keen soldier, a fine sportsman, and a very successful big game hunter. The wounds which proved fatal were received while he was carrying a wounded brother officer out of the firing line into safety.

OUR HEROES

1. LT. GEORGE C. JULER,
5th Royal Irish Lancers.

2. CAPT. LORD RICHARD WELLESLEY,
Grenadier Guards.

3. 2nd LIEUT. CHARLES M. STANUELL,
Durham Light Infantry.

4. CAPT. HARRY H. KELLY, F.R.G.S.,
Royal Engineers.

5. MAJOR GEORGE E. BOLSTER,
Royal Field Artillery.

6. CAPT. WILLIAM R. FREND,
2nd Sherwood Foresters.

7. LIEUT. HENRY F. T. RENNY-TAILYOUR,
Royal Engineers.

8. CAPT. RAYMOND H. NOLAN,
Royal Army Medical Corps.

9. LIEUT. JOHN FRASER,
Connaught Rangers.

DIED FOR THEIR COUNTRY.

2nd Lieutenant Maurice Charles Day, 13th Rajputs, Indian Army, killed in action in East Africa, November 4th, 1914. He was the eldest son of the Very Rev. Maurice W. Day, Dean of Waterford. He was gazetted as 2nd Lieutenant, September, 1911. He was educated at Aravon School, Bray; Marlborough College, and Trinity College, Cambridge (B.A. Wrangler, 1913).

◇ ◇ ◇

Lieutenant Geoffrey Russell Fenton, 2nd Battalion Connaught Rangers, killed in action. He was the youngest son of Mr. W. Russell Fenton and Mrs. Fenton, of Ardaghowen, Sligo. He was educated at Cheltenham College and Sandhurst and joined his regiment in 1909. He married the elder daughter of Lt.-Col. E. H. Montresor, commanding the 2nd Batt. Royal Sussex Regiment, who was killed at the battle of the Aisne.

◇ ◇ ◇

Captain Philip Godfrey Barrett, Royal Munster Fusiliers, was killed in action. He served with the Militia in the South African War, and was transferred to the Royal Munster Fusiliers, being gazetted Lieutenant in 1902 and obtained his Captaincy in 1908. Between November, 1907, and September, 1908, he acted as Adjutant in the Militia and the Special Reserve. He received the Queen's Medal with two clasps after the South African War.

◇ ◇ ◇

Major Francis Maxwell Chenevix-Trench, R.F.A., killed in action on October 31st. He was the son of Colonel C. Chenevix-Trench, of Broomfield, Camberley. He was born in September, 1879, and joined the Army in 1898, being gazetted Lieutenant in the Royal Artillery in 1901 and obtaining his Captaincy in May, 1907. He served in South Africa from 1899 to 1901, and took part in the defence of Ladysmith and the various operations in Natal, including the actions at Talana, Lombard's Kop and Laing's Nek. During the war he had two Staff appointments, that of A.D.C. to the Lieutenant-General commanding the Infantry Division and A.D.C. to the Lieutenant-General commanding the 1st Army Corps. He was twice mentioned in despatches and received the Queen's Medal with six clasps. From November of 1907 until December, 1910, he was employed with the Egyptian Army. During the Sudan Campaign of 1908 he took part in the operations of the Blue Nile Province, receiving the Egyptian Medal. In August of last year he was appointed Brigade-Major, Royal Artillery, 2nd Division, in the Aldershot command.

◇ ◇ ◇

Captain Lachlan Gordon Duff, Gordon Highlanders. He was the eldest son of Mr. T. Gordon Duff, of Drummuir, and Park House. He was born in January, 1880, and entered the Military College at Sandhurst 1898. A year later he was gazetted to the Gordon Highlanders, joining the 1st Battalion as 2nd Lieutenant. In January, 1900, he was promoted Lieutenant and had attained Captain's rank when he retired. On the outbreak of hostilities he at once rejoined his regiment and was killed in an engagement in the North of France on the 24th October. In April, 1908, he married Miss Lydia Dorothy Muriel Pike, daughter of Mr. Joseph Pike, D.L., of Dunsland, Co. Cork, where he was well known in the Southern hunting fields, and was a member of the United Hunt Club. During the South African War he saw a good deal of service and had both medals with clasps.

◇ ◇ ◇

Captain Hamilton Hugh Berners, Irish Guards, who was killed in action, was the third son of Mr. C. H. Berners, J.P., Woolverstone Park, Suffolk. He entered the Army in November, 1905, as 2nd Lieutenant and six months later was gazetted Lieutenant, and in December, 1912, he obtained his Captaincy.

◇ ◇ ◇

Lieutenant F. W. J. M. Miller, Grenadier Guards, killed in action on October 23rd. Mr. Miller was the elder son of Sir William Miller, Bart., of Glenlee, and Lady Miller, youngest daughter of Mr. Charles John Manning, brother of Cardinal Manning. Mr. Miller was educated at Sandhurst and gazetted to the Grenadier Guards in February, 1912, and obtained his Lieutenancy in August last.

◇ ◇ ◇

Lieutenant Vivian T. T. Rea, B.A., 2nd Batt. Royal Irish Rifles, killed in action at Neuve Chapelle on October 25th. He was the only son of Mr. Henry Tighe Rea, of Glandore Park, Belfast, and grandson of the late Mr. Hugh Rea, of Clifton Lodge, Belfast. He joined the 4th Batt. of the Royal Irish Rifles two years ago and was promoted and selected for service with the 2nd Batt., which he joined at the front on September 27th. He was a very popular student at Trinity College, Dublin, where he had a distinguished career, gaining many honours, including the medal of the Theological Society for oratory, which was awarded this year and was only sent to his parents after his death. He was Hon. Secretary of the Ulster Provisional Council of Baden-Powell's Scouts, and an enthusiastic Scoutmaster and an earnest worker amongst the young men and boys of Bangor, Co. Down.

◇ ◇ ◇

Captain Walter Mellor, 2nd Battalion Royal Irish Regiment. He was born in 1878 and entered the Army in 1899, obtaining a commission in the Lancashire Fusiliers through the Militia. He obtained his Captaincy in 1905 and was transferred to the Royal Irish Regiment three years later. He served in the South African War and took part in the operations in the Transvaal in Natal and in the Orange River Colony, later acting as railway officer in the Transvaal from January, 1901, to May, 1902. He received the Queen's Medal with four clasps and the King's Medal with two clasps.

1. 2nd LIEUT. MAURICE C. DAY, 13th Rajputs, Indian Army.	2. LIEUT. GEOFFREY R. FENTON, 2nd Connaught Rangers.	3. CAPT. PHILIP G. BARRETT, Royal Munster Fusiliers.
4. MAJOR FRANCIS MAXWELL CHENEVIX-TRENCH, 2nd Division, Royal Artillery.	5. CAPT. LACHLAN GORDON DUFF, Gordon Highlanders.	6. CAPT. HAMILTON H. BERNERS, Irish Guards.
7. LIEUT. F. W. J. M. MILLER, Grenadier Guards.	8. LIEUT. VIVIAN T. T. REA, B.A., 2nd Royal Irish Rifles.	9. CAPT. WALTER MELLOR, 2nd Royal Irish Regiment.

DIED FOR THEIR COUNTRY.

Lieutenant Robert Harold Bond, King's Royal Rifle Corps, killed in action at the Battle of the Aisne, September 14th, 1914. He was the only son of Colonel R. J. Bond, R.E. He was a keen soldier, and a fine horseman and athlete. He was educated at Wellington College, and joined the 2nd Battalion of the K.R.R.C. in 1903, and was gazetted 1st Lieutenant in 1907.

◇ ◇ ◇

Staff-Surgeon G. C. C. Ross, R.N., eldest son of Surgeon-Colonel G. C. Ross, late I.M.S., and grandson of the late Charles A. Ross, M.D., of Castlecomer, Co. Kilkenny. He was lost in H.M.S. "Hawke," which was sunk by a German submarine on 15th October, 1914. He was educated at Warwick and Trinity College, Dublin. Served in H.M.S. "Magnificent," in the Ambassador's Yacht, H.M.S. "Hussar" (Constantinople), and in H.M.S. "Niobe." He was in medical charge at Devonport Dockyards, and also at Whale Island School of Gunnery, and was appointed to the "Hawke" on the outbreak of the war. He was just forty years of age, and was a very skilful and successful surgeon, and was very popular in the Navy.

◇ ◇ ◇

2nd Lieutenant Victor A. Lentaigne, Connaught Rangers, killed in action at the Battle of the Aisne. He was the youngest son of Sir John Lentaigne, F.R.S.C.I., Merrion Square, Dublin, and grandson of the Right Hon. Sir John F. Lentaigne, P.C., D.L. Mr. Lentaigne was only twenty-one years of age, and was gazetted to the Connaught Rangers in January, 1914.

◇ ◇ ◇

Captain Thomas M. Phillips, R.A.M.C., was a native of Belfast, and a graduate of the Queen's University of that city.

◇ ◇ ◇

Major Charles George Pack-Beresford, 1st Battalion Queen's Own Royal West Kent Regiment, was killed in action near Mons. He entered the army in 1889; saw service on the north-west frontier of India (1897-98); was present at the action at Landakai and the operations in Bajaur and in the Mamund country; he was also in the attack and capture of the Tanga Pass, and was awarded a Medal with clasp. He served in the South African War (1899-91), taking part in the operations in the Orange River Colony and in the Transvaal. He was mentioned in despatches, and was awarded the Queen's Medal with four clasps.

◇ ◇ ◇

Surgeon-Captain Cecil A. E. Conyngham, Royal Army Medical Corps, killed in action in East Africa. He was the son of Mr. Henry Conyngham, of 40 Waterloo Road, Dublin, and a graduate of Trinity College, where he received the M.B. Degree. He was for some time in charge of the Loyal North Lancashire Regiment, and was stationed at Bangalore. On the outbreak of war he at once applied to be sent to the front, and left Bombay for East Africa on the 16th October. He was a keen athlete and a good Rugby player, and during his college career was noted as a swimmer.

◇ ◇ ◇

2nd Lieutenant Claude O'Conor Mallins, 2nd Battalion Connaught Rangers, killed in action November 2nd. He was the elder son of the late Captain Frederick W. Mallins, 3rd Battalion East Lancashires, and Mrs. Henry O'Connell-Fitzsimon, 31 Pembroke Road, Dublin.

◇ ◇ ◇

Captain T. J. Reynolds, Royal Irish Rifles, only son of the late Mr. T. J. Reynolds, C.E., Ceylon, entered the army April, 1900; obtained his Captaincy in 1909, and was appointed Adjutant of the 3rd Battalion May, 1914. Early in his military career he was recommended for service with the Housas force in West Africa, and took part in the Ashanti Expedition, for which he received the Medal. Appointed a Lieutenant in the Royal Dublin Fusiliers, he joined his battalion in India, where he was later appointed to the Staff. On obtaining his company he was transferred to the 2nd Battalion Royal Irish Rifles, where he was again recommended for service as Adjutant to the Territorial Forces, and held this appointment for one year. Last January he was appointed to the 3rd Battalion Royal Irish Rifles, and accompanied the regiment from Belfast to Dublin on the outbreak of the war, leaving Dublin for the front on September 24th. He was a well-known cricketer, and at one time played for the Leinster Cricket Club.

◇ ◇ ◇

The Earl Annesley, Royal Flying Corps, was lost in an aeroplane accident when crossing from the South of England to France on his return to the front. During the campaign he rendered valuable services both in scouting and conveying messages. He was the only son of the fifth Earl. He was born in February, 1884, and was married in September, 1909, to Evelyn Hester, eldest daughter of Mr. Alfred E. Miller Mundy, of Shipley Hall, Co. Derby.

◇ ◇ ◇

Lieutenant Rhys Ivor Thomas, Connaught Rangers, who was killed in action, is amongst the officers mentioned in Sir John French's first despatches. He entered the service in April, 1910, and obtained his promotion as 1st Lieutenant in 1912 and was regarded as a very smart and efficient officer.

Supplement to Irish Life, December 4th, 1914.

1. LIEUT. ROBERT H. BOND, King's Royal Rifles.
2. STAFF-SURGEON G. C. C. ROSS, R.N., H.M.S. "Hawke."
3. 2nd LIEUT. VICTOR A. LENTAIGNE, Connaught Rangers.
4. CAPT. THOMAS M. PHILLIPS, Royal Army Medical Corps.
5. MAJOR CHARLES G. PACK-BERESFORD, Queen's Own Royal West Kent Regiment.
6. SURGEON-CAPT. CECIL A. E. CONYNGHAM, Royal Army Medical Corps.
7. LIEUT. CLAUDE O'CONOR MALLINS, 2nd Connaught Rangers.
8. CAPT. T. J. REYNOLDS, Royal Irish Rifles.
9. THE EARL ANNESLEY, Royal Flying Corps.

MENTIONED IN DESPATCHES.

Lieutenant R. J. H. Purcell, 2nd Battalion King's Royal Rifles, mentioned in Sir John French's despatches for gallantry in the Battle of the Aisne. He was severely wounded in the engagement, and unfortunately his wounds are of such a nature as to prevent his return to the firing line for some time.

Lieutenant Cecil Crampton Holmes, 1st Lincolnshire Regiment, son of Captain H. W. Holmes, late North Staffordshire Regiment, of Rockwood, Galway. He entered the army October, 1907, and was promoted 1st Lieutenant in November, 1911. He took part in the action at Fourmies, near Mons, on August 24th, when he was wounded. He was maxim gun officer on that occasion, and displayed great bravery and coolness under fire, causing considerable loss to the enemy, and putting two of their guns out of action. While lying wounded he continued to direct and encourage his men, and his services were mentioned in Sir John French's despatches.

Captain Viscount Gort, M.V.O., Grenadier Guards. Lord Gort is the sixth holder of the title, and was born in July, 1886, and educated at Harrow and Royal Military College, Sandhurst, and was gazetted to the Grenadier Guards in 1905. He was A.D.C. from 1913 to this year to Major-General Sir Francis Lloyd, K.C.B., C.V.O., D.S.O., Commanding the London District. On the outbreak of the war Lord Gort was appointed A.D.C to Major-General C. H. Munro, Commanding the 2nd Division, and was mentioned in Sir John French's despatches. He was married in February, 1910, to his cousin, Corinne, only daughter of Mr. George M. Vereker, of Abbeyfeale, Co. Limerick, and Sharpitor, Salcombe, South Devon.

Lieut.=Colonel Ernest Fitzwilliam Taylor, Army Service Corps, entered the service August, 1888, being gazetted Lieutenant Royal Irish Fusiliers. Served in the South African War; took part in the advance on Kimberley, and was in action at Belmont, Enslin and Modder River; was engaged in the operations in Cape Colony and Orange River Colony, and was twice mentioned in despatches during the campaign. He received the Queen's Medal with three clasps and the King's Medal with two clasps. He left the Royal Barracks, where he had been stationed a considerable time, on the declaration of war, and proceeded to the front with his corps, and has been mentioned in despatches.

Captain A. F. Pery=Knox=Gore, Army Service Corps, obtained his Commission November, 1902, and was promoted Captain in May, 1911. Joined the service from the Militia, and was mentioned in Sir John French's despatches.

Captain Hugh Stewart, R.A.M.C., son of the late Hugh Stewart, Cheshire Regiment, joined the Army Medical Service in 1905, and has since served five years in India. Since the outbreak of hostilities he has been attached to the 10th Field Ambulance (4th Division), and has been mentioned in despatches.

Lieutenant Julian Watson, R.E., who was stationed for a considerable time in Dublin on Post Office duty at Aldborough House, and who has been carrying out important work in connection with the Field Telephones at the front, and has been mentioned in Sir John French's despatches.

2nd Lieutenant Charles Jasper Martin, A.S.C., son of the late Lieutenant Charles F. Martin, Connaught Rangers, and grandson of the late Mr. James Martin, D.L., of Ross, Co. Galway. He was educated at Wellington College, and served in the Special Reserve (3rd Battalion) of the Connaught Rangers for two years, passing into the Army Service Corps in December, 1912. He has been mentioned in Sir John French's despatches.

Captain Francis F. Waldron, Flying Commander, Royal Flying Corps, was gazetted 2nd Lieutenant 19th Hussars in May, 1907, and was promoted Captain in June of the present year. He is a son of General Waldron, Handicapper to the Turf Club and I.N.H.C., and is distinguished in many fields of sport besides being a skilled aeronaut.

1. LIEUT. R. J. H. PURCELL, 2nd King's Royal Rifles.
2. LIEUT. CECIL C. HOLMES, 1st Lincolnshire Regiment.
3. CAPT. VISCOUNT GORT, M.V.O., Grenadier Guards.
4. LIEUT.-COL. ERNEST FITZWILLIAM TAYLOR, Army Service Corps.
5. CAPT. A. F. PERY-KNOX-GORE, Army Service Corps.
6. CAPT. HUGH STEWART, Royal Army Medical Corps.
7. LIEUT. JULIAN WATSON, Royal Engineers.
8. 2nd LIEUT. CHARLES J. MARTIN, Army Service Corps.
9. CAPT. FRANCIS F. WALDRON, Flying Commander, Royal Flying Corps.

MENTIONED IN DESPATCHES.

2nd Lieutenant William Hugh Coulter, 5th Royal Irish Lancers, entered the service February, 1912, and accompanied the Regiment to France on the outbreak of hostilities, and was mentioned in Sir John French's despatches. He is a member of the Subaltern's Regimental Polo Team, and is a good all-round sportsman.

✧ ✧ ✧

Captain Gerald Farrell Boyd, D.S.O., Leinster Regiment, entered the service May, 1900, and obtained his captaincy in March, 1904; served in the South African War from 1899 to 1902; was present at the Relief of Ladysmith and the action at Colenso; took part in the operations of the Orange River Colony, and in the Transvaal and Cape Colony. He was employed with the Mounted Infantry, and was mentioned in despatches upon three occasions, receiving the Medal for distinguished service in the field; he had the Queen's Medal with three clasps and the King's Medal with two clasps.

✧ ✧ ✧

Lieutenant the Hon. Hugh William Gough, Irish Guards, only son of Viscount Gough, K.C.V.O. He entered the service in January, 1912, and was promoted 1st Lieutenant in 1913. He took part with his Regiment in the various actions during the present campaign, in which the Irish Guards acquitted themselves so magnificently. He has been mentioned in Sir John French's despatches.

✧ ✧ ✧

Major Charles Allix Lavington Yate, King's Own Yorkshire Light Infantry, entered the service in 1892, and obtained his majority in July, 1899; served on the north-west frontier of India and with the Tirah Expeditionary Force, receiving the Medal and clasp; served through the South African War, and took part in the advance on Kimberley, being in action at Belmont and Enslin, where he was dangerously wounded. He was also present during the operations in the Transvaal from February to May, 1902, and was mentioned in despatches, and received the Queen's Medal with four clasps. During the Russo-Japanese campaign he was attached to General Kuroki's army in Manchuria, and received the Japanese War Medal and the Order of the Sacred Treasure, 4th Class. He was mentioned in Sir John French's despatches.

✧ ✧ ✧

Brigadier-General Spring R. Rice, C.B.R.E., entered the service in 1877, and after a most distinguished career was promoted Lieutenant-Colonel in 1903 and full Colonel in 1908. He served in the South African War, and took part in the operations in Natal, including the action at Lombard's Kop, and as Chief Royal Engineer greatly distinguished himself in the defence of Ladysmith. He was responsible for perfecting the blockhouse system, which played such an important part in the Boer War. He was mentioned twice in despatches, and obtained the Queen's Medal with three clasps and the King's Medal with two clasps. He held the position of Chief Engineer at Aldershot, and is now serving with the Headquarters 1st Army. He has been mentioned in Sir John French's despatches.

✧ ✧ ✧

Major Viscount Massereene and Ferrard, D.S.O., North Irish Horse, formerly 17th Lancers, entered the army in 1895; served through the South African War, and was mentioned twice in despatches. He was promoted Brevet-Major, and received the Queen's Medal with four clasps and the King's Medal with two clasps and the D.S.O. He retired in 1907, having married in 1905 Jean Barbara, daughter of Mr. Stirling-Ainsworth, M.P. He has been mentioned in Sir John French's despatches.

✧ ✧ ✧

Lieutenant Hon. Harold Rupert Leofric George Alexander, Irish Guards, third son of the late Earl of Caledon, entered the service in September, 1911, and was promoted 1st Lieutenant in December, 1912. He accompanied his Regiment abroad, and has had the Croix de Chevalier conferred on him by the President of the French Republic.

✧ ✧ ✧

Captain Arthur E. Newland, R.F.A., son of the late Canon E. Newland, and great-grandson of Major Arthur Newland, 40th Regiment, of Ballintemple, Garvagh, entered the army in May, 1900, and received his captaincy in 1910. He served in the South African War, and also in Somaliland, and has been mentioned in Sir John French's despatches.

✧ ✧ ✧

Lieutenant A. A. A. Knight, 3rd Battalion Royal Munster Fusiliers, who took part in the campaign, including the Battle of Mons, where he was wounded and invalided home. He joined the army in July, 1912, and has been awarded the Legion of Honour.

1. 2nd LIEUT. WM. HUGH COULTER, 5th Royal Irish Lancers.	2. CAPT. GERALD F. BOYD, D.S.O., Leinster Regiment.	3. LIEUT. THE HON. HUGH W. GOUGH, Irish Guards.
4. MAJOR CHARLES A. L. YATE, King's Own Yorkshire Light Infantry.	5. BRIGADIER-GENERAL SPRING R. RICE, C.B., Royal Engineers.	6. MAJOR VISCOUNT MASSEREENE AND FERRARD, D.S.O., North Irish Horse.
7. LIEUT. HON. HAROLD R. L. G. ALEXANDER, Irish Guards.	8. CAPT. ARTHUR E. NEWLAND. Royal Field Artillery.	9. LIEUT. A. A. A. KNIGHT, 3rd Royal Munster Fusiliers.

DIED FOR THEIR COUNTRY

Lieutenant George Creagh Jenings, 1st Battalion King's Shropshire Light Infantry, killed in action November 6th, youngest son of Lieut.-Colonel and Mrs. Ulick Jenings, of Mervue, Monkstown, and Ironpool, Co. Galway. Passed into Sandhurst from Wimbledon College. Was assistant adjutant for the full period and was given a six months' extension. He was a keen sportsman, won the subaltern's cup in his battalion four times, and was second and third in the six events which took place since the cup was instituted.

Lieutenant John Bloomfield Gough, Royal Horse Artillery, gazetted as 2nd Lieutenant, 1906, and first Lieutenant, 1909. He was the eldest son of the late Col. Bloomfield Gough, 9th Lancers, and of Mrs. Gough of Belchester, Berwickshire. His grandfather, General Sir John Bloomfield Gough, the distinguished Indian soldier, who fought at Sobraon and in the Gawlior campaign, was a member of the family which has given and still gives so many of its sons to the Army. Lieut. Gough was only 28 years of age and was killed in action early in September.

Major Hubert F. Crichton, Irish Guards, the only son of Col. the Hon. Charles Crichton, of Mullaboden, Co Kildare. Entered the service in January, 1896, served with the Nile Expedition, took part in the battle of Khartoum, received the Egyptian medal with clasps. He also served in the South African war, and was employed with the Imperial Yeomanry, receiving the Queen's Medal with two clasps. He was well-known in hunting circles in Co. Kildare, and was very popular with his men as well as with his brother officers. He married in 1903 a daughter of the late Mr. Llewelyn and Lady Rachel Saunderson.

Major P. A. Charrier, Royal Munster Fusiliers, fell in action while leading his regiment against overwhelming odds. Entered the service in June 1890, obtaining his majority in 1909. He took part in the operations in Ashanti and was mentioned in despatches. He served in the South African War, was employed with the Imperial Yeomanry and was present during the operations in Cape Colony in May, 1902, receiving the Queen's Medal with two clasps, served in East Africa in 1903-1904, served in operations in Somaliland, and was appointed on the staff as special service officer.

Major William Griffith Phibbs, Royal Irish Fusiliers, who died of acute pneumonia contracted in the trenches. He was the only son of the late Lieut.-Col. George Griffith Phibbs, of Knockbrack, Co. Sligo. Entered the service in 1892, was gazetted Captain in 1900, and obtained his majority in August, 1902. Served with the Nile Expedition in 1899, receiving Egyptian Medal with clasps; served in the South African War, taking part in the operations in Natal, including the actions at Talana and Lombard's Kop, also in the Orange River Colony in 1900, and in the Transvaal the same year; again in the Orange River Colony in 1901, and the operations on the Zulu frontier in the same year. Served as adjutant with the Second Batt. Royal Irish Fusiliers from May, 1901-2. Was mentioned in despatches, receiving Queen's Medal with four clasps and King's Medal with two clasps.

Captain William Mountcharles Crofton Vandeleur, Essex Regiment, entered the service 1889, and obtained his Company September, 1904. Served on the North-west frontier of India, 1897-8, also with the Tirah Expeditionary Force, receiving the medal with three clasps; served throughout the South African War, being detailed for special service on various occasions, acting as assistant to staff officer Colonial forces and as intelligence officer, afterwards being appointed to the Staff. He took part in practically all the actions near Johannesburg and Pretoria during the progress of the war. Served in Orange River Colony in 1901, and also in Cape Colony in September, 1901. He received the Queen's Medal with four clasps and the King's Medal with two clasps.

Lieutenant Edwin W. Robinson, 5th Royal Irish Lancers, was gazetted in December, 1911, and was promoted first Lieutenant on 5th August, 1914. He was killed in action on October 26th. He was a good sportsman, a keen polo player and a hard rider to hounds, and was most popular amongst his brother officers and men.

Lieutenant C. F. Murphy, Oxfordshire and Buckinghamshire Light Infantry, who was killed in action on the 20th October at the beginning of the battle of Ypres. He was the younger son of the Rev. Canon and Mrs. R. W. Murphy, Clifden, Co. Galway, and was gazetted in 1908 to the R.F.A. Special Reserve, and the following year was attached to the 35th Battery, Clonmel; in 1910 he obtained a commission in the 1st Batt. of the Oxfordshire and Buckinghamshire Light Infantry, and joined the Regiment at Wellington, Madras. In the spring of 1912 he "captained" his regimental team in the contest for the cross-country challenge cup at Bangalore, which they secured, coming in third of his team and 5th of the division.

Captain the Hon. Andrew Edward Somerset Mulholland, 1st Battalion Irish Guards, killed in action on November 1st, during the engagement round Ypres. He joined the Imperial Yeomanry in 1903, and served under the command of the Earl of Shaftesbury in the North Irish Horse. In 1906 he was gazetted to the Irish Guards. He was the eldest son of Lord and Lady Dunleath, and was recently married to Lady Joan Byng, youngest daughter of the Earl and Countess of Strafford.

1. LIEUT. GEORGE C. JENINGS, 1st King's Shropshire Light Infantry.
2. LIEUT. JOHN B. GOUGH, Royal Horse Artillery.
3. MAJOR HUBERT F. CRICHTON, Irish Guards.
4. MAJOR P. A. CHARRIER, Royal Munster Fusiliers.
5. MAJOR WILLIAM G. PHIBBS, Royal Irish Fusiliers.
6. CAPT. WM. M. C. VANDELEUR, Essex Regiment.
7. LT. EDWIN W. ROBINSON, 5th Royal Irish Lancers.
8. LIEUT. C. F. MURPHY, Oxfordshire and Buckinghamshire Light Infantry.
9. CAPT. THE HON. A. E. S. MULHOLLAND, 1st Battalion Irish Guards.

DIED FOR THEIR COUNTRY

Lieut. A. N. A. J. de L. Teeling, 3rd Batt. Norfolk Regiment. Entered the service in July, 1912, and was killed in action early in the war.

✧ ✧ ✧

Capt. Miles Bertie Cunninghame Carbery, Royal Irish Fusiliers, killed in action. Son of the late Mr. William Carbery and Mrs. Carbery, of 17 Hartingdon Mansions, Eastbourne. He entered the service from the Militia in December, 1897, being commissioned as 2nd Lieutenant to the Royal Irish Fusiliers. In December, 1899, he was promoted Lieutenant, and received his Captaincy in February, 1903. In the South African War he saw service, taking part in the operations in Natal, including the action at Talana, where he was dangerously wounded. He had the Queen's Medal with one clasp.

✧ ✧ ✧

Lieutenant Cecil Francis Blacker, 2nd Batt. Connaught Rangers, was born in 1889, and entered the Army in 1909, and was promoted first Lieutenant in January, 1911.

✧ ✧ ✧

Captain Simms, M.V.O., Royal Munster Fusiliers, 2nd Battalion, son of the late Mr. George Simms, Sumner Grange, Sunninghill, Berks. Born in 1875, joined the Royal Munster Fusiliers in 1897, and served through the South African War, obtaining the medal and two clasps. Killed in action.

✧ ✧ ✧

Lieutenant-Colonel P. McClear, Royal Dublin Fusiliers. Obtained his commission in 1895, served through the South African War, was present at the Relief of Ladysmith and at Laing's Nek, received the Queen's Medal with five clasps and the King's Medal with two clasps. Served with the West African Frontier Forces from April, 1903, to March, 1908, also in Southern Nigeria. appointed to command the West African Field Forces last April, and commanded the second Brigade of the Nigerian Force in the recent engagement.

✧ ✧ ✧

Captain Frank Henry Mahony, 3rd Battalion Cheshire Regiment. Was killed in action. Served through the South African War in 1900, being attached to the Army Service Corps. He took part in the operations in the Orange Free State from February to May, 1900, including the actions at Dreifontein, Vet River, and Zand River. He saw service in the Transvaal in May and June of the same year, taking part in the actions near Johannesburg and Diamond Hill. He was again in the Transvaal east of Pretoria from July to November, 1900, and was in the action at Belfast. He obtained the Queen's Medal with five clasps. He served in Northern Nigeria, 1901, and was present in the operations against the Emir of Yola, receiving the medal with clasp. He also obtained an additional clasp for the Aro expedition.

✧ ✧ ✧

Lieut. Charles Barry Gibbons, Royal Irish Regiment, who was killed in action. He was born in 1892, and received his commission in 1913.

✧ ✧ ✧

Captain Charles Lionel Master, 2nd Battalion Royal Irish Rifles. Killed in action. He was son of the late Mr. William Edgar Master, and was born in Ceylon on 24th March, 1881. He was educated at Bradfield, and entered the Royal Irish Rifles as second Lieutenant from the Militia in January, 1901, and became Lieutenant four years later. He obtained Adjutancy of his Regiment in January, 1908, and was promoted Captain in June of the same year. He saw service in South Africa during the war of 1901-2 in the Orange River Colony, and received the Queen's Medal with five clasps. On the outbreak of the present war he accompanied his Regiment to the front, where it was continuously engaged and suffered severely. Captain Master was killed by shrapnel while leading his Company in the attack on La Couture on the 12th October, 1914. He was mentioned in Sir John French's despatches of October 8th.

✧ ✧ ✧

Lieut. Arthur Noel Whitfield, Royal Irish Rifles, who was killed in action. He was the eldest son of the Rev. A. L. Whitfield, Hughenden Vicarage, High Wickham. He joined the Army in October, 1910, as second Lieutenant, and obtained his promotion in March of this year. He was a very keen and promising young soldier, and was mentioned in Sir John French's despatches.

1. LT. A. N. A. J. DE L. TEELING, 3rd Norfolk Regiment.
2. CAPT. M. B. C. CARBERY, Royal Irish Fusiliers.
3. LT. CECIL F. BLACKER, 2nd Connaught Rangers.
4. CAPT. SIMMS, M.V.O., 2nd Royal Munster Fusiliers.
5. LT.-COLONEL P. McCLEAR, Royal Dublin Fusiliers.
6. CAPT. FRANK H. MAHONY, 3rd Cheshire Regiment.
7. LT.-CHARLES BARRY GIBBONS, Royal Irish Regiment.
8. CAPT. CHARLES LIONEL MASTER, 2nd Royal Irish Rifles.
9. LT. ARTHUR N. WHITFIELD, Royal Irish Rifles.

DIED FOR THEIR COUNTRY.

Lieutenant Maximilian Francis Broadwood, Royal West Kent Regiment, killed in action. He entered the Army on September 4th, 1912, and was stationed for some time in Dublin, where he was well-known as a keen golfer and became a member of the Royal Dublin Golf Club.

◇ ◇ ◇

Captain Gerard Lourdes Edward Sherlock, 3rd King's Own Hussars, killed in action in Togoland on August 25th, 1914. Captain Sherlock, who was the second son of Mr. David Sherlock, D.L., of Rahan, King's Co., entered the service through the Militia Artillery with which he had been in action in South Africa. He was gazetted 2nd Lieutenant in the 3rd Hussars in July, 1906, and first Lieutenant in December, 1908. He was seconded for special service in Nigeria, and during a short leave last year he entered the Army Flying School at Brooklands, where he qualified in an incredibly short time and obtained his Pilot's certificate. Returning to Nigeria he took part in several small expeditions and accompanied the British Force to Togoland on the outbreak of hostilities.

◇ ◇ ◇

Sir Richard William Levinge, Bart., attached to the First Life Guards, who was killed in action, was the representative of a very old Irish family. He was born in July, 1878, and succeeded his father as 10th Baronet in 1900. He formerly held a Lieutenancy in the 8th King's Royal Irish Hussars, and also in the 6th Batt. of the Rifle Brigade, and more recently had served in the South Irish Horse. On the outbreak of war he rejoined the army, and was attached to the First Life Guards. He was Deputy Lieutenant for the County of Westmeath, where he resided at Knockdrin Castle, near Mullingar. He was well-known in hunting and sporting circles in Ireland.

◇ ◇ ◇

Lieut.-Colonel Charles Dalton, R.A.M.C., who has died of wounds sustained in the battle of the Aisne. He was born at Monkstown, Co. Dublin, 1867, educated at Clongowes. After serving in the Merchant Service, where his gallantry in saving life procured him the Arnott Medal, Dr. Dalton passed into the Army Medical Corps. He saw active service in Burma, Chitral, Sierra Leone and South Africa. At the battle of Colenso he was seriously wounded, his recovery being short of marvellous. He took part in most of the operations in the Orange River Colony, and also in Cape Colony, and was mentioned in despatches, February, 1901. He obtained the Queen's Medal with three clasps. He was Deputy Assistant Director of the Irish Medical Command.

◇ ◇ ◇

Captain Gerald Hugh FitzGerald, 4th Royal Irish Dragoon Guards, who was killed in action. He was the only son of the late Lord Maurice FitzGerald and Lady Maurice FitzGerald, and grandson of the fourth Duke of Leinster. He entered the Army in December, 1907, was gazetted first Lieutenant in November, 1908, and obtained his Captaincy in November, 1913. He was a brilliant young officer and keen sportsman, and was well-known in hunting circles in County Wexford, where his mother, Lady Maurice FitzGerald, resides at Johnstown Castle. He was married last August to Miss Charrington, and left almost immediately after the ceremony for the front.

◇ ◇ ◇

Capt. Michael Joseph Lochrin, R.A.M.C., entered the service in July, 1906, and was promoted Captain in January, 1902. He was a native of Drogheda, Co. Louth.

◇ ◇ ◇

Lieut. Challoner Francis Trevor Chute, Royal Munster Fusiliers, who was killed in action on August 27th, 1914, was born on April 2nd, 1885, and received his commission from the Militia in the Royal Munster Fusiliers in November, 1905, being gazetted Lieutenant in February, 1908. He was the son of the late Mr. Francis Blennerhassett Chute, of Chute Hall, Tralee, and was a most promising young officer. Captain Jervis, the senior officer, in a letter has given a spirited account of Mr. Chute's bravery in covering the withdrawal of Captain Jervis' Company with his machine guns, bringing them back at a gallop along the road under a hail of lead. Having successfully accomplished this daring feat, he was shot and fell dead.

◇ ◇ ◇

Lieutenant Frederick H. L. Rushton, Royal Irish Regiment, entered the service in December, 1909, and was promoted first Lieutenant in October, 1911. Killed in action.

◇ ◇ ◇

Captain Henry Telford Maffett, Leinster Regiment, killed in action on October the 21st. He was the youngest son of the late Mr. Wm. Hamilton Maffett, Barrister-at-Law, of St. Helena, Finglas, Co. Dublin. He was born in March, 1872, and received his commission in the Leinster Regiment from the Militia in June, 1894, was gazetted Lieutenant, 1895, and Captain in August, 1900. He saw service in Northern Nigeria in August, 1901, and received the medal with clasp. In 1908 he was serving in India, and took part in the operations on the North West Frontier, for which he received the medal with clasp. From November, 1898, to July, 1899, he discharged the duties of garrison adjutant at St. Lucia, later he was employed with the West African Frontier force and acted as Provost-Marshal of the Mohmand Field Force for a short period in 1908.

1. LT. MAXIMILIAN F. BROADWOOD,
Royal West Kent Regiment.

2. CAPT. GERARD L. E. SHERLOCK,
3rd King's Own Hussars.

3. SIR RICHARD W. LEVINGE, BT.,
1st Life Guards.

4. LT.-COL. CHARLES DALTON,
Royal Army Medical Corps.

5. CAPT. GERALD H. FITZGERALD,
4th Royal Irish Dragoon Guards.

6. CAPT. MICHAEL J. LOCHRIN,
Royal Army Medical Corps.

7. LT. CHALLONER F. T. CHUTE,
Royal Munster Fusiliers.

8. LT. FREDERICK H. L. RUSHTON,
Royal Irish Regiment.

9. CAPT. HENRY T. MAFFETT,
Leinster Regiment.

DIED FOR THEIR COUNTRY.

Lieutenant William Ormsby Wyndham Ball, M.B., R.A.M.C., killed in action on the 26th September. He was the younger son of the late Henry Wyndham Ball and of Mrs. Ball, 5 Palmerston Park, Dublin. He had a distinguished career in Trinity College, Dublin, entering in 1907 and obtaining his medical degree in 1912. While in College he was well-known in the hockey world, he played two seasons in the colour team, and represented Ireland six times in International matches. He entered the Royal Army Medical Corps in January, 1913, as Lieutenant. On the outbreak of the war he was attached to the 2nd Battalion South Staffords, and left England on the 13th August. On the 26th September, when our position on the Aisne was being shelled, he went out to attend a wounded soldier. When kneeling beside him he was killed by a shell which burst close to him. He was in his 25th year.

✧ ✧ ✧

Lieutenant Kennether Ronald Mathieson, 1st Battalion Irish Guards, elder son of Mr. and Mrs. Kenneth Mathieson, of 50 Prince's Gate, London, S.W., was killed at Ypres on November 1st. He was formerly in the Royal Fusiliers and was gazetted into the Irish Guards on August 14th, 1914. He was well-known in Co. Meath and Co. Down, particularly in the neighbourhood of Castlewellan, where his brother-in-law, Mr. H. Armitage-Moore, resides.

✧ ✧ ✧

Captain J. H. Brennan, Royal Welsh Fusiliers, killed in action at Zonnebeke. He belonged to the special reserve of the R.W.F., which he joined in 1902, and was very keen about his military service, obtaining special honours on the completion of his course at the Hythe School of Musketry. He was well-known in Dublin, where he held a similar billet in the Irish Land Commission Court. He was educated at St. Columba's College, and matriculated at Trinity College, where he was a prominent member of the cricket club.

✧ ✧ ✧

Captain Richard Dominick O'Connor, R.A.M.C., killed in action on 25th October, was the third son of the late Mr. F. W. O'Connor, F.R.C.S.I., of Limerick. He entered the service in January, 1907, and was promoted to Captain's rank in July, 1910. He was attached to the Sherwood Foresters. He was educated at Clongowes Wood College and at St. Bartholomew's Hospital, London.

✧ ✧ ✧

Captain H. O. Davis, of the Royal Irish Rifles, eldest son of the late Mr. Henry Davis, of Holywood, Co. Down, was killed in action on October 27th. He was born in 1884, and educated at Protora Royal School, Enniskillen, from which he passed direct into the R.M.C., Sandhurst. He was gazetted to the 2nd Batt. Royal Dublin Fusiliers in August, 1905. He resigned his commission four years later. On the outbreak of the war he was gazetted as Captain in the Royal Irish Rifles. He was a member of the Headquarter Staff of the Ulster Volunteer Force.

✧ ✧ ✧

Captain Daniel George Harold Auchinleck, Royal Inniskilling Fusiliers, killed in action, was born on September 18th, 1877, and received his commission in the Royal Inniskilling Fusiliers on the 14th September, 1898, being gazetted Lieutenant in March, 1900, and Captain in January, 1904. He served in the South African War, 1899-1901, being present at the relief of Ladysmith, the actions at Colenso, Spion Kop, Tugela Heights, Belfast and Lydenberg, for which he received the Queen's Medal with four clasps. He was Adjutant to a Militia Battalion from October, 1904, to March, 1908. He was the son of Mrs. Auchinleck, of Omagh.

✧ ✧ ✧

Lieutenant Ronald Elphinstone Parker, Royal Horse Artillery, killed in action. He was the youngest son of Mr. R. G. Parker, J.P., and Mrs. Parker, of Bally Valley, Killaloe, Co. Clare. Gazetted to the R.H.A. on the 25th May, 1907, and became Lieutenant on 25th May, 1910. Lieutenant Parker was well-known in Limerick, where he was very popular.

✧ ✧ ✧

Lieutenant Cecil Glendower Percy Gilliat, 1st Royal Warwickshire Regiment, was mortally wounded on October 13th near the Belgian frontier, and died at Hasebrouke the following day. He was the eldest son of Mr. and Mrs. Cecil Gilliat, of Arch Hall, Co. Meath. He was gazetted to the first Battalion Royal Warwickshire Regiment from the Militia in November, 1906, and served with that Regiment for about five years in India. Lieut. Gilliat comes of a fighting family on his mother's side, being a nephew of the late Major Singleton, of Aclare House, Meath, and of the late Admiral Singleton, C.B., and of Colonel F. C. Singleton, Bombay Native Infantry, who took part in the march to Kandahar.

✧ ✧ ✧

Captain Samuel George Roe, 2nd Battalion Royal Inniskilling Fusiliers, killed in action on October 21st, was the elder son of Lieut.-Col. Roe, of Sion House, Glenageary, Co. Dublin. He joined the service in January, 1899, was gazetted Lieutenant in April, 1900, and obtained his Captaincy in July, 1904.

1. LIEUT. WILLIAM O. W. BALL, M.B., Royal Army Medical Corps.	2. LIEUT. KENNETHER R. MATHIESON, 1st Irish Guards.	3. CAPT. J. H. BRENNAN, Royal Welsh Fusiliers.
4. CAPT. RICHARD D. O'CONNOR, Royal Army Medical Corps	5. CAPT. H. O. DAVIS, Royal Irish Rifles.	6. CAPT. DANIEL G. H. AUCHINLECK, Royal Inniskilling Fusiliers.
7. LIEUT. RONALD E. PARKER, Royal Horse Artillery.	8. LIEUT. CECIL G. P. GILLIAT, 1st Royal Warwickshire Regt.	9. CAPT. SAMUEL G. ROE, 2nd Royal Inniskilling Fusiliers.

DIED FOR THEIR COUNTRY.

2nd Lieutenant James Cyril Baptist Crozier, Royal Munster Fusiliers, killed on the 27th August, 1914. He only joined the Army last June when he was gazetted 2nd Lieutenant. He was a nephew of the Right Rev. Dr. Crozier, the Primate of Ireland.

◇ ◇ ◇

Commander Arthur Tudor Darley, R.N., H.M.S. "Good Hope," who was killed in the naval action off the coast of Chile on November 1st. He joined the "Britannia" in November, 1890, passing in 7th out of 57 candidates. He became midshipman in 1898 and Lieut. in 1898, and Commander in Dec., 1909. The following month he was appointed Flag-Commander to Admiral Winsloe, Commander-in-Chief on the China Station, and in June, 1912, he was one of the fifteen Commanders selected for the special appointment to the newly formed War Staff. In March last he was temporarily appointed to the "Good Hope," while waiting to take up an appointment to the Flag Ship of the China Squadron. He was the elder son of Mr. and Mrs. Wellington Darley, of Violet Hill, Bray, Co. Wicklow, and in November, 1910, he married Charlotte Sinclair, elder daughter of Major-General E. S. May, C.B., C.M.G.

◇ ◇ ◇

Lieutenant Maurice Dease, V.C., 4th Battalion, Royal Fusiliers, killed in action at the Battle of Mons on the 23rd August, 1914. Lieutenant Dease was the only son of Mr. Edmund F. Dease, Culmullen, Co. Meath. He was born in 1889, and was educated at Stonyhurst and Wimbledon, whence he passed into Sandhurst in 1909, and was gazetted to the Royal Fusiliers in 1910. Lieutenant Dease was machine gun officer of his Battalion, and was in command of the guns which were placed to protect the crossing of Canal Bridge at Nimy, north of Mons; he was wounded several times while working the guns until he and nearly all the machine detachment were killed. He was mentioned in Despatches by Sir John French and awarded the V.C. Lieutenant Dease was heir presumptive to his uncle, Major Dease, of Turbotston, Co. Meath, who also served in the Royal Fusiliers.

◇ ◇ ◇

Captain Lord Arthur John Hamilton, Irish Guards. He is the fifth son of the late Duke of Abercorn, and was born in August, 1883. His death was reported early in the campaign, but it transpired that he had been badly wounded but was still alive. He recovered sufficiently to rejoin his regiment, and his death in action recently has been much regretted.

◇ ◇ ◇

Major Lord Charles George Francis Fitz=Maurice Nairne, M.V.O., 1st Dragoons, killed in action. He was the second son of the Marquis of Lansdowne and grandson of the first Duke of Abercorn. He was Equerry in Ordinary to King George the 5th when Prince of Wales and Equerry to His Majesty from 1910, having formerly acted as A.D.C. to Field-Marshal Lord Roberts.

◇ ◇ ◇

Capt. C. Paget O'Brien=Butler, R.A.M.C., attached to the 5th Royal Irish Lancers, died of wounds received in action. He was a son of the late Major Pierce O'Brien-Butler, King's Royal Rifle Corps. Prior to Captain Butler obtaining his Commission in the R.A.M.C. he had achieved the distinction of being classed amongst the first Gentlemen riders in the United Kingdom. Shortly after he entered the service he was ordered to India, and there continued his racing successes. On returning from abroad some eighteen months ago he was sent to the Curragh Camp where he was able to indulge in his love of riding to the utmost. He was always keen for a mount, and was present at all the well-known race meetings through the country. He was just as keen as soldier as he was a sportsman, and his care of his men in peace and war constituted a record.

◇ ◇ ◇

Lieutenant David Cecil Bingham, Coldstream Guards, younger son of Brig.-General Hon. Cecil Edward Bingham, C.V.O., and grandson of the late Earl of Lucan. He was born in 1887, and entered the service in August, 1906. He was promoted first Lieutenant in March, 1909, and accompanied his regiment to the front last August, and was killed in action in September.

◇ ◇ ◇

Captain Norman Jerome Beauchamp Leslie, Rifle Brigade, who was killed in action, was the eldest son of Colonel John Leslie and grandson of Sir John and Lady Constance Leslie, of Glasslough, Co. Monaghan. Capt. Leslie entered the Rifle Brigade as second Lieutenant in September, 1905, being promoted Lieutenant in October, 1909, and last May he obtained his promotion as Captain. During the period from September, 1908, to April, 1910, he acted as A.D.C. to the General Officer Commanding in Egypt, and in April, 1912, he was gazetted A.D.C. to the Governor of Bengal. He was exceedingly popular both in the Army and in his own county. He was a first class polo player, a brilliant swordsman and very fond of sport.

◇ ◇ ◇

2nd Lieutenant Howard A. Bligh St. George, First Life Guards, was killed in action on November 15th. He was the second son of Mr. and Mrs. St. George, of Ashbourne Hill, Leamington, formerly of Clonsilla Lodge, Co. Dublin. Entered the service on the 14th January, 1914, and accompanied his regiment to the front where it was engaged in the attack on the German Guards a short time ago. It was in this charge that Mr. St. George was killed.

1. 2nd LIEUT. JAMES C. B. CROZIER,
Royal Munster Fusiliers.

2. COMM. ARTHUR T. DARLEY, R.N.,
H.M.S. "Good Hope."

3. LIEUT. MAURICE DEASE, V.C.,
4th Royal Fusiliers.

4. CAPT. LORD ARTHUR JOHN HAMILTON,
Irish Guards.

5. MAJOR LORD CHARLES G. F. F. NAIRNE, M.V.O.,
1st Dragoons.

6. CAPT. C. PAGET O'BRIEN-BUTLER, R.A.M.C.,
5th Royal Irish Lancers.

7. LIEUT. DAVID C. BINGHAM,
Coldstream Guards.

8. CAPT. NORMAN J. B. LESLIE,
Rifle Brigade.

9. LIEUT. HOWARD A. BLIGH ST. GEORGE,
First Life Guards.

DIED FOR THEIR COUNTRY.

Lieutenant H. J. S. Shields, R.A.M.C., attached to the Irish Guards, killed in action. Was gazetted Lieutenant in July, 1912. He was a graduate of Cambridge, where he was known as an oarsman, and rowed stroke in the Cambridge Boat in 1910.

✦ ✦ ✦

2nd Lieutenant Philip Hamilton Sulivan, 1st Batt. Royal Munster Fusiliers, was killed in action on his 20th birthday near Etreux, France. He was the fourth son of Colonel Sulivan, of Woking. He was gazetted 2nd Lieutenant in February, 1914.

✦ ✦ ✦

Major Peter Martin Connellan, Hampshire Regiment, killed in action, was the only son of Major J. H. F. H. Connellan, Coolmore, Thomastown, Co. Kilkenny, who was formerly a Captain in the Hampshire Regiment. Major P. Connellan was gazetted 2nd Lieutenant in January, 1901, a first Lieutenant in November, 1903, and Captain in 1907. He served at Aden in 1903-4, and took part in the operations in the interior. He acted as Brigade Signalling Officer to the Aden Boundary Delimitation Column, and in 1909 Adjutant of the third Battalion of the Hampshire Regiment, and acted as Adjutant in the Special Reserve from January, 1911, to January, 1914.

✦ ✦ ✦

Major Thomas Roche, Wiltshire Regiment, 1st Battalion, killed in action on November 19th. He was the third son of the late Mr. Thomas Roche, J.P., of Annakissa House, Castletownroche, Co. Cork, and joined the Wiltshire Regiment from the Militia (9th Batt. K.R.R.) in 1895. His promotion to Captain's rank followed five years later, and he was gazetted Major in April, 1913. He served in the South African War from 1898 to 1901, took part in the operations in the Transvaal from November, 1900, to January, 1901. He was also present during the operations in Cape Colony, and was mentioned in despatches, obtaining the Queen's Medal with four clasps. He was Adjutant for four years, and held the post of Brigade-Major for the regulation period. Sir John French, telegraphing to Lord Kitchener, said, "The counter attack was gallantly lead by Major Roche, Wiltshire Regiment, and I regret to say he was killed."

✦ ✦ ✦

Major Robert Alexander Gray, Royal Irish Fusiliers, killed in action. He was gazetted 2nd Lieutenant in 1891, and became first Lieutenant in 1895, obtaining his Captaincy in February, 1900, and his Majority in 1910. He served through the South African War and took part in the operations in the Transvaal, the Orange River Colony and in Cape Colony, receiving the Queen's Medal with three clasps and the King's Medal with two clasps.

Captain Francis H. Barton, 2nd Gurkha Rifles, who was killed in action, was the son of the late Mr. James Barton, of Farndreg, Dundalk. He obtained his commission in the Irish Rifles in 1901, and was gazetted two years later to the Indian Army. He served in the South African War, taking part in the operations in the Transvaal and in the Orange River Colony. He was mentioned in despatches, and received the Queen's Medal with three clasps and the King's Medal with two clasps.

✦ ✦ ✦

Lieutenant Robert Burton Benison, 2nd Battalion Connaught Rangers, killed in action at the battle of the Aisne on September 20th. He was the youngest son of the late Mr. J. J. Benison, of Slieve Russell, Ballyconnell, Co. Cavan. He was born in 1891, educated at Portora School, Enniskillen, and St. Paul's School, London, from which he went to Sandhurst. In 1911 he was gazetted to the Connaught Rangers, joining that Regiment at the Curragh. While in Kildare he was a prominent follower of hounds and a smart cross-country runner, and for some time he kept the Regimental Beagles. Lieutenant Benison was Signalling officer to the Regiment, and while in France held the post of Intelligence officer. He was killed in the trenches of La Soupire whilst rallying his men who were being raked by terrific rifle and artillery fire.

✦ ✦ ✦

Lieutenant Percy Stuart Banning, 2nd Battalion Royal Munster Fusiliers, killed in action in Belgium. He was the only son of Lieutenant-Colonel S. G. Banning, late Royal Munster Fusiliers, and Mrs. S. T. Banning, of 50 Kensington Mansions, Earls Court. He was born in 1887, and received his commission in the Royal Munster Fusiliers in September, 1908, and was gazetted Lieutenant in March, 1910. He was married in March, 1913, to Mona Mary, only daughter of the late Mr. Alfred Chaplin, of Henfield, Sussex. His services were mentioned in despatches of November 11th.

✦ ✦ ✦

Captain Francis William Mowbray Leader, Connaught Rangers, was killed in action on August 26th. He was the elder son of Mr. F. H. M. Leader, J.P., late R.A., and Mrs. F. H. Leader, of Alassas, Coachford, Co. Cork. He was gazetted to his Regiment in January, 1903, passing from the Manchester Militia, with which Corps he had served through the Boer War, and obtained the Queen's Medal with four clasps. He also took part in the Southern Nigerian Campaign, and received the medal with clasps. He was gazetted Lieutenant in 1905 and Captain in August, 1914.

1. LIEUT. H. J. S. SHIELDS, R.A.M.C., Irish Guards.	2. 2nd LIEUT. PHILIP H. SULIVAN, 1st Royal Munster Fusiliers.	3. MAJOR PETER M. CONNELLAN, Hampshire Regiment.
4. MAJOR THOMAS ROCHE, Wiltshire Regiment.	5. MAJOR ROBERT A. GRAY, Royal Irish Fusiliers.	6. CAPT. FRANCIS H. BARTON, 2nd Gurkha Rifles.
7. LIEUT. ROBERT B. BENISON, 2nd Connaught Rangers.	8. LIEUT. PERCY S. BANNING, 2nd Royal Munster Fusiliers.	9. CAPT. FRANCIS W. M. LEADER, Connaught Rangers.

MENTIONED IN DESPATCHES.

Captain the Hon. A. R. Hewitt, D.S.O., East Surrey Regiment, second son of Viscount Lifford, has been mentioned in Sir John French's despatches and awarded the D.S.O. He joined the army in October, 1900; was gazetted 1st Lieutenant in 1904, and received his captaincy in May, 1910.

Captain William Ingham Macauley, A. V. Dept., attached to the Queen's Bays, mentioned in General French's despatches, is a son of Mr. C. J. Macauley, formerly of Monaghan, and now residing at Cliftonville, Belfast. Captain Macauley received his commission about eight years ago, and has been five years in India. He has been at the front since the beginning of the war, and after one engagement was personally thanked by the General in command for saving a comrade under severe fire.

Captain R. G. Douglas Small, Prince of Wales' Leinster Regiment (Royal Canadians), is the son of Colonel Small, of Prince of Wales Mansions, Battersea. He entered the service in 1902, and was promoted Flying Commander with the rank of Captain. He has been mentioned in despatches for distinguished service.

Major G. A. Moore, Royal Army Medical Corps, has been mentioned in despatches. He is the son of the late Mr. William Moore, of Moore Lodge, Ballymoney. He served in the South African War, also in India; received the Queen's Medal with 4 clasps and the King's Medal with 2 clasps, and has seen considerable service in different parts of the Empire.

Major=General Edward S. Bulfin, C.V.O., C.B., Commanding 2nd Infantry Brigade at Aldershot since 1913, was mentioned in Sir John French's despatches, and promoted on October 26th to the rank of Major-General for distinguished services in the field. He is the second son of the late Mr. P. Bulfin, J.P., of Woodtown Park, Rathfarnham. He was educated at Stoneyhurst and Trinity College, Dublin. He entered the army in 1884, and has had a most distinguished career. He has been three times mentioned in despatches prior to the present war, and has the Queen's Medal with 4 clasps and the King's Medal with 2 clasps. He was wounded at Ypres on the 1st November, but has recovered sufficiently to rejoin his Brigade.

Colonel R. J. Ross, Middlesex Regiment, who has been mentioned in Sir John French's despatches, and decorated by President Poincaré with the Legion of Honour, Croix d'Officier, has been residing at Newcastle, Co. Down, since retiring from the army, which, however, he rejoined on the outbreak of hostilities, and was given a Lieutenant-Colonelcy and attached to the Middlesex Regiment. His eldest son, Lieutenant Robert K. Ross, has likewise been doing good service at the front.

Captain Lionel Warren De Vere Sadlier=Jackson, D.S.O., 9th Queen's Royal Lancers, entered the army in May, 1898; obtained his lieutenancy in October, 1900, and was gazetted Captain in December, 1904. He served with much distinction in the South African War, and was mentioned in despatches on three occasions. He received the Queen's Medal with 7 clasps, the King's Medal with 2 clasps, and the D.S.O. He has been mentioned in Sir John French's despatches.

Captain the Hon. Francis Reginald Denis Prittie, Rifle Brigade. He has been mentioned in Sir John French's despatches. He was seconded as Assistant Commissioner to the Uganda Boundary Commission. He is the second son of Lord Dunally, and was born in 1880. He has received the Cross of the Legion of Honour in recognition of his bravery in holding a trench under terrific fire, and thus saving many French lives. He has been in constant action since his arrival in France, and his brigade has done splendid service.

Captain William Maurice Armstrong, 10th Hussars, who has been mentioned in despatches for distinguished service, entered the army in February, 1910, and gazetted 1st Lieutenant, January, 1914. He is the son of Mr. Marcus Beresford Armstrong, D.L., of Mealiffe, Co. Tipperary.

Lieutenant=Colonel John Joshua Russell, Royal Army Medical Corps, who has been mentioned in Sir John French's first despatch, entered the service in 1886, and served through the South African War, being present during the operations in Cape Colony, 1899-1900, and again in Cape Colony from November, 1900, to January, 1902. He obtained the Queen's Medal with clasp, and the King's Medal with two clasps.

1. CAPT. THE HON. A. R. HEWITT, D.S.O.,
East Surrey Regiment.

2. CAPT. WILLIAM I. MACAULEY, A. V. DEPT.,
Queen's Bays.

3. CAPT. R. G. DOUGLAS SMALL,
Prince of Wales' Leinster Regiment.

4. MAJOR G. A. MOORE,
Royal Army Medical Corps.

5. MAJOR-GENERAL EDWARD S. BULFIN, C.V.O., C.B.,
Commanding 2nd Infantry Brigade.

6. COLONEL R. J. ROSS,
Middlesex Regiment.

7. CAPT. LIONEL W. DE VERE SADLIER-JACKSON, D.S.O.,
9th Queen's Royal Lancers.

8. CAPT. THE HON. FRANCIS R. D. PRITTIE,
Rifle Brigade.

9. CAPTAIN WILLIAM M. ARMSTRONG,
10th Hussars.

Our Heroes

DIED FOR THEIR COUNTRY.

Lieutenant John Henry Loftus Reade, 2nd Battalion Manchester Regiment, who was killed in action on the 29th October, was the only son of the late Mr. John Henry Loftus Reade, Barrister-at-Law, Lincoln's Inn, and grandnephew of the late John Dawson Brien, D.L., of Castletown, Co. Fermanagh, to whose property he succeeded. He was born in 1881, and was educated at St. Columba's College, Rathfarnham. He entered the service in December, 1900, receiving a commission in the 5th Royal Irish Rifles, and served in the South African Campaign from 1901 to 1902. In January, 1902, he was gazetted to the Manchester Regiment. From 1909-1912 he was adjutant of the 2nd Batt. Manchester Regiment. He left the Curragh with his regiment on 13th August, and after the battle of Le Cateau became acting adjutant. He was mentioned in Sir John French's despatches.

◊ ◊ ◊

Second Lieutenant Richard Somerset Maxwell, The Black Watch, only son of Colonel the Hon. Henry E. Maxwell, Secretary of the Grand Orange Lodge of Ireland, and grandson of Colonel Cosby, of Stradbally Hall, Queen's County. He only joined his regiment last year and proceeded to the front and was killed in action.

◊ ◊ ◊

Captain H. V. Hare, 2nd Batt. Durham Light Infantry, son of the late Admiral Hon. Richard Hare and Hon. Mrs. Hare, and nephew of Lord Listowel. He joined the Army in 1900, became Captain in 1912, and accompanied his regiment to France in the early part of the War. A week later he was in the firing line and was killed whilst leading his men in a desperate charge against the enemy, being mortally wounded within thirty yards of the German trenches on September 20th at the battle of the Aisne. In 1909 he married Miss Hudson-Kinahan, by whom he leaves two little children, a boy and a girl.

◊ ◊ ◊

Captain Frederick George Brown, 101st Grenadiers (Indian Army), second son of the late Mr. Vere Ward Brown, J.P., of Balnagowan, Palmerston Park, and Mrs. Vere Ward Brown, 22 Highfield Road, Rathgar. He was killed in action on 4th November in German East Africa. He married a few years ago Miss Ivy Wright, youngest daughter of Mr. A. M. Wright, LL.D., Peafield, Blackrock.

◊ ◊ ◊

Captain George Hume-Kelly, North Staffordshire Regiment, was born on the 13th November, 1879, and was gazetted Second Lieutenant from the Militia in May, 1899. He became Lieutenant in June, 1900, and obtained his Captaincy in February, 1906. He was adjutant in the Special Reserve from August, 1908, to February, 1912. In the South African War Captain Hume-Kelly was employed with the Mounted Infantry being present at Paardeberg and Dreitfontein. He received the Queen's Medal with four clasps and the King's Medal with two clasps. He was the youngest son of Major and Mrs. Hume-Kelly, Glencara, Mullingar.

◊ ◊ ◊

Lieutenant Frederick Ernest Styles, Royal Munster Fusiliers, who was killed in action on August 27th at Etreux, France, was the eldest son of the late Mr. Frederick Styles and of Mrs. Styles, of Blackmoor, Four Elms. He was born in 1884, was educated at Harrow and Sandhurst, and gazetted as Second Lieutenant to the Munster Fusiliers in 1903. He obtained his promotion as Lieutenant in 1906, and retired from the Army in April, 1914, but rejoined on the outbreak of the War. Lieut. Styles was killed while gallantly leading his men under a heavy fire.

◊ ◊ ◊

Lieutenant Commander Walter B. Watkins Grubb, R.N., of H.M.S. "Cressy," son of Lieutenant-Colonel Alexander Grubb, late R.A., and grandson of the late Mr. Richard Grubb, Cahir Abbey, Cahir, Co. Tipperary. Entering the Navy at an early age, he was advanced through the various steps of his profession until his promotion as Lieutenant-Commander, when his career was terminated in his thirty-fifth year in the naval action which resulted in the loss of the "Cressy" and the "Hogue."

◊ ◊ ◊

Lieutenant G. de M. Armstrong Lushington-Tulloch, Connaught Rangers, son of Mrs. Lushington-Tulloch, Shanbolard, Letterfrack, Co. Galway, was killed in action on November the 7th whilst attacking a German trench near Neuve Chapelle. He was gallantly leading his men against great odds, and though wounded continued to encourage them to his last moments, but though the task was only accomplished with great loss, it was carried out to the complete satisfaction of the General. Mr. Lushington-Tulloch was a very popular officer, and his men were so attached to him that they would have followed him into any zone of danger.

◊ ◊ ◊

Second Lieutenant A. J. F. de Courcy Williams, 4th Battalion of the Middlesex Regiment, was severely wounded at Bethune on October the 20th, and only lived till the following day. He was the only son of Dr. Almericus de Courcy Williams, of St. Etchins, Killucan, Co. Westmeath. He was born in 1895, and passed out of Sandhurst only last July. He had already proved himself to be a fearless and brilliant soldier, and was seen encouraging his men even while fatally wounded, his last words being, "Men, give it them."

Supplement to Irish Life, January 22nd, 1915.

1. LIEUT. J. H. L. READE,
2nd Battalion Manchester Regiment.

2. 2nd LIEUT. R. S. MAXWELL,
The Black Watch.

3. CAPT. H. V. HARE,
2nd Batt. Durham Light Infantry.

4. CAPT. F. G. BROWN,
101st Grenadiers, Indian Army.

5. CAPT. G. H. KELLY,
North Staffordshire Regiment.

6. LIEUT. F. STYLES,
Royal Munster Fusiliers.

7. LIEUT. G. DE M. LUSHINGTON-TULLOCH,
Connaught Rangers.

8. 2nd LT. DE COURCY WILLIAMS,
4th Batt. Middlesex Regiment.

9. LT.-COMMANDER GRUBB, R.N.,
H.M.S. "Cressy."

DIED FOR THEIR COUNTRY.

Lieutenant N. G. S. McGrath, 2nd Dragoon Guards (Queen's Bays), entered the Service in 1912, and was promoted in October of the same year to the rank of Lieutenant. He accompanied his regiment abroad, where he was killed in action, and a promising career was thus sadly cut off.

✧ ✧ ✧

2nd Lieut. Alan James Ramsay Anderson, 3rd Battalion Royal Irish Regiment, who was killed in action at Le Pelly, near Lille, last October. He was the third son of Mr. Anderson, Secretary of the Irish Agricultural Organization Society. He was educated at Bedford Grammar School, and like his two elder brothers, had held one of the public school boxing championships. Afterwards he studied at Oxford with the object of devoting his life to the service of the Irish co-operative movement. When the war broke out, however, he was amongst the first to answer the call, and with his regiment was ordered to the front in October and shortly afterwards was killed in action.

✧ ✧ ✧

Captain Hugh Mortimer Travers, late of the Leicestershire Regiment, attached to the Duke of Wellington's Regiment, who was killed in action on the 8th November near Ypres while gallantly leading a bayonet attack, retaking a trench from which the French had retired. Captain Travers was born in 1873, and was a son of Lieut.-Colonel Travers, who had served through the Crimean campaign and was a Knight of the Legion of Honour, and came of a Co. Cork family. He was educated at Wellington College and entered the service in 1896, receiving his Captaincy in the Royal Munster Fusiliers in 1902. He retired in 1907 but rejoined on the outbreak of the War. He served through the South African campaign and was on an armoured train for the last thirteen months of the war, for which he and the other officers received the thanks of Lord Kitchener. He received the Queen's Medal with five clasps and the King's Medal with two clasps.

✧ ✧ ✧

Captain Frederick Henry Mahony, 3rd Battalion Cheshire Regiment, entered the Service in August, 1896, was gazetted Lieutenant in June, 1900, and Captain in 1906. He served through the South African War, taking part in the operations in the Orange Free State at Dreitfontein, Vet River and Zand River. Later in the Transvaal, where he took part in the operations near Johannesburg, Pretoria, and Diamond Hill, receiving the Queen's Medal with five clasps; in 1901 he was in Northern Nigeria, and in 1902 in Southern Nigeria, receiving a medal and clasp and an extra clasp for the Ara Expedition. He was a typical Irishman and a born soldier, showing extraordinary bravery and courage during the present campaign, and when his senior officers were put out of action he commanded the first Cheshires and led a brilliant and successful bayonet charge at La Bassée under heavy German artillery fire. He was killed fighting bravely and is buried at Bethune.

✧ ✧ ✧

Major George Geoffrey Prendergast Humphreys, who died from wounds received in action October 30th, was the youngest son of the late Mr. T. W. D. Humphreys, of Donoughmore House, Castlefinn, Co. Donegal. He received his commission in the Welsh Regiment in July, 1893, was transferred to the Bombay Command of the Indian Staff Corps, and received all passes and certificates associated with the Indian Service. His corps was the 127th Queen Mary's Own Baluch, Light Infantry. He served for a considerable time with the Sind Volunteer Rifles as Adjutant, and on promotion he took over a Double Company in the 127th. His war record is of a specially brilliant character. In 1897 he was Staff Officer commanding the troops in Uganda during the operations there, and received the medal with clasp. He served in East Africa, proceeding to China with his regiment in 1903.

✧ ✧ ✧

Captain Edward Hugh Bagot Stack, 2nd Batt. 8th Gurkha Rifles, who was killed in action in France on November 1st, 1914. He was the only son of the late Mr. Edward Stack of the Bengal Civil Service, and of Mrs. Luttman-Johnson, of Redhill House, Petworth, Surrey. He entered the Army in August, 1905, and was promoted to the rank of Lieutenant in August, 1907, and acted as A.D.C. to King George at the Coronation Durbar in India. He married the only daughter of General Sir James Bell, Governor of Aden, and leaves three children.

✧ ✧ ✧

Second Lieutenant Patrick McDonagh, Royal West Kent Regiment, who was killed in action on the Belgian frontier on the 19th November, 1914, was one of the Clongowes boys who has added lustre to the rolls of that well-known school. He was the second son of Mrs. McDonagh, of Loughgall, Co. Armagh, and nephew of Mr. James Fenning, of Gladstone Street, Waterford.

✧ ✧ ✧

Second Lieutenant A. Montgomery, Connaught Rangers, who was killed in action, was only appointed on probation from the second battalion to the third battalion in August last, and was one of the promising young soldiers who lost his life in the early part of the campaign.

✧ ✧ ✧

Captain B. Allgood, Royal Irish Rifles, who obtained his Captaincy in February, 1904, was for a considerable time in the Reserve of Officers, and was employed with the 3rd Batt. of his regiment. He rejoined on August 14th, 1914, in time to accompany his corps to the front, where he was killed in action in one of the mid-autumn engagements.

1. LIEUT. N. G. S. McGRATH, 2nd Dragoon Guards.
2. LIEUT. A. ANDERSON, Royal Irish Regiment.
3. CAPT. H. M. TRAVERS, Leicestershire Regiment.
4. CAPT. F. H. MAHONY, 1st Cheshire Regiment.
5. MAJOR G. G. P. HUMPHREYS, 1st Cheshires.
6. CAPT. BAGOT STACK, 2nd Batt. 8th Gurkha Rifles.
7. LIEUT. PATRICK McDONAGH, Royal West Kent Regiment.
8. 2nd LT. A. MONTGOMERY, 3rd Batt. Connaught Rangers.
9. CAPT. B. ALLGOOD, Royal Irish Rifles.

MENTIONED IN DESPATCHES.

Lieutenant Thomas de Burgh, 31st D.C.O. Lancers, who has been mentioned in despatches. He entered the Service on the 9th September, 1908, and obtained his promotion on the 9th December, 1910.

⋄ ⋄ ⋄

The Right Rev. Mgr. Francis Bickerstaffe=Drew, K.H.S., Senior Chaplain to the Forces (R.C.), who has been mentioned in despatches. He was born in Headingly, Leeds, in 1858, and was a son of the late Rev. Harry Lloyd Bickerstaffe and Mona Brougham, daughter of the late Rev. Pierce William Drew, of Heathfield Towers, Youghal. In 1879 he assumed the additional surname of Drew. He was educated at Edward VI. Grammar School, Lichfield; St. Chad's College (A.S.N.C. 1st Class Honours), and Oxford. He was ordained Priest in 1884, and was Assistant Priest of Pro-Cathedral, Kensington, from 1884 to 1886, Acting Chaplain to the Forces, 1886-93, and was Chaplain to the Forces, Plymouth, from 1893 to 1899; Senior R.C. Chaplain, Malta, 1899-1905 and 1909, and Chaplain to the Forces, Salisbury Plain, from 1905 to 1909. He was Private Chamberlain of his late Holiness Pope Leo XIII and of his late Holiness Pope Pius X. He was created a Knight of the Sacred Military Order of the Holy Sepulchre and Count in 1909. He is the well-known writer of several books, under the name of John Ayscough.

⋄ ⋄ ⋄

Lieutenant R. Annesley West, North Irish Horse, who has been mentioned in despatches, is the youngest son of the late Aug. G. West, of White Park, Brookeborough. He served in the Boer War in 45th (Irish Hunt) Co. Imperial Yeomanry, January, 1900, till disbanded in March, 1901. He returned to South Africa in July, 1901, and enlisted in Kitchener's 2nd Fighting Scouts, and shortly afterwards he was given a commission. He obtained the Queen's and King's Medal with three clasps.

⋄ ⋄ ⋄

Captain Claude L. Davis, Army Service Corps, entered the Service in the year 1902, receiving his promotion as Captain in 1912. On the outbreak of the war he accompanied his regiment to the front and has been mentioned in despatches by General Sir John French.

⋄ ⋄ ⋄

Lieutenant=Colonel Wilkinson Dent Bird, D.S.O., 2nd Battalion Royal Irish Rifles, who has been mentioned in despatches by General Sir John French. He was a son of the late Captain J. D. Bird, of the 20th Hussars, and in 1902 he married Winifred Editha, daughter of Major J. B. Barker. He was educated at Wellington College and R.M.C., Sandhurst. In 1888 he entered the Queen's Royal West Surrey Regiment, and became Captain and Brevet Major in 1897. He served in the Niger Expedition in 1897, and was mentioned in despatches, and was awarded the medal with clasp and was made Brevet Major. He also served in the North-West Frontier of India, for which he was awarded the medal with two clasps. During the South African War he was present at the Relief of Mafeking, where he was severely wounded. He was mentioned in despatches and awarded the D.S.O. In 1909 he was made Brevet Lieutenant-Colonel. Lieut.-Colonel Bird has the Diploma of the Royal Geographical Society, and has published Lectures on the Strategy of the Franco-German and Russo-Japanese Wars, and also the Précis of Strategy.

⋄ ⋄ ⋄

Captain O. H. L. Nicholson, D.S.O., the Staff at No. 1 Bast., who has been mentioned in despatches, is a son of the late General Sir Lothian Nicholson, K.C.B., R.E., formerly Governor of Gibraltar, and is a son-in-law of Major-General A. S. Montague Browne, of St. John's Point, Killough, Co. Down. Captain Nicholson entered the Service in September, 1897, became Lieutenant in 1899, obtaining his Captaincy in 1904. He served during the South African War, took part in the operations at Natal, and was present at the Relief of Ladysmith, including the action at Colenso, Spion Kop, and Vaal Kranz. He was also present during the operations at Tugela Heights and the action at Pieters Hill. He was mentioned three times in despatches, and obtained the Queen's Medal with three clasps, the King's Medal with two clasps and the D.S.O.

⋄ ⋄ ⋄

Sergeant William Boyd, 2nd Battalion Royal Irish Regiment, who has been mentioned in General Sir John French's despatches, is a son of Mr. William Boyd, of Brockley Park, Stradbally, Queen's County. Sergeant Boyd joined the Service about eight years ago, and until the present war broke out he was chiefly engaged at the Headquarters of his regiment in Staff work.

⋄ ⋄ ⋄

Captain Hubert Knox, 2nd Battalion Manchester Regiment, who has been mentioned in Sir John French's despatches, entered the Army in 1900, and obtained his Captaincy in April, 1909. He served in the South African War, 1900-2, and obtained the Queen's Medal with three clasps and the King's Medal with two clasps. He was wounded at Le Cateau on August 26th during the retreat from Mons. He is the youngest son of the late Mr. Fitzroy Knox, D.L., of Brittas Castle, Thurles.

⋄ ⋄ ⋄

Sergeant Carson D. Jones, 1st Battalion Royal Irish Fusiliers, who was killed at Armentieries, France, on the 20th October, 1914. Sergeant Jones had been in the fighting line from the beginning of the war, and had been granted the "Distinguished Service Medal" for conspicuous gallantry in the field. Sergeant Jones was a native of Drumaloor, near Belturbet, Co. Cavan.

1. LIEUT. THOMAS DE BURGH, 31st D.C.O. Lancers.	2. THE RIGHT REV. MONS. BICKERSTAFFE-DREW, Senior Chaplain to the Forces.	3. LIEUT R. ANNESLEY WEST, North Irish Horse.
4. CAPT. CLAUDE L. DAVIS, Army Service Corps.	5. LIEUT.-COL. WILKINSON DENT BIRD, D.S.O., 2nd Royal Irish Rifles.	6. CAPT. O. H. L. NICHOLSON, D.S.O., 1st Division.
7. SERGT. WM. BOYD, 2nd Royal Irish Regiment.	8. CAPT. HUBERT KNOX, 2nd Batt. Manchester Regiment.	9. SERGT. CARSON D. JONES, 1st Royal Irish Fusiliers.

DIED FOR THEIR COUNTRY.

Second Lieutenant H. A. Boyd, Royal Inniskilling Fusiliers, obtained his commission in 1913. On the outbreak of the war he accompanied his regiment to the front, where he was killed in action.

✧ ✧ ✧

Cadet Charles Huband Wilson, of H.M.S. *Bulwark*, the younger son of Mr. Charles J. Wilson, of Ailesbury Park, Dublin, was born on the 2nd January, 1899. He was for four years at the preparatory school, Connaught House, Weymouth, and from there entered Osbourne in September, 1911. He was Chief Cadet Captain at Osbourne when he entered Dartmouth in September, 1913. On the outbreak of war in August last, he was made a Cadet Captain at Dartmouth before being sent for service on the *Bulwark*, in the explosion of which he lost his life.

✧ ✧ ✧

Lieutenant C. E. Gaitskell, Leinster Regiment, who was killed in action, obtained his commission on the 1st January, 1913.

✧ ✧ ✧

Captain the Hon. Charles Henry Stanley Monck, 3rd Battalion Coldstream Guards, who was killed in action on the 21st October, 1914. Captain Monck, who was born on the 9th November, 1876, was the elder and only surviving son of Viscount Monck, of Charleville, Enniskerry, Co. Wicklow. He was educated at Eton, and received his commission in the Coldstream Guards in May, 1897, becoming Lieutenant in November, 1898, and Captain in November, 1903. During the South African War he saw much service, being present at the engagements at Paardeberg, Poplar Grove and elsewhere, receiving the Queen's Medal with seven clasps and the King's Medal with two clasps. Captain Monck married in 1904 Mary Florence, daughter of Sir William Wyndham Portal, Bart., and leaves a son and two daughters.

✧ ✧ ✧

Major Edmund Peel Thomson, 2nd Battalion Royal Munster Fusiliers, killed in action, was the youngest son of the late William Thomson, of Manchester, and of Mrs. Thomson, of 30 Saunders Street, Southport, Leeds. He entered the Service in October, 1893, became Lieutenant on the 1st of October, 1896, Captain in July, 1901, and obtained his promotion as Major in February, 1912. He served through the South African War, taking part in the operations in the Transvaal, being mentioned in despatches and obtaining the Queen's Medal with two clasps. Major Thomson was a very distinguished school athlete. He captained the Cricket Eleven for two years, 1891 and 1892, and was in the Fives Team, the Gymnastic Eight and the Rugby Fifteen. He was a contemporary (and in the same house) at Fettes with Sir John Simon, the Attorney-General.

Captain Charles Edward Hack, 1st Battalion Connaught Rangers, who was killed in action on the 5th November, 1914, near Neuve Chapelle. He was the second son of the late William Lionel F. Hack and of Mrs. Hack, Thruxton, near Andover, and was a great grandson of Sir Joseph Burke, 11th Baronet, of Glinsk, Co. Galway. Captain Hack entered the Service in December, 1897, obtaining his promotion as Lieutenant in April, 1900, and his Captaincy in May, 1904. He served in the South African War from 1899-1902, being present at the Relief of Ladysmith, including the action at Colenso. He was also present at Spion Kop and Vaal Kranz, the operations at Tugela Heights and the action at Pieters Hill. In May, 1900, he took part in the actions in the Orange Free State and in the Transvaal and in several other actions including the operations at the Orange River Colony and in Cape Colony. He was mentioned in despatches and obtained the Queen's Medal with five clasps and the King's Medal with two clasps.

✧ ✧ ✧

Lieut. Robert de Stacpoole, Connaught Rangers, fourth son of the Duke de Stacpoole, was born in 1892 at Mount Hazel, Co. Galway, and went to Downside School in September, 1902. In the autumn of 1902, he left school and entered Sandhurst in the following year. He was gazetted to the Connaught Rangers in September, 1911. When the hostilities broke out he accompanied his regiment to the front. He was killed in action at the battle of the Aisne on Sunday, the 20th September. Of the Duke's five sons, three others are now on active service; in the Connaught Rangers, the Prince of Wales Leinster Regiment, and the Royal Field Artillery, respectively.

✧ ✧ ✧

Captain John Percy Whelan, 1st Battalion the Royal Irish Rifles, who was killed in action on the 11th December, 1914, was the son of Mr. and Mrs. J. P. Whelan, Barna, Osbourne Park, Belfast. He was born in May, 1879. After serving in the Militia he was gazetted Second Lieutenant in the Royal Garrison Artillery in August, 1902, and obtained his promotion as Lieutenant the following year. Transferring to the Royal Irish Rifles in 1905, he became Captain in the year 1910. From that date till November, 1912, Captain Whelan was employed as adjutant in the Territorial Force. On the outbreak of the war he became attached to the 2nd Battalion of the Royal Irish Regiment.

✧ ✧ ✧

Lieutenant Hughes, Sussex Regiment, killed in action, was a son of Captain Hughes, late of Cappy, Enniskillen, and who now resides in Birr. Lieutenant Hughes was gazetted on the 22nd May, 1912. On the outbreak of the war he accompanied his regiment to the front, where he died fighting for his country.

1. 2nd LIEUT. H. A. BOYD, Royal Inniskilling Fusiliers.	2. CADET C. HUBAND WILSON, H.M.S. "Bulwark."	3. LIEUT. C. E. GAITSKELL, Leinster Regiment.
4. CAPT. THE HON. H. C. S. MONCK, 3rd Batt. Coldstream Guards.	5. MAJOR E. PEEL THOMSON, 2nd Batt. Royal Munster Fusiliers.	6. CAPT. CHARLES E. HACK, 1st Batt. Connaught Rangers.
7. LT. ROBERT DE STACPOOLE, Connaught Rangers.	8. CAPT. JOHN PERCY WHELAN, 1st Batt. Royal Irish Rifles.	9. LIEUTENANT HUGHES, Sussex Regiment.

DIED FOR THEIR COUNTRY.

Lieutenant S. B. Combe, North Irish Horse, who was killed on the 29th September, 1914, on refusing to surrender to a party of Germans who surrounded him. He was a son of Mr. Abram Combe, J.P., of Donaghloney House, Co. Down, and son-in-law of Captain Holt Waring, D.L., Waringstown, of the North Irish Horse. Lieut. Combe was well-known in Co. Down, where he had been for some years Master of the Co. Down Staghounds.

◇ ◇ ◇

Lieutenant Commander William Crawford Harrison, H.M.S. "Formidable," who lost his life in the sinking of that vessel, of which he was the First and Navigating Officer. He was 33 years of age, and was the second surviving son of Mr. C. L. Harrison, of the Indian Civil Service, and the son-in-law of Dr. T. J. Browne, of Atherstone, Temple Road, Rathmines, Dublin. Entering the Navy in 1895, he attained the rank of Lieutenant on the 31st December, 1910. On January 24th, 1912, he was appointed to the "Formidable" from the repair ship "Cyclops." While serving as Lieutenant in the "Blonde" on the 15th of June, 1904, he received the Royal Humane Society's Medal for a gallant attempt to save a stoker's life. As a Lieutenant in the "Fox" he was employed in blockading the Warsangli Coast, Somaliland, September, 1908, to February, 1909, and in suppression of the arms traffic in the Persian Gulf from 1909 to 1910, during which time four dhows were captured. Officers and men received the thanks of the Colonial Office for their services in Somaliland.

◇ ◇ ◇

Lieutenant James Crosbie Caulfield, 2nd Manchester Regiment, killed in action on the 18th November, 1914, was the youngest son of Brig.-General and Mrs. James E. Caulfield, of Corozal, Jersey. He was born on the 22nd February, 1892, and was appointed Lieutenant in the Army Service Corps in September, 1911.

◇ ◇ ◇

Captain Geoffrey Stewart, Coldstream Guards, who was killed in action on the 22nd December, 1914, was the only surviving son of Major-General Sir Herbert Stewart and the late Lady Stewart, and brother of the Countess of Lanesborough and Mrs. Boyce Combe.

◇ ◇ ◇

Major Herbert Arthur Herbert-Stepney, Irish Guards, who was killed in action on the 7th November, whilst commanding the Irish Guards. Major Herbert-Stepney obtained his first commission in the Coldstream Guards in 1898, and became Lieutenant in December, 1899, and was transferred to the Irish Guards in February, 1901. He was Adjutant from the 1st January, 1902, to the 31st December, 1903. He was promoted to the rank of Captain in September, 1904, and received his majority in February, 1912. He served in the South African War from 1900 to 1901, where he was slightly wounded, and received the Queen's Medal with three clasps.

◇ ◇ ◇

Captain R. C. Orr, Somerset Light Infantry, who has been killed in action, was reported missing on the 19th December. He was a son of the late Mr. R. H. Orr, Solicitor, Belfast and Ballymena, who was joint secretary of the Ulster Unionist Convention, 1892, and a nephew of His Honor James Orr, K.C. He is a member of the firm of Messrs. F. and H. Orr, Solicitors, Ballymena, and before the war he was Adjutant of the North Antrim Regiment Ulster Volunteer Force. Captain Orr was educated at Rugby, and was admitted as a Solicitor in 1903. In December, 1911, he received his commission as Lieutenant in the 3rd Batt. Somerset Light Infantry, and was promoted Captain in August last.

◇ ◇ ◇

Lieutenant W. E. Hope, who has been killed in action, was a Captain on retired pay when he was appointed Lieutenant of the Special Reserve, Irish Guards, in January, 1910. From December, 1912, he had held the post of A.D.C. to the Earl of Aberdeen, Lord Lieutenant of Ireland.

◇ ◇ ◇

Captain Francis William Durand, 3rd Battalion Royal Munster Fusiliers, who was killed in action in December, 1914, was the son of the late Rev. Havilland Durand, of Earley, and of Mrs. Durand, of Moulin Huet, Guernsey. He was born in January, 1875, and was educated at Elizabeth College, Guernsey. In 1891 he was gazetted 2nd Lieutenant in the 3rd Royal Guernsey Light Infantry (Militia), and in 1895 he joined the Rhodesian Horse and served with the Gwelo Field Force in the Matabele campaign of 1896, and the Mashona campaign of 1897, being awarded the medal and clasp. From 1899 to 1902 he served with the African Transcontinental Telegraph Survey through German East Africa. In 1906 he obtained his Company in the Royal Munster Fusiliers, and was seconded under the Foreign Office for the above service. He was employed under both the military and civil Administration of Zanzibar until 1913, when he retired on pension. During his service in Zanzibar he was awarded the Order of El Aliyeh (4th class) and the Brilliant Star of Zanzibar (3rd class). In 1903 he married Geraldine Vesey, youngest daughter of the late Rev. John W. Hawtrey, of Aldin House, Slough. In September last he joined the 2nd Battalion Royal Munster Fusiliers, and was present at the actions on the Aisne, the Marne and at Ypres.

◇ ◇ ◇

Lieutenant Geoffrey Dyett Abbott, Connaught Rangers, who has been killed in action, received his commission as Second Lieutenant on the 4th March, 1911, and was promoted to the rank of Lieutenant on the 9th June, 1914.

Supplement to Irish Life, January 22nd, 1915.

1. LIEUT. S. B. COMBE. North Irish Horse.	2. LT.-COMMANDER HARRISON, H.M.S. "Formidable."	3. LIEUT. J. C. CAULFIELD. Manchester Regiment.
4. CAPTAIN G. STEWART. Coldstream Guards.	5. MAJOR HERBERT STEPNEY. Irish Guards.	6. CAPTAIN R. C. ORR. Somerset Light Infantry.
7. LIEUT. W. E. HOPE, 1st Irish Guards.	8. CAPT. F. W. DURAND, Royal Munster Fusiliers.	9. LIEUT. G. D. ABBOTT, 1st Connaught Rangers.

DIED FOR THEIR COUNTRY

Lieutenant James Francis O'Brien, Royal Munster Fusiliers, who was killed in action, was a son of Mr. Denis O'Brien, late of Thurles, and now residing at Ramsgate. Lieutenant O'Brien received his commission in the Royal Munster Fusiliers in 1910, being promoted to the rank of Lieutenant in 1913.

✧ ✧ ✧

Lieutenant=Colonel the Hon. George H. Morris, Irish Guards, who was killed in action on the 1st September, 1914. He fell in an engagement fought by the Fourth Brigade near Villiers Catterels, towards the end of which a final charge by the Irish Guards and Grenadiers was made, Colonel Morris leading. He was a brother of Lord Killanin and heir presumptive to the barony. Born in 1872, he joined the Rifle Brigade when he was twenty years of age, became Major in the Irish Guards, and was promoted Colonel in 1913. He was D.A.A.G. in Belfast in 1904, and Staff Captain Headquarters of the Army, 1904-6. Colonel Morris saw active service in India, 1897-8, and also went through the South African War. His decorations included the Queen's Medal with four clasps. Last year he married Dora Wesley, daughter of the late Mr. J. Wesley Hall, Melbourne.

✧ ✧ ✧

Captain G. R. Fitzpatrick, 2nd Welsh Regiment, who has been killed in action, obtained his commission on the 1st August, 1909, and obtained his Captaincy recently.

✧ ✧ ✧

Captain Godfrey Malcolm Bentley, 1st Northamptonshire Regiment, who died on the 29th October, 1914, from wounds received in action, was the fifth son of Lieutenant-Colonel A. W. Bentley, J.P., of the Grove, Monken Hadley, Middlesex, and the son-in-law of Mr. W. H. Gallway, of Belgravia, Bangor, Co. Down. Captain Bentley entered the Service in January, 1903, being promoted Lieutenant in 1904, and obtaining his Captaincy in 1910. He served in the South African War, taking part in the operations in Cape Colony, June, 1901, to January, 1902, and served in St. Helena from January to 31st May, 1902. He obtained the Queen's Medal with two clasps.

✧ ✧ ✧

Brevet=Major Edward Martin Panter= Downes, who has been killed in action, entered the Army as Second Lieutenant on the 10th October, 1894, being promoted Lieutenant in September, 1897, and obtaining his Captaincy in 1901. He served in the South African War from 1899 to 1902 on the Staff. He took part in the operations in the Orange Free State, Transvaal, east of Pretoria, including actions at Belfast, and in various other actions for which he was mentioned in despatches and made Brevet-Major. He received the Queen's Medal with three clasps and the King's Medal with two clasps.

✧ ✧ ✧

Captain C. O'Brien Butler, R.A.M.C., attached to the 5th Royal Irish Lancers, died of wounds received in action. He was son of the late Major Pierce O'Brien-Butler, King's Royal Rifle Corps. Prior to Captain Butler obtaining his commission in the R.A.M.C. he had achieved the distinction of being classed amongst the first Gentlemen riders in the United Kingdom. Shortly after he entered the Service he was ordered to India, and there continued his racing successes. On returning from abroad some eighteen months ago he was sent to the Curragh Camp where he was able to indulge in his love of riding to the utmost. He was always keen for a mount, and was present at all the well-known race meetings through the country. He was just as keen a soldier as he was a sportsman, and his care of his men in peace and war constituted a record.

✧ ✧ ✧

Second Lieutenant John S. Eldred, Royal Irish Rifles, who died of wounds in hospital at Boulogne. He was gazetted to the Leinster Regiment in August on joining the Army, but owing to the Rifles being short of officers, through numerous casualties, he was attached to them and was serving with them when he was mortally wounded. He was the second son of Fleet Paymaster Edward N. Eldred, late of H.M.S. "Hogue," and grandson of Mr. Edward Eldred, of the Gables, Petersfield, Hants, and of the late Commander Richard Sturgess.

✧ ✧ ✧

Lieutenant John Lionel Wordsworth, 5th Royal Irish Lancers, who was killed in action, was gazetted to the 5th Lancers in May, 1906, obtaining his promotion as Lieutenant in May, 1908.

✧ ✧ ✧

Lieutenant Neville Leslie Woodroffe, who has been killed in action, was gazetted to the Irish Guards on the 12th February, 1913, and was appointed to the 1st Battalion on the 5th August last.

Supplement to Irish Life, January 22nd, 1915.

OUR HEROES

1. LIEUT. J. F. O'BRIEN, Royal Munster Fusiliers.
2. LT.-COL. THE HON. GEORGE MORRIS, Irish Guards.
3. CAPT. G. R. FITZPATRICK, 2nd Welsh Regiment.
4. CAPT. GODFREY MALCOLM BENTLEY, 1st Northamptonshire Regiment.
5. BREVET-MAJOR EDWARD MARTIN PANTER-DOWNES, Royal Irish Regiment.
6. CAPT. C. O'BRIEN BUTLER, R.A.M.C., Attached to 5th Royal Irish Lancers.
7. 2nd LIEUT. JOHN S. ELDRED, Royal Irish Rifles.
8. LIEUT. J. L. WORDSWORTH, 5th Royal Irish Lancers.
9. LIEUT. NEVILLE LESLIE WOODROFFE, Irish Guards.

MENTIONED IN DESPATCHES.

Sergeant Patrick McEnroy, of the Irish Guards, who has been mentioned in despatches by General Sir John French. Previous to the war Sergt. McEnroy was an enthusiastic boxer, having won the Navy and Army Middle-weight Championship, N.S.C., in 1911, and he was the finalist in the Navy and Army Middleweight, 1909-10. He also was the winner of the " Best Shot " (all ranks) at Aldershot in 1910.

◇ ◇ ◇

Lieutenant-Colonel A. Parker, of the 5th (Royal Irish) Lancers, who has been mentioned in despatches. He was gazetted in 1887, became Lieutenant in 1889, Captain in 1894, Major in 1903, and Lieutenant-Colonel in 1913. Colonel Parker served in the South African campaign and took part in the defence of Ladysmith as well as the actions at Elandslaagte, Rietfontein and Lombard's Kop, which preceded the investment of Sir George White's force and the sorties from the beleaguered town. He was mentioned in despatches several times and obtained the Queen's Medal with five clasps and the King's Medal with two clasps. He was wounded early in the present war.

◇ ◇ ◇

Corporal Roberts, of the 5th Lancers, who has been awarded the Medaille Militaire by the President of the French Republic in recognition of his gallantry during the operations between August 21st and 30th.

◇ ◇ ◇

Second Lieutenant David Nelson, V.C., who has been mentioned in despatches by General Sir John French, belongs to the famous L Battery Royal Horse Artillery. Second Lieutenant Nelson is a native of Monaghan, and he was awarded the Victoria Cross for " helping to bring the guns into action under heavy fire at Nery on the 1st September, 1914, and while severely wounded remaining with them until all the ammunition was expended, although he had been ordered to retire to cover."

◇ ◇ ◇

Col. Thomas Joseph O'Donnell, D.S.O., R.A.M.C., who has been mentioned in despatches. He was born in January, 1858, and was the third son of the late Mr. P. O'Donnell, High Constable of the Barony of Glenquin, of Killeedy, Ashford, Co. Limerick. He was educated at St. Stanislaus' College, Tullabeg, King's County, which was amalgamated with Clongowes Wood College in 1886. Colonel O'Donnell served with the Egyptian Expedition, 1881-2, for which he obtained the medal, Khedive's Star. He served with the Kimberley Light Horse under Sir C. Warren, Bechuanaland Expedition, 1885-86, and with the Inniskilling Dragoons in the operations in Zululand, 1887-88, and with the 3rd Batt. Rifle Brigade, Tirah campaign, 1897-98, for which he obtained the medal with clasp. He also served with the 12th Royal Lancers during the South African War, being mentioned in despatches twice and obtaining the medal with six clasps, and King's Medal with two clasps. He was decorated for attending the wounded under fire.

◇ ◇ ◇

Captain Michael Patrick Leahy, R.A.M.C., entered the service as Lieutenant in 1907, being promoted to the rank of Captain in 1910. He has been mentioned in General Sir John French's despatches.

DIED FOR THEIR COUNTRY

Lieutenant Patrick Maxwell Murray, Sherwood Foresters, who has been killed in action, entered the service on the 18th September, 1909, and was promoted to the rank of Lieutenant on the 16th August, 1911.

◇ ◇ ◇

Captain Leo Creagh, Manchester Regiment, who has been killed in action, entered the Army in January, 1899, being promoted to the rank of Lieutenant in September of the same year, and obtaining his Captaincy in 1901. He served in the South African War, 1899, taking part in the operations in Natal, including the action at Lombard's Kop. He was also present at the defence of Ladysmith, including the sorties of the 7th and 10th December, 1899. He obtained the Queen's Medal with clasp.

◇ ◇ ◇

Private Edward Richardson, of the 17th Lancers, who gave up his life, when a prisoner in the hands of the Germans, in order that a patrol of his comrades, who were walking into a trap, might be saved. Private Richardson is the fourth son of Mr. Henry Richardson, of Torca Hill, Dalkey.

Supplement to Irish Life, January 22nd, 1915.

OUR HEROES

1. SERGT. PATRICK McENROY, Irish Guards.

2. LIEUT.-COL. A. PARKER, 5th Royal Irish Lancers.

3. CORPORAL ROBERTS, 5th Royal Irish Lancers.

4. 2nd LIEUT. DAVID NELSON, L Battery R.H.A.

5. COL. THOMAS J. O'DONNELL, D.S.O. Royal Army Medical Corps.

6. CAPTAIN MICHAEL LEAHY, R.A.M.C.

7. LIEUT. PATRICK MAXWELL MURRAY, Sherwood Foresters.

8. CAPTAIN L. CREAGH, Manchester Regiment.

9. PTE. EDWARD RICHARDSON, 17th Lancers.

MENTIONED IN DESPATCHES.

Lieutenant the Hon. Herbrand Charles Alexander, 5th Lancers, who has been mentioned in despatches, is the brother and heir-presumtive of the 5th Earl of Caledon. He was born on the 28th November, 1888, and was educated at R.M.C., Sandhurst. He entered the service on the 27th January, 1909, and obtained his promotion as Lieutenant on the 1st March, 1910.

◇ ◇ ◇

Brigadier-General the Earl of Cavan, M.V.O., D.S.O. Frederick Rudolph Lambart, 10th Earl, was born in 1865. He acted for some time as A.D.C. to the Governor-General of Canada and served with distinction in the South African War, when he was mentioned in despatches. In the present war, to quote from General Sir John French's despatch, "he was conspicuous for the skill, coolness and courage with which he led his troops."

◇ ◇ ◇

Lieutenant Lord Holmpatrick, 16th Lancers, who has been mentioned in despatches, was born in 1886, and was the son of the 1st Baron and Lady Victoria Alexandrina, daughter of General Lord Charles Wellesley. Lord Holmpatrick succeeded his father as 2nd Baron in 1898. He entered the 16th Lancers as Lieutenant in March, 1909, being gazetted from the 16th Hussars.

◇ ◇ ◇

Captain John Joseph O'Keeffe, Army Service Corps, who has been mentioned in despatches, entered the service in 1906, when he was gazetted Lieutenant, obtaining his Captaincy in 1910.

◇ ◇ ◇

Major General Henry H. Wilson, C.B., D.S.O., Sub-Chief, Head Quarter, British Expeditionary Force, who has been twice mentioned in General Sir John French's despatches, is the second son of the late Mr. James Wilson, D.L., of Currygrane, Co. Longford. He was educated at Marlborough College and was a graduate at the Staff College. In 1884 he entered the service, being gazetted to the Royal Irish Regiment and was transferred the same year to the Rifle Brigade. In December, 1893, he obtained his Captaincy, and on December 1st, 1901, his Majority, being promoted as Lieutenant-Colonel the following day. In 1904 he became Colonel and in 1913 Major-General. He served with the Burmese Expedition, 1886-8, during which campaign he was wounded, and was awarded the medal with two clasps. He also served during the South African War, on the Staff, and was present at the Relief of Ladysmith, including the actions at Colenso, Spion Kop, and Vaal Kranz, and in most of the important actions of that campaign. He was mentioned in despatches four times, and was awarded the medal with five clasps and was made Brevet Lieutenant-Colonel on promotion to Major. He was also awarded the D.S.O. From 1902-3 he commanded the 9th Provisional Batt., D.A.A.G., Army Headquarters, 1903; A.A.G., Army Headquarters, 1903-6. From 1904-1906 he was Assistant Director Staff Duties in the War Office and from 1907-10 Commandant Staff College. Two years ago he was decorated with the Order of the "Legion d'Honneur." From August 1st, 1910, he has been Director of Military Operations on the Imperial General Staff.

◇ ◇ ◇

Captain George Eric Burroughs Dobbs, R.E., who has been awarded the Cross of the Legion of Honour for distinguished service, is a son of Mr. Joseph Dobbs, of Coolbawn House, Castlecomer, and entered the service as 2nd Lieutenant in March, 1904, obtaining his promotion as Lieutenant in 1906.

◇ ◇ ◇

Lieutenant Richard Lambart, who has been awarded the D.S.O., is the first actor to gain this distinction. He has been leading man with Sir Charles Wyndham and Sir John Hare in London and with Mr. Charles Frohman in New York. He comes of a fighting family, for he is a son of the late Major Frederick Lambart, Royal Scots Fusiliers, and great-grandson of the 9th Earl of Cavan. His family is well represented in the great war: his cousin, Brigadier-General Lord Cavan is at the front, and his uncle, Brig.-General Lambart, is training Kitchener's new army at Bordon.

◇ ◇ ◇

The Rev. Percy Wyndham Guinness, who is the first clergyman to receive the D.S.O., is the second son of the Rev. Wyndham Guinness, Rector of Rathdrum. He is a Graduate of Cambridge University, and entered the Church of England, undertaking duty in the diocese of Birmingham. Some years ago he obtained an army chaplaincy, and accompanied the Expeditionary Force to France, where his coolness and bravery under fire were fittingly rewarded by the above distinction.

◇ ◇ ◇

Lieutenant Inglis F. Rowley Miller, 2nd Royal Inniskilling Fusiliers, who has been mentioned in General Sir John French's despatches, is a son of Major Rowley A. Miller, Registrar of the Tyrone County Court. He is an officer of the 3rd (Special Reserve) Battalion, Omagh, and has been serving with the 2nd Battalion in the war. Lieutenant Miller was wounded at Cambrai.

Supplement to Irish Life, January 22nd, 1915.

1. LT. HON H. C. ALEXANDER, 5th Lancers.
2. BRIG.-GEN. THE EARL OF CAVAN, 4th Guards Brigade.
3. LIEUT. LORD HOLMPATRICK, 16th Lancers.
4. CAPT. JOHN J. O'KEEFFE. Army Service Corps.
5. MAJOR-GEN. H. H. WILSON, C.B., D.S.O.
6. CAPTAIN G. ERIC B. DOBBS, Royal Engineers.
7. LT. R. LAMBART, D.S.O.
8. REV. P. W GUINNESS. Chaplain to the Forces.
9. LIEUT. INGLIS F. ROWLEY MILLER, 2nd Batt. Inniskilling Fusiliers.

DIED FOR THEIR COUNTRY.

Lieutenant Denis Duncan Philby, who was killed in action near Ypres on the 12th November, 1914, was appointed 2nd Lieutenant of the Royal Dublin Fusiliers in June, 1910, and obtained his promotion as Lieutenant in March, 1912, and was afterwards attached to the Royal Munster Fusiliers. He was twenty-five years of age.

✧ ✧ ✧

2nd Lieutenant Gerard Ribton Gore, 1st Royal Sussex Regiment, who was killed in action on the 19th December, 1914. He was the only son of the late Lieut.-Colonel Ribton Gore, of the Royal Sussex Regiment, and Mrs. Ribton Gore, of Thornfields, Co. Limerick. He was educated at Cheltenham College. Lieut. Gore was wounded during the retreat from Mons and returned shortly afterwards to the front. He was a nephew of Col. Gore, King's Royal Body Guard, of Erleigh, Devon.

✧ ✧ ✧

2nd Lieutenant Lawrence Ernest Pelham Grubb, Yorkshire Light Infantry, who was killed in action near Ypres on the 15th November, 1914, was a great-grandson of the late Mr. Richard Grubb, of Cahir Abbey, Co. Tipperary. He was educated at Rugby and at Brasenose College, Oxford, where he had recently obtained his B.A. degree with honours. Lieut. Grubb went to the front early in August, and for over three months was a despatch rider. He fell when gallantly leading a charge.

✧ ✧ ✧

Captain Eric John Fletcher Gough, Irish Guards, who was killed in action on the 30th December, 1914, was the only son of the late Major Thomas Armstrong Gough and of Mrs. Claude Langley, of 9 Onslow Crescent, London, S.W. Captain Gough entered the army on the 1st February, 1911, being promoted Lieutenant the following November. He was recently promoted to the rank of Captain.

✧ ✧ ✧

Major William Stopford Sarsfield, 2nd Batt. Connaught Rangers, who died on the 20th September, 1914, of wounds received in the battle of the Aisne when, owing to the capture and imprisonment of Colonel Abercrombie, he was in temporary command of the regiment. Major Sarsfield was the third son of the late Mr. D. R. P. Sarsfield, of Doughcloyne, Co. Cork. He joined the 1st Battalion of the Connaught Rangers in September, 1888, and served all through the South African War, where he took part in the relief of Ladysmith and the actions at Colenso, Spion Kop, Vaal Kranz and Tugela Heights. He was appointed Assistant Press Censor in South Africa and Deputy Assistant Adjutant-General. He received the Queen's Medal with three clasps and the King's Medal with two clasps.

✧ ✧ ✧

Captain Hugh Conor Henry O'Brien, Royal Munster Fusiliers, who has been killed in action, was born on the 19th November, 1880. He became 2nd Lieutenant in August, 1900, Lieutenant in March, 1903, and was promoted to the rank of Captain in April, 1910. He was present at many operations in the South African War, and had the Queen's Medal with clasp. On the North-West Frontier of India in 1908 he was Brigade Signalling Officer, and received the medal with clasp.

✧ ✧ ✧

2nd Lieutenant R. A. Young, of the Munster Fusiliers, who has been killed in action, is a son of Mr. A. Young, of 3, The Green, St. Leonards-on-Sea.

✧ ✧ ✧

Captain Hon. Arthur Annesley, 10th Hussars, who has been killed in action, is the eldest son of Viscount Valentia, and entered the service in April, 1900, being promoted to the rank of Lieutenant the following year and obtaining his Captaincy in 1907. He served in the South African War, taking part in the operations in the Transvaal from October to November, 1900, also in the Transvaal from the 30th November, 1900, to July, 1901. He was in Cape Colony from July, 1901, to March, 1902. He was awarded the Queen's Medal with three clasps and the King's Medal with two clasps.

✧ ✧ ✧

Lieutenant Hubert William Brown, Royal Irish Regiment, who has been killed in action, entered the service as 2nd Lieutenant in November, 1909, and obtained his promotion as Lieutenant on the 9th March, 1910.

OUR HEROES

1. LT. DENIS DUNCAN PHILBY, Royal Munster Fusiliers.
2. 2nd LIEUT. GERARD RIBTON GORE, 1st Royal Sussex Regiment.
3. 2nd LIEUT. LAWRENCE E. PELHAM GRUBB, Yorkshire Light Infantry.
4. CAPT. ERIC JOHN FLETCHER GOUGH, Irish Guards.
5. MAJOR WILLIAM STOPFORD SARSFIELD, 2nd Connaught Rangers.
6. CAPT. HUGH C. H O'BRIEN, Royal Munster Fusiliers.
7. 2nd LIEUT. R. A. YOUNG, Munster Fusiliers.
8. CAPT. THE HON. ARTHUR ANNESLEY, 10th Hussars.
9. LIEUT. HUBERT W. BROWN, Royal Irish Regiment.

MENTIONED IN DESPATCHES.

Lance-Corporal Henry Murray, Royal Irish Rifles, who has been mentioned in Sir John French's Despatches. Had seen previous war service and is in possession of the Queen's Medal for the South African campaign. On his discharge he qualified as chauffeur and obtained employment with Mr. J. McCaughey, Dunbarton, Belfast. On the outbreak of war he at once rejoined the Colours, and after distinguishing himself in the early portion of the campaign was unfortunately wounded at the battle of the Aisne and was invalided home.

✧ ✧ ✧

Major George Hercules Forster Tailyour, Royal Horse Artillery, who has been mentioned in Sir John French's First Despatch. He entered the service in 1896, was promoted Lieutenant 1899, his Captaincy following three years later, and in September, 1913, he was gazetted Major.

✧ ✧ ✧

Lance-Corporal James Delaney, 2nd Battalion Royal Irish Regiment, was amongst the twenty-three Non-Commissioned Officers and men who were awarded the medal for Distinguished Conduct on the Field. During an important point in the operations at Orloy, Delaney greatly distinguished himself by smart scouting in the vicinity of the River Petit Morin and discovering the position of the enemy in time to warn the advance guard of danger.

✧ ✧ ✧

Brigadier-General Charles Toler McMurrough Kavanagh, who has been mentioned in Sir John French's Despatches, late of the 10th Hussars, entered the service in 1884, became Captain in 1890, Major in January, 1900; Lt.-Col. in the winter of the same year, and Colonel in August, 1905. He served through the South African campaign, being mentioned twice in Despatches, receiving a Brevet Colonelcy, the Queen's Medal with five clasps, the King's Medal with two clasps, and the Distinguished Service Order. In addition to the distinctions already mentioned, General Kavanagh has been given the C.B., the M.V.O., and C.V.O.

✧ ✧ ✧

Brigadier-General Aylmer Hunter Weston, C.B., D.S.O., J.P., D.L., who has been mentioned in Despatches, acted as assistant director of Military Training on the General Staff of the War Office from 1911. He entered the army in 1884, being gazetted Lieutenant to the Royal Engineers; his promotion as Captain followed in 1892; he became Brevet Major in 1895; Brevet Lt.-Col. in 1900, and Brevet Col. in 1906. He was a member of the Dongola Expeditionary Force in 1896, being mentioned in despatches and obtaining the fourth class Medjidieh, the Khedive's Medal with clasp, and the Queen's Medal. In the South African War, 1899 to 1902, he took part in most of the operations during the campaign, being mentioned in despatches and obtaining the medal with seven clasps, the D.S.O. and his Brevet Lieutenant-Colonelcy.

✧ ✧ ✧

Brigadier-General Norman Reginald McMahon, D.S.O., entered the service in May, 1885, became Captain in November, 1896; Major in November, 1901; and was gazetted Lieut.-Col. in May, 1911. He served in the Burmese expedition, 1886 to 1887, as special service officer, receiving the Medal and clasp. In the South African war he was attached to the staff, was present at the relief of Ladysmith, took part in the action at Colenso, also at the Tugela Heights and at Pieter's Hill. He was mentioned in despatches, received the Queen's medal with five clasps, the King's Medal with two clasps, and the D.S.O. He is the son of the late General Sir Thomas McMahon, 3rd Bart., C.B.

✧ ✧ ✧

Gunner C. B. Carry, R.H.A., who has been awarded the Distinguished Conduct Medal for conspicuous gallantry on September 8th in France. When his section was under heavy fire Gunner Carry displayed great bravery, particularly in assisting to carry a wounded man under cover. Gunner Carry has been in the service for about seven years and is a good athlete.

✧ ✧ ✧

Lieutenant T. W. Fitzpatrick, 2nd Batt. Royal Irish Regiment, who has been mentioned in Sir John French's Despatches for conspicuous gallantry in the fighting line from August 21st to the 30th. He has also been decorated with the Legion of Honour by the President of the French Republic for coolness and bravery in the field. Lieutenant Fitzpatrick was Regimental Quartermaster Sergeant when going on active service; on the 1st October he was commissioned Second Lieutenant and again promoted on the field in November as Lieutenant.

✧ ✧ ✧

Lance-Corporal Noel Fernie, 2nd Batt. Royal Irish Regiment, who has been mentioned in Sir John French's Despatches and promoted Lance-Corporal, is a son of Mr. Fernie, Rosemount, Tramore, Waterford, and of Mrs. Fernie, Waterford. Noel Fernie is only 18 years of age.

1 LANCE-CORP. H. MURRAY. Royal Irish Rifles.	2. MAJOR GEO. H. F. TAILYOUR, Royal Horse Artillery.	3. LANCE-CORPORAL J. DELANY, Royal Irish Regiment.
4. BRIG.-GEN. McMURROUGH KAVANAGH, C.B., C.V.O.	5. BRIG.-GEN. WESTON, C.B., D.S.O.	6. GENERAL McMAHON, D.S.O.
7. GUNNER C. B. CARRY, Royal Horse Artillery.	8. LIEUT. FITZPATRICK, Royal Irish Regiment.	9. LANCE-CORP. NOEL FERNIE, Royal Irish Regiment.

MENTIONED IN DESPATCHES.

Captain Guy St. George Robinson, Northampton Regiment, son of the late Mr. St. George C. W. Robinson and Mrs. Robinson, Woodville, Sligo, and nephew of the Right Honourable Sir Edward Carson, M.P., was amongst the officers mentioned in Sir John French's first despatch. He was gazetted in May, 1907, became Lieutenant in April, 1909, and obtained his Captaincy in 1914. The announcement has now been made that he has been awarded the new Military Cross.

◇ ◇ ◇

Lieut.=Col. St. John Augustus Cox, Royal Irish Regiment, entered the service in November, 1889, was gazetted Lieutenant in 1891, Captain 1898, obtained his Majority in July, 1898, his promotion as Lieutenant-Colonel being gazetted in February, 1913. He served through the South African war and took part in many important operations, including the actions near Johannesburg, Pretoria, and Diamond Hill in June, 1900, and later the same year near Pretoria and at Belfast. He obtained the Queen's Medal with six clasps He has been mentioned in Sir John French's despatches.

◇ ◇ ◇

Captain the Hon. William Andrew Nugent, 15th King's Hussars, son of the 10th Earl of Westmeath, and brother and heir presumptive to the present Earl of Westmeath. He was born in March, 1876, and married in 1913, Kathleen, eldest daughter of Mr. J. J. Stein. He entered the army in 1896, became Lieutenant in June, 1897, and obtained his Captaincy in March, 1900. He has been mentioned in Sir John French's despatches.

◇ ◇ ◇

Brigadier=General Beauchamp J. C. Doran, C.B. Entered the service in January, 1880, was gazetted Lieutenant in 1881 and Captain in May, 1887, obtaining his Majority the same week. In November, 1900, he became Lieut.-Colonel and obtained his full Colonelcy in October, 1905. He is the eldest son of the late General Sir John Doran, K.C.B., a distinguished Irish officer. He has seen considerable service, having served in the Afghan War, the Sudan expedition, the Hazara expedition, the Miranzai expedition. In 1899-1902 he was taking part in the South African War, acting as Press censor in Natal, also discharging staff duties and later acting as Commandant at Rustenberg. He was present at the relief of Ladysmith, was engaged in the Transvaal in November, 1900, to April, 1901, and in Cape Colony, where he was severely wounded. In 1903 he married Mary, widow of the late William M'Geough Bond, and they have resided from time to time at their town house, 50 Stephen's Green, Dublin, and at the family seat, Ely House, Co. Wexford. He was mentioned in Sir John French's despatches.

◇ ◇ ◇

Admiral David Beatty, C.B., D.S.O., M.V.O. This distinguished officer is the son of Captain V. L. Beatty, of Borodale, Co. Wexford, and was born in 1871. He entered the Navy in 1884, and was promoted Commander in 1898. He served in the Sudan in the campaign of that year and obtained the D.S.O., the medal and the fourth-class Medjidieh. His next service was in China in 1900, where he was mentioned in despatches, received the medal and clasp, and was promoted Captain. In 1910 he was made Rear-Admiral, after which he acted as Naval Secretary to the First Lord of the Admiralty, and in 1912 was appointed to command the First Cruiser Squadron. Since the outbreak of the war he has been conducting naval operations with the squadron under his command.

◇ ◇ ◇

Brigadier=General F. S. Maude, C.M.G., D.S.O. (1900), late Coldstream Guards, who has been mentioned in Sir John French's despatches, son of the late General Sir Frederick Maude, V.C., G.C.B. He entered the army in 1884, passed the Staff College 1896, obtained his Majority in 1899, Lieut.-Colonelcy in 1907, and Colonel in 1911. He was promoted Brigadier-General this year. He served in the Sudan 1885; took part in the South African War, and was present during the operations in the Orange Free State and in the Transvaal. He was mentioned in despatches, receiving the Queen's medal with six clasps and the D.S.O. He was chief Staff Officer of the 5th Division at the Curragh 1912 to 1914, and was Staff Officer with the Third Army Corps from August to October of this year, when he was appointed Brigadier-General commanding the 14th Infantry Brigade.

◇ ◇ ◇

Sergeant Edward Henry, son of Colour-Sergeant Robert Henry, late of the 5th Batt. Royal Irish Rifles (Royal South Downs), who has been mentioned in despatches amongst the officers and men of the Royal Irish Rifles.

◇ ◇ ◇

Major the Hon. Leslie Probyn Butler, Irish Guards, second son of Lord Dunboyne, Knoppogue Castle, Quin, Co. Clare. Major Butler entered the service in March, 1900, became Lieutenant two years later, obtained his Captaincy in March, 1909, and was promoted Major in July, 1913. He acted as Brigade Major in the 8th Infantry Brigade, Southern Command, in the early part of 1913. He served through the South African War and took part in the operations south of the Orange River in 1899 and 1900, receiving the Queen's Medal and clasp. His marriage with Mary Christal, youngest daughter of Sir John Heathcote-Amory, took place in 1907. He has been mentioned in Sir John French's despatches.

◇ ◇ ◇

Lieutenant W. H. Leisching, 2nd Batt. Royal Irish Fusiliers, who has been mentioned in Sir John French's despatches, and awarded the Legion of Honour by the President of the French Republic. He entered the service in September, 1913, and has been on active service with his regiment from the beginning of the present campaign.

1. CAPT. GUY ST. G. ROBINSON. Northamptonshire Regiment.
2. LIEUT.-COL. ST. J. A. COX, Royal Irish Regiment.
3. HON. W. A. NUGENT, 15th Hussars.
4. GENL. B. J. C. DORAN, C.B.
5. ADMIRAL BEATTY, C.B., D.S.O., M.V.O.
6. BRIG.-GEN. F. S. MAUDE, C.M.G., D.S.O.
7. SERGEANT HENRY, Royal Irish Rifles.
8. MAJOR THE HON. LESLIE BUTLER, Irish Guards.
9. LIEUT LEISCHING, Royal Irish Fusiliers.

CORRECTIONS IN PART I. OF ALBUM.

Lieut. H. V. Gerrard, whose portrait appeared in our first part, should have been Captain H. V. Gerrard.

In our first part it was stated that Captain H. Ansley Davis was educated at Portora Royal School, Enniskillen, from which he passed direct into the Royal Military College, Sandhurst. This is incorrect. Capt. Davis after leaving Portora went to Campbell College, Belfast, from which he passed direct into the Royal Military College.

The late Capt. Auchinleck, whose portrait appeared in our first part, was the son of Mrs. Auchinleck, of Omagh.

The initials of the late Capt. Conyngham were erroneously given in our first part as C. A. E. They should have been C. A. T. Capt. Conyngham was medical officer in charge of the Loyal North Lancashire Regiment, and left with them at the beginning of the war for Mombassa. He was killed in action near the German East African frontier, when the English forces attempted unsuccessfully to take a railway junction. He was 31 years of age.

FOR VALOUR.

FIVE IRISH V.C's.

OUR HEROES.

Captain Robert Foster Dill, D.S.O., 129th D. C. O. Baluchis, Indian Army, was killed in action on April 11th. He was the second son of the Very Rev. Marcus Dill, D.D., Alloway, ex-Moderator of the Church of Scotland, and formerly of First Presbyterian Church, Ballymena. Having received his education at Marlborough College and the Royal Military College, Sandhurst, he obtained a commission in the Indian Army in 1904, and was gazetted to his captaincy in 1912. On the outbreak of the war his regiment, along with the Lahore Division, arrived in France, and it has since then been at the front. In October, when fighting in the trenches, he was wounded, but in a few weeks he was able to return to his military duty. For his brilliant conduct on that occasion he was mentioned in the despatches of the Commander-in-Chief, and the King bestowed upon him the Distinguished Service Order.

✧ ✧ ✧

Captain George O'D. F. Thomas-O'Donel, 4th Battalion Royal Fusiliers (City of London Regiment), who has been mentioned in despatches and has recently been awarded the Military Cross, is the only child of Mr. and Mrs. Thomas-O'Donel, of Newport, County Mayo, and great-grandson of Sir Richard O'Donel, Bart., on the death of whose son and successor, Sir George O'Donel, without male issue, the baronetcy became extinct. Captain Thomas-O'Donel, who is Adjutant of his regiment, has been engaged in the operations in France since the early stages of the war, and has distinguished himself on various occasions.

✧ ✧ ✧

Captain Dudley G. Johnson, D.S.O., of the South Wales Borderers, received his Captaincy in March, 1914. He was serving with his regiment in China when war broke out, and was engaged in the operations at Tsing-Tau, where he greatly distinguished himself, and was granted the Distinguished Service Order, which was bestowed, according to *The Gazette,* "for conspicuous ability on the night of November 5th-6th, 1914, during the operations against the German positions at Tsing-Tau, and for great gallantry in rescuing several wounded men whilst exposed to heavy machine-gun fire."

✧ ✧ ✧

Major Gilbert John Anthony Ormsby, of the Royal Army Medical Corps, who received the D.S.O. and was mentioned in despatches. This officer served all through the South African War, and was educated at the Meath Hospital and Co. Dublin Infirmary and the University of Dublin. Major Gilbert Ormsby is the only son of Sir Lambert H. Ormsby, senior surgeon to the Meath Hospital and Co. Dublin Infirmary, and of Merrion Square.

Brigadier-General Beauchamp J. C. Doran, C.B., who has been twice mentioned in despatches and promoted, is the eldest son of the late General Sir John Doran, K.C.B., a distinguished Irish officer. He has seen considerable service, having served in the Afghan War, the Sudan expedition, the Hazara expedition, the Miranzai expedition. In 1899-1902 he was taking part in the South African War, acting as Press censor in Natal, also discharging staff duties and later acting as Commandant at Rustenberg. He was present at the relief of Ladysmith, was engaged in the Transvaal in November, 1900, to April, 1901, and in Cape Colony, where he was severely wounded. In 1903 he married Mary, widow of the late William M'Geough Bond, and they have resided from time to time at their town house, 50 Stephen's Green, Dublin, and at the family seat, Ely House, Co. Wexford.

✧ ✧ ✧

Lord Massereene and Ferrard, who has been mentioned in Sir John French's despatches for distinguished service in the field, has been in command of the contingent of the North Irish Horse, who have been acting as General's guard since the beginning of the war.

✧ ✧ ✧

Staff-Sergeant T. R. Collins, of the Royal Scots Regiment, who was specially mentioned by the late Lord Justice Moriarty at the opening of the Co. Mayo Assizes for his distinguished service in the war. He was wounded and ordered to hospital, but refused to go, and remained on duty, and was again wounded and fell into the hands of the Germans. He was mentioned in despatches. He is a brother of Mr. J. J. Collins, P.L.G., Castlebar.

✧ ✧ ✧

Captain James Arundel Nixon, 1st Royal Lancaster Regiment (King's Own), joined February, 1899; served through the Boer War in South Africa; mentioned in despatches; promoted Captain in 1902; wounded at Le Cateau August 26th, 1914. He is the eldest son of Major-General Nixon, D.L., retired, late R.A., Clone, Ballyragget, Co. Kilkenny.

✧ ✧ ✧

Lt. Geo. Neville Patrick Young, second son of George L. Young, J.P., of Culdaff House, Co. Donegal, and Millmount, Randalstown, Co. Antrim. Born 17th March, 1893, educated at Castle Park Preparatory School, St. Columba's College, and Dover College, from where he entered Sandhurst, 1912, gaining a Prize Cadetship. Gazetted 2nd Lieutenant Leinster Regiment, September, 1913. Went out with Expeditionary Force, September, 1914. Mentioned in despatches and awarded Military Cross, February, 1915.

1. CAPT. R. F. DILL, D.S.O., 129th D.C.O. Baluchis.	2. CAPT. G. O'D. F. THOMAS-O'DONEL, 4th Royal Fusiliers.	3. CAPT. D. G. JOHNSON, D.S.O., South Wales Borderers.
4. MAJOR G. J. A. ORMSBY, R.A.M.C.	5. BRIG.-GEN. BEAUCHAMP J. C. DORAN, C.B.	6. LORD MASSEREENE AND FERRARD, North Irish Horse.
7. STAFF-SERGT. T. R. COLLINS, Royal Scots Regiment.	8. CAPT. J. ARUNDEL NIXON, 1st Royal Lancaster Rgt.	9. LT. GEORGE NEVILLE PATRICK YOUNG, Leinster Regiment.

OUR HEROES.

Lieutenant Joseph Charles Tyndall, 4th Dublin Fusiliers. In his 22nd year, and after a brief fortnight in the trenches, Lieutenant J. Charles Tyndall was killed in action on March 2nd. Second son of Mr. and Mrs. J. P. Tyndall, Monkstown, Lieut. Tyndall followed his elder brother, Lieut. W. E. Tyndall, to the front. He belonged to the 4th Dublin Fusiliers, but was transferred to the Royal Irish Rifles in February, and it was with them, in the early morning of March 2nd that Lieutenant Tyndall gloriously met his end. A soldier to his finger tips, Lieutenant Tyndall gave promise of a brilliant career.

◆ ◆ ◆

Second Lieutenant Alfred Francis Bate, Royal Dublin Fusiliers, was the youngest son of Mr. E. R. Bate, Solicitor to the Post Office in Ireland. He was educated at St. Columba's College, Rathfarnham, Co. Dublin, and he took his degree at Trinity College, Dublin, in 1913. He received his commission in August last and, at the time of his death, was attached to the 2nd Leinster Regiment. He was in his 23rd year.

◆ ◆ ◆

Lieutenant Thomas Musgrave, Irish Guards (killed in action on February 6), was born in 1889 and obtained his commission in the Guards in August, 1912. He retired, but on the outbreak of the war he rejoined his regiment, and was gazetted to the 2nd Battalion last September. He was the only child of the late Capt. Archer Musgrave, R.N., and the late Mrs. Musgrave.

◆ ◆ ◆

Captain Dudley Eyre Persse, 4th Battalion Dublin Fusiliers, who died from wounds received in active service in France in February last, was the son of Mr. Alfred Lovain Persse and Mrs. Persse, late of Rose Park, County Galway, and grandson of the late Mr. Dudley Persse, of Roxborough, County Galway. He was gazetted Second Lieutenant in April, 1911, was promoted Lieutenant in 1912 and Captain in February, 1915. His father has received a telegram from their Majesties expressing their regret and sympathy in the loss he has sustained on the death of his son.

◆ ◆ ◆

Lieutenant=Colonel A. Loveband, 2nd Batt. Royal Dublin Fusiliers, joined the 1st Battalion at the Curragh in 1889, and shortly afterwards transferred to the 2nd Battalion in India. There he quickly established a reputation as a first-class, all-round sportsman. He entered into all the sports of the country, including ibex-shooting, massur-fishing and racing. His many successes in the last named earned for him a place amongst the best soldier riders in India at the time. Later as a Captain—in which capacity he was serving at the Regimental Depôt at Naas—he was appointed Adjutant of the 3rd Battalion, which position he held for six years. Here again he became one of the most prominent men to hounds among a particularly hard-riding field. The late Mr. Robert Rynd told the writer he always considered "The Littleman," as his friends always call him, the third best man to hounds he had ever known. At Punchestown he also had successes, while his splendid horsemanship and marvellous eye for country enabled him to establish an extraordinary record at point-to-point riding. At the outbreak of the war he was commanding the Depôt at Naas, and was almost immediately given command of the 6th Service Battalion. Towards the end of October, when the command of the 2nd Battalion at the front became vacant, he was appointed to fill the vacancy. Arriving at the front early in November he evidently did not take long to obtain the recognition of the authorities, where sterling merit and efficiency are the sole qualifications for reward. He also served in the South African War.

◆ ◆ ◆

Captain H. C. H. O'Brien, Royal Munster Fusiliers, who was killed in action, was a son of the late Colonel O'Brien, of Queenstown, and a brother-in-law of the late Capt. O'Brien Butler. He had seen much service both in South Africa and on the North-west Frontier of India.

◆ ◆ ◆

Lieutenant Philip Maurice Ramsay Ander=son was the eldest son of Mr. R. A. Anderson, of the Irish Agricultural Organisation Society, whose youngest son, Lieut. Alan Anderson, as recorded in the last part of "Our Heroes," had also fallen in the field of honour. At the outbreak of the war Mr. Anderson's eldest son, Philip Maurice Ramsay, held an important position on a great estate in the Argentine. He came home immediately and joined King Edward's Horse. When the news of his brother's death was received, Philip Anderson, with the cheerful consent of his father, who has done such admirable work for the Dublin Veterans' Corps, applied for and received a commission in the Royal Irish Regiment. He stepped, as it were, into the shoes of his dead brother. Lieutenant Anderson was soon sent to the front. He was severely wounded in action on 14th February, and he died on Wednesday at a base hospital in France.

◆ ◆ ◆

Captain William Graham Montgomerie received his first commission as Second Lieutenant in the Prince of Wales's Leinster Regiment (Royal Canadians) in September, 1897, became Lieutenant in 1900, and got his Captaincy in November, 1903.

◆ ◆ ◆

Lieutenant John Fraser was gazetted to the Connaught Rangers in 1905 and was appointed Lieutenant in April, 1906.

OUR HEROES

1. LT. J. C. TYNDALL, 4th Dublin Fusiliers.	2. 2nd LT. A. F. BATE, Royal Dublin Fusiliers.	3. LT. THOMAS MUSGRAVE, Irish Guards.
4. CAPT. DUDLEY E. PERSSE, 4th Dublin Fusiliers.	5. COLONEL LOVEBAND, Royal Dublin Fusiliers.	6. CAPT. H. C. H. O'BRIEN, Royal Munster Fusiliers.
7 LT. PHILIP MAURICE RAMSEY ANDERSON, Royal Irish Regiment.	8. CAPT. W. G. MONTGOMERIE, Leinster Regiment.	9. LT. JOHN FRASER, Connaught Rangers.

OUR HEROES.

Captain H. Brudenell Bruce, Norfolk Regiment, mentioned in Sir John French's despatch, and promoted Brevet-Major for Distinguished Service in the field, is the third son of the late Lord Robert Brudenell Bruce, R.N.

◇ ◇ ◇

Captain William Augustine Gallagher, 2nd Battalion East Lancashire Regiment, who was killed in action on March 14th, was the only surviving child of Mr. and Mrs. William Gallagher, Charlemont Place, Armagh. He was born in 1882, obtained his commission in the East Lancashire Regiment in August, 1906, and was promoted Lieutenant in 1908 and Captain in 1914.

◇ ◇ ◇

Captain Henry Russell Goodman, 2nd Battalion Royal Irish Rifles, was gazetted 2nd Lieutenant on 7th March, 1900, Lieutenant on 28th May, 1903, and Captain on the 28th June, 1908. He served in the South African War, 1899-1902, being attached to the Army Service Corps from April, 1900. He took part in the several operations in the Transvaal, Orange River Colony and Cape Colony from November, 1900, to May, 1902, and was slightly wounded. He received the Queen's medal with four clasps and the King's medal with two clasps.

◇ ◇ ◇

Captain Francis William Durand, 3rd Battalion Royal Munster Fusiliers, who was killed in action on the night of December 22-23, was the son of the late Rev. Havilland Durand, of Earley, and of Mrs. Durand, of Moulin Huet, Guernsey. He was born in January, 1875, and was educated at Elizabeth College, Guernsey. Gazetted Second Lieutenant, 3rd Royal Guernsey Light Infantry (Militia) in 1891, he joined the Rhodesian Horse in 1895 and served with the Gwelo Field Force in the Matabele Campaign of 1896 and the Mashona Campaign of 1897, being awarded the medal and clasp. From 1899 to 1902 he served with the African Transcontinental Telegraph Survey through German East Africa, and in the Tanganyika Concessions Expedition to Katarga Congo Free State. In 1903 he married Geraldine Vesey, youngest daughter of the late Rev. John W. Hawtrey, of Aldin House, Slough, and of Mrs. J. W. Hawtrey. In September last he joined the 2nd Battalion Royal Munster Fusiliers, and was present at the actions on the Aisne, the Marne, and at Ypres.

◇ ◇ ◇

Major Charles Arthur Tisdall, Irish Guards, of Charlesfort, County Meath, who was killed in action near Villers Cotterets, France, on September the 1st, was gazetted Second Lieutenant (from the Militia) in 1900. He joined the Royal Irish Rifles and was transferred in 1901 to the Irish Guards. He was gazetted Lieutenant in 1901 and Captain in 1909. He saw active service in South Africa, and was present during the operations in the Orange River Colony, January to August, 1901. He received the Queen's Medal, with two clasps. He was the eldest son of the late Captain John Knox Tisdall, Royal Engineers, and Mrs. Tisdall, and succeeded his grandfather, the late Mr. John Tisdall, of Charlesfort, J.P., D.L., in 1892. He married, 1904, Gwynneth May, only child of Mr. Charles Adshead, and leaves two daughters. He was in his 40th year.

◇ ◇ ◇

Captain Gerald Maurice Ponsonby, of the 2nd Battalion Royal Inniskilling Fusiliers, was gazetted 2nd Lieutenant in May, 1898, Lieutenant in March, 1899, and received his Captaincy in 1908 (Captain Royal Warwickshire Regiment, 1902). He served in the South African War, 1902, where he was employed with Mounted Infantry. He was slightly wounded, and obtained the Queen's medal with four clasps.

◇ ◇ ◇

Lieutenant Richard Apjohn Fitzgibbon, 128th Pioneers, who was killed in the fighting on the Suez Canal, February 3rd and 4th, was the only son of Captain H. Macaulay Fitzgibbon, of Greystones, and grandson of a former Recorder of Belfast and County Court Judge of Antrim. He was born in Dublin, July, 1889, and was educated first at Strangways School and subsequently at Radley College. Whilst at Radley he twice "coxed" the College boat at the Henley Regatta. On leaving school he entered Christ Church, Oxford, taking his degree in 1911. He was for a time cox of the Christ Church boat and subsequently stroke of their second eight. He steered in the University trial eights and was a member of Leander Rowing Club. On leaving Oxford he was appointed to the Indian Army (Unattached List)), and after serving for a year with the 3rd Battalion of the Royal Fusiliers, he joined the 128th Pioneers (Indian Army) as a double Company Officer. He was severely wounded in the action near Ismalia on the Suez Canal on February 3rd, notwithstanding which he continued to direct his men for several hours, leading a bayonet charge in which he appears to have lost his sword. It then became necessary to transmit a very important message to the Artillery, which Lt. Fitzgibbon undertook to do, having to traverse a quarter of a mile exposed to heavy maxim and rifle fire. He delivered the message and then, for the first time, mentioned he was wounded. He succumbed to his injuries next morning on the way to the base hospital in Ismalia, where he was buried with full military honours, the General in Command of the Canal defences attending in person as a tribute of respect and gratitude for his services. Dublin people may like to know that his maternal grandfather was Surgeon John Kellock Barton, principal Surgeon to the Adelaide Hospital for many years, his maternal grandmother being a daughter of Professor Apjohn, the eminent Professor of Chemistry in Dublin University for many years.

OUR HEROES

1. CAPT. R. H. BRUDENELL BRUCE, Norfolk Regiment.	2. CAPT. W. A. GALLAGHER, 2nd East Lancashires.	3. CAPT. H. RUSSELL GOODMAN, Royal Irish Rifles.
4. CAPT. F. W. DURAND, Royal Munster Fusiliers,	5. MAJOR CHAS. A. TISDALL, Irish Guards.	6. CAPT. H. T. RADCLIFFE. 5th Royal Leinster Regiment.
7. CAPT. GERALD MAURICE PONSONBY, 2nd Royal Inniskilling Fusiliers.	8. LIEUT. R. A. FITZGIBBON, 128th Pioneers, Indian Army.	9. CAPT. HYACINTH A. ROCHE, Royal Munster Fusiliers.

OUR HEROES.

Second Lieutenant Charles Richard Griffin Vance, youngest son of the Rev. Chancellor Vance, M.A., Rathronan, Ardagh, County Limerick, killed in action near Ypres, March 9th, aged 21 years. He was educated at Campbell College, Belfast, where he was one of the original members of the contingent of the Officers' Training Corps in 1909. Before joining the Cheshire Regiment at the outbreak of war, he was a premium apprentice at Crewe Loco. Works. He went to the front in November, and had only returned a week—after being home on furlough—when he was killed. He is the fifth old Campbellian to lose his life in the present war.

✧ ✧ ✧

Captain John Pitt Kennedy, 2nd Scottish Rifles (Cameronians), who was killed in action at Neuve Chapelle on March 10th, belonged to a North of Ireland family, one of his ancestors being famous in the Siege of Derry. His father, the late Charles Napier Kennedy, was an artist chiefly known as a portrait painter, and was an Associate of the Royal Hibernian Academy. His grandfather, Col. John Pitt Kennedy, was the friend and contemporary of the three Lawrence brothers, and was Military Secretary to Sir Charles Napier when he was Commander-in-Chief in India. He married Norah, daughter of Lieutenant-Colonel Baddeley, R.E., and leaves a son. At the battle of Neuve Chapelle his company was in the first line of advance, and he was the first officer to fall, killed by shell fire as he climbed out of the trench. He was in his thirty-first year.

✧ ✧ ✧

Brigadier-General John Edmond Gough, V.C., C.B., C.M.G., A.D.C., who died from wounds received in action, was on the staff at Aldershot as principal General Staff Officer to Sir Douglas Haig at the time of the mobilisation in August, and went out for Staff work with the Army Corps. In the great retreat from the Mons line to Paris he did admirable work, and was mentioned in despatches on October 8th by the Commander-in-Chief. John Gough was a brilliant officer, and won by his work in action the V.C., C.B., C.M.G., and brevet promotion. He was an A.D.C. to the King, and greatly interested himself in the Public Schools training camps. The death of Brigadier-General J. E. Gough places several families in and around Clonmel in mourning. He was born on 25th October, 1871, and in 1907 he married Dorothea, daughter of General Keyes.

✧ ✧ ✧

Captain Edward Radcliffe Nash, of the 16th (the Queen's) Lancers, was killed in action. He was the eldest son of Colonel Edward Nash, late Essex Regiment, and Mrs. Nash, of Ballycarty, County Kerry, and 56 Sloane Street, London. He went to Eton in 1902, to Miss Evans, from Mr. Bull's at Westgate. In 1905, at the age of 16, he won the Junior Sculling, and his fine rowing at stroke took his Junior House Four up to "Head" the last time the colours of Miss Evans' were destined to be run on the river. In September of the same year, at the earliest possible age, he passed into Sandhurst, giving up for sake of seniority all that another two years at Eton would have meant for him. At Sandhurst he showed himself a remarkable athlete, winning against competitors considerably older than himself the equivalent of the Victor Ludorum Cup. A keen sportsman, a hard rider to hounds and a fine horseman, conspicuous for dash and energy and endurance, he was the ideal cavalry officer, and seemed to have a distinguished career before him; and one who knew him well on receiving the news that he had been killed said: "Of all the deaths in this war, his death is the hardest to realize." He was killed near Ypres on February 21st.

✧ ✧ ✧

Lieutenant Mervyn T. Johnson, South Wales Borderers, who died of wounds received in action at the battle of the Aisne, on September 14th, 1914, was a member of a family distinguished for its brilliant and loyal services. This promising young officer, who had displayed great courage and fortitude in the various stages of the campaign leading up to the above-named battle, was a son of the late Captain William Johnson, 6th Inniskilling Dragoons, and Mrs. Johnson, of Oddington, Moreton-in-Marsh Gloucestershire.

✧ ✧ ✧

Lieutenant William Hugh Coulter, 5th (Royal Irish) Lancers, was killed in action on 22nd April at Ypres. He appeared in our last part as one of the officers mentioned in despatches.

✧ ✧ ✧

Captain H. O. D. Becher, of the Cameronians, was the elder son of the Rev. Harry Becher, Rector of Rosscarbery, County Cork, and was killed in action near Armentieres, at Bois Grenier, on March 13th, 1915. He was born at Houghton-le-Spring, where his father was curate to the late Hon. John Grey, and was in his 26th year at the time he fell. He was educated at Marlborough College, where he was in the XV., also captain in College House, and one of the four heavy-weights in the boxing competition. After leaving Marlborough he was cramming under Messrs. Beasley and Jackson, of Bedford, entering Sandhurst, January, 1909, and passing out in the following December. His grandfather, the late John Richard Hedges Becher, was formerly in the 27th Inniskilling Fusiliers, and his maternal grandfather, the late Ralph M. Hudson, shipowner, of Sunderland, whose fifth daughter Zoé Louisa, was Captain Becher's mother

Supplement to Irish Life, May 14th, 1915.

1. LT. R. E. CUSACK.
4th Batt. Royal Dublin Fusiliers.

2. LT. C. R. G. VANCE,
1st Cheshire Regiment.

3. CAPT. JOHN PITT KENNEDY,
2nd Scottish Rifles.

4. MAJOR R. E. BOND,
4th Rajputs.

5. BRIG.-GEN. JOHN E. GOUGH,
V.C.

6. CAPTAIN E. R. NASH,
16th (Queen's) Lancers.

7. LT. M. T. JOHNSON.
South Wales Borderers.

8. WILLIAM HUGH COULTER,
5th Lancers.

9. LT. H. O. BECHER,
Cameronians.

OUR HEROES.

Captain Robert Edward Michael Pakenham, of the Royal Munster Fusiliers, who died of wounds received in action, was a son of Major Charles Pakenham, of Headon Hall, Isle of Wight, and a member of the family of which the Earl of Longford is head. He was born in 1874; got his first commission in 1897. He was for sometime Adjutant of the 3rd Royal Irish Fusiliers; and retired in 1912. He joined from the Reserve of Officers on the outbreak of the war, and was appointed to a Captaincy in the Munster Fusiliers.

Captain N. P. Clarke, 2nd Royal Dublin Fusiliers, joined from the Warwickshire Regiment on the 20th May, 1908. He fought through the South African War and already must be familiar to readers of IRISH LIFE as the officer who succeeded in leading the remnants of the half battalion cut off at Le Cateau through the German lines to safety. He, as will be remembered, brought his small command to the coast and thence to England. He quickly returned to the front and found himself in command of the regiment, in which capacity he acted until severely wounded. He has now fortunately recovered sufficiently to join the 3rd Battalion at Cork for light duty.

Captain H. Leslie Homan was gazetted to the Middlesex Regiment as Second Lieutenant in May, 1900. He was promoted Lieutenant in 1901 and got his Captaincy in August, 1909. He was killed in action at Neuve Chappelle on March 10th. He was a son of Canon Homan, of Eglington Park, Kingstown.

Lieutenant-Colonel George Brenton Laurie, of the 1st Battalion Royal Irish Rifles, fell in action at the head of his Battalion near Neuve Chappelle. He was born in 1867 and was gazetted to the Royal Irish Rifles in 1885. He became Captain in 1893, Major in 1904, and Lieut.-Colonel in 1912. During the South African war he served as Special Service Officer (including command of a mounted Infantry Battalion) and took part in the operations in the Transvaal, Orange River Colony, and Cape Colony. He was mentioned in despatches and received the Queen's Medal with five clasps. He was the eldest surviving son of Lieut.-General Laurie, C.B., and of Mrs. Laurie, of Oakfield, Nova Scotia, and was closely connected by marriage with the North of Ireland, having been married at Rostrevor, in 1905, to Florence Clementine Vere, daughter of the Hon. Sydney Skeffington, third son of the tenth Viscount Masserene and Ferrard. He was also related to Lady Ross of Bladensburg. His wife is a great granddaughter of Mr. John Forster (Lord Oriel), the last Speaker of the Irish House of Commons. Colonel Laurie's father, Lt.-General Laurie, C.B., served with great distinction in the Crimea, in the Indian Mutiny, and in the Transvaal. "If he had not been a great soldier," writes an intimate friend, "the late Colonel would have been a great historian. His knowledge of history, more especially of military history, was profound, and his memory was singularly retentive. He had moreover a very sound judgment in the marshalling of facts. He had written with a pen of light the history of his regiment, which he loved, and which loved him, and on which in life and in death he had shed an additional lustre."

Captain James Robert Moffatt, the Leinster Regiment, was born in April, 1869, in India, his father being Lieutenant-Colonel Moffatt, of the Yorkshire Regiment, who fought in the Crimea with great distinction. Captain Moffatt enlisted as a private in 1887, at Gosport, and served in the ranks for seven years, receiving his commission in January, 1895, at Jersey. He served throughout the South African war and had the Queen's Medal with three clasps. He had also served in India and the Bermudas. He received his Captaincy in 1901, and in 1909 he retired. After five years in the Reserve he got a company in the 3rd Battalion of the Leinsters (the old King's County Militia) on the outbreak of the war in August last.

Second Lieutenant Brendan Joseph Fottrell, Royal Irish Regiment, received his commission from the Officers' Training Corps in September last. He was a son of Mr. John G. Fottrell, Crown Solicitor for the County Meath, and was a member of the eminent firm of solicitors, Messrs. Fottrell. He was married only a year ago, and was home on short leave only a fortnight before he was killed in action.

Lieutenant Rowland Auriol James Beech was gazetted a Second Lieutenant 16th Lancers on the 17th October, 1908, and became Lieutenant in January, 1911, consequently most of his life in the Army was spent at the Curragh, where the 16th Lancers were stationed up to the outbreak of the war. As a sportsman he was well known in Ireland and highly popular.

Lieutenant George W. Coates was gazetted to the Royal Field Artillery in July, 1914, so that his life in the Army may be said to have been entirely spent on active service. He was killed in action on the 10th March last. He was a son of Mr. G. Coates, manager of the Royal Avenue branch of the Northern Bank, Belfast.

1. CAPT. ROBERT E. M. PAKEN-HAM, Royal Munster Fusiliers.

2. CAPT. N. P. CLARKE, Royal Dublin Fusiliers.

3. CAPT. H. LESLIE HOMAN, Middlesex Regiment.

4. CAPT. C. V. LESLIE POE, 4th King's Royal Rifle Corps.

5. LT.-COL. GEORGE BRENTON LAURIE, 1st Royal Irish Rifles.

6. CAPTAIN J. R. MOFFATT, Royal Leinster Regiment.

7. 2nd LT. BRENDAN J. FOTTRELL, Royal Irish Regiment.

8. LIEUT. R. A. BEECH, 16th Lancers.

9. LIEUT. GEORGE W. COATES, Royal Field Artillery.

OUR HEROES.

Lieutenant J. M. Stewart, who was killed in action, was a promising young officer who was gazetted to the Irish Guards on August 14th last.

✧ ✧ ✧

Lieutenant Hon. John de Blaquiere was the eldest son of the sixth Baron de Blaquiere, Great Alnager of Ireland. He received his commission in the Scottish Rifles in November, 1909, and obtained his Lieutenancy in January, 1913. He was born in 1889, and was therefore 26 years of age when he fell in action.

✧ ✧ ✧

Captain Bertram Weldon Moloney was gazetted to the 2nd Battalion of the East Lancashire Regiment in 1908, was promoted to Lieutenant in January, 1911, and got his Captaincy last November. He was in his 27th year when he was killed. He belonged to a well-known County Clare family, the Moloneys of Kiltannon, of which Captain William Beresford Moloney is the representative.

✧ ✧ ✧

Second Lieutenant A. C. Walsh, Royal Horse Artillery, obtained his first Commission in July, 1912, and fell in action in his 23rd year.

✧ ✧ ✧

Brigadier General Fitzclarence, V.C., Irish Guards, was killed in action at Ypres. He got his first Commission in May, 1886, became Captain in April, 1888, Brevet-Major, November, 1900, Major in May, 1904, Lt.-Col., July, 1909, Colonel, March, 1913, Officer Commanding Regiment and Regimental District, July, 1913. His father, the late Captain the Hon. G. Fitzclarence, R.M., was the third son of the first Earl of Munster. Brigadier-General Fitzclarence served with distinction in South Africa, taking part in the defence of Mafeking, where his daring won for him the sobriquet of "The Demon." It was there he won his V.C. by three acts of valour; relieving an armoured train under a furious fire and saving his handful of men by his skill; leading an attack on Boer trenches in a night sortie and himself killing four of the enemy, and displaying great courage in the action at Game Tree, where he was shot through both legs. He was married in 1898 to Violet, daughter of the late Lord Alfred Spencer Churchill, and leaves a son and daughter.

Second Lieutenant Alexander R. Newton-King was gazetted to the Royal Irish Regiment on the 24th January, 1914. He took part in the retreat from Mons and the battles of the Marne and the Aisne. He was one of the first officers to receive the French military decoration. He fell in action in April near Ypres.

✧ ✧ ✧

Second Lieutenant R. A. Young received his first Commission in the 2nd Battalion of the Royal Munster Fusiliers on August 15th, 1914, and was aged twenty when he fell in action in March last.

✧ ✧ ✧

Captain William Augustine Gallagher, East Lancashire Regiment, was the son, and last surviving child, of Mr. William Gallagher, Charlemont Place, Armagh. He was educated at Clongowes Wood and at Trinity College, Dublin, where he graduated. He received his Commission as Second Lieutenant in the East Lancashire Regiment on 20th August, 1906, as a University Candidate, and proceeded to India to join the 2nd Battalion, then stationed at Poona. He was promoted Lieutenant 26th September, 1908, and after serving about five years in different stations in India, he moved with his regiment to South Africa. For nearly two years he was employed with Mounted Infantry at Harrismith, Orange River Colony. At the outbreak of the war he had rejoined his regiment and was stationed at Wynberg, near Cape Town, and was selected by the General there to bring home the horses of the 10th Hussars, a duty which he performed to the entire satisfaction of the Colonel of that regiment. He got his Captaincy on 5th August, 1914, and went to France on the Staff of Brigadier-General Carter. He was killed on the night of 10th March, 1915, at the battle of Neuve Chapelle, whilst carrying orders to the Generals in the firing line. His General described him as a fearless officer and the best fellow he had ever met.

✧ ✧ ✧

Second Lieutenant R. D. Ford was gazetted to the Royal Irish Regiment shortly after the outbreak of the war. He fell in the battle of Neuve Chapelle, in which the Royal Irish Regiment behaved with great gallantry but had very severe losses.

1. LIEUT. JOHN MAURICE STEWART, Irish Guards.	2. LIEUT. THE HON. JOHN DE BLAQUIERE, The Cameronians.	3. 2nd LIEUT. R. A. YOUNG, 2nd Royal Munster Fusiliers.
4. CAPT. BERTRAM W. MOLONEY, East Lancashire Regiment.	5. BRIG.-GEN. C. FITZCLARENCE, V.C., Irish Guards.	6. CAPT. W. A. GALLAGHER, East Lancashire Regiment.
7. 2nd LIEUT. A. C. M. WALSH, Royal Horse Artillery.	8. 2nd LT. A. R. NEWTON-KING, Royal Irish Regiment.	9. 2nd LIEUT. R. D. FORD, Royal Irish Regiment.

OUR HEROES.

Lieutenant H. Sheehy Keating, Irish Guards, who was killed in action on January 20th, was the only son of the late Rt. Hon. Sir H. Keating and grandson of Lady Ward, 16 Cadogan Gardens, London. He joined the Special Reserve as Second Lieutenant on 12th August, 1914.

Captain Hugh Conor Henry O'Brien, Royal Munster Fusiliers, who has been killed in action, was born on the 19th November, 1880. He became Second Lieutenant in August, 1900, Lieutenant in March, 1903, and was promoted to the rank of Captain in April, 1910. He was present at many operations in the South African War, and had the Queen's Medal with clasp. On the North-West Frontier of India in 1908 he was Brigade Signalling Officer, and received the medal with clasp.

Lieutenant G. E. G. Stackpoole, Royal Irish Regiment, who was killed in action on January 27th, was born in January, 1892, and was gazetted in November, 1911. He was posted to the 1st Battalion at Nasiribad, which until recently was in Major-General K. S. Davison's Brigade of the Mhow Division. While in India he had gone in for transport work and passed the appointed course. He obtained his Lieutenancy in August last year. Lieutenant Stackpoole was the eldest son of Mr. and Mrs. R. G. Stackpoole, 26 Walton Place, London, S.W., and of Co. Clare.

Captain Eric John Fletcher Gough, Irish Guards, who was killed in action on the 30th December, 1914, was the only son of the late Major Thomas Armstrong Gough and of Mrs. Claude Langley, of 9 Onslow Crescent, London, S.W. Captain Gough entered the army on the 1st February, 1911, being promoted Lieutenant the following November. He was recently promoted to the rank of Captain.

Major Francis Innes Day, Royal Munster Fusiliers, received his commission in February, 1895, became Lieutenant in November, 1900, and got his Captaincy in the Middlesex Regiment in September, 1902. He took part in the operations on the Niger in 1897 and in the expedition to Beda and Ilorin, where he took part in the action of Beda, obtaining the medal with clasp. He served again in West Africa in 1898 during the Niger operations, and was engaged with the Imperial Yeomanry in the South African War. He also took part in the operations in Cape Colony up to May, 1902, obtaining the Queen's Medal with two clasps.

Captain Hyacinth Albert Roche, Flight Commander Royal Flying Corps, and Royal Munster Fusiliers, was the youngest son of Sir John and Lady Roche, 76 Merrion Square, Dublin. Captain Roche met his death as he was setting out with three of his comrades on a bomb-dropping raid in Belgium. When he was only a few miles out an explosion took place in his machine and Captain Roche had to drop his whole stock of bombs at once. The aeroplane fell into the sea and Captain Roche's dead body was found a few hours later on the sands.

Lieutenant Frederick Ernest Styles, Royal Munster Fusiliers, who was killed in action on August 27th at Etreux, France, was the eldest son of the late Mr. Frederick Styles and of Mrs. Styles, of Blackmoor, Four Elms. He was born in 1884, was educated at Harrow and Sandhurst, and gazetted as Second Lieutenant to the Munster Fusiliers in 1903. He obtained his promotion as Lieutenant in 1906, and retired from the Army in April, 1914, but rejoined on the outbreak of the war. Lieut. Styles was killed while gallantly leading his men under a heavy fire.

Captain Charles Vernon Leslie Poë, of the 4th Battalion King's Royal Rifle Corps, was gazetted as Second Lieutenant in May, 1900, Lieutenant in 1901, and Captain in November, 1910. He served in the South African war, taking part in the operations in the Orange River Colony from January to 31st May, 1902, and had the Queen's Medal with two clasps. He was a son of Captain George Leslie Poë, J.P., and Mrs. Poë, of Santry Court, County Dublin. He was killed while leading an attack on a German trench on the night of the 1st and 2nd March. Although wounded in the advance, he still continued to lead his men till he fell mortally wounded.

Lieutenant W. L. Ringrose Hatch was gazetted to the Royal Irish Fusiliers on the 25th March, 1911, and promoted Lieutenant April 16th, 1913. He was the son of Lieut.-Colonel W. K. Hatch, Indian Medical Service (retired), 8 Earlham Road, Norwich, and was in his 24th year when killed in action in Flanders.

1. LIEUT. H. S. KEATING, Irish Guards.	2. CAPT. H. C. H. O'BRIEN, Royal Munster Fusiliers.	3. LT. G. E. G. STACKPOOLE, Royal Irish Regiment.
4. CAPT. E. J. F. GOUGH, Irish Guards.	5. MAJOR FRANCIS I. DAY, Royal Munster Fusiliers.	6. CAPT. HYACINTH A. ROCHE, Royal Munster Fusiliers (Royal Flying Corps).
7. LIEUT. FREDERICK E. STYLES, Royal Munster Fusiliers.	8. CAPT. C. V. LESLIE POE, King's Royal Rifle Corps.	9. LT. W. L. RINGROSE HATCH, Royal Irish Fusiliers.

OUR HEROES.

Lieutenant A. W. Wylie, 2nd Battalion Lincolnshire Regiment, who died from wounds received in action, was a son of the Rt. Hon. Mr. Justice Wylie and a nephew of the Rev. R. B. Wylie, M.A., LL.D., Portstewart. He received his commission in the Lincolnshire Regiment in July, 1914, and was at the front with his regiment almost from the beginning of the war to the time of his death.

✧ ✧ ✧

Dr. Percy Netterville Gerrard, M.D., T.C.D., Malay States Volunteers and Colonial Medical Service, was the eldest son of the late Thomas Gerrard, Crown Solicitor, and of Mrs. Gerrard, 5 Appian Way, Leeson Park, Dublin. Dr. Gerrard was in charge of the internment camp of the German prisoners at Singapore, where he stood to his post after the first attack of the mutineers in order to communicate by telephone to headquarters. In this he was successful, and therefore must be considered to have very materially minimised the effects of the mutiny.

✧ ✧ ✧

Lieutenant William Knox Humfrey, 2nd Battalion Lancashire Fusiliers, who was killed in action in France, was the eldest surviving son of the late Colonel B. G. Humfrey, of Cavanacor, Ballindrait, Co. Donegal. He was gazetted as Second Lieutenant on 5th October, 1910, and became Lieutenant in September, 1914.

✧ ✧ ✧

Captain Herbert Travers Radcliffe, 5th Leinster Regiment, was killed in action at Neuve Chapelle on March 15th last. Prior to the war the deceased officer occupied the position of Petty Sessions Clerk for the districts of Kells, Moynalty, and George's Cross, where he was extremely popular. He volunteered for service at the outbreak of the war.

✧ ✧ ✧

Major Edwyn Fetherstonhaugh, fourth son Mr. S. R. Fetherstonhaugh, Clerk of the Peace, County Westmeath; born 2nd Nov., 1867; educated Chard Grammar School, Somerset; entered the Army, 1888, from Sandhurst; served all through the South African War with the 2nd Dublin Fusiliers, and was present at battles of Talana Hill, Willow Grange, Colenso, Spion Kop, Val Krantz, Pieter's Hill, Relief of Ladysmith, Inderichsted, and subsequent operations under Lord Methuen in Western Transvaal. Subsequently served in Arabia, Egypt, Soudan, and India. Mentioned in despatches, South Africa; Queen's Medal with six clasps; King's Medal, two clasps. Adjutant, 2nd Dublin Fusiliers, 1900-1905. Was attached at outbreak of war. Killed 25th April, 1915, at landing at Dardanelles.

✧ ✧ ✧

Captain Edward R. Lloyd, Adjutant, Royal Inniskilling Fusiliers, died in hospital at Cambrai of wounds received in action. He was the eldest surviving son of Lieut.-Colonel Lloyd and Mrs. Lloyd, of Bedford. He was noted as a good all-round sportsman, and represented his school in the Public Schools' Boxing Competition held at Aldershot in 1899. He was a keen follower of the hounds and a frequent rider in point-to-point hunt steeplechases. He was a good shot, both with gun and rifle, and an enthusiast in all outdoor games.

✧ ✧ ✧

Lieutenant S. B. Combe, North Irish Horse, who was killed on the 29th September, 1914, on refusing to surrender to a party of Germans who surrounded him. He was a son of Mr. Abram Combe, J.P., of Donaghloney House, County Down, and brother-in-law of Major Holt Waring, D.L., Waringstown, of the North Irish Horse. Lieutenant Combe was well-known in County Down, where he had been for some years Master of the County Down Staghounds.

✧ ✧ ✧

Mr. George Poole Soady, third surviving son of the late Mr. William B. Soady, Financial and General Secretary, His Majesty's Board of Public Works, Ireland, was born in Dublin, and came over from Canada with the 14th Battalion of the 1st Canadian contingent. He was killed in the fighting at Neuve Chapelle.

✧ ✧ ✧

Lieutenant Robert St. J. Blacker Douglass was the elder son of Mr. V. Blacker Douglass, Barrister-at-Law, Bellevue Park, Killiney. He was born in November, 1892, was gazetted to the Irish Guards in February, 1912, and was promoted to Lieutenant in the 2nd Battalion in January, 1913. He was wounded at the end of last year, and had only just returned to the front on his recovery when, in taking part in an attack on a German post, he was again severely wounded, and shortly afterwards died from the effects. He was 22 years of age at the time of his death and was regarded by his superiors as a young officer of great promise.

1. LIEUT. A. W. WYLIE, Lincolnshire Regiment.	2. PERCY NETTERVILLE GERRARD, M.D., T.C.D., Malay States Volunteers (Colonial Medical Service).	3. LIEUT. W. K. HUMFREY, 2nd Lancashire Fusiliers.
4. CAPT. HERBERT T. RADCLIFFE, 5th Royal Leinster Regiment.	5. MAJOR EDWYN FETHERSTON-HAUGH, 2nd Royal Dublin Fusiliers.	6. CAPT. EDWARD R. LLOYD Royal Inniskilling Fusiliers.
5. LIEUT. S. B. COMBE, North Irish Horse.	8. MR. GEORGE POOLE SOADY, Canadians.	9. LIEUT. R. ST. J. BLACKER DOUGLASS, Irish Guards.

OUR HEROES.

Second Lieutenant Maurice Wookey, who was 27 years of age, was the eldest surviving son of Mr. Frederick Wookey, J.P., of Weston Lodge, Leixlip. Shortly after the outbreak of war Mr. Maurice Wookey went out as a despatch rider. Recently he was given a commission in the 18th Royal Irish Regiment, and returned to the front after a short leave. Only ten days later the news was received that he had fallen in action. He was educated at Campbell College.

✧ ✧ ✧

Lieutenant Haldane Day Stokes, M.V.O., of the King's Own (Royal Lancaster) Regiment, was the son of Lieut.-Colonel Henry Haldane Stokes (formerly of the Royal Army Medical Corps), of Devonshire House, Cowley, Oxford. Educated at Tonbridge School, he entered the Royal Lancaster Regiment from the Militia in July, 1907, and received the step three years later. Lieutenant Stokes was rated M.V.O. in 1905. His age was 29.

✧ ✧ ✧

Captain R. McG. Bowen-Colthurst, Prince of Wales's Leinster Regiment (Royal Canadians), who was killed in action on March 15, was the younger son of the late Mr. R. W. T. Bowen-Colthurst and Mrs. Bowen-Colthurst, of Oakgrove and Dripsey Castle, Co. Cork. He was born in September, 1883, and was educated at Harrow and Trinity College, Cambridge. From 1905 to 1912 he was on the staff of the Earl of Aberdeen, Lord Lieutenant of Ireland, and was Justice of the Peace for Co. Cork.

✧ ✧ ✧

Captain Lord Northland, 2nd Batt. Coldstream Guards, who was killed in action in February at La Bassee, was the only son of the Earl of Ranfurly, and had been engaged for a considerable time on active service in the trenches and was severely wounded in the heavy fighting at La Bassee. He was 32 years of age. He was married in 1912 to Miss Hilda Susan Cooper, daughter of Sir Daniel Cooper, Bart., and leaves two sons, the Hon. Thomas D. Knox and the Hon. Edward Paul Uchter Knox.

✧ ✧ ✧

Major Cecil Thomas Wrigley Grimshaw, D.S.O., Royal Dublin Fusiliers, who was killed in the Dardanelles April 29th, was the sixth son of the late Mr. Thomas Wrigley Grimshaw, C.B., Registrar-General of Ireland, and Mrs. Grimshaw, of The Lodge, Waterbeach, Cambridgeshire. He was educated at Eastman's, the Royal Naval Academy, and Trinity College, Dublin, where he graduated B.A.

✧ ✧ ✧

Captain Roger Charles Noel Bellingham, who was killed in action near Ypres, was second son of Sir Henry Bellingham, Bart., H.M.L. for Co. Louth, and went to the front with the First Expeditionary Force in August. He was educated at the Royal Military Academy, whence he passed into the 37th Battery, R.F.A., to which he was attached when he met his death. For two years he was Aide-de-Camp to the late Viceroy, the Marquis of Aberdeen, and discharged the duties of that office with tact and courtesy. Hardly any of the casualties of the war has evoked more sincere and widespread regret in Ireland than the loss of this gallant officer, whose kindly disposition and unassuming manner had endeared him to all with whom he came in contact, and whose high character and genuine ability marked him as one whom the country could ill afford to lose.

✧ ✧ ✧

Lieutenant Anthony Gerald Malpas Roberts was born in London and was only 19 years of age last July. As a boy at his junior schools he was always an athlete. He went to Ardingly College, Haywards Heath, Sussex, in 1910, and in 1911 joined the Officers' Training Corps, was made Lance-Corporal and Sergeant in 1912, and was awarded Certificate A in 1913. He also received a Life Saving Certificate in 1911 and Life Saving Medallion in 1912. He obtained Victor Ludorum, 1911, 1912, 1913 (World's Record) School Prefect, 1912. He was gazetted to Inniskilling Fusiliers (Special Reserve) in May, 1913, and on mobilisation was gazetted to 2nd Battalion as Second Lieutenant.

✧ ✧ ✧

Lieutenant James Herbert Buchanan was a native of County Down. He entered the Queen's University, Belfast, in 1910, where he was a member of the Officers' Training Corps, in which he got rapid promotion. In June last he received a commission in the Reserves, Royal Irish Fusiliers, and in February last was sent to the front in charge of 200 men. He was five days at the base, and was then sent up to the trenches. On the evening of March 14th he very bravely led an attack on a German trench, which was captured and held all night. At dawn next morning it was found the trench was untenable and the order was given to retreat. Lt. Buchanan was gathering up the rear of his men when he was struck in the body by two bullets from snipers.

✧ ✧ ✧

Captain Arthur Grove Colles was among those reported killed in the action at Neuve Chapelle on the 14th April. He was only son of Mr. and Mrs. Alex. Colles, of 3 Elgin Road, Dublin. About four years ago he joined the Royal Dublin Fusiliers, and was attached for a year to the Connaught Rangers at the Curragh. In November last he was sent to the front with the 1st Battalion Royal Irish Rifles, to which regiment he was subsequently gazetted. Since he went out he had been continuously in the trenches until this last action.

Supplement to Irish Life, May 14th, 1915.

OUR HEROES

1. 2nd LT. MAURICE WOOKEY, 18th Royal Irish Regiment.
2. LT. HALDANE DAY STOKES, 2nd King's Own Regiment.
3. CAPT. R. M'G. BOWEN-COLTHURST, Leinster Regt. (Royal Canadians).
4. LORD NORTHLAND, Coldstream Guards.
5. MAJOR C. T. W. GRIMSHAW, Royal Dublin Fusiliers.
6. CAPTAIN ROGER C. N. BELLINGHAM, Royal Field Artillery.
7. LT. ANTHONY G. M. ROBERTS, Inniskilling Fusiliers.
8. LT. J. H. BUCHANAN, Royal Irish Fusiliers.
9. CAPT. ARTHUR G. COLLES, Royal Dublin Fusiliers.

OUR HEROES.

Captain P. R. Butler, Royal Irish Regiment, is a son of the late Major-General Sir William Butler, K.C.B., and Lady Butler, *née* Thompson, the famous painter of *The Roll Call* and many other celebrated pictures of military subjects. He has been mentioned in Sir John French's despatches for distinguished conduct in the field.

✧ ✧ ✧

Major John Gage Lecky, Army Service Corps, has been mentioned for the second time in Sir John French's despatches. He served in the South African war, taking part in the advance on Kimberley, including actions at Belmont, Modder River and Maagersfontein, and was present during the operations in Orange River Colony from April to August, 1900, including actions at Bethlehem and Wittebergen. He was in the Transvaal operations in the autumn of 1900 and again in the autumn of 1901, and received the Queen's Medal with four clasps and the King's Medal with two clasps. Major Lecky is a son of Col. George Lecky (retired), Indian Army.

✧ ✧ ✧

Captain S. G. de Courcy Wheeler, Royal Dublin Fusiliers, who is reported wounded in the recent fighting at Hill 60, has been in France since the commencement of hostilities in August, and was recently mentioned in despatches. Captain de Courcy Wheeler is a Graduate in Arts and Engineering of Trinity College, Dublin. He served in the South African war with his regiment, and his medals bearing seven clasps. Captain de Courcy Wheeler was well known in Dublin, where he was for three years Adjutant of the Dublin University, and Royal College of Surgeons Officers' Training Corps. He is the son of the late Mr. W. I. de Courcy Wheeler, President of the Royal College of Surgeons, and a brother of the present Dublin surgeon.

✧ ✧ ✧

Major=General Allenby, who commands the Cavalry Expeditionary Force, was born in 1861. He first of all entered the Inniskilling Fusiliers, and served with the Bechuanaland Expedition in 1884-5, and took part in the operations in Zululand in 1888. He served in the South African War, 1899-1902, and was present at the relief of Kimberley. Major-General Allenby has been several times mentioned in despatches, and wears the Queen's Medal with six clasps and the King's Medal with two clasps. He was in active command of the 5th Lancers from 1902-1905, when he commanded the 4th Cavalry Brigade until 1910. Major Allenby married Adelaide Mabel, daughter of Mr. H. E. Chapman, of Donhead House, Salisbury. He was educated at Haileybury.

✧ ✧ ✧

Major=Gen. C. T. McMorrough Kavanagh, who has been mentioned in despatches and promoted to his present rank during the war, has had a very distinguished military career. He greatly distinguished himself in the South African War in almost every sphere of those operations, and was in command of a mobile column in Cape Colony from July, 1901, to May, 1902. He was mentioned in despatches and obtained the Queen's Medal with five clasps and the King's Medal with two clasps, and also the D.S.O. He belongs to the distinguished Carlow family, of which Walter McMorrough Kavanagh, of Borris, is the distinguished representative.

✧ ✧ ✧

Lieutenant=Colonel A. Parker, of the 5th (Royal Irish) Lancers, who has been a second time mentioned in despatches. He was gazetted in 1887, became Lieutenant in 1889, Captain in 1894, Major in 1903, and Lieut.-Colonel in 1913. Colonel Parker served in the South African campaign and took part in the defence of Ladysmith as well as the actions at Elandslaagte, Rietfontein and Lombard's Kop, which preceded the investment of Sir George White's force and the sorties from the beleaguered town. He was mentioned in despatches several times and obtained the Queen's Medal with five clasps and the King's Medal with two clasps. He was wounded early in the present war.

✧ ✧ ✧

Lieutenant W. Tyrrell, M.B., R.A.M.C., who has been mentioned in Sir J. French's despatches, will be remembered for the distinguished name he had made for himself in Rugby football, representing Ireland on many occasions in International matches.

✧ ✧ ✧

Second Lieutenant M. E. Dennis, R.H.A., is the eldest son of Colonel M. J. C. Dennis, R.A., and Honble. Mrs. Dennis, of Fort Granite, Baltinglass, Co. Wicklow, and has been mentioned in despatches and awarded the Military Cross.

✧ ✧ ✧

Lieutenant J. H. K. Richardson, Royal Horse Artillery, who has been mentioned in despatches. Educated at Clifton and R.M.A., Woolwich, he was gazetted to the Royal Field Artillery, December 23rd, 1911, and went to the front last August with the 65th Battery R.F.A. He obtained his promotion in February, 1915; wounded near Ypres February 5th.

Supplement to Irish Life, May 14th, 1915.

OUR HEROES

1. CAPT. P. R. BUTLER, Royal Irish Regiment.
2. MAJOR JOHN GAGE LECKY, Army Service Corps.
3. CAPT. S. G. De C. WHEELER, Royal Dublin Fusiliers.
4. MAJOR-GEN. E. H. H. ALLENBY.
5. MAJOR-GENERAL C. T. McMORROUGH KAVANAGH.
6. LT.-COLONEL A. PARKER, 5th Lancers.
7. LT. W. TYRRELL, M.B., R.A.M.C.
8. 2nd LT. M. E. DENNIS, R. H. Artillery.
9. LT. J. H. K. RICHARDSON, Royal Horse Artillery.

OUR HEROES.

Second Lieutenant E. G. Dunscombe Masters Phillips is the only son of Major J. H. Phillips, of Carrigrohane, Cork, and grandson of the late George Colthurst Dunscombe, of Mount Desert, Cork. He was educated at Portora Royal School, and entered the 3rd Battalion Royal Regiment (old Tipperary Light Infantry). On the mobilisation he was attached to the 2nd Battalion Royal Irish Regiment, to which regiment he has since been gazetted. He has been twice wounded, at Le Cateau and subsequently.

✧ ✧ ✧

Lieutenant Walter Borrowes was the youngest son of the late Sir Erasmus Borrowes, Bart., of Barretstown Castle, County Kildare, and Florence, daughter of the late William Ruxton, Esqre., Ardee House, Co. Louth, and half-brother of Sir Kildare Borrowes. He was born in 1892, and was appointed Midshipman in 1910, Sub-Lieutenant on H.M.S. "Antrim," 1913; promoted Lieutenant, 1914; killed on active service in H.M. Submarine, January, 1915. Aged 22.

✧ ✧ ✧

Lieut. Gerrard Ferrers Nixon, Royal Artillery, was killed in action in France on October 25th last; was the son of Major-Gen. Nixon, D.L., of Clone, Ballyragget, County Kilkenny. He joined the Artillery in December, 1910, and was 23 years of age at the time of his death. He was a keen sportsman and well known with the Kilkenny hounds.

✧ ✧ ✧

Lieut. E. J. Cormac Walshe, 2nd Leinsters, died of wounds received in action last November. He was a son of Mr. Ed. C. Walshe, D.L., of Castle Hill, Crossmolina, County Mayo; was educated at Stoneyhurst, where he was captain of the football team and a commissioned officer of the Officers' Training Corps. He was also a B.A. of Trinity College, Dublin.

✧ ✧ ✧

Major Jasper J. Howley, D.S.O., of the 2nd Lincoln Regiment, was killed in action at Neuve Chapelle on March 11th. He was the third son of Colonel John Howley, D.L., of Rich Hill, Co. Limerick. He was educated at Oscott and Sandhurst and joined the Lincoln Regiment in March, 1888. With his two brothers he served in the South African War, in which campaign he was severely wounded. He was twice mentioned in despatches and received the D.S.O. He was in Bermuda with his regiment when the war broke out, and the regiment, of which he was second in command, was brought to France about the 1st November.

✧ ✧ ✧

Lieutenant W. J. Meredith, 3rd Battalion Royal Munster Fusiliers, who died on February 20th from wounds received in action in France, where he was serving with the British Expeditionary Force since last November, was the eldest son of the late Richard Meredith, Esq., of Dicksgrove, Kerry, whom he succeeded about two years ago. Dicksgrove, the family residence, has been in the possession of the Merediths since the year 1656, but the property has been, in common with other Kerry properties, sold under the Land Purchase Acts. The late Lieut. Meredith was a magistrate of the county and was most popular with everyone who knew him, and his early decease has caused very widespread regret. He joined the Kerry Militia, which is now the 3rd Battalion of the Royal Munster Fusiliers (Special Reserve) in the year 1906.

✧ ✧ ✧

Lieutenant Pierce M. J. Power, R.A.M.C., passed into the Army in August, 1911, taking first place in marks in all Ireland. At the outbreak of the war he was attached to the 1st Battalion Wiltshire Regiment. He was with his regiment at Mons and in the retreat had his horse wounded under him and put out of action. He was in the advance to the Aisne and subsequently to Belgium. He arrived home on short leave on 21st February, hunted with the County Limerick Hounds at Adare, 24th, attended the Limerick Races 25th, and returned that night to the front and was killed in action a few days afterwards.

✧ ✧ ✧

Captain T. McC. Phillips, R.A.M.C., died on November 4th, 1914, from wounds received in action while attending the wounded in Flanders. He was 34 years of age, and was the second son of the late Rev. J. G. Phillips, B.A., Damascus, Syria, where Capt. Phillips was born. He received his early education at Trent College, Nottinghamshire, and then at Campbell College, Belfast, where he played in the famous Schools' Cup team of 1897-8. He was a distinguished student of Queen's College, Belfast, and took the degrees of M.B., B.Ch., B.A.O., Royal University of Ireland.

✧ ✧ ✧

Lieutenant William Armstrong Burges was born in 1889, June 3rd, and was the second son of the late Mr. Francis L. Burges, of Irwin House, West Australia, and of Mrs. Scroope, stepson of Mr. Frederic Scroope, and grandson of the late Francis Carlton Burges, M.D., of Fethard, County Tipperary. His school career began at the Grammar School, Clonmel. He was at Campbell College, Belfast, for a short time, and the remainder of his school days were spent at the Royal School, Armagh, where he was immensely popular with his masters and schoolfellows alike. Lieutenant Burges' elder brother is on his way home with the West Australian Light Horse, and his younger brother has, since December, been at the front with the Irish Guards.

1. LIEUT. E. G. D. MASTERS PHILLIPS, 2nd Batt. Royal Irish Regiment.	2. LIEUT. WALTER BORROWES, Royal Navy.	3. LT. GERRARD EERRERS NIXON, Royal Artillery.
4. LIEUT. E. J. C. WALSHE, 2nd Leinsters.	5. MAJOR JASPER J. HOWLEY, 2nd Lincolns.	6. LT. W. J. MEREDITH, 3rd Batt. Royal Munster Fusiliers.
7. LT. PIERCE M. J. POWER, R.A.M.C.	8. CAPT. T. McC. PHILLIPS, R.A.M.C.	9. LT. W. A. BURGES, 2nd Batt. Royal Irish Rifles.

Our Heroes

OUR HEROES.

Lieutenant James Gardiner McCormick, 2nd Worcestershire Regiment, was killed on May 15-16. Lieutenant McCormick, who was the youngest son of Mr. S. S. McCormick, J.P., Shandon, Monkstown, Dublin, entered Sandhurst in 1913. He joined the Expeditionary Force on January 4th, 1915. His Commanding Officers report of him: "He died, as he would have wished, at the head of his men whom he led with the greatest gallantry and fell close to the German works which we had orders to take."

◇ ◇ ◇

Captain John Hugh Gardiner McCormick, Royal Warwickshire Regiment, was reported in April as having died in a German hospital on October 19th of wounds received on same day, while attacking a German battery. Capt. McCormick, who was the eldest son of Mr. S. S. McCormick, J.P., Shandon, Monkstown, Dublin, received his commission in 1906 and his Captaincy in September, 1914. He joined the Expeditionary Force on October 4, and lost his life leading his troops in an attack on the German trenches.

◇ ◇ ◇

Lieutenant A. B. P. McClenaghan, 1st Wilts. Regiment, was the eldest son of the Rev. G. R. and Mrs. McClenaghan, Thistlehurst, Ipswich, and a grandson of the Rev. Canon McClenaghan, Athlone. He was educated at Marlborough College, Wilts., where he was an officer of the O.T.C. for some time. He obtained his commission in the 1st Wilts. Regiment in September, 1914, and in December left with his regiment for the front. On June 16th he was shot whilst leading his men on a charge.

◇ ◇ ◇

Captain Richard C. G. M. Kinkead, Royal Army Medical Corps, was the only son of Professor and Mrs. Kinkead, of Galway. He was educated at Galway Grammar School and afterwards at Portora. He then entered Galway College, where he graduated. He was resident pupil at the Richmond Hospital, Dublin, in 1908, and afterwards House Surgeon to the Coventry and Warwickshire Hospital. He landed at Ostend on October 9th and was in the thick of the fighting until October 30th, when he was killed while attending the wounded.

◇ ◇ ◇

Major Giles Rooke, 10th Gurkha Rifles, who was killed in action on May 9th, had served during the winter with the 3rd Battalion Royal Irish Rifles in Dublin, commanding B Company. He was ordered from Dublin to France several months ago and was wounded shortly after his arrival. He was born on June 16th, 1874, joined the service as Second Lieutenant in August, 1893, became Captain of the 10th Gurkha Rifles in August, 1902, and was promoted to the rank of Major in August, 1911. He was a son of Major-General Rooke, Ellerslie, Ryde.

◇ ◇ ◇

Captain John Wilfrid Jenkinson, M.A., D.Sc., 12th Worcestershire Regiment, who was killed in the trenches in Gallipoli on June 7th, was in 1909 elected Lecturer in Comparative and Experimental Embryology to the University of Oxford and to a Research Fellowship at Exeter College. His death is an irreparable loss to the world of science, for he was a pioneer in a most important part of embryological discovery. Soon after the outbreak of the war he was offered a commission. He was attached to the 2nd Royal Dublin Fusiliers and fell shortly after landing at the Dardanelles. Captain Jenkinson married a daughter of the late Mr. John Stephenson, of Ballyrohan and Ballydineen, County Limerick.

◇ ◇ ◇

Lieutenant Edward Crawford, 3rd Royal Inniskilling Fusiliers, died on 27th May, in the British Hospital at Wimereux from gas poisoning and wounds received in action in Flanders about 24th May. He was the son of the late Robert Crawford, D.L., of Stonewold, Ballyshannon, an eminent Civil Engineer, Professor of Engineering in Trinity College, Dublin, 1882-1887, by his wife Anna, daughter of the late Thomas Troubridge Stubbs, of Ballyshannon. He went to the front in October last, when he was attached to the 2nd Royal Irish Rifles.

◇ ◇ ◇

Captain Damer Wynyard, 1st Battalion East Surrey Regiment, born 1890, was educated at Wellington College, and joined from the Royal Military College at Sandhurst in 1909. He was killed in action at Hill 60 in Flanders, 20th April, 1915. On May 31st he was mentioned in despatches by Field-Marshal Sir John French "for gallant and distinguished service in the field." The only son of Lieut.-Colonel Richard Damer Wynyard (formerly of the same regiment), he married on 12th December, 1914, Olive, youngest daughter of His Honour Judge Wakely, K.C., D.L., of Ballyburly, in the King's County. Captain Wynyard was the sixth in direct succession from father to son of a family of soldiers.

◇ ◇ ◇

Second Lieutenant C. E. Cooke, 1st Batt. Royal Irish Fusiliers, who was killed in action at Ypres on May 26th, was the second surviving son of Mr. Alexander Cooke, of Notting Hill, Belfast. He joined the Ulster Volunteer Force in May last on his return from a trip round the world, and volunteered for service at the front the day after war was declared. He went to the front in the end of September, was wounded in November, and after six weeks in hospital returned to the front. Lieutenant Cooke was mentioned in despatches by Sir John French in February last for gallantry in the field.

1. LIEUT. J. G. McCORMICK, 2nd Worcestershire Regiment.
2. CAPT. J. H. G. McCORMICK, Royal Warwickshire Regiment.
3. LIEUT. A. B. P. McCLENAGHAN, Wiltshire Regiment.
4. CAPT. R. C. G. KINKEAD, R.A.M.C.
5. MAJOR GILES ROOKE, 10th Gurkha Rifles.
6. CAPT. J. W. JENKINSON, M.A., 2nd Royal Dublin Fusiliers.
7. LIEUT. ED. CRAWFORD, Royal Inniskilling Fusiliers.
8. CAPT. DAMER WYNYARD, East Surrey Regiment.
9. LIEUT. C. E. COOKE, Royal Irish Fusiliers.

OUR HEROES.

Second Lieutenant H. B. Hodges, 2nd Battalion King's Own Yorkshire Light Infantry, was killed in action on 18th April, 1915, at Hill 60, when leading his men in a charge against the Germans. He was the younger son of Mr. J. F. W. Hodges, J.P., of Glenravel House, Glenravel, County Antrim. He was born in 1895, and educated at Sherborne School, Dorset, where he was in the first XV. football team, and won numerous prizes for swimming and boxing. He left for the front in the middle of March, and had been five weeks in the trenches when he was killed.

◇ ◇ ◇

Captain Hugh Lefroy Crofton, 1st Batt. Inniskilling Fusiliers, who was killed in action at the Dardanelles about the 26th May, was the eldest son of Captain Duke Crofton, R.N., D.L., and Mrs. Crofton, of Lakefield, Mohill, County Leitrim, and a grandson of the late General Sir J. H. Lefroy, K.C.M.G., C.B., R.A. He received his commission as Lieutenant in the Inniskilling Fusiliers in October, 1906, and was gazetted Captain on September 4th, 1914. He had served with his regiment in Crete, Malta, North China, and India.

◇ ◇ ◇

Lieutenant Mervyn Kebble Anderson, 2nd Batt. Royal Irish Regiment, was the fourth son of Mr. James Anderson, of Brentford, Orwell Park, Rathgar, County Dublin. Lieutenant Anderson joined the 3rd Batt. (Special Reserve) of his regiment in August, 1914, was confirmed in rank and proceeded to the front in January, 1915; gazetted to the Regular Army on 28th February, 1915, and promoted Lieutenant on the 27th April, 1915. Lieutenant Anderson was very severely wounded in the neighbourhood of Ypres on the 7th May, 1915, and on the 11th May succumbed to these wounds.

◇ ◇ ◇

Captain D. Gaussen, 2nd Batt. Highland Light Infantry, who was killed in action in France on May 17th, belonged to an old Irish family, and had a wide circle of friends in Dublin, where for many years he was attached to the Headquarters Staff. His mother resides at Upton, Bagenalstown, and his wife, whom he leaves surviving, was Miss Marguerite Kelly, daughter of the late Judge Kelly. Though only in his 40th year, Captain Gaussen had seen much active service during the operations on the North-West Frontier of India, including the attack and capture of the Tanga Pass, for which he received the Medal with clasp, and afterwards in the South African War, for his services in which he received the Queen's Medal with three clasps and the King's Medal with two clasps.

◇ ◇ ◇

Major St. John Adcock, 3rd Batt. Leinster Regiment, was killed on May 9th while gallantly leading his men into action at Rue de Bois, Richebourg, St. Vaast. He was the second surviving son of the late Mr. St. John Adcock and Mrs. Adcock, of Loughnavala, Merrion, Co. Dublin. In 1901 he enlisted in the Longford Horse and proceeded to the front where he took part in the campaign against the Boers, and before the termination of the war obtained a commission in the 3rd Battalion Leinster Regiment. He was gazetted Captain in May, 1906, and Major in the early part of this year. He was officially reported missing after the engagement of May 9th, and a few days later it was notified that he had been killed.

◇ ◇ ◇

Captain Claude Alexander French, 2nd Batt. Royal Irish Regiment, who died on May 8th, from wounds received in action in France, was the second son of Mr. John A. French, St. Ann's, Donnybrook, Dublin. He was educated at Mr. Strangways and Shrewsbury School and Trinity College, Dublin. He served in the South African War and gained the King's Medal with three clasps. He went to Flanders in September, 1914, and was wounded in October at Le Pilley, but rejoined and again went to the front on January 12th, and on May 8th was seriously wounded by shell and succumbed shortly afterwards in the Australian Hospital at Wimereux.

◇ ◇ ◇

Lieutenant Robert A. Finlay, 5th Batt. Royal Dublin Fusiliers, was the younger son of Colonel H. F. Finlay, D.L., of Corkagh, Clondalkin, High Sheriff of the Co. Dublin. Lieutenant Finlay was gazetted to the 3rd Royal Dublin Fusiliers in July, 1913, and in March, 1915, was attached to the 1st Royal Irish Rifles in Flanders, where he was killed on May 9th, during an attack on the German trenches.

◇ ◇ ◇

Second Lieutenant Maurice C. Rogers, Royal Engineers, was killed in the trenches on February 25th, only three or four weeks after he had been sent to the front. He was the only son of Mr. John C. Rogers, Inspector of National Schools in Ireland, and was educated at Campbell College, Belfast, where he won many distinctions, including a Junior and Senior Exhibition, as well as the McNeill Memorial Prize.

◇ ◇ ◇

Lieutenant Christopher D. Considine, 5th Royal Dublin Fusiliers, was killed in action in Flanders on May 25th. He was the third son of the late Sir Heffernan Considine, C.B., M.V.O., D.L., Derk, County Limerick. Lt. Considine met his death in trying to bring the Major commanding his company out of danger under a murderous artillery and machine-gun fire, Lieutenant Considine being killed instantaneously and his Major died shortly afterwards.

Supplement to Irish Life, July 30th, 1915.

1. LIEUT. H. B. HODGES, King's Own Yorkshire Light Infantry.
2. CAPT. H. L. CROFTON, 1st Batt. Inniskilling Fusiliers.
3. LIEUT. M. K. ANDERSON, Royal Irish Regiment.
4. CAPT. D. GAUSSEN, Highland Light Infantry.
5. MAJOR ST. JOHN ADCOCK, Leinster Regiment.
6. CAPT. CLAUDE A. FRENCH, Royal Irish Regiment.
7. LIEUT. R. A. FINLAY, Royal Dublin Fusiliers.
8. LIEUT. MAURICE C. ROGERS, Royal Engineers.
9. LIEUT. C. D. CONSIDINE, Royal Dublin Fusiliers.

OUR HEROES.

Lieutenant Charles Sealy King, 2nd Royal Munster Fusiliers, who was killed in action on May 9th, at Neuve Chapelle, in his 20th year, was a son of Mr. Charles Sealy King, Richmount, Bandon, County Cork, where the news of his death has been received with regret. Lieutenant Sealy King was killed while leading his platoon in an attack on the German trenches, when he dashed forward ahead of his men and was killed right up against the German parapet.

◇ ◇ ◇

Captain Annesley St. George Gore, who is reported unofficially as having fallen in action, was the son of Colonel Charles Gore, late Commanding the Duke of Wellington's West Riding Regiment. Captain Gore was educated at Aravon School, Bray, and Cheltenham, from whence he entered Sandhurst, where he captained the Rugger XV. in 1905. He first joined the Royal Irish Regiment at Rawal Pindi, and afterwards the 110th Mahratta Light Infantry (Gurkhas). He exchanged later into the 2nd Battalion of the 9th Rifles, with whom he was serving when he fell at the head of his men on Saturday, June 26th, leading an attack to recover the body of one of his Scouts, and to drive the Germans back. Captain Gore, who came of a well-known Irish family, the Gores of Derrymore, County Clare, was a keen all-round sportsman.

◇ ◇ ◇

Lieutenant Francis M. D. Morrogh, Royal Munster Fusiliers, who has been killed in the Dardanelles, was a son of the late Mr. John Morrogh, M.P. for South East Cork. Lieutenant Morrogh was educated at Castleknock College, and joined the Munster Fusiliers at the outbreak of the war. He was a County Councillor for Cork, and was well-known as a prominent member of the South Union Hunt and a cricket player.

◇ ◇ ◇

Major R. D. Johnson, Royal Dublin Fusiliers, joined the Militia Battalion (now the 3rd Special Reserve) in 1900 and served in the 11th Mounted Infantry through the South African War, receiving the Queen's Medal with four clasps. He was wounded on April 25th, during the fighting near Ypres, but returned again to the front on May 10th and was killed in action a fortnight later, on May 24th, in Flanders. Major Johnson's name has since been mentioned in despatches, dated May 31st, and published on June 23rd. He was the younger son of the late Mr. E. M. Johnson, of St. Mary's, York, and leaves a widow, Mrs. Claudine Johnson, Camoys, Braintree, Essex, and two children, surviving.

◇ ◇ ◇

Major Richard Saker, Connaught Rangers, was wounded at the memorable landing in Gallipoli on April 25th, but returned to the firing line and was killed in action the following day. He had served in the South African War and obtained the Queen's Medal with four clasps. He became Captain of the Connaught Rangers in 1907. At the outbreak of the war he was in Australia, but became attached to the 5th Batt. Australian Corps, and proceeded with them to the Dardanelles.

◇ ◇ ◇

Major F. G. Richards, R.A.M.C., who has been killed in action in France, served in the South African (1900-2) War; was present at the relief of Ladysmith, including the action at Spion Kop, during the operations on Tugela Heights and action at Pieter's Hill, and in the action at Laing's Nek. He obtained the Queen's Medal with four clasps and the King's Medal with two clasps. He was a brother of Colonel Richards, Arno's Vale, Rostrevor.

◇ ◇ ◇

Lieutenant T. F. Brown, 7th Batt. Manchester Regiment, who has been killed in action at the Dardanelles, was the elder son of Mr. and Mrs. Brown, 204 Shankill Road, Belfast. He was a member of the Officers' Training Corps of Queen's University, Belfast, and on the outbreak of the war received his commission in the Manchester Regiment. His battalion left England for Khartoum, where he was stationed until transferred to the Dardanelles.

◇ ◇ ◇

Lieutenant George Joseph Weldrick, R.N.R,. was the second son of Mr. and Mrs. John F. Weldrick, of Booterstown. He was born at Idrone House, Blackrock, Co. Dublin, on the 2nd May, 1883; was educated at Blackrock College. He had a distinguished career in the Mercantile Marine Service, and in July, 1914, he was appointed in H.M.S. "Hannibal," and in November, 1914, was transferred to the H.M.S. "Clan McNaughton," in which he lost his life in the service of his country on or about 3rd February, 1915.

◇ ◇ ◇

Dr. Geoffrey M. M. Fleming, M.B., T.C.D., Lieut. R.A.M.C., who was killed in action in France on 16th June, 1915, was the only son of Mr. A. G. Fleming, Deputy Cashier of the Bank of Ireland, and Mrs. Fleming, Beechfield, Blackrock, County Dublin. He was educated at Avoca School, Blackrock, and Trinity College, Dublin. He was Resident Surgeon at the Meath Hospital when war broke out, and felt it his duty to volunteer. He was in several serious battles, and at the time of his death was attached to the 2nd Bedford Regiment. During our attack he was in his Advanced Dressing Station when a shell burst through the roof, instantly killing him and the poor fellow whose wounds he was dressing at the moment.

Supplement to Irish Life, July 30th, 1915.

OUR HEROES

1. LIEUT. CHAS. SEALY KING, Royal Munster Fusiliers.
2. CAPT. ANNESLEY ST. GEORGE GORE, 9th Gurkha Rifles.
3. LIEUT. FRANCIS M. D. MORROGH, Royal Munster Fusiliers.
4. MAJOR R. D. JOHNSON, Royal Dublin Fusiliers.
5. MAJOR RICHARD SAKER, Connaught Rangers.
6. MAJOR F. G. RICHARDS, Royal Army Medical Corps.
7. LIEUT. T. F. BROWN, 7th Batt. Manchester Regiment.
8. LIEUT. G. J. WELDRICK, Royal Naval Reserve.
9. LIEUT. G. M. M. FLEMING, Royal Army Medical Corps.

OUR HEROES.

Lieutenant Claude Lysaght Mackay, 5th Worcestershire Regiment, who was wounded on May 28th and died in hospital on June 7th was a nephew of Mr. and Mrs. Wakefield Richardson, of Moyallen, County Down, and a son of the late Edward Vansittart Mackay and Mrs. Mackay, of Clifton, Gloucestershire. Lieutenant Mackay was on the Old Cliftonian Cricket Tour the day war was declared and before the day was over he had returned home and filled in his papers for a commission.

✧ ✧ ✧

Captain Gerard Arthur O'Callaghan, 2nd Battalion Royal Irish Regiment, who was killed by poisonous gas in France on the morning of May 25, entered the Service from Sandhurst, where he had been a Queen's Cadet in 1899. He served in the South African War, receiving the Queen's and King's Medals, with five clasps. He acted as Provost-Marshal to General (now Sir Horace) Smith-Dorrien, and also served with Dammant's Horse ("Rimington's Tigers") during the latter part of that campaign. He was promoted Captain, and joined the Egyptian Army in 1907, and served in the Soudan with the rank of Bimbashi for seven years. The only son of Major-General Sir Desmond and the late Lady O'Callaghan, he was born at Shoeburyness in April, 1880, and in October, 1914, married Joan Mary, daughter of Mr. S. R. and Mrs. Grubb, of Castle Grace, Clogheen.

✧ ✧ ✧

Lieutenant Frederick C. P. Joy, 2nd Batt. Royal Irish Rifles, of Grove House, Stillorgan, County Dublin, was killed in action on June 16th. Lieutenant Joy obtained his commission on August 15th, and went to the front with a draft several months ago. Lieutenant Joy was a young officer of much promise, and the news of his death has been received with much regret. His brother, Dr. H. A. Joy, is also in the service of his country.

✧ ✧ ✧

Captain Robert Arthur Revell, 1st Batt. Essex Regiment, who was dangerously wounded at Dardanelles about June 4th, and died at Deaconesses Hospital, Alexandria, on June 12th, was the second son of the late John A. Revell, Esq., of Newcastle House, County Wicklow, and of Mrs. Revell, Bray. He received his commission in 1st Essex Regiment in 1912, and joined his regiment at Quetta, in November, from there he accompanied it to Mauritius, returning to England last December to join 29th Division, which sailed for Dardanelles on March 22nd. He was promoted Lieutenant, February, 1913, and was given his company a short time before his death.

✧ ✧ ✧

Colonel R. Fitzgerald Uniacke, Royal Inniskilling Fusiliers, who is reported killed, was a member of an old Cork family, and a son of the Rev. Fitzgerald Uniacke, Stone Cross House, Wadhurst. Colonel Uniacke entered the Inniskillings from the Militia in 1891, received his Captaincy in 1899, and was gazetted to field rank two years ago. Colonel Uniacke was mentioned in Sir John French's despatches at the same time as his cousins, Brigadier-General H. C. Uniacke, R.H.A., and Lieutenant-Colonel H. P. Uniacke, commanding the 2nd Batt. Gordon Highlanders, who also fell in action.

✧ ✧ ✧

Captain J. Goold=Adams, only son of the Ven. J. M. Goold-Adams, Archdeacon of Derry, who has been killed in action in Flanders, was born in October, 1883, and was educated at Rugby School and Sandhurst. He obtained his commission in the Prince of Wales' Leinster Regiment (Royal Canadians) in 1903, became Lieutenant in 1904 and Captain in 1912. He was wounded in February, 1915, and killed on the 4th May, in the memorable action on Hill 60. Captain Goold-Adams married in August, 1913, Irene, daughter of Assheton Biddulph, Esq., and Mrs. Biddulph, Moneyguyneen, King's County.

✧ ✧ ✧

Lieutenant Francis Stuart Verschoyle, Royal Engineers, youngest son of Mr. W. H. F. and Mrs. Frances Verschoyle, of Woodley, Dundrum, County Dublin, was born 9th April, 1896; educated at Castle Park, Dalkey, and Marlborough College. Leaving the latter at the end of the summer term, 1914, he entered Trinity College, Dublin. He left Chatham for France on the 13th December, 1914, and was killed in action on Sunday night, 25th April, near Ypres, defending a trench, with only four others, against overwhelming odds. His C.O. wrote from the battlefield, "that he behaved like a soldier, did his duty well, and fought to the end."

✧ ✧ ✧

Lieutenant Cecil J. F. Black, Royal Marine Light Infantry, who gave his life for his King and Country in the Dardanelles on May 9th, was a son of Mr. W. Black, High Sheriff for the Co. Monaghan. Lieutenant Black was only 18 years of age, and his kindly disposition, unassuming manner and absolute fearlessness had endeared him to all with whom he came in contact.

✧ ✧ ✧

Lieutenant R. B. Buchanan, 5th Royal Scots Fusiliers, was the younger son of Mr. R. Eccles Buchanan, C.E., Londonderry, and Mrs. Buchanan, Warwick Terrace, Leeson Park, Dublin. He was gazetted to a Lieutenancy in the Royal Army Medical Corps on August 16th, but finding he would not be permitted to go on active service until he had completed his medical course, he applied for a transfer to the Royal Scots Fusiliers. He landed at the Dardanelles on May 30th and almost immediately proceeded to the trenches where he was killed.

Supplement to Irish Life, July 30th, 1915.

1. LIEUT. C. L. MACKAY, Worcestershire Regiment.	2. CAPT. GERARD O'CALLAGHAN, Royal Irish Regiment.	3. LIEUT. C. P. JOY, Royal Irish Rifles.
4. CAPT. R. A. REVELL, 1st Batt. Essex Regiment.	5 COL. R. FITZGERALD UNIACKE, Royal Inniskilling Fusiliers.	6. CAPT. J. GOOLD-ADAMS, Prince of Wales' Leinster Regiment.
7. LIEUT. F. S. VERSCHOYLE, Royal Engineers.	8. LIEUT. CECIL J. F. BLACK, Royal Marine Light Infantry.	9. LIEUT. R. B. BUCHANAN, 5th Royal Scots Fusiliers.

OUR HEROES.

Lieutenant J. E. Bruce Miller, 5th Royal Irish Rifles, who died in France on May 24th, of wounds received in action, was the only son of Dr. and Mrs. J. E. Miller, of Londonderry, and grandson of the late Major Stewart Hervey Bruce, Argyll and Sutherland Highlanders. He was 20 years of age and was gazetted to a Lieutenancy in the 5th Royal Irish Rifles in January last, and shortly afterwards proceeded with his regiment to France. His early death has caused much regret in his native town.

◇ ◇ ◇

Captain the Hon. Ernest W. Brabazon, 3rd Batt. Coldstream Guards, the youngest son of the Earl and Countess of Meath, has been killed in action in France. He was born in 1884, received his commission in 1904, was promoted Lieutenant in 1906 and Captain in 1912. In December last year he was mentioned in despatches, and received the D.S.O. for "conspicuous efficiency in Staff duties and in keeping up communications with a long line of front composed of many units, where communication was often difficult. He carried and delivered messages under fire with promptness and despatch." Lord Meath's three other sons are all on active service.

◇ ◇ ◇

Lieutenant A. W. Battersby, Connaught Rangers, who died of fever on active service in West Africa on June 8th, had only arrived there in April last, being attached to the 2nd Nigerian Regiment in Kamerun. He was the second son of the late John Radcliffe Battersby, of Loughbawn, Westmeath, and was educated at Trinity College, Dublin. His younger brother is also in Africa, serving with the East African Mounted Rifles.

◇ ◇ ◇

Captain E. G. Harvey, 1st Wiltshire Regiment, who was killed in action in France on June 16th, was a son of Mr. J. G. M. Harvey, of Creglorne, Londonderry, had served in the South African War, taking part in the operations in the Transvaal and receiving the Queen's Medal with two clasps. He was in 1913 recorded for service in the Royal Flying Corps, and in 1914 was promoted to Flight Commander. At the outbreak of the war he rejoined his regiment, and was with them at the front until his death.

◇ ◇ ◇

Lieutenant-Colonel Francis G. Jones, Royal Inniskilling Fusiliers, who died of wounds received in action, was 51 years of age and had seen service in India and Africa. He took part in the operations in Northern China Hills, being awarded a Medal and clasp, and also served in the operations on N.W. Frontier of India in 1897-8. He went through the South African War, taking part in the relief of Ladysmith and the actions at Colenso and Spion Kop, also in the operations on Tugela Heights. For his services in the South African War Colonel Jones was mentioned in despatches and was awarded the Queen's Medal with three clasps.

◇ ◇ ◇

Captain H. Edgar Goodbody, 4th Battalion Leinster Regiment, eldest son of Mr. T. H. Goodbody and husband of Mrs. Goodbody, Sheerwater, Monkstown, County Cork, obtained his Lieutenancy in August, 1912, was appointed Assistant Commissioner of Police on the Gold Coast in 1913, and subsequently received his Captaincy. He went with his regiment to the front and was killed in the action near Ypres on May 12th.

◇ ◇ ◇

Lieutenant William P. Heffernan, 3rd Royal Irish Regiment, who was killed in action at Richebourg, France, on May 9th, in his 29th year, was the second son of Dr. Wm. K. Heffernan and Mrs. Heffernan, Killenaule, Tipperary, and 11 Harlow Moor Drive, Harrogate. Lieutenant Heffernan was a well-known athlete in Trinity College, winning, amongst other valuable prizes, the Viceroy's Cup, presented on the occasion of the King's visit in 1911. He also possessed high musical talent, and was an expert horseman, well-known in the hunting field in Tipperary. He was wounded at La Bassée in January, but returned to the front, where he had only been a short time when he fell in action.

◇ ◇ ◇

Captain H. M. Finegan, 8th (Irish) Battalion King's Liverpool Regiment, who was killed in action in Flanders, was gazetted Lieutenant in July, 1912. He went to the front shortly after the outbreak of the war, and at the time of his death was in charge of his company.

◇ ◇ ◇

Lieutenant R. L. Neill, 5th Batt. Royal Irish Rifles, who was killed in action in France on the 9th May, was the younger son of Mr. Sharman D. Neill, 22 Donegall Place, Belfast. He was educated at Campbell College, where he joined the Officers' Training Corps, and completed his studies at Neuchatel, Switzerland. On his return home he joined the Holywood contingent of the 1st Battalion North Down Regiment, Ulster Volunteer Force. He obtained a commission in the Royal South Downs early in August and left for the front on March 22nd, to join the 1st Battalion, taking out a draft of Princess Charlotte of Wales's Royal Berkshire Regiment.

1. LIEUT. J. E. BRUCE MILLER, Royal Irish Rifles.
2. CAPT. HON. E. W. BRABAZON, 3rd Batt. Coldstream Guards.
3. LIEUT. A. W. BATTERSBY, 4th Batt. Connaught Rangers.
4. CAPT. E. G. HARVEY, 1st Batt. Wiltshire Regiment.
5. COL. F. G. JONES, Royal Inniskilling Fusiliers.
6. CAPT. H. E. GOODBODY, 4th Batt. Leinster Regiment.
7. LIEUT. W. P. HEFFERNAN, 3rd Royal Irish Regiment.
8. CAPT. H. M. FINEGAN, 8th Batt. King's Liverpool Regiment.
9. LIEUT. R. L. NEILL, 5th Batt. Royal Irish Rifles.

OUR HEROES.

Lieutenant Gerald C. Moran, 5th Battalion Royal Dublin Fusiliers, was the only surviving son of Mr. and Mrs. Stanislaus Moran, of Moatecharie, Greystones. He was born in 1888, and was educated at Clongowes and Trinity College, Dublin. In 1910 he was attached to the 28th Brigade Royal Field Artillery, and two years later was gazetted to the 5th Batt. Royal Dublin Fusiliers. He went to the Front on May 2nd, and on the 25th was brought to the hospital at Rouen, suffering from gas poisoning, from the effects of which he died the following morning.

❖ ❖ ❖

Major James Woods, Indian Medical Service, was the youngest son of the late Mr. William Woods, Waring Street, Belfast. He was gazetted to the 53rd Sikhs, now serving in Egypt, and saw some active service on the North-West Indian frontier. On the outbreak of war in August last he joined the first Indian Expeditionary Force and was attached to the 39th Gharwal Rifles, a regiment which has won many distinctions since it landed in France in October last. Major Woods was invalided home, suffering from influenza a few months ago, but returned to the front and fell in the fierce fighting on May 9th.

❖ ❖ ❖

Lieutenant F. G. Kerridge Judd, 2nd Batt. Royal Dublin Fusiliers, was killed in action on May 25th, with seven other officers of his battalion. He was only 18 years of age, and was the second son of Mr. H. Kerridge Judd, of Stanhope Works, Clerkenwell Close, London. Lieutenant Judd came of an Irish family on his mother's side. He received his commission in the 2nd Battalion of the Royal Dublin Fusiliers, and it was while in the trenches with the " B " Company of his regiment that this very promising young officer met his death.

❖ ❖ ❖

Captain Thomas Villiers Thacker Neville, 3rd Dragoon Guards, was the eldest son of the late Mr. Joseph William Thacker, of 40 Upper Fitzwilliam Street, Dublin, and a grandson of the late Mr. Thomas Neville, of Borrismore, County Kilkenny, whose surname he took last year. He reached the rank of captain in 1909, was adjutant of the Yorkshire Dragoons, after which he rejoined his regiment and proceeded to Egypt. At the outbreak of the present war his regiment was ordered to the front. He was killed fighting in the trenches near Ypres on May 13th, 1915, in a very severe engagement, in which his squadron, though heavily bombarded and attacked both in front and rear, held its ground.

❖ ❖ ❖

Major Charles Conyers, 2nd Batt. Royal Irish Fusiliers, who died of wounds received whilst gallantly fighting with his regiment in France, was born in 1867, received his commission in 1889, was promoted captain in 1899 and major in 1909. Major Conyers saw service in the Transvaal, Orange River Colony and Cape Colony during the South African War and received the Queen's Medal with five clasps. By his death the army has been deprived of a brave and able officer.

❖ ❖ ❖

Captain Arthur Moore O'Sullivan, 1st Royal Irish Rifles, who was killed in action in France on May 9th, was the only son of the late Mr. Patrick O'Sullivan, Advocate-General, Madras Presidency, and Mrs. O'Sullivan, Auburn, Greystones, Co. Wicklow. He was born in 1878 in Ootacamund, India, and was educated at Bedford Grammar School and Hertford College, Oxford. He enlisted in 1900 in the Oxfordshire Light Infantry and served in the South African War, receiving the Queen's Medal with four clasps. He obtained a commission in the Royal Irish Rifles in 1902, was promoted lieutenant in 1906, captain in 1910, and was adjutant of his regiment in 1910-12. In 1905-7 he was seconded for service with the Northern Nigerian regiment of the West African Frontier Force. Captain O'Sullivan went to the front with his regiment in November, 1914, and was wounded at Neuve Chapelle and mentioned in despatches.

❖ ❖ ❖

Lieutenant J. R. Fitzgibbon Hall, 2nd Royal Dublin Fusiliers, the only surviving son of Mr. and Mrs. Fitzgibbon Hall, The Bank House, Tipperary, was only in his 21st year when he was killed in action near Ypres on May 24th. He was much beloved by the officers and men of his fine old regiment, and had already established a reputation as a reliable soldier.

❖ ❖ ❖

Surgeon James Barrett, R.N., who was drowned while on active service off the Orkneys on December 14th, 1914, was the eldest son of the late Mr. Denis Barrett, Tralee. He was educated at Clongowes College and afterwards at University College, Dublin, taking out his degrees at an exceptionally young age. He took his medical degree in the Royal University of Ireland and entered the Navy about seven years ago. When the war broke out he was surgeon in charge of the Royal Marine Barracks at Plymouth and applied to be sent to a ship on active service. He was surgeon on the " Imperieuse " at the time of his death.

❖ ❖ ❖

Lieutenant Oliver Babington Macausland, who was killed on May 9th, was the younger son of Lieutenant-Colonel Macausland, of Woodbank, Garvagh, County Derry. He was educated at Haileybury and the Royal Military College, Sandhurst (prize cadet), and was gazetted in August last as Second Lieutenant on the unattached list for the Indian Army. He was, however, posted to the 4th Royal Irish Rifles, and in March gazetted to the 1st Royal Irish Rifles in France.

1. LIEUT. G. C. MORAN, 5th Batt. Royal Dublin Fusiliers.	2. MAJOR JAMES WOODS. Indian Medical Service.	3. LIEUT. F. G. K. JUDD, 2nd Batt. Royal Dublin Fusiliers.
4. CAPT. T. V. T. NEVILLE, 3rd Dragoon Guards.	5. MAJOR CHAS. CONYERS, 2nd Batt. Royal Irish Fusiliers.	6. CAPT. A. M. O'SULLIVAN, 1st Royal Irish Rifles.
7. LIEUT. J. R. FITZGIBBON HALL, 2nd Royal Dublin Fusiliers.	8. SURGEON JAMES BARRETT, Royal Navy.	9. LIEUT. O. B. MACAUSLAND, 4th Royal Irish Rifles.

OUR HEROES.

Lieutenant Henry Colpoys Gloster, 6th Gordon Highlanders, was the only son of Dr. and Mrs. Gloster, of Phillimore Place, Kensington, London. His mother is a County Clare lady, and Lt. Gloster was well known in Kilkee. At the outbreak of the war he left Caius College, Cambridge, to serve his country and was killed in the action at Neuve Chapelle in his twentieth year.

◇ ◇ ◇

Captain F. W. Wood-Martin, who has been killed in action in Flanders, was well known in County Sligo, where the intelligence of his death has occasioned widespread regret. He was the youngest son of Col. Wood-Martin, A.D.C., Clevenagh, Sligo, was educated at Cheltenham and entered the Army in August, 1899. He took part in the operations in the Transvaal, where he acted as Station Officer from 1899 to 1902; he was taken prisoner in January, 1900, but was released in the following June, when Lord Roberts entered Pretoria. He also took part in the operations in the Orange River Colony, in Cape Colony, and at Colesburg. He was promoted to the rank of Captain in 1906, and held the Queen's Medal with three clasps and the King's Medal with two clasps.

◇ ◇ ◇

Lieutenant J. O'Grady Delmege, 4th Royal Irish Dragoons, who was only in his 21st year, died on the 27th May last, from the effects of gas poisoning. He was educated at Clifton, Bath College and Trinity College. He was a very promising young officer, a fine horseman, and devoted to cricket and football. Much sympathy is felt with his father, Mr. J. O'Grady Delmege, Castle Park, Limerick.

◇ ◇ ◇

Captain E. Stafford King-Harman, of the Irish Guards, who has been missing since November last, is now officially reported to have been killed near Ypres on the 6th November last. On that date he was with Captain Lord John Hamilton in the front trench with a company of their regiment, when they were surrounded and cut off by the Germans. Captain King-Harman was a very keen soldier and a good sportsman. He played polo for the regimental team and hunted his own pack of harriers, was a good rifle shot and a member of the Eton eight for two years. His death has caused widespread regret in the County Roscommon, where he was extremely popular with all classes. He was the eldest son of Sir Thomas and Lady Stafford, of Rockingham, Boyle, and married in July, 1914, Olive, only child of Henry Packenham Mahon, of Strokestown Park, Roscommon, and leaves a daughter born in April, 1915.

◇ ◇ ◇

Lieutenant-Colonel Derrick A. Carden, who died of wounds received in action in Flanders on May 25th, was the youngest son of the late Sir John Carden, Bt., of Templemore Abbey, County Tipperary, and Lady Carden, of Weston, Straffan. He was educated at Wellington College, and was gazetted to the Seaforth Highlanders in 1895. He took part in the Soudan campaign, receiving the Medal and two clasps, and in the North-West Indian Frontier expedition in 1908. He was wounded at the Aisne in September last, but returned to the front in December.

◇ ◇ ◇

Captain Basil Maclear, 2nd Royal Dublin Fusiliers, has been killed in action in France. The news has been received with great regret in Ireland, where he was well known as the famous Irish International Rugby footballer. He represented Ireland on a number of occasions in the international series and distinguished himself by his play, his fine physique and pace making him a conspicuous figure. He learned his football at Bedford Grammar School and figured in many military teams, both in England and South Africa, where he was with the Dublin Fusiliers during the South African War. Capt. Maclear's brother, Lt.-Col. Percy Maclear, formerly of the Royal Dublin Fusiliers, was killed last August in the Cameroons while in command of a battalion of the Nigeria Regiment. The deceased officers were two of the five sons of Mrs. Maclear, Bedford, and the three remaining sons are also in service. They are nephews of Mrs. Moore, Flowerfield, Portstewart.

◇ ◇ ◇

Second Lieutenant A. McLaughlin, Royal Irish Rifles, who has been killed in action, was a son of Mr. W. H. McLaughlin, D.L., Macedon, Whitehouse, principal of the firm of McLaughlin and Harvey, of Belfast and Dublin. He received his commission on the 15th August and was posted to the 3rd Battalion of the Rifles at Dublin, in which regiment his brother, Captain McLaughlin, is also an officer. Lieutenant McLaughlin had only been a short time at the front when he fell. His brother, George, was killed in the Boer War.

◇ ◇ ◇

Second Lieutenant A. W. Bourke was the only son of Mr. and Mrs. C. E. Bourke, "Killala," Belfast. Lieutenant Bourke was a medical student of Queen's University, Belfast, and received his commission in the 3rd Royal Irish Fusiliers in August last. He was killed in action near Ypres on May 9th whilst gallantly leading a bomb party of the 1st Royal Irish Rifles to which he had been attached.

◇ ◇ ◇

Second Lieutenant Ray Lancaster Bell, who was killed in action near Ypres on the 17th May, in his nineteenth year, was the only son of Mr. and Mrs. Alfred Bell, of 33 Morehampton Road, Dublin, and late of Ardcarne, Ballinasloe.

1. LIEUT. H. C. GLOSTER, 6th Gordon Highlanders.
2. CAPT. F. W. WOOD-MARTIN, Suffolk Regiment.
3. LIEUT. J. O'GRADY DELMEGE, 4th Dragoon Guards.
4. CAPT. E. STAFFORD KING-HARMAN, Irish Guards.
5. LT.-COL. DERRICK A. CARDEN, Seaforth Highlanders.
6. CAPT. BASIL MACLEAR, Royal Dublin Fusiliers.
7. LIEUT. A. M. M'LAUGHLIN, Royal Irish Rifles.
8. LIEUT. A. W. BOURKE, Royal Irish Fusiliers.
9. LIEUT. RAY LANCASTER BELL, Royal Dublin Fusiliers.

OUR HEROES.

Lieutenant W. La Nauze, 4th Royal Irish Rifles, was the youngest son of the late Mr. T. S. La Nauze and Mrs. G. Scott-Mansfield. He was educated at the Abbey School, Tipperary, and joined the Special Reserve in June, 1914. He went with his regiment to the front on May 2nd and was only a fortnight there when he was killed in action on May 16th, in his 19th year.

✧ ✧ ✧

Captain Edward Graham Mylne, 1st Irish Guards, who died in No. II. Red Cross Hospital, Rouen, on June 12, of wounds received on May 13, was the eldest son of the Right Rev. L. G. Mylne, Rector of Alvechurch, Worcestershire, formerly Bishop of Bombay. He ran for Oxford against Cambridge in the 100 Yards in 1905. In the same year he received an appointment in the Royal Irish Constabulary, in which he served with distinction, obtaining special good service pay and other honours.

✧ ✧ ✧

Second Lieutenant Francis William Lynch, who was killed in action on April 26, near Ypres, was the third son of Mr. Henry C. Lynch, of Seaview House, Donnybrook, Ireland, and grandson of the late Mr. Commissioner Lynch. He was born on October 6, 1895, and was educated at the Oratory School, Edgbaston, where he won distinction. In October, 1913, he entered Trinity College, Dublin, and was a member of the Officers' Training Corps. On the outbreak of the war he joined the 4th Batt. Connaught Rangers, and fell at Neuve Chapelle, at the head of his platoon, cheering his men on in an endeavour to capture a German trench north of Ypres.

✧ ✧ ✧

Captain Eustace G. W. Bourke, King's Royal Rifles, who was killed in Belgium on June 16th, was the eldest son of Mr. Walter Bourke, of Monycrower, Maidenhead, and great-grandson of the 5th Earl of Mayo. He went to the front on August 12th, 1914. Was in command of the Machine Gun section of his battalion, and on October 26th he received a bullet wound in the foot and was sent home. Subsequently he was appointed Adjutant of the 6th (Reserve) Battalion of his Regiment, but at his urgent request he was transferred as Adjutant to the 9th (Service) Battalion, and on the 19th of that month he again proceeded to the front. He was killed within half-a-mile of the same place where he was previously wounded.

✧ ✧ ✧

Lieutenant-Colonel Ivon D'Esterre Roberts, R.F.A. (promoted to above rank previous to his death). He commanded the "Anson" Battalion of the Naval Division, and was killed in action on June 3rd, at Gallipoli, Dardanelles. He served through the South African War with distinction; also in Nigeria, India, Central Africa and Egypt. He was a member of an old Cork family; younger son of the late Major Richard Roberts, Norfolk Regiment, and grandson of Lieutenant R. Roberts, Royal Navy, who commanded the "Sirius," the first steamship to cross the Atlantic from Europe to America. Lieutenant-Colonel Ivon D'Esterre Roberts commanded the Egyptian Artillery at the Suez Canal, when they repulsed the Turkish Army, for which he received the congratulations and thanks of the Sultan and Government of Egypt.

✧ ✧ ✧

Captain Valentine Knox Gilliland, attached 2nd Battalion Royal Irish Rifles, aged 25, killed in action on May 8th, was the youngest surviving son of the late G. K. Gilliland, D.L., of Brook Hall, Londonderry. At the outbreak of the war Captain Gilliland was posted to the 3rd (Reserve) Battalion Royal Irish Rifles, stationed at Dublin, and proceeded to the front on January 18, having been promoted Captain two days previously from the rank of Second Lieutenant.

✧ ✧ ✧

Second Lieutenant Harold Charles Des Vœux, aged 19½ years, unattached Indian Army, attached to Royal Munster Fusiliers, killed at the Dardanelles on June 11, was the son of the late Lieutenant-General Sir Charles Hamilton Des Vœux, K.C.B., and Lady Des Vœux, of Palace Mansions, Kensington. He was educated at Wellington College, Sandhurst, and received his commission from Sandhurst last August.

✧ ✧ ✧

Captain James Hugh Christie, Royal Irish Regiment, was killed in action in France on May 24th. He was a son of Mr. Hugh Christie, of Woolton Manor, Yorkshire, and married in 1907 Miss Phyllis Beecher, daughter of Colonel Sullivan Beecher, 2nd King Edward's Own Gurkhas. Captain Christie served in the South African War and received both the King's and Queen's Medals. He was recommended for the V.C., but his colonel was shot in the same action before his intentions could be carried out. Captain Christie hunted for several seasons with the Duhallows, Limerick, Tipperary, Muskerry, South Union and several other packs.

✧ ✧ ✧

Lieutenant J. Rowe Dill, 69th Punjabs, Indian Army, was killed in action on Sunday, June 6th, in France. He was the third son of the Very Rev. Marcus Dill, D.D., Alloway, ex-Moderator of the General Assembly of the Church of Scotland, and formerly of the Presbyterian Church, Ballymena, County Antrim. Lieutenant Dill was in his 26th year. He joined the North Staffordshire Regiment in 1910, and was transferred to the Indian Army in 1911.

1. LIEUT. W. LA NAUZE, 4th Royal Irish Rifles.
2. CAPT. E. G. MYLNE, 1st Irish Guards.
3. LIEUT. F. W. LYNCH, Connaught Rangers.
4. CAPT. E. G. W. BOURKE, King's Royal Rifles.
5. LIEUT.-COL. I. D'ESTERRE ROBERTS, Royal Field Artillery.
6. CAPT. V. K. GILLILAND, Royal Irish Rifles.
7. LIEUT. H. C. DES VŒUX, Royal Munster Fusiliers.
8. CAPT. J. H. CHRISTIE, Royal Irish Regiment.
9. LIEUT. J. ROWE DILL, 69th Punjabs, Indian Army.

OUR HEROES.

Lieutenant H. K. O'Kelly, D.S.O., is the youngest son of Mr. W. H. O'Kelly, of Monkstown Castle, County Dublin. He left for the front early in August with his regiment, the 2nd Duke of Wellington's, was mentioned in Sir John French's first despatch for coolness and gallantry at the battles of Mons and Le Cateau. Later he was awarded the Distinguished Service Order for bravery at Crêcy ou Valois, on which occasion he and a few men captured some armoured motor cars containing the Headquarter Staff of the 1st German Cavalry Division. He was afterwards very severely wounded at Ypres.

✧ ✧ ✧

Colonel G. W. Brazier Creagh, C.M.G., who has recently been mentioned in despatches and has received the personal thanks of Sir John French for his organisation and care of the wounded on Ambulance Train Service, is an old Trinity College man and a well-known follower of "The Duhallows." This officer has seen much service in the Indian Frontier campaign and in the South African War, in connection with which he was thrice mentioned in despatches. He also conducted two political missions in Persia, Baluchistan, and again in China. Colonel Creagh takes a great interest in horse-breeding and racing in Ireland. He has been at the front since the outbreak of the war.

✧ ✧ ✧

Lieutenant Francis P. Freeman, R.A.M.C., has been mentioned in Sir John French's despatches. He is a son of Mr. David Freeman, Tudor House, Monkstown, and was educated at Clongowes College. He qualified as a Doctor just before the outbreak of the war and was for a short time House-Surgeon at the City of Dublin Hospital. He went to the front in October, attached to the 22nd Brigade, Royal Field Artillery, and has ever since been in the thick of the fighting.

✧ ✧ ✧

Captain M. L. Lakin, 11th Hussars, who has been mentioned in despatches for distinguished service in the field, is a son of Sir Michael and Lady Lakin, and married in July last the only daughter of Lady Maurice Fitzgerald, of Johnstown Castle, Wexford. Captain Lakin served in the South African War and in the Mediterranean and received a Medal. He is well known in the hunting field, being the popular Master of the Wexford Hunt.

✧ ✧ ✧

Surgeon-General M. W. O'Keeffe, R.A.M.C., who has been mentioned in despatches for his services on the Headquarters Staff, is a son of the late William O'Keeffe, M.D., who practised in Mallow, County Cork. He is a graduate of the old Queen's College, Cork. He served during the first Egyptian campaign, also in some Indian Frontier campaigns, and held the position of Inspector of Medical Service for four years, until the war opened when he was appointed one of the Assistant Medical Directors. The Order of the Bath has been conferred on Surgeon-General O'Keeffe.

✧ ✧ ✧

Captain Charles V. Fox, 2nd Scots Guards, has been awarded the D.S.O. for "conspicuous gallantry at Kruiseik, in which he captured five officers and 200 men." His previous record is a remarkably brilliant one. He has been mentioned in despatches at least seven times. He has the West African Medal and seven clasps, the Soudan Medal and one clasp, and the Mejidieh, a decoration bestowed on him by the Khedive of Egypt for his success in the Bier and Annak Expeditions. Captain Fox was educated at Clongowes College, and is a son of Mrs. Fox, Brookfield, Milltown, Dublin.

✧ ✧ ✧

Lieutenant George Rowland Patrick Roupell, 1st Battalion, East Surrey Regiment, who was recently awarded the Victoria Cross, is the second son of Colonel F. Fyler-Roupell, of Chartham, Westbourne, Bournemouth. Lieutenant Roupell was born in Tipperary when his father, Colonel Fyler-Roupell, was with his regiment at that town. Lieutenant Roupell, on securing his commission, joined this regiment at Kinsale and accompanied it from Dublin, whence he proceeded to the front in the early weeks of the war.

✧ ✧ ✧

Captain D. Nelson, Royal Field Artillery, is yet another Irishman who has been awarded the V.C. Captain Nelson landed in France on August 16th, 1914, was slightly wounded at the battle of Mons on August 24th, whilst doing the work of a section officer and another officer, both of whom had been wounded. At Nery, on September 1st, he brought, with the assistance of a gunner, the first gun into action in the "L" Battery exploit, and continued to serve it until the enemy's eight guns, 600 yards away, were silenced. He was wounded slightly in the leg and seriously in the right lung and ribs. He was taken prisoner on September 2nd, but escaped on the 5th and reached the French Hospital at Dinan on the 9th. He was granted convalescent leave after an operation, and returning home was gazetted Captain Instructor in Gunnery at Shoeburyness on March 1st, 1915, which post he at present holds.

✧ ✧ ✧

Lieutenant J. F. Ruttledge, eldest son of Lieutenant-Colonel A. Ruttledge, of The Woodlands, Castleconnell, was gazetted on 24th February, 1914, to his father's old regiment, the 2nd Batt. Prince of Wales's Own (West Yorkshire) Regiment. He was awarded the Military Cross for great coolness and gallantry near Neuve Chapelle on December 19th, 1914, for rescuing, under very heavy machine and rifle fire, wounded men lying in the open " on no man's land."

1. LIEUT. H. K. O'KELLY,
2nd Duke of Wellington's.
D.S.O.

4. CAPT. M. L. LAKIN,
11th Hussars.

7. LIEUT. G. R. P. ROUPELL,
East Surrey Regiment.
V.C.

2. COL. G. W. BRAZIER CREAGH,
C.M.G.

5. SURG.-GEN. M. W. O'KEEFFE,
R.A.M.C.

8. CAPT. D. NELSON,
Royal Field Artillery.
V.C.

3. LIEUT. FRANCIS P. FREEMAN,
R.A.M.C.

6. CAPT. C. V. FOX,
2nd Scots Guards.
D.S.O.

9. LIEUT. J. F. RUTTLEDGE,
2nd Battalion Prince of Wales' Own.
Military Cross.

OUR HEROES.

Captain the Hon. A. M. Henley, 5th Lancers, served in the South African War and took part in the operations in the Transvaal in May and June, 1900, including actions near Johannisberg and Pretoria. He was also present during the operations on the Zululand Frontier of Natal in September and October, 1901, and in Cape Colony in May, 1902. He then obtained the Queen's Medal with three clasps and the King's Medal with two clasps. Capt. Henley has been promoted to the rank of Brevet-Major for distinguished service in the field.

✧ ✧ ✧

Lieutenant Herbert Francis Otway, Prince of Wales's Leinster Regiment (Royal Canadians), has been awarded the Military Cross for the conspicuous ability he showed in making important reconnaissances under heavy shell fire. His reconnaissances were of the greatest value to the Divisional Commander at Potijze and were always carried out at considerable risk. Lieutenant Otway is a graduate of Trinity College, Dublin, and obtained his commission from the O.T.C. in the 1st Batt. Leinster Regiment in the autumn of 1913. He is a son of Mr. J. Otway, 18 Westby Road, Boscombe, Hants.

✧ ✧ ✧

Captain C. Ridings, 1st Batt. Royal Inniskilling Fusiliers, who has been awarded the D.S.O. for gallantry and devotion to duty in connection with the operations at the Dardanelles, served in the South African War and took part in the relief of Ladysmith and the action at Colenso. He also took part in the operations on the Tugela Heights in February, 1900, and subsequently in the Transvaal and Orange River Colony. For his services during that period he was awarded the Queen's Medal with five clasps and the King's Medal with two clasps.

✧ ✧ ✧

Major W. H. Odlum, of the Indian Medical Service, who was attached to the 112th Indian Field Ambulance, has been mentioned in Sir John French's despatches for gallant and distinguished service in the field. He is a brother of Mrs. Gardiner, wife of Mr. A. G. Gardiner, sub-agent of the Bank of Ireland, Roscommon.

✧ ✧ ✧

Major T. E. Fielding, Royal Army Medical Corps, who has been awarded the D.S.O., is a son of Major Fielding, late Adjutant of the Royal Hospital, Dublin. He served in the South African War and took part in the operations in the Transvaal, in the Orange River Colony and in Cape Colony. Also during the operations on the Zululand Frontier of Natal, September and October, 1901, including the defence of Fort Itala. On that occasion Major Fielding was mentioned in despatches and obtained the Queen's Medal with three clasps and the King's Medal with two clasps.

Major Baptist Johnston Barton, D.S.O., Duke of Wellingon's Regiment, joined the Duke of Wellington's Regiment, from Sandhurst, in 1896, and retired in 1911. On the outbreak of war he rejoined the 2nd Battalion, and was present at the battles of the Marne and Aisne, the fighting near La Bassée and Festubert, and the first battle of Ypres. He was wounded, mentioned in despatches, and awarded the D.S.O. He also served with the 2nd Battalion during the months of March, April and May, in the fighting near Ypres, including the taking of Hill 60. He was again mentioned in despatches and promoted Major in the Reserve of Officers. He is the eldest son of the late Colonel Baptist Johnston Barton, D.L., A.D.C., of Portsalon, County Donegal.

✧ ✧ ✧

Captain H. C. Crozier, 1st Batt. Royal Dublin Fusiliers, was with his regiment in the landing at the Dardanelles, when he was dangerously wounded and awarded the Military Cross. Lieutenant Crozier is the second son of the late Mr. James Crozier, Montpelier Hill, Dublin, and was educated at High School, Harcourt Street, and Dublin University. He was a well known member of Bohemian Football Club, and maintained his interest in the game after joining his regiment, captaining the regimental team which won the Egyptian Shield, the principal Association trophy in Egypt. When in Egypt Captain Crozier was awarded the Medal of the Royal Humane Society for trying to save the life of a brother officer who had fallen into the Nile.

✧ ✧ ✧

Lieutenant J. F. Hodges, 2nd Batt. Royal Irish Fusiliers, who has recently been mentioned in Sir John French's despatches and awarded the Military Cross, is a son of Mr. J. F. W. Hodges, Glenravel House, County Antrim. Lieutenant Hodges went to the front in December, 1914, from India, where he had been with his regiment for two years previous to the outbreak of war. He has again returned to the front on his recovery from a severe wound received at St. Eloi. His younger brother, Lieutenant H. B. Hodges was killed in action on June 15th.

✧ ✧ ✧

Captain J. J. Kavanagh, 3rd Batt. Connaught Rangers, has been promoted Captain for distinguished conduct and bravery on the battlefield. He was gazetted temporary Lieutenant in the Connaught Rangers and left for the front on March 4th. He took part in the battle of Neuve Chapelle and has since been in many engagements. He is the eldest son of Mr. P. J. Kavanagh, solicitor, Cork.

1. CAPT. HON. A. M. HENLEY,
5th Royal Irish Lancers.

2. LIEUT. H. F. OTWAY,
Prince of Wales's Leinster Regiment.
Military Cross.

3. CAPT. C. RIDINGS,
1st Batt. Royal Inniskilling Fusiliers.
D.S.O.

4. MAJOR W. H. COLUM,
Indian Medical Service.

5. MAJOR T. E. FIELDING,
R.A.M.C.
D.S.O.

6. MAJOR B. J. BARTON,
Duke of Wellington's Regiment.
D.S.O.

7. CAPT. H. C. CROZIER,
Royal Dublin Fusiliers.
Military Cross.

8. LIEUT. J. F. HODGES,
Royal Irish Fusiliers.
Military Cross.

9. CAPT. J. J. KAVANAGH,
3rd Batt. Connaught Rangers.

OUR HEROES.

Lieutenant V. D. French, 5th Battalion, Shropshire Light Infantry, died on June 16th of wounds received in action in France on the previous day. He was the third son of the Hon. John French, Resident Magistrate, Queenstown. He had served previously in the 5th Munster Fusiliers, but went to Malay, where he was for seven years manager of the Shelford Rubber Estates. On the outbreak of war he returned home and joined the Shropshire Light Infantry, and left with his regiment for the front on the 20th May. Only a short time previously his cousins, Lord de Freyne and the Hon. John French were killed in the same action.

❖ ❖ ❖

Captain Reginald H. C. Gilliat, 5th Battalion Leinster Regiment (attached to the 1st Batt. Connaught Rangers), was killed in action in France on April 6th, in his 30th year. He was the second son of Mr. Cecil Gilliat and Mrs. Gilliat, Arch Hall, County Meath, and twin brother of Captain C. G. P. Gilliat, 1st Batt. Royal Warwickshire Regiment, who was killed in action on October 13th last.

❖ ❖ ❖

Lieutenant J. A. R. M'Cormick, Royal Naval Volunteer Reserve, was killed in action in the Dardanelles. He joined the Volunteer Reserve about the end of September and was first in the "Hawk" Battalion and afterwards transferred to the "Nelson" Battalion. He was afterwards sent to Egypt, but was there only a few weeks when he was ordered to the Dardanelles and was in the second landing there. He was the only son of Mr. T. C. M'Cormick, Blackrock House, Blackrock.

❖ ❖ ❖

Captain Sylvester Cecil Rait Kerr, R.F.A., was the second son of Sylvester Rait Kerr. He was born at Rathmoyle, Edenderry, King's County, on October 14th, 1887, and was educated at Arnold House, Llanddulas; Rugby School, and the Royal Military Academy, Woolwich. He was gazetted Second Lieutenant on December 18th, 1907; First Lieutenant on December 18th, 1910, and Captain on November 4th, 1914. Most of his service was spent abroad. He was home on leave from India when war broke out and went to the front in "G" Battery R.H.A. in November, 1914, and was afterwards transferred to 41st Battery, 42nd Brigade R.F.A. In April, 1915, he was given command of a trench Howitzer Battery and fell near La Brique, north of Ypres, on May 13th, shot by a German sniper. He is said to have done splendid work with his battery.

❖ ❖ ❖

Rev. Father Finn, the heroic Chaplain of the 1st Battalion, Royal Dublin Fusiliers, was killed in the Dardanelles whilst gallantly attending to the wounded. He insisted on landing with the troops in face of a terrible cannonade of field artillery, machine-guns and rifles. Father Finn was requested to remain on board the troopship *Clyde,* but insisted on accompanying his men, and was killed in the boat before they reached the shore. In the same action the Colonel, the two Majors, and all the senior officers were either killed or wounded. Father Finn was on the Yorkshire Mission before joining the army.

❖ ❖ ❖

Captain William Charles Rait Kerr, D.S.O., R.F.A., eldest son of Sylvester Rait Kerr, was born at Rathmoyle, Edenderry, King's County, on August 6th, 1886. He was educated at Arnold House, Llanddulas; Rugby School, and the R.M. Academy, Woolwich. He was gazetted Second Lieutenant on July 28th, 1907, and First Lieutenant on July 10th, 1910. On August 16th, 1914, he went to the front, and was through the retreat from Mons, fought on the Marne and on the Aisne and at Ypres. On the morning of November 10th, 1914, he was killed by a German sniper at Veldhoek, four miles east of Ypres, while in command of an advanced gun, having just gained the D.S.O. for " gallant conduct in bringing up a gun to within 250 yards of the enemy in a wood and blowing down a house in which the enemy were working a machine gun." Captain Rait Kerr had passed most of his service in Ireland, and had hunted with the Kildare, Westmeath and Tipperary hounds.

❖ ❖ ❖

Lieutenant R. M. B. Gamble, 7th Batt. King's Liverpool Regiment, was killed at Festurbet on May 16th, in a successful attack on the German trenches by his regiment. He joined at the outbreak of the war and received his commission in September, 1914. He was the eldest son of Mrs. Richard K. Gamble, 51 Fitzwilliam Square.

❖ ❖ ❖

Captain Eric Lockhart Hume Henderson, 1st Royal Munster Fusiliers, was the son of Colonel W. Hume Henderson, I.M.S., and Mrs. Hume Henderson; grandson of Dr. Samuel Gordon, of 13 Hume Street, Dublin. He was educated at Loretto, was gazetted to 1st Royal Munster Fusiliers in 1900, and served through part of the Boer War. The greater part of his service was spent in India and Burmah. He was amongst the very first to land at Gallipoli, and was severely wounded whilst leading his men, and died from the effects of wounds on 20th May, at Alexandria.

❖ ❖ ❖

Lieutenant Bernard Conroy, 4th Batt. Royal Dublin Fusiliers, who was killed in action in Flanders, was a son of a former Chief Clerk to the Maryborough District Asylum. He joined the Army at the age of 18 and served in Egypt, India, Malta, and through the South African campaign. He held two medals with five clasps. His mother, who lives at Elm Park Avenue, Ranelagh, has received letters from the officers of the regiment expressing their regret at the loss the regiment has sustained by the death of "a most gallant and capable officer."

1. LIEUT. V. D. FRENCH, Shropshire Light Infantry.
2. CAPT. R. H. C. GILLIAT, Leinster Regiment.
3. LIEUT. J. A. R. M'CORMICK, R.N.V.R.
4. CAPT. S. C. RAIT KERR, Royal Field Artillery.
5. REV. FATHER FINN, 1st Batt., Royal Dublin Fusiliers.
6. CAPT. W. C. RAIT KERR, Royal Field Artillery.
7. LIEUT. R. M. B. GAMBLE, King's Liverpool Regiment.
8. CAPT. E. L. HUME HENDERSON, Royal Munster Fusiliers.
9. LIEUT. BERNARD CONROY, Royal Dublin Fusiliers.

OUR HEROES.

Lieutenant E. J. K. Pemberton Pigott, 1st Royal Irish Regiment, was the third son of Surgeon-Colonel F. K. Pemberton Pigott, of Belmont House, Shrewsbury, and grandson of the late Captain George P. Pigott, of Slavoy Castle, County Wexford. He was gazetted in January, 1914, to the 1st Batt. Royal Irish Regiment, which he joined in India. At the outbreak of the war he returned with his regiment and went to the front. He was made Machine Gun Officer, and was killed in action on June 24th, having saved his guns.

✧ ✧ ✧

Captain Frank Robertson, 2nd Royal Fusiliers, was wounded on June 4th at the Dardanelles and succumbed the following day. He joined Queen Victoria's Rifles at the outbreak of the war and afterwards received a commission in the 12th Worcestershire Regiment. He was very quickly promoted to the rank of Captain and at the time of his death was attached to the 2nd Royal Fusiliers. He was the youngest son of the late James Robertson, Newtown Lodge, Waterford.

✧ ✧ ✧

Lieutenant Charles Frederick Fearn, 4th Batt. Royal Inniskilling Fusiliers, died from the effects of wounds received in the engagement at Noyelles on July 4th. He was the elder son of Mr. and Mrs. Charles Fearn, of Stanwell, Middlesex, and was educated at St. Andrew's, Eastbourne and Malvern College. He was gazetted on August 15th to the 4th Royal Inniskilling Fusiliers, but was attached to the 2nd Royal Munster Fusiliers and was with that regiment at the time of his death.

✧ ✧ ✧

Captain Stephen Ussher, 129th Duke of Connaught's Own Baluchis, Indian Army, was killed at Givenchy on December 16th last. Captain Ussher came of an Irish family, his father, Rev. Richard Ussher, Vicar of Westbury, North Hants, being a native of County Waterford. Captain Ussher was educated at St. Edward's School, Oxford, and the Royal Military College, Sandhurst. He was first attached to the Buffs at Poona in 1902, and in 1904 was appointed to the Baluchis; he received his Captaincy in 1911 and served as Adjutant to the regiment for four years.

✧ ✧ ✧

Captain G. Smith, Gordon Highlanders, who was recently mentioned in despatches by Sir John French, was killed on June 6th in action in France. Captain Smith received his commission in the Gordon Highlanders in 1911. He had been through several engagements before his death on June 6th. He was a grandson of the late Mr. R. Workman, Ceara, Belfast, and a cousin of Mr. G. S. Clark, of Messrs. Workman, Clark & Co., Ltd.

Captain Beverley Ussher, Leinster Regiment, went out with the Mediterranean Expeditionary Force as Staff Captain and was killed at the Dardanelles. Captain Ussher was a son of the Rev. R. Ussher, Vicar of Westbury, Brackley, Northampton. He was born in 1879, was educated at St. Edward's School and Wadham College, Oxford, and in 1900 received a University commission in the Leinsters. For service in the South African War he received the Queen's Medal with four clasps. His brother, Captain Stephen Ussher, 129th Baluchis, was killed in action in France in December last.

✧ ✧ ✧

Lieutenant Henry d'Esterre Head, 2nd Batt. Royal Dublin Fusiliers, died from the effects of gas poisoning in France on June 1st. He was appointed to the Royal Dublin Fusiliers in October last and went to the front with his regiment in December, and had been through much severe fighting. Lieutenant Head was educated at Monkstown Park School, and at Bromsgrove, and passed into the Royal Military College, Sandhurst. He was the eldest son of Mr. d'Esterre Prittie Head, M.I.C.E., who is Chief Engineer on the Government Railways in South Africa. Lieutenant Head is a grandson of Mrs. Head, Clarinda Park, Kingstown.

✧ ✧ ✧

Captain Harold Gordon Wilmer, 14th Sikhs, who was killed in action at the Dardanelles, was the elder son of Colonel John Randal Wilmer, 91 Warwick Road, London, and husband of Mrs. Violet Wilmer, 23 Pembroke Park, Dublin. He had seen active service in East Africa in 1903-4, when he took part in operations in Somaliland and received the Medal with clasp. He entered the Indian Staff College in February, 1914, but rejoined his regiment at the outbreak of the war and left with it for service in Egypt, but was shortly afterwards appointed Staff Captain to the Indian Infantry Brigade and proceeded to the Dardanelles, where he took part in the memorable landing in April last.

✧ ✧ ✧

Lieutenant A. E. C. T. Dooner, 1st Batt. Royal Welsh Fusiliers, was killed in action at Zanvoorde, near Ypres. The deceased officer was 22 years of age and was the third son of Colonel Dooner, of Ditton Place, Maidstone, Kent, who was well known in Dublin and the North of Ireland a few years ago, having served as Brigade Major at the Curragh and afterwards in command of the Royal Irish Fusiliers Depôt at Armagh. Lieut. Dooner was a magnificent athlete and a splendid rifle shot. Lieutenant Dooner was shot while returning to his Colonel after having given an order to another trench, Colonel Cadogan, who went to his assistance, being shot at the same time.

1. LIEUT. E. J. K. PEMBERTON PIGOTT, Royal Irish Regiment.	2. CAPT. H. G. WILMER, 14th Sikhs.	3. LIEUT. C. F. FEARN, Royal Inniskilling Fusiliers.
4. CAPT. STEPHEN USSHER, 129th Baluchis.	5. CAPT. BEVERLEY USSHER, Leinster Regiment.	6. CAPT. G. SMITH, Gordon Highlanders.
7. LIEUT. H. d'ESTERRE HEAD, 2nd Batt. Royal Dublin Fusiliers.	8. CAPT. FRANK ROBERTSON, 2nd Royal Fusiliers.	9. LIEUT. A. E. C. T. DOONER, Royal Welsh Fusiliers.

Our Heroes

OUR HEROES.

Captain Gerald Robert O'Sullivan, V.C., 1st Royal Inniskilling Fusiliers, who was reported missing on August 21st, is now believed to have been killed on that date during the attack on Hill 70, or Burnt Hill, at Suvla Bay. He was seen to advance at the head of his men to the second line of Turkish trenches, where he fell. Captain O'Sullivan was the son of the late Lieutenant-Colonel George Lidnill O'Sullivan, 91st Argyle and Sutherland Highlanders, and of Mrs. O'Sullivan, Rowan House, Dorchester. He passed into Sandhurst in 1907, and was gazetted to his regiment, 1st Royal Inniskilling Fusiliers, on May 15, 1909. Captain O'Sullivan was awarded the V.C. for conspicuous gallantry on two occasions at the Dardanelles on June 18th-19th and July 1st-2nd. The official record of his deeds is as follows:—" For most conspicuous bravery during operations south-west of Krithia, on the Gallipoli Peninsula. On the night of July 1st-2nd, 1915, when it was essential that a portion of a trench which had been lost should be regained, Captain O'Sullivan, although not belonging to the troops at this point, volunteered to lead a party of bomb-throwers to effect the recapture. He advanced in the open under a very heavy fire, and, in order to throw his bombs with greater effect, got up on the parapet, where he was completely exposed to the fire of the enemy occupying the trench. He was finally wounded, but not before his inspiring example had led on his party to make further efforts, which resulted in the recapture of the trench. On the night of June 18th-19th, 1915, Captain O'Sullivan saved a critical situation in the same locality by his great personal gallantry and good leading."

Lieutenant George Arthur Boyd Rochfort, Scots Guards, has just returned to the front from a well-earned rest spent at his family seat, Middleton Park, Westmeath. Lieutenant Rochfort won his V.C. by a brilliant exploit. He was in a trench with about forty of his men when a mortar bomb from the German lines hurtled over the parapet. He at once realised the danger and springing forward caught the bomb just before it reached the ground and flung it back over the parapet, where it exploded with a terrific report, burying Lieut. Rochfort and his comrades under the falling earth, but fortunately without inflicting any injuries. Lieutenant Rochfort's father, Major R. H. Boyd Rochfort, 15th Hussars, was formerly High Sheriff for the County Westmeath, and a member of the old Grand Jury. Lieut. Rochfort is well known not alone in Westmeath but throughout Ireland as an expert polo player and has frequently played in inter-county matches and on All-Ireland teams, and is also a well-known follower of the Westmeath hounds. He is the second Westmeath soldier to receive the V.C.

Sergeant James Somers, 1st Batt. Inniskilling Fusiliers, was awarded the V.C. for conspicuous gallantry displayed in the retaking of a trench by throwing bombs amongst the Turks from the open though exposed to heavy rifle fire. When the trench was finally captured he advanced and held back the enemy until the barricade was re-established. Sergeant Somers was in the retreat from Mons, where he received a wound from the effects of which he was in hospital for some time. He went with the 1st Inniskillings to the Dardanelles in March last and took part in the memorable landing. He was born in Belturbet, Co. Cavan, but at present his parents reside at Cloughjordan, Co. Tipperary.

Corporal William Cosgrave, Munster Fusiliers, has been awarded the V.C. for distinguished gallantry. When in the attack on the Turkish position at Cape Helles he, disdaining cover, rushed forward in advance of his section and pulled up the stakes holding up the enemy's wire entanglements. He is yet another Irishman who has upheld the splendid traditions of his country and his regiment.

Private Robert Morrow, 87th Royal Irish Fusiliers, was awarded the V.C. for gallantry at Messina on April 12th last in rescuing on his own initiative wounded soldiers whilst exposed to heavy shell fire. The gallant young hero was killed thirteen days afterwards at St. Julien before he actually received the Victoria Cross, which has been sent to his widowed mother who resides at Sessia, Newmills, Co. Tyrone. The Emperor of Russia has also conferred on the gallant young hero the Medal of St. George, 3rd Class. The Faugh-a-Ballaghs, though a renowned fighting regiment never before earned the V.C., and are naturally proud of the young soldier who has obtained for the regiment the coveted distinction. A portrait of Private Morrow, V.C., is being included in a large commemoration painting which is being executed for the French Government, by M. Cairier-Belleux.

FOR VALOUR

FIVE IRISH V.C'S.

OUR HEROES.

Major H. E. O'Brien Traill, of Westview, Portallintrae, Co. Antrim, has been at the front for the past twelve months, and has been mentioned in Sir John French's despatches for distinguished service. Major Traill also served with distinction in the South African War, for which he obtained the Queen's Medal.

Father Gill, S.J., who was mentioned in Sir John French's despatches, belongs to a well-known Dublin family. He gave up some very important scientific work in order to go to the front. He is an M.A. of Cambridge University, where he obtained a research degree through an important discovery in electricity. Father Gill has been attached to the 2nd Royal Irish Rifles since he went out in November last, and has been with the regiment at the front ever since.

Major Burns=Lindow, South Irish Horse, has on several occasions been mentioned in Sir John French's despatches for gallantry and distinguished service. Previous to the outbreak of the war he was Master of the South Union Hunt. In his absence Mrs. Burns-Lindow has acted as master.

Major Elliott Beverley Bird, R.A.M.C., who has been mentioned in despatches, is the only son of Mr. Geo. Beverley Bird, King's Own Yorkshire Light Infantry, and nephew of the late Captain Hollway Steeds, of Clonsilla, Co. Dublin. Major Bird married, in 1909, the Hon. Gladys Rice, eldest daughter of the 6th Baron Dynevor. He was educated at Cheltenham College and Trinity College, Dublin, and is a Licentiate of the Royal College of Physicians and Surgeons of Ireland.

Lieutenant=Colonel Arthur Milton Bent, C.M.G., 2nd Royal Munster Fusiliers, only surviving son of the late Lieutenant-Colonel George Bent, King's Own Borderers, was appointed to the command of his battalion a year ago when serving as senior Major of the 1st Battalion of his regiment at Rangoon. He joined the 2nd Munsters in France, and was with them during the first battle of Ypres, and was dangerously wounded at Festubert on 22nd December, being twice mentioned in despatches. He was made a Companion of the Order of St. Michael and St. George. Colonel Bent has spent most of his service in the East, and has the South African and Mohmand campaigns to his credit. He was educated at Wellington, and joined the Royal Munster Fusiliers from Sandhurst in 1890.

Major E. Neville Townsend, 2nd Duke of Wellington's Regiment, has been mentioned in Sir John French's despatches, and is now a prisoner of war in Germany. Major Townsend served in the South African War and was present at the relief of Kimberley and the operations in the Transvaal and Orange Free State, in the course of which he was dangerously wounded and received the Queen's Medal with six clasps. Major Townsend left Dublin in August, 1914, with his regiment for the front, and was severely wounded at the battle of Mons.

Captain W. W. Boyce, R.A.M.C., who has been mentioned in despatches, is a son of Dr. Wallace Boyce, St. Kilda, Blackrock, Co. Dublin. He was educated at Avoca School, Blackrock, and Trent College, Derbyshire. He obtained his commission in 1906 and served in the Punjab for some years. He left for France on the outbreak of the war, and was attached to the Guards Brigade, and is at present in command of a motor ambulance convoy.

Major Baptist Barton Crozier, D.S.O., R.F.A., is the eldest son of the Most Rev. Dr. Crozier, Archbishop of Armagh. He received the Companionship of the Distinguished Service Order for his conduct on March 10th and 11th, 1915, being specially noted in the Army order as "conspicuous for gallantry and coolness under fire throughout the campaign." He has been twice wounded in action. Major Crozier served with distinction in the South African War, and now commands the 56th (Howitzer) Battery Royal Field Artillery in Flanders.

Lieutenant J. L. Whitty, Prince of Wales's Leinster Regiment, has been mentioned in Sir John French's despatches, and awarded the Military Cross. He is the third son of Lieut.-Colonel M. J. Whitty, R.A.M.C., M.I.R., and one of four sons serving in the regular army.

1. MAJOR H. E. O'BRIEN TRAILL, Royal Artillery.	2. REV. FATHER GILL, S.J. 2nd Royal Irish Rifles.	3. MAJOR BURNS-LINDOW, South Irish Horse.
4. MAJOR E. B. BIRD, 26th Field Ambulance Corps.	5. COLONEL A. M. BENT, 2nd Royal Munster Fusiliers.	6. MAJOR E. NEVILLE TOWNSEND, 2nd Duke of Wellington's Regiment.
7. CAPT. W. W. BOYCE, R.A.M.C.	8. MAJOR BAPTIST B. CROZIER. Royal Field Artillery.	9. LIEUT. J. L. WHITTY, 1st Batt. Leinster Regiment.

OUR HEROES.

Second Lieut. Hugh Maurice MacDermot, 6th Batt. Royal Irish Fusiliers, aged 19, who was killed in action at the Dardanelles between August 7th and 10th last, was the eldest son of The MacDermot, D.L. (Prince of Coolavin), Vice-Chairman of the Irish Prisons Board, and grandson of the Rt. Hon. The MacDermot, P.C., D.L., late Attorney-General for Ireland. He was educated at the Oratory School, Edgbaston, Birmingham. He was a very promising cricketer and played on his school eleven in 1914, when he won the Edgbaston Cup for the highest bowling average.

◇ ◇ ◇

Lieutenant James Edward Thornhill Nelis, 5th Inniskilling Fusiliers, who was killed in action at the Dardanelles on August 15th last, was the only son of Lieut.-Colonel and Mrs. J. A. Nelis, 1 Seaview Terrace, Donnybrook. Lieut. Nelis was educated at Haileybury. He subsequently entered Trinity College, Dublin, and became a member of the Officers' Training Corps. Shortly after the outbreak of the war he received his commission in the Inniskillings.

◇ ◇ ◇

Lieutenant Andrew Hubert Fairnbairn, 3rd Batt. Royal Irish Regiment, attached to the 2nd Batt., died on June 5th last at Oost Nieukerke of wounds received in action near Ypres on May 24th. Lieut. Fairnbairn was in his 22nd year, and was the elder son of Mr. and Mrs. A. C. Fairnbairn, 25 Campden Grove, Kensington, London. He was educated at Cheltenham College, where he was a member of the Officers' Training Corps, and at Wye Agricultural College in Kent. Shortly after the outbreak of the war he obtained his commission in the 5th Royal Irish Lancers. After serving for some months on embarkation duty at Dublin he was gazetted to the 3rd Royal Irish, being subsequently attached to the 2nd.

◇ ◇ ◇

Major William Fortescue Colborne Garstin, 5th Batt. Royal Irish Fusiliers, was killed in action at the Dardanelles between the 7th and 10th August last. Major Garstin was born at Glasthule House, Kingstown, in 1875, and was the only son of Mr. John R. Garstin, D.L., Braganstown, Co. Louth. Major Garstin took part in the South African War with the 2nd Batt., obtaining the Queen's Medal with two clasps. The Garstin family, which has been associated with the Co. Louth since the 17th century, has a long and distinguished military record.

◇ ◇ ◇

Lieutenant-Colonel J. Clark, C.B., K.C., D.L., 9th Batt. Argyle and Sutherland Highlanders, was killed in action in France on May 10th last while gallantly leading his men in action. Colonel Clark was the eldest son of the late Mr. James Clark, Chapel House, Paisley, and a brother of Mr. George S. Clark, D.L., Dunlambert, Belfast. He was a well-known and popular figure in the North of Ireland and a very eloquent and effective speaker. He was educated at Pau (France), Paisley, and the Glasgow and Edinburgh Universities, being an M.A. of the former and an LL.B. of the latter. At the outbreak of the war he offered his services and was given command of the 9th Argyle and Sutherland Highlanders, and went with his regiment to France in February last.

◇ ◇ ◇

Captain John Miller, 6th Royal Welsh Fusiliers, who has been killed in action, was well known in Ireland in connection with engineering and scientific work. He was for many years member of the engineering staff of Messrs. A. Guinness, Son & Co., and was one of the founders of the Engineering and Scientific Association of Ireland. He was the eldest son of Mr. and Mrs. John J. Miller, Dalesworth House, Mansfield, Nottingham, and was educated at Mansfield Grammar School and Nottingham University.

◇ ◇ ◇

Second Lieutenant P. Sidney Snell was killed in action at the Dardanelles on August 9th last. He was in his 22nd year and was the only son of Mr. Philip W. Snell, 32 Upper Mount-street, Dublin. Lieut. Snell was educated at Campbell College, Belfast, where he was a member of the Officers' Training Corps and a very fine cricketer. He subsequently entered Trinity College Medical School and joined the Officers' Training Corps there. On the outbreak of the war he at once volunteered and was given a commission in the 6th Royal Irish Fusiliers.

◇ ◇ ◇

Lieutenant H. M'Cormac, 5th Batt. Royal Inniskilling Fusiliers, was killed in action at the Dardanelles, was a son of the late Mr. Samuel H. M'Cormac, Cnoc Aluin, Dalkey, and was well known in Rugby football circles in Dublin, with his twin-brother Fred, of the Wanderers' team, who is also at the front with the Inniskilling Fusiliers. On the outbreak of war Lieut. M'Cormac at once offered his services to his country and obtained his commission in the 5th Inniskillings.

◇ ◇ ◇

Second Lieutenant Frederick Hamilton Norway, 2nd Batt. Duke of Cornwall's Light Infantry, has died in hospital in France from the effects of wounds sustained on June 13th, when the section of the trench of which he was in command was blown up by a German mine. Lieut. Norway thereupon collected a few unwounded men and led them out over the parapet of the trench under heavy shell-fire to dig out their comrades, in doing which he was struck by a shell, from the effects of which he died later. Lieut. Norway was the elder son of Mr. Arthur H. Norway, South Hill, Blackrock, and was only in his 19th year. He was educated at Rugby and subsequently entered Trinity College, but on the outbreak of the war he at once volunteered and left for the front.

Supplement to Irish Life, September 24th, 1915.

1. LIEUT. H. M. MacDERMOT,
6th Batt. Royal Irish Fusiliers.

2. LIEUT. J. E. T. NELIS,
5th Batt. Royal Inniskilling Fusiliers.

3. LIEUT. A. H. FAIRNBAIRN,
3rd Batt. Royal Irish Regiment.

4. MAJOR W. F. C. GARSTIN,
5th Batt. Royal Irish Fusiliers.

5. LT.-COL. J. CLARK, C.B., K.C.,
9th Batt. Argyle and Sutherland Highlanders.

6. CAPT. J. MILLER,
6th Batt. Royal Welsh Fusiliers.

7. LIEUT. P. S. SNELL,
6th Batt. Royal Irish Fusiliers.

8. LIEUT. H. McCORMAC,
5th Batt. Royal Inniskilling Fusiliers.

9. LIEUT. F. H. NORWAY,
2nd Batt. Duke of Cornwall's Light Infantry.

OUR HEROES.

Lieutenant Peyton Tollemache Warren, R.A.M.C., who has been killed in action at the Dardanelles, was the eldest son of Mr. Peyton Warren, Rosario, Sandymount-avenue, and grandson of the late Serjeant Armstrong. Dr. Warren was a Licentiate of the College of Surgeons of Ireland, and was 26 years of age at the time of his death. His brothers are also in the Army; Lieut. H. P. Warren in the 56th Canadians and Second-Lieut. R. P. Warren in the Army Service Corps.

◇ ◇ ◇

Captain Hubert John Coddington, 2nd Durham Light Infantry, who was killed in action on July 7th last, was the second son of Lieut.-Colonel Coddington, D.L., Oldbridge, Drogheda. Captain Coddington served in the South African War and took part in the operations in the Transvaal and Orange River Colony in 1901 and 1902. He was a very able officer, and for his services in the South African War, in the course of which he was wounded, he obtained the Queen's Medal with four clasps.

◇ ◇ ◇

Second Lieutenant Gilbert Kennedy, Cameronians, 16th Scottish Rifles, who was killed in action at Festurbet on the 15th June last, was the eldest son of the Rev. Gilbert Kennedy, parish minister of Cambusnethan, Lanarkshire. Lieut. Kennedy was born in the Manse of Aghadoey, Co. Derry, on the 5th March, 1895, where his father was minister at that time. He was a nephew of Dr. John Kennedy, medical officer, Portstewart, Co. Derry. On the outbreak of the war he immediately volunteered and received his commission. He fell whilst leading his men in an attack on the German trenches.

◇ ◇ ◇

Captain A. D. Talbot, 1st Batt. Lancashire Fusiliers, who has been killed in action at the Dardanelles in his 28th year, was the only son of Colonel J. S. Talbot (late Shropshire Light Infantry), of Ashgrove, Borrisokane, Co. Tipperary, and of Mrs. Talbot, Camberley, Surrey, and was a brother of Mrs. F. Montgomery, Millburn, Coleraine. Capt. Talbot joined the 1st Batt. Lancashire Fusiliers (then quartered in India) in December, 1908, was gazetted Lieutenant in June, 1910, and received his Captaincy a short time before his death.

◇ ◇ ◇

Major Edgar Philip Conway, 6th Battalion Munster Fusiliers, has been killed in action at the Dardanelles. Major Conway, who belonged to the 2nd Battalion, had 15 years' service, having been gazetted Second Lieutenant on 18th April, 1900. In November last he was appointed Major of the 6th (Service) Battalion. Major Conway saw a good deal of the fighting in South Africa in 1900. He was present during the operations in the Orange River Colony, and was severely wounded. He was mentioned in despatches and received the Queen's Medal and two clasps.

◇ ◇ ◇

Captain Gilbert Page-Leschelles, 7th Royal Dublin Fusiliers, who was killed in action at the Dardanelles on August 15th, was the second son of the late Mr. Henry Page-Leschelles and Mrs. Leschelles, of Highams, Windlesham, Surrey. He was educated at Radley and at Trinity College, Cambridge, where he took his degree in 1901. He married, in 1905, Edith, younger daughter of the late Rev. J. W. Bennett, of Newchurch-in-Rossendale, and formerly of St. Paul's, South Hampstead. Capt. Page-Leschelles served for five years in the Inns of Court Mounted Infantry, and in September last was gazetted to the Dublin Fusiliers, obtaining his Captaincy in the following January. He leaves surviving a widow and a little son and daughter.

◇ ◇ ◇

Lieutenant Guy W. Burrowes, 6th Royal Munster Fusiliers, who was killed in action at the Dardanelles on August 16th, 1915, was 28 years of age, and belonged to a well-known Cork family, his father being a celebrated oarsman. Prior to the war Lieut. Burrowes spent several years in Central Africa, from where, immediately war was declared, he volunteered and was gazetted Lieutenant in the 6th Munsters in January last, and appointed machine gun officer. He was a son of Mrs. Burrowes, Carrig Lee, Sunday's Well, Cork.

◇ ◇ ◇

Lieutenant N. J. Figgis, 6th Batt. Leinster Regiment, who was killed in action at the Dardanelles on August 10th, was the elder son of Mr. and Mrs. Charles E. Figgis, Ingle Field, Greystones. Lieut. Figgis was educated at Portora and entered T.C.D. in 1910, where he had a distinguished career, taking honours in Modern Literature. He was in the University O.T.C. for about 2½ years. When Lord Kitchener called for men he was amongst the first to offer his services, obtaining his commission on August 26th, 1914. He was gazetted to the 6th Leinsters on September 28th, 1914, and received his Lieutenancy on January 8th, 1915. He was a very keen and promising soldier, a good rifle shot, and took a great interest in his work.

◇ ◇ ◇

Second Lieut. George Frederick Dobbin, who was killed in action at the Dardanelles on the 16th August last, within two days of his 21st birthday, was the son of Mr. and Mrs. Dobbin, 115 Morehampton Road, Dublin. He was educated at Strangways School and entered the Medical School, T.C.D., in 1912, where he was a member of the Officers' Training Corps. On the outbreak of the war he at once offered his services and obtained his commission in the Royal Irish Fusiliers in September last.

OUR HEROES

1. LIEUT. P. T. WARREN, R.A.M.C.	2. CAPT. H. J. CODDINGTON, 2nd Durham Light Infantry.	3. LIEUT. G. KENNEDY, 16th Scottish Rifles.
4. CAPT. A. D. TALBOT, 1st Batt. Lancashire Fusiliers.	5. MAJOR E. P. CONWAY, 6th Batt. Royal Munster Fusiliers.	6. CAPT. G. PAGE-LESCHELLES, 7th Batt. Royal Dublin Fusiliers.
7. LIEUT. G. W. BURROWES, 6th Royal Munster Fusiliers.	8. LIEUT. N. J. FIGGIS, 6th Batt. Leinster Regiment.	9. LIEUT. G. F. DOBBIN, 6th Batt. Royal Irish Fusiliers.

OUR HEROES.

Lieutenant Henry Greene, 92nd Punjabs, attached to the 16th Gurkha Rifles, has been killed in action at the Dardanelles. Lieutenant Greene, who was 24 years of age, was the second son of Mr. George Greene, St. Lawrence Road, Clontarf. He was educated at Dean Close School, Cheltenham, and at Trinity College. He was gazetted to the Indian Army in August, 1913. He was sent with his regiment to the Suez Canal in November last, and was killed in action on April 4th.

✧ ✧ ✧

Captain William Reeves Richards, 6th Royal Dublin Fusiliers, was killed in action at the Dardanelles on August 15th last. He was the elder son of Mr. John W. Richards and Mrs. Richards, 7 Lower Fitzwilliam-street, and Rath, Greystones. Captain Richards was educated at the Chilterns, Wendover, Malvern College, and Trinity College, Dublin, obtaining in May, 1914, the gold medal and first place at the Final Examination of the Incorporated Law Society. He joined the Trinity College Officers' Training Corps in August, 1914, after the outbreak of the war, and obtained his commission in September last, being promoted Captain and Adjutant last July.

✧ ✧ ✧

Lieutenant Ernest M. Harper, 7th Batt. Munster Fusiliers, has been killed in action at the Dardanelles. Lieut. Harper had just been appointed a Demonstrator in Chemistry in Queen's University, Belfast, at the outbreak of the war, but at once volunteered for active service and obtained a commission in the 7th Munsters. He was a son of Mr. Henry M. Harper, Northland Place, Dungannon, and was educated at Dungannon Royal School, afterwards entering the Royal University, where he had a brilliant record. He was in his 25th year when he fell in action whilst gallantly leading his men, and although wounded at the time he insisted on continuing the attack until he fell.

✧ ✧ ✧

Captain Bernard M'Auley, 1st Batt. Border Regiment, has been killed in action at the Dardanelles. Capt. M'Auley resided at Leopardstown, Foxrock, and was the fourth son of the late Mr. W. M'Auley and Mrs. M'Auley, Kilcock. He had served 28 years in the 1st Border Regiment, during which time he saw service in India, Malta, Gibraltar and South Africa, and was severely wounded in the action at Spion Kop. On the 1st March, 1915, he was appointed Captain of the 6th Batt. of his regiment, and proceeded with them to the Dardanelles.

✧ ✧ ✧

Major Hugo Mascie Taylor, 6th Royal Irish Fusiliers, who was killed in action at the Dardanelles between August 6th and 10th last, was the son of Mr. H. Mascie Taylor, late of the 51st King's Own Light Infantry, and Mrs. Mascie Taylor, Besselsleigh, Cheltenham. He was born in 1870 at Clonmel, Co. Tipperary, and was educated at Cheltenham College. He served through the South African War and was twice mentioned in despatches and received the Queen's Medal with two clasps. On the outbreak of war he at once applied to be allowed to rejoin, and in September, 1914, was appointed Major of the 6th Royal Irish Fusiliers. Major Taylor married, in 1911, Miss Josephine Madeline de Courcy, daughter of Col. Berkeley M'Calmont, C.B., of Warborne, Hants.

✧ ✧ ✧

Captain Robert H. Cullinan, B.A., 7th Royal Munster Fusiliers, was killed in action at the Dardanelles on August 8th. He was the second son of Mr. John Cullinan, Ennis, and was called to the Bar in 1904. He was one of a number of young barristers who at the outbreak of the war offered their services to their country. He obtained a commission in the 7th Royal Munsters, and in February last was promoted Captain.

✧ ✧ ✧

Lieutenant C. H. Lambert, A.V.C., died in hospital in Alexandria on 16th August last from wounds received in action at the Dardanelles, where he had been through much severe fighting since he landed with his regiment in June last. Lieut. Lambert was the eldest son of Mr. J. H. Lambert, Redmount, Ballinasloe. On the outbreak of the war he was attached to the 58th Brigade, R.F.A.

✧ ✧ ✧

Lieutenant Edward J. C. Supple, 6th Batt. Duke of Wellington's Regiment, died of wounds received in action in France on August 20th. He was educated at Ripon Grammar School. He held a mastership at Belvedere School, Brighton, where he was keenly interested in the Cadet Corps, raising it to a very high standard of efficiency. Lieut. Supple was the youngest son of Mr. E. K. Supple, Glenmore, Greystones.

✧ ✧ ✧

Second Lieutenant Edwin S. Frizelle, 5th Battalion Lancashire Fusiliers, was killed in action at the Dardanelles on Tuesday, 3rd August. Lieut. Frizelle was the son of Mr. William G. Frizelle, Drumreagh, Alliance-avenue, Belfast, and was educated at the Antrim-road Baptist School. He had a most distinguished career in the Queen's University, having been a scholar and exhibitioner right through his Arts course. Mr. Frizelle had intended studying for the medical profession, but upon the outbreak of war he volunteered for active service, and received his commission in the Lancashire Fusiliers in August last. About two months ago he was wounded and sent to the base hospital at Alexandria, but returned to the front and had been in the trenches and firing line for some weeks previous to the action in which he was killed.

1. LIEUT. H. GREENE, 92nd Punjabs.	2. CAPT. W. R. RICHARDS, 6th Batt. Royal Dublin Fusiliers.	3. LIEUT. ERNEST M. HARPER, 7th Batt. Royal Munster Fusiliers.
4. CAPT. B. M'AULEY, 6th Batt. Border Regiment.	5. MAJOR H. M. TAYLOR, 6th Batt. Royal Irish Fusiliers.	6. CAPT. R. H. CULLINAN, B.A., 7th Batt. Royal Munster Fusiliers.
7. LIEUT. C. H. LAMBERT, Army Veterinary Corps.	8. LIEUT. E. J. C. SUPPLE, 6th Batt. Duke of Wellington's Regt	9. LIEUT. E. S. FRIZELLE, 5th Batt. Lancashire Fusiliers.

OUR HEROES.

Lieutenant G. P. Costello, Royal Engineers, who was killed in action at the Dardanelles, was a son of Mr. and Mrs. Costello, The Croft, Galway. Lieut. Costello was educated in Galway University, where he took his degree as Bachelor of Engineering. On the outbreak of war he at once volunteered and left with his regiment for the Dardanelles, where he fell in action on the 16th August last.

◇ ◇ ◇

Major William Eastwood, 6th Batt. Royal Irish Rifles, who has been killed in action at Gallipoli, was a son of Major Eastwood, Castletown Castle, Dundalk. Major Eastwood entered the Royal Irish Rifles from the Militia in February, 1900. He obtained his Captaincy in 1908, and in January last was detached from the regular battalions for service with the 6th (Service) Battalion. He served through the South African War, and received the Queen's Medal with three clasps and the King's Medal with two clasps.

◇ ◇ ◇

Second Lieutenant James H. Bruce Levis, 6th Batt. Royal Irish Rifles, was killed in action at the Dardanelles about the 12th August last. Lieut. Levis was only in his 19th year, and was the elder son of Mr. Bruce Levis, Glenview, Skibbereen, Co. Cork. Prior to the war Lieut. Levis had been a medical student of Trinity College, and had passed through half his course with distinction, but on the outbreak of war he at once volunteered and was gazetted to the 6th Royal Irish Rifles in November, 1914.

◇ ◇ ◇

Captain James Smyth, 3rd Batt. Lancashire Fusiliers, who was killed in action in Flanders on July 8th last, was the second son of Colonel James Smyth, Gaybrook, Mullingar. He was in his 29th year, and was educated at Rugby and Lincoln College, Oxford. Captain Smyth was gazetted to the 3rd Batt. Lancashire Fusiliers in 1908 and obtained his Lieutenancy in 1911. On the outbreak of war he was attached to the 2nd Batt. Lancashire Fusiliers, and left with his battalion for France in August, 1914.

◇ ◇ ◇

Colonel A. R. Cole-Hamilton, 6th Batt. East Lancashire Regiment, was killed at the Dardanelles on August 9th last while leading his men into action. The deceased officer was Deputy Lieutenant of Co. Tyrone, and resided at Beltrim Castle, Gortin. He was the eldest son of the late Captain William Claude Cole-Hamilton, and was a kinsman of the Earl of Castlestuart and the Earl of Enniskillen. Colonel Cole-Hamilton began his career in the Shropshire Light Infantry and obtained his Captaincy into the 7th Hussars. He then exchanged into the Royal Scots Fusiliers and subsequently retired from the Army, but later joined the Militia and had command of the 6th Louth Irish Rifles until they were disbanded. In 1882 he took part in the defence of Alexandria and the occupation of Kafr Dowar. On the outbreak of war he was chosen to command the 6th Batt. of the East Lancashire Regiment.

◇ ◇ ◇

Captain Bertram Walter Bourke, 5th Royal Dublin Fusiliers, was killed in action near Ypres on May 9th, 1915, while gallantly leading his men. Captain Bourke was in his 33rd year, and had served with the Royal Engineers (Militia), from which he exchanged into the 5th Batt. Royal Dublin Fusiliers in 1904, and received his Captaincy in 1908. He left for the front on May 2nd, and was attached to the 2nd Batt. R.D.F. Captain Bourke married, in 1913, Eileen, daughter of Mr. G. Neville Ussher, Carlow. He was a son of the late Major William H. Bourke, Connaught Rangers, Heathfield, Ballina, Co. Mayo.

◇ ◇ ◇

Second Lieutenant W. S. Collen, 6th Royal Inniskilling Fusiliers, was killed in action on August 7th last at Suvla Bay. Lieut. Collen was a son of Mr. Joseph Collen, Homestead, Dundrum, and was very well known and popular in golfing circles around Dublin. He was one of the competitors at the Irish Close Championship last year. At the outbreak of war he at once volunteered and obtained his commission in the 6th Inniskillings.

◇ ◇ ◇

Captain W. G. M. Eagar, 1st Batt. Royal Munster Fusiliers, was killed in action at the Dardanelles on August 21st last, in his 23rd year, whilst gallantly leading his company. His commanding officer bears a high tribute to his courage and gallantry. Although hit through the shoulder he bravely carried on, leading and encouraging his men, and fell mortally hit afterwards. The few survivors left of his company declare that Captain Eagar was "absolutely magnificent." Captain Eagar was educated at St. Columba's College and obtained his commission in the 3rd Munsters in 1909. In 1913 he was appointed Assistant Conservator, Forest Department, at Siam, where he was when war was declared, but returned home immediately, obtained his Captaincy in March, 1915.

◇ ◇ ◇

Second Lieutenant Harold Gordon Jameson, Royal Engineers (65th Field Company), was killed in action at the Dardanelles on August 16th, 1915, in his 26th year. He was the sixth son of Mr. and Mrs. Jameson, Campfield House, Dundrum, and was educated at Monkton Combe School, Bath, and afterwards at Trinity College, Dublin, where he passed through the Engineering School. He was appointed to the Sudan Irrigation Service, but was in Ireland when the war broke out, and at once volunteered.

1. LIEUT. G. P. COSTELLO, Royal Engineers.	2. MAJOR W. EASTWOOD, 6th Batt. Royal Irish Rifles.	3. LIEUT. J. H. B. LEVIS, 6th Batt. Royal Irish Rifles.
4. CAPT. J. SMYTH, 3rd Batt. Lancashire Fusiliers.	5. COL. A. R. COLE-HAMILTON, 6th Batt. East Lancashire Regt.	6. CAPT. B. W. BOURKE, 5th Batt. Royal Dublin Fusiliers.
7. LIEUT. W. S. COLLEN, 6th Batt. Royal Inniskilling Fusiliers.	8. CAPT. W. G. M. EAGAR, 1st Batt. Royal Munster Fusiliers.	9. LIEUT. H. G. JAMESON, Royal Engineers.

OUR HEROES.

Second Lieutenant Francis Evans Bennett, 7th Batt. Royal Munster Fusiliers, was killed in action at the Gallipoli Peninsula on August 7th last. Lieut. Bennett obtained his commission in the 6th Batt. Royal Munster Fusiliers in April and was afterwards transferred to the 7th Batt. He went out with the 10th Division in July. He was shot whilst gallantly endeavouring to assist his Captain, who had been mortally wounded. Lieut. Bennett was educated at The Manor School, Fermoy, and The Abbey, Tipperary, and was a son of Mr. Frank Bennett, Cregane Manor, Rosscarbery, Co. Cork.

◆ ◆ ◆

Captain Edward Crump Dorman, 1st Batt. Royal Munster Fusiliers, who was killed in action at the Dardanelles, was the third son of the late J. W. Dorman, C.E., and Mrs. Dorman, Raffin, Kinsale. Previous to entering the Army he was a student of medicine in the Royal University. In 1908 he received his lieutenancy, and in 1914 was promoted Captain. Captain Dorman was a fine athlete and an excellent shot, and had won several important prizes in sabre and bayonet contests and for rowing while in India. He fell while rallying his men during a night attack of the Turks on the 4th May, 1915.

◆ ◆ ◆

Lieutenant Kevin E. O'Duffy, 7th Munster Fusiliers, who was killed in action at the Dardanelles on August 15th, was a son of Mr. Kevin O'Duffy, 85 Harcourt-street. He was educated at Athlone and Belvedere before entering Stonyhurst, where he held the Senior Scholarship and gained four gold medals and one silver. He entered Trinity College in 1914, was Librarian of the College Historical Society and one of the ablest cadets of the O.T.C. He joined the 7th Munsters shortly after the outbreak of the war and obtained his lieutenancy in January last.

◆ ◆ ◆

Captain J. C. Johnston, 6th Batt. Royal Irish Fusiliers, has been killed in action at the Dardanelles. Captain Johnston served through the Boer War with the 14th Hussars, and was private secretary to the Earl of Aberdeen during the last three years of his Viceroyalty. He was educated at Charterhouse and Sandhurst, and was a Resident Magistrate for the Co. Meath. His family residence was Magheramena Castle, Co. Fermanagh, of which county he was High Sheriff in 1910.

◆ ◆ ◆

Major William Hawtrey White, 1st Batt. Royal Irish Regiment, who was killed in action on February 14th last, when gallantly leading his men in a night attack on a trench held by the Germans near St. Eloi, and was mentioned in Sir John French's despatches, was a son of the Rev. James White, late Vicar of St. Peter's, Paddington, a member of an old Co. Wexford family. Major White entered the Army in 1892, took part in the operations on the North-West Frontier of India in 1897-8, receiving the medal with two clasps. He served in the South African War, 1899-1902, and received the Queen's Medal with three clasps and King's Medal with two clasps. He married, in 1911, Muriel, daughter of Major Braddon, of Skisdon, Cornwall, and leaves two daughters.

◆ ◆ ◆

Captain Charles Edward Granville Vernon, 5th Batt. Inniskilling Fusiliers, was killed in action at the Dardanelles on the 15th August last. He was the only child of Colonel and Mrs. Granville Vernon, 34 Rosary Gardens, London, S.W., and grandson of the late John Edward Venables Vernon, J.P., D.L., Clontarf Castle, Dublin, and of Major Shairp, of Kirkton, J.P., D.L. for Linlithgow. He was educated at Wellington College, and passed thence into the Royal Military Academy, Woolwich. He was posted to the Royal Inniskilling Fusiliers, with whom he served in Egypt, where he contracted malarial fever, was invalided home and eventually obliged to resign his commission. On the declaration of war he was given a commission in the 5th (Service) Batt. of his old regiment, with whom he served continuously until he fell whilst gallantly leading his company in their first action against the Turks.

◆ ◆ ◆

Second Lieutenant J. N. H. Murphy, 3rd Royal Dublin Fusiliers, aged 20, was the only son of the late Rev. W. A. E. Murphy, of Desertmartin, Co. Derry, and Mrs. Murphy, Blackrock. He was educated at St. Columba's College, Rathfarnham, and when the war broke out was in the Medical School, Trinity College, Dublin. He went to the Front on 2nd May, was attached to the 2nd Royal Dublin Fusiliers, and was killed in action on 9th May near Ypres.

◆ ◆ ◆

Captain J. V. Dunn, 7th Royal Munster Fusiliers, was killed in action at the Dardanelles on August 15th last. He was a son of Mr. Valentine Dunn, solicitor, Dublin, and was educated at Belvedere and Clongowes Wood College. Having gone through a very successful course of law lectures in Trinity he adopted the profession of solicitor, and on the outbreak of the war joined the Officers' Training Corps, T.C.D., obtaining his commission in the Munsters in October last. He was promoted Captain in April last, and left with his regiment in July for the Dardanelles.

◆ ◆ ◆

Second Lieutenant J. V. Y. Willington, 6th Batt. Leinster Regiment, was killed in action at the Dardanelles between August 6th and 12th. He was the eldest surviving son of Mr. James Willington, of St. Kieran's, Birr, and was educated at Chesterfield School, Birr, and Cheltenham. On the outbreak of the war Lieut. Willington at once offered his services to his country and received his commission in the 6th Leinsters in September last.

1. LIEUT. F. E. BENNETT, 7th Batt. Royal Munster Fusiliers.
2. CAPT. E. C. DORMAN, 1st Batt. Royal Munster Fusiliers.
3. LIEUT. K. E. O'DUFFY, 7th Batt. Royal Munster Fusiliers.
4. CAPT. J. C. JOHNSTON, 6th Batt. Royal Irish Fusiliers.
5. MAJOR W. H. WHITE, 1st Batt. Royal Irish Regiment.
6. CAPT. C. E. G. VERNON, 5th Batt. Royal Inniskilling Fusiliers.
7. LIEUT. J. N. H. MURPHY, 5th Royal Dublin Fusiliers.
8. CAPT. J. V. DUNN, 7th Royal Munster Fusiliers.
9. LIEUT. J. V. Y. WILLINGTON, 6th Batt. Leinster Regiment.

OUR HEROES.

Second Lieutenant Walter Stanley Currie Griffith, 6th Leinster Regiment, was killed in action at the Dardanelles. Lieut. Griffith was educated at Hurst Court and Winchester. He took a great interest in social work, and was for some time Secretary of the Christian Social Union. He had been a member of the Inns of Court Volunteers, and at the outbreak of war obtained a commission. He was the eldest son of Mr. and Mrs. Griffith, 22 Victoria Park, Dover.

❖ ❖ ❖

Captain J. F. Martyr, 1st Batt. Royal Irish Rifles, has died of wounds received in action at the Dardanelles on August 11th last. Capt. Martyr was attached to the 6th Batt. Royal Irish Rifles at the time of his death. He had served in the South African War in 1901 and 1902, where he was employed with the Mounted Infantry, and obtained for his valuable services the Queen's Medal with five clasps. He was the elder son of the late Mr. Peter Martyr and Mrs. Martyr, "Hillside," Fleet, Hants, and husband of Mrs. Violet Martyr, Bray, Co. Wicklow.

❖ ❖ ❖

Lieutenant Harry Jackson Cummins, 5th Gurkha Rifles, was killed in action at the Dardanelles. He was a son of Professor and Mrs. Ashley Cummins, St. Patrick's Place, Cork, and was in his 27th year. Lieutenant Cummins was educated at Cheltenham College, whence he passed into Sandhurst and entered the Indian Army in 1908. He joined the 5th Gurkha Rifles in India and returned with his regiment to Egypt, whence he was invalided home, but returned to the front, and was killed in action on August 21st.

❖ ❖ ❖

Captain George Grant Duggan, 5th Batt. R. I. Fusiliers, who died from wounds received in action at Gallipoli on August 16th last, was the third son of Mr. George Duggan, Manager of the Provincial Bank, College-street, Dublin. He was educated at the High School and subsequently entered Trinity, where he had a brilliant University career. He was a member of the Officers' Training Corps, where he showed exceptional efficiency. In September, 1914, he joined the 5th Batt. Royal Irish Fusiliers. Capt. Duggan was a noted athlete and one of the finest long-distance and cross-country runners that Trinity College has ever possessed.

❖ ❖ ❖

Colonel Arthur Sandars Vanrenen, 5th Batt. Inniskilling Fusiliers, who was killed in action on August 15th last at the Dardanelles, was the second son of the late General Donald Vanrenen, R.A. (Indian Army). He was born in December, 1862, and was educated at Cheltenham. In 1883 he was gazetted to the Lincolnshire Regiment, with whom he served until 1897, when he was seconded for service with the Malay States Guides, and appointed Commandant. Last February he was given command of the 5th Batt. Inniskilling Fusiliers, and left with the 31st (Irish) Brigade for the Dardanelles in July last.

❖ ❖ ❖

Lieutenant J. R. Duggan, 5th Batt. Royal Irish Regiment, was killed in action at Gallipoli on August 16th last, the same day on which his elder brother, Captain Duggan, received the wounds from the effects of which he died. He was the youngest son of Mr. J. R. Duggan, Provincial Bank, College-street, who has thus lost two sons in the service of their country. Two other sons are also on active service. Lieut. J. R. Duggan was educated at the High School and subsequently at Trinity College, where he entered the Medical School. On the outbreak of the war he at once offered his services and was gazetted to the 5th Batt. Royal Irish Regiment.

❖ ❖ ❖

Second Lieutenant Archibald R. Toomey, 6th Leinster Regiment, who was killed in action at the Dardanelles on August 10th last, was the eldest son of Mr. Archibald Toomey, 20 Palmerston Park, Dublin. He was educated at St. Stephen's Green School and Portora Royal School, subsequently entering Trinity Medical School. On the outbreak of the war he applied for and was granted a commission in the 6th Batt. Leinster Regiment from the Officers' Training Corps, T.C.D.

❖ ❖ ❖

Captain Arthur John Dillon Preston, 6th Batt. Royal Dublin Fusiliers, only son of Major A. J. Preston, late Duke of Wellington's Regiment, and Mrs. Preston, Swainston, Co. Meath, was born in 1885 and received his first commission in the Militia Battalion, Durham Light Infantry. In 1907 he was gazetted to the Royal Dublin Fusiliers and served with the 1st Batt. in Egypt. At the outbreak of the war he was ordered to Naas to raise the 6th Batt., and was with this battalion at the Dardanelles when he fell in action.

❖ ❖ ❖

Second Lieutenant Donald James Grubb, 5th Royal Inniskilling Fusiliers, who was killed in action at the Dardanelles on August 15th, 1915, was the only son of Rev. James and Mrs. Grubb, Donegall Square, Belfast, and nephew of Captain J. J. Grubb, late Royal West Surrey Regiment. Lieutenant Grubb was educated at Wesley College, Dublin. On the outbreak of the war he joined the Queen's University (Belfast) Officers' Training Corps, and was gazetted to the Inniskillings in September, 1914, and landed with his regiment at Suvla Bay on August 7th last. His Commanding Officer in writing of Lieut. Grubb says "he met his death while bravely attending the wounded at great personal risk under a very heavy fire."

OUR HEROES

1. LIEUT. W. S. C. GRIFFITH, 6th Batt. Leinster Regiment.
2. CAPT. J. F. MARTYR, 1st Batt. Royal Irish Rifles.
3. LIEUT. H. J. CUMMINS, 5th Gurkha Rifles.
4. CAPT. G. G. DUGGAN, 5th Batt. Royal Irish Fusiliers.
5. COLONEL A. S. VANRENEN, 5th Batt. Royal Inniskilling Fusiliers.
6. LIEUT. J. R. DUGGAN, 5th Batt. Royal Irish Regiment.
7. LIEUT. A. R. TOOMEY, 6th Batt. Leinster Regiment.
8. CAPT. A. J. DILLON PRESTON, 6th Batt. Royal Dublin Fusiliers.
9. LIEUT. D. J. GRUBB, 5th Batt. Royal Inniskilling Fusiliers.

OUR HEROES

Second Lieutenant Thomas Alexander David Deane, Royal Marine Light Infantry, was killed in action on May 3rd last at the Dardanelles (Gaba Tepe), whilst ascending a hill with others of his (Portsmouth) battalion going to the assistance of the Australians. Lieut. Deane was the only son of Sir Thomas Manly and Lady Deane, of Ailesbury Park, Dublin, and was in his 22nd year. He was educated at Mr. Bookey's School, Aravon, Bray, and at Trent College, Derbyshire, afterwards entering Trinity College, Dublin, where he belonged to the Officers' Training Corps. He received his commission in September, 1914, and left England to join the Mediterranean Expeditionary Force on February 27 last.

◊ ◊ ◊

Captain Henry Desmond O'Hara, D.S.O., 1st Batt. Royal Dublin Fusiliers, who will be remembered for the part he took in the memorable landing at Sedd-el-Bahr on April 25th last, when, though the junior officer, he took command of the remnant of his battalion, all the officers of which, with the exception of Captain (then Lieutenant) O'Hara, having been either killed or wounded, on which occasion his initiative and resource and the coolness and gallantry he displayed earned for him the D.S.O. and special mention in despatches, was wounded in action on August 12th last at the Dardanelles and died on the hospital ship *Arcadian* near Gibraltar on the 29th. The gallant young soldier was laid to rest in the cemetery at Gibraltar with full military honours. He was the only son of Mr. W. J. O'Hara, R.M., Oriel House, Ballincollig, Co. Cork.

◊ ◊ ◊

Lieutenant William Major Gilliland, 1st Batt. Royal Inniskilling Fusiliers, who was killed in action at the Dardanelles on April 28th, 1915, was the only son of the late Mr. and Mrs. Louis Gilliland, of Eschol, Londonderry, and was only in his 21st year. He was educated at Baymount School, Dollymount, Dublin, and Shrewsbury, from whence he passed direct into the Royal Military College, Sandhurst, in January, 1913, and was gazetted to the 2nd Battalion of his Territorial Regiment, the Royal Inniskilling Fusiliers. He was wounded at the battle of Le Cateau on August 26th, 1914, and on his recovery joined the 1st Battalion at Rugby on its return from India, and was with them in the landing at Gallipoli in April last.

◊ ◊ ◊

Captain R. Maxwell Pike, Royal Flying Corps, who was reported missing on August 9th last, is now reported dead. Captain Pike, who was a son of Mr. R. L. Pike, Kilnock, Co. Carlow, entered the Navy when a young man, but owing to an injury to his knee had to leave the service. On the outbreak of the war he joined the Royal Flying Corps. He was a most daring and skilful aviator, and his place in the corps will be difficult to fill.

Major Algernon H. Cuthell, 9th Batt. Prince of Wales's Own (West Yorkshire) Regiment, was killed in action at the Dardanelles on the 22nd August last. Major Cuthell was well known in the North of Ireland. He was a son of Lieutenant-Colonel Cuthell, late of the 13th Hussars, and had 16 years' service in the Army, obtaining his first commission in 1899. He served in the South African War, for his services in which he was awarded the Queen's Medal with three clasps and the King's Medal with two clasps. When war broke out he assisted in training the new army in Lincolnshire, and was afterwards gazetted to the 9th Batt. of the West Yorks, with whom he served until he fell in action.

◊ ◊ ◊

Captain W. Robinson, 5th Royal Inniskilling Fusiliers, who was killed on August 15th at the Dardanelles, was the third son of Mr. R. A. Robinson, D.L. Captain Robinson was educated at St. Paul's School and Royal School of Mines. He was for some years in the London Scottish and served in the South African War. He subsequently became a Lieutenant in the Rhodesian Volunteers, but on the outbreak of the war he joined the Inniskilling Fusiliers, with whom he served until he fell in the severe fighting in Gallipoli about August 15th last.

◊ ◊ ◊

Lieutenant A. A. Raymond, 3rd R. Irish Rifles, who has died from wounds received in action at Gallipoli on April 28th last, was the only surviving son of the late Captain H. W. Raymond, Royal Irish Rifles, and was only in his 19th year. Lieut. Raymond was educated at Wellington College and Sandhurst, and obtained his commission in the Royal Irish Rifles shortly after the outbreak of the war. He was wounded in the attack on June 16, but continued to serve until August 2nd, when he fell.

◊ ◊ ◊

Lieutenant K. R. Forde, 3rd Batt. East Kent Regiment, who was killed in action in Flanders on July 23rd, was a son of the Rev. Canon Hugh Forde, LL.D., Finlagan Rectory, Ballykelly, Londonderry. Lieut. Forde was in Japan when the war broke out, and when the call for volunteers came he resigned a lucrative post and came home to offer his services to his country.

◊ ◊ ◊

Lieutenant J. H. F. Leland, 5th Batt. Royal Welsh Fusiliers, was killed in action at the Dardanelles on August 10th last. He was the eldest son of Mr. and Mrs. Henry Leland, Blackrock, and was an ex-Scholar and Moderator of Trinity College and a member of the Irish Bar. At the outbreak of the war he volunteered and was gazetted to the 5th Royal Welsh Fusiliers in August, 1914, and served with them until killed in action at the Dardanelles on August 10th, 1915.

Supplement to Irish Life, September 24th, 1915.

1. LIEUT. T. A. D. DEANE, Royal Marine Light Infantry.
2. CAPT. DESMOND O'HARA, D.S.O., 1st Batt. Royal Dublin Fusiliers.
3. LIEUT. W. M. GILLILAND, 1st Batt. Royal Inniskilling Fusiliers.
4. CAPT. MAXWELL PIKE, Royal Flying Corps.
5. MAJOR A. H. CUTHELL, 9th Batt. Prince of Wales's Regiment.
6. CAPT. R. W. ROBINSON, 5th Batt. Royal Inniskilling Fusiliers.
7. LIEUT. A. A. RAYMOND, 3rd Batt. Royal Irish Rifles.
8. LIEUT. K. R. FORDE, 3rd Batt. East Kent Regiment.
9. LIEUT. J. H. F. LELAND, 5th Batt. Royal Welsh Fusiliers.

OUR HEROES.

Second Lieutenant Edward Theaker Weatherill was killed in action at the Dardanelles on the 15th August last. He was educated at Fettes College, Edinburgh, and Armstrong College (Durham University), Newcastle-on-Tyne, where he obtained his B.Sc. degree and later gained a first-class marine engineer's certificate. In the course of his duties as marine engineer he made several voyages in the Far Eastern and Pacific Trades, and was well acquainted with the features of the Dardanelles and Constantinople. At its formation in September, 1914, he joined the "Football Company" of the 7th Royal Dublin Fusiliers. Lieutenant Weatherill was in his 28th year, and was a son of Captain and Mrs Weatherill, 6 Ailesbury-road.

Captain Poole Henry Hickman, who fell in action at Gallipoli on August 15th last, was one of the many members of the Irish Bar who on the outbreak of the war joined the 7th Batt. Royal Dublin Fusiliers. He was called to the Bar in 1909, and was hon. secretary of the Munster Circuit. His short professional career was full of promise, and he was highly esteemed by his colleagues. Captain Hickman was a son of Mr. F. W. Hickman, D.L., Kilmore, Knock, and was educated at Tipperary Grammar School and Trinity College.

Mr. William Purefoy Bridge was a son of Mrs. Bridge, 64 Morehampton-road, and nephew of Dr. Purefoy, of Merrion-square, and was a member of a well-known Tipperary family. On the outbreak of the war he enlisted with the "Football" Company of the 7th Dublins and served with his "Pals" until he fell in action on August 10th. Mr. Bridge was a solicitor by profession. His younger brother, Captain R. F. Athol Bridge, is also at the front.

Captain R. P. Tobin, only son of Dr. R. F. Tobin, St. Stephen's Green, Dublin, had just passed his 21st birthday when, on August 15th, at Gallipoli, he, with so many of his gallant "Pals," gave his life in his country's cause. Captain Tobin was much beloved by his company, and the letters received from his comrades tell how bravely he took his part on that fatal day, which will be ever remembered with pride and grief by "all that was left of them."

Major C. H. Tippet, whose coolness and bravery inspired his junior officers and men in the action at Suvla Bay, in which he fell, was a son of the late Mr. H. V. Tippet, Stone Grange, Maltoy. He was originally in the 4th Batt. Royal Dublin Fusiliers, and served as Major through the last two years of the South African campaign, receiving the Queen's Medal with five clasps. On the outbreak of the war he rejoined his old regiment as Major in the 7th Batt., and sailed for the Dardanelles on July 11th. His son, Captain H. C. C. Tippet, is serving with the 4th Batt. Royal Dublin Fusiliers.

Captain M. J. Fitzgibbon was the youngest son of Mr. John Fitzgibbon, M.P., Castlerea, and previous to the outbreak of the war was a law student, but immediately volunteered and obtained his commission in the 7th Batt. Royal Dublin Fusiliers in August, 1914, and sailed with his regiment for Gallipoli, where he fell in the action on August 15th last. Captain Fitzgibbon was a very popular young officer, and admired for his many sterling qualities.

Mr. Cecil W. Murray, who was killed in action at the Dardanelles, was the eldest son of Mr. W. D. and Mrs. Murray, 17 Dartmouth Square, Dublin. On the formation of the "D" Company of the 7th Batt. Royal Dublin Fusiliers he at once joined his comrades and served as a private until he fell in action on August 16th last.

Sergeant Francis A. Marrable was one of those who in September, 1914, joined the "D" Company, 7th Royal Dublin Fusiliers. He was the younger son of Mr. Arthur Marrable, B.L., Druid Hill, Cabinteely, and was educated at Aravon School, Bray, and Trinity College. Previous to the outbreak of the war he was a chartered accountant, but when the urgent call of King and Country came he enlisted and, like many of his comrades, declined a commission out of loyalty to his "Pals."

Sergeant Edward C. Millar, who fell in action at the Dardanelles on August 9th last, was the fourth son of Mr. Fitzadam Millar, Monkstown, Co. Dublin. He entered Trinity College in 1906, and in 1907 rowed for the University junior eight. Mr. Millar was a prominent footballer. On its formation in August last he joined the "D" Company of the 7th Royal Dublin Fusiliers, and, like many others of this company, refused to accept a commission, preferring to be amongst his comrades. His company officer, Capt. Poole-Hickman, who was killed shortly afterwards, made special mention of Sergeant Millar's gallantry.

7th BATT. ROYAL DUBLIN FUSILIERS.

1. LIEUT. E. T. WEATHERILL.	2. CAPT. POOLE HENRY HICKMAN.	3. PTE. WM. PUREFOY BRIDGE.
4. CAPT. R. P. TOBIN.	5. MAJOR C. H. TIPPET.	6. CAPT. M. J. FITZGIBBON.
7. PTE. CECIL W. MURRAY.	8. SERGT. F. A. MARRABLE.	9. SERGT. E. C. MILLAR.

OUR HEROES.

Lance-Corporal Charles E. Dowse was the third son of Canon and Mrs. Dowse, Seafield Lodge, Monkstown. He was educated at Trent College, Derbyshire, where he was a member of the Officers' Training Corps, and on the outbreak of war he joined the 7th Dublins, and though offered a commission in another regiment he refused to leave his "Pals," and was with them in the landing at Suvla Bay and the subsequent fighting until he fell in action on August 16th, within a few months of his 20th birthday.

Mr. Walter Paul joined the "Pals" Battalion with his younger brother on the outbreak of the war, and was with them at the landing at Suvla Bay, and on the following day fell in action with many of his brave comrades. Mr. Paul was an enthusiastic footballer and took a great interest in dramatic art. He was a son of Mr. C. J. Paul, Sydenham, Howth-road.

Mr. Walter D. Appleyard was the third son of the late Mr. William Appleyard, Representative Church Body, and Mrs. Appleyard, Sandford. He was educated at the High School, Dublin, and on leaving school entered the Civil Service. He was on the staff of the Irish Land Commission, but when war broke out he joined the "Pals" and left with them for the Dardanelles in July. He was with them in the landing at Suvla Bay and the fierce fighting of the following week, but fell on August 16th. His brother, Mr. George Appleyard, is serving with the Cadet Corps, 7th Batt. Leinster Regiment.

Lieutenant Ernest Lawrence Julian was the only surviving son of Mrs. Julian, 28 Lower Leeson-street, and had a distinguished career in Trinity College. He was called to the Irish Bar in 1903 and was Reid Professor of Law in Trinity. When the war broke out he was quick to answer his country's call and obtained his commission in the 7th Royal Dublin Fusiliers, with whom he went to the Dardanelles, where he fell in action. His death is a loss to scholarship and to the law, and cut short a most promising career.

Major R. S. H. Harrison was the only son of the Rev. A. R. Harrison, Vicar of Tattenhall, Staffs. He was born in 1883 and was educated at Clifton and Sandhurst. He entered the Indian Army and was appointed to the 22nd Punjabs and was later transferred to the 51st Sikhs. He was at home on leave when war broke out and was attached to the 7th Battalion Royal Dublin Fusiliers, with whom he sailed for the Dardanelles in July and took part in the landing at Suvla Bay and the subsequent heavy fighting, in which his battalion won for itself such a glorious name, though at the cost of many gallant lives. Where all were brave, Major Harrison's coolness and bravery were conspicuous, and he died at the head of his men in the action on August 16th. He had endeared himself to his company, who received the news of his death with the keenest regret.

Mr. Charles J. MacDonald was the only son of the late Mr. Thomas J. MacDonald and Mrs. MacDonald, 104 Marlborough-road, Donnybrook. On the outbreak of the war he joined the "Pals" Company of the 7th Dublins, and fell in the action at the Dardanelles on August 16th last, when so many of his comrades gave their lives for their country.

Mr. T. A. Symes, who died in hospital at Alexandria on August 18th, was the seventh son of Mr. and Mrs. Sandham J. Symes, Hill View, Tinahely, Co. Wicklow. He went to the Dardanelles with the "Pals" Company of the 7th Royal Dublin Fusiliers, which he had joined on the outbreak of the war. He was attached to the machine gun section of his battalion, and was a very keen and promising soldier.

Mr. Thomas Cecil Moore Elliott, only son of Mr. John Elliott, solicitor, Strabane, was killed in a bayonet charge of his company at the Dardanelles on August 16th. He was only in his 21st year when he joined the now famous "D" Company of the 7th Royal Dublin Fusiliers. Mr. Elliott was educated at Strabane Academy and Portora Royal School, and subsequently entered Trinity College Medical School. He was a prominent athlete, and won the All-Ireland School Shield for rifle shooting. He had been through two severe engagements, in which his battalion greatly distinguished itself, prior to the action in which he fell.

Mr. John J. McGrath, who died on August 8th from wounds sustained in action at the Dardanelles on the same day, was another of those who on the outbreak of war joined the 7th Dublins, and served with his comrades in the ranks, where he was promoted Company Quarter-Master-Sergeant, and cheerfully and bravely gave his life for his country. He was a brother of Mrs. Bermingham, wife of Mr. E. J. Bermingham, L.D.S., Harcourt-street.

7th BATT. ROYAL DUBLIN FUSILIERS.

1. LCE.-CPL. C. E. DOWSE.
2. MR. WALTER PAUL.
3. MR. WALTER D. APPLEYARD
4. LIEUT. E. L. JULIAN.
5. MAJOR R. S. H. HARRISON.
6. MR. T. C. M. ELLIOTT.
7. MR. CHAS. MacDONALD.
8. MR. T. A. SYMES.
9. MR. JOHN J. McGRATH.

OUR HEROES.

Lieutenant S. R. V. Travers, 7th Batt. Royal Munster Fusiliers, who was killed in action at the Dardanelles, is the third of his name to give his life in the service of his country. There are sixteen members of his family in the fighting line, his brother, Lieut. A. S. Travers, being in the 7th Munsters. On the day he met his death Lieut. Travers had kept his gun working on a communication trench all day though under a hot fire the whole time, but at the close of the day he was hit and died soon afterwards. His General and brother-officers in their letters to his relatives speak highly of Lieut. Travers' bravery and devotion to duty. He was a son of Mr. and Mrs. Travers, Mill Cove, Rosscarbery, Co. Cork.

✧ ✧ ✧

Lieutenant Duncan Boyd Wallis, 3rd Batt. Connaught Rangers (attached to the 2nd Batt. Royal Munster Fusiliers), died of wounds received in action in France on July 23rd, 1915, on his 24th birthday. He was the fifth son of the late Mr. H. Boyd Wallis and Mrs. Wallis, of Graylands, Horsham, Sussex, and 48 Holland Park, London. Lieut. Wallis was educated at St. Ronan's, Cheltenham College, and Cambridge, where he took his degree in Engineering. Shortly after the outbreak of the war he joined the 3rd Connaught Rangers and left for the front on May 14th.

✧ ✧ ✧

Lieutenant J. R. Whitsitt, 5th Batt. Royal Inniskilling Fusiliers, who died on August 16th last from wounds received in action at the Dardanelles, was in his 24th year, and was the eldest son of Mr. Finlay Whitsitt, 2 Montebello Terrace, Bray. He was educated at the Methodist College, Belfast, and Trinity College, Dublin, where he was a member of the Officers' Training Corps, and was well known in Rugby football circles in Belfast and Dublin.

✧ ✧ ✧

Lieutenant William F. C. McGarry, 6th Batt. Royal Dublin Fusiliers, who was killed in action at Suvla Bay, was the second son of the late Mr. Frederick McGarry and Mrs. McGarry, 4 Belfast Terrace, Phœnix Park. Lieut. McGarry joined shortly after the outbreak of the war, and was only in his 21st year when he fell in action.

✧ ✧ ✧

Major Sir William Lennox Napier, 4th South Wales Borderers, was killed at the Dardanelles on August 13th, aged 47. He was a grandson of the late Sir Joseph Napier, Lord Chancellor of Ireland, and succeeded his father as third baronet in 1884. He was educated at Uppingham and Jesus College, Cambridge. In 1894 he was called to the Bar. For some time Lieutenant-Colonel of the 7th Royal Welsh Fusiliers, he retired in 1912, but at the outbreak of war rejoined the service as Major in the 4th South Wales Borderers. Sir Lennox married in 1890 Mabel Edith Geraldine, daughter of the Rev. C. T. Forster. His eldest son, Joseph W. L. Napier, who succeeds to the baronetcy, is a Second Lieutenant, also in the 4th South Wales Borderers, and his second son, Charles M. Napier, is in the Royal Field Artillery and is now fighting in Flanders.

✧ ✧ ✧

Captain John Clarke, R.A.M.C., Welsh Field Ambulance, Territorial Division, died of wounds received in action on the 9th September. Captain Clarke, who was the third son of Mr. William Clarke, High-street, Ballymena, and a brother of Mr. James Clarke, solicitor, Ballymena, was aged 32. He was educated at Ballymena Academy and Edinburgh University, and took his degree at Queen's University, Belfast. He volunteered for active service in the autumn of 1914.

✧ ✧ ✧

Lieutenant J. C. Hawkes, M.D., R.A.M.C., was killed in action in France on July 31st, 1915. Dr. Hawkes qualified at Edinburgh University and was practising at Nottingham when he joined the Army. Dr. Hawkes was the second son of Mr. William Hawkes, Manager Munster and Leinster Bank, Castletown-Berehaven, Co. Cork. Dr. Hawkes was much beloved in his regiment for his skill and devotion in attending to his wounded comrades. He was killed instantaneously by a shell.

✧ ✧ ✧

Lieutenant Thomas Alfred Peel, M.B., B.S., R.A.M.C., was the third son of Mr. Joshua E. Peel, solicitor, Armagh. Previous to the outbreak of war Dr. Peel was house surgeon in a large infirmary in Stoke-on-Trent. He was amongst the first of the surgeons to volunteer his services for his country, and in August, 1914, was appointed to a commission in the R.A.M.C. A very short time afterwards he was gazetted as Surgeon-in-general to the 5th Dorset Regiment. This regiment was attached to the 11th Division, which was sent out to the Dardanelles. Lieutenant Peel was wounded in action on August 19th and died on 24th August, 1915. His eldest brother, Mr. John A. Peel, solicitor, and Coroner for the mid-division of Co. Armagh, in September, 1914, joined the Royal Engineers, Ulster Division, as a despatch rider.

✧ ✧ ✧

Lieutenant John J. Doyle, 6th Royal Dublin Fusiliers, was killed in action at the Dardanelles about the 7th August last. He was the fourth son of Mr. Joseph Doyle, Fairview, Clontarf, and a grandson of the late Mr. Edward Fegan, Killashee, Naas. His brother, Captain E. C. Doyle, A.N.C., is well known in racing circles in India. Lieut. Doyle was only 22 years of age at the time of his death, and previous to receiving his commission had been an engineering student of the National University. He was well known in Dublin football circles.

1. LIEUT. R. S. V. TRAVERS,
7th Batt. Royal Munster Fusiliers.

2. LIEUT. D. BOYD WALLIS,
3rd Batt. Connaught Rangers.

3. LIEUT. J. R. WHITSITT,
5th Royal Inniskilling Fusiliers.

4. LIEUT. W. F. C. MacGARRY,
6th Batt. Royal Dublin Fusiliers.

5. MAJOR SIR WILLIAM LENNOX NAPIER,
4th South Wales Borderers.

6. CAPTAIN J. CLARKE,
R.A.M.C.

7. LIEUT. J. C. HAWKES,
R.A.M.C.

8. LIEUT. T. A. PEEL,
R.A.M.C.

9. LIEUT. J. J. DOYLE,
6th Batt. Royal Dublin Fusiliers.

OUR HEROES.

Second Lieut. Frank Brendan O'Carroll, 6th Batt. Royal Dublin Fusiliers, was killed in action on August 10th at Gallipoli. He was the youngest surviving son of Dr. O'Carroll, Merrion Square, and was educated at St. Mary's College, Rathmines, and Shrewsbury School. He subsequently entered University College, Dublin, and intended adopting the Bar as his profession, but immediately war broke out he at once applied for and obtained a commission in the 6th Dublin Fusiliers.

Captain C. B. Williams, 3rd Batt. Royal Irish Rifles, who has been killed in action in Flanders, was a son of Mr. J. A. Williams, The Willows, Northland Road, Londonderry. He was educated at Foyle College and Trinity, where he was a student when war broke out. He immediately volunteered and received his lieutenancy in May last. He left for the front with a draft of the 2nd Battalion on the 1st May last, and fell in action on August 29th. Captain Williams was a keen Rugby footballer and a capital swimmer, and was looked on in his regiment as a young officer of exceptional promise.

Second Lieutenant J. J. Beasley, 6th Batt. Royal Irish Fusiliers, who is reported killed in action at the Dardanelles, was a son of Mr. G. Beasley, Main-street, Limavady, Co. Londonderry. He was educated at Foyle College and Trinity, where he was a member of the Officers' Training Corps and rowed in the senior eights. He was in the second year of his medical course when on the outbreak of the war he joined the Royal Irish Fusiliers.

Captain Gerald William Nugent, Royal Irish Rifles and 29th Infantry Brigade, who has been killed in action, was the second son of Sir John Nugent, Bart., of Cloncoskoraine, Co. Waterford. He was formerly in the Worcestershire Regiment, and was gazetted temporary Captain in September, 1914, and Staff Captain in January of this year. Capt. Nugent married Norah, daughter of the late Dr. W. H. Bagnell, and leaves one daughter.

Captain Kingsmill William Jones, M.D., R.A.M.C., attached to 1st Batt. East Kent Regiment, has been mentioned in despatches for distinguished service on August 9th and 10th at Hooge, when during the entire day and night he was attending to the wounded in the front trenches, constantly exposing himself to shell and rifle fire. He was twice slightly wounded, but stuck to his work, and it was entirely owing to his efforts that the crater was successfully evacuated of wounded. Captain Jones is the only surviving son of Mrs. Perceval Jones, Glenmore, Orwell Park, Rathgar, and was educated at Trinity College.

Captain H. W. L. Waller, Brigade-Major, Royal Artillery, was recently presented with the Military Cross at Buckingham Palace by the King for gallant and distinguished service in the field. Captain Waller is a son of the Dean of Kildare, and is a keen and very popular officer.

Mr. James Edward Quin, 13th Batt. Royal Canadian Highlanders, who has been missing since the battle of St. Julien in Flanders, is now reported killed. He was the elder son of the late Mr. John Quin, D.L., Limerick, and was educated at Stonyhurst College and Louvain University. He was in Canada at the outbreak of the war, but immediately joined the Canadian contingent and was killed on the Ypres road, where his battalion having refused to surrender were practically annihilated, having fought until their ammunition was expended.

Lieut. John Hartley Schute, 6th Batt. Royal Irish Fusiliers, was killed in action at the Dardanelles on the 15th August last in his 22nd year. He was the younger son of the late Mr. Frederick Schute, C.E., and Mrs. Langley, and was very popular in Dublin sporting circles, being an excellent swimmer and footballer. He was educated at Strangways School and afterwards at Trinity College, where he graduated in 1914. He was a good sportsman, a gallant officer, and known to a large circle of friends as "one of the best."

Second Lieutenant C. E. S. Dobbs, Army Service Corps, has been mentioned in Sir John French's despatches and awarded the Military Cross. He is a son of Mr. and Mrs. J. S. Dobbs, Knockrath, Greystones, and great grandson of the late Major-General Dobbs. He was educated at Marlborough and Trinity College, Dublin. He joined the A.S.C. Special Reserve in January, 1914, and on August 4th was attached to the 1st Division of the Expeditionary Force, receiving his commission in November.

OUR HEROES

1. LIEUT. F. B. O'CARROLL,
6th Batt. Royal Dublin Fusiliers.

2. CAPT. C. B. WILLIAMS,
3rd Batt. Royal Irish Rifles.

3. LIEUT. J. J. BEASLEY,
6th Batt. Royal Irish Fusiliers.

4. CAPT. G. W. NUGENT,
Royal Irish Rifles.

5. CAPT. K. W. JONES, M.D.,
1st Batt. East Kent Regiment.

6. CAPT. H. W. L. WALLER,
Royal Artillery.

7. MR. F. E. QUIN,
13th Batt. R. Canadian Highlanders.

8. LIEUT. J. H. SCHUTE,
6th Batt. Royal Irish Fusiliers.

9. LIEUT. C. E. S. DOBBS,
Army Service Corps.

OUR HEROES.

Lieutenant Irving M. Palmer, R.N., in command of H.M.S. *Comet,* has been awarded the Distinguished Service Cross for service on the river Tigris, Mesopotamia, especially for the capture of a battalion of Turkish officers and men—twenty-five officers, including a general, and three hundred and seventeen men. He is youngest son of Surgeon I. M. Palmer, Armagh, and has two brothers in the Royal Navy—Commander Alex. R. Palmer and Acting-Commander E. M. Palmer.

◇ ◇ ◇

Captain Francis Percy Freeman, R.A.M.C., has been awarded the Military Cross for conspicuous gallantry and devotion to duty during operations near Hulluch, from 25th to 29th September, 1915. For four consecutive days and nights he brought in and attended to the wounded, repeatedly going out under heavy fire. By his personal bravery and energy he set a splendid example to his men. He was mentioned in despatches after Neuve Chapelle. He is the eldest son of the late Mr. David Freeman, and Mrs. Freeman, Saravan, Morehampton-road. His two brothers are also with the forces.

◇ ◇ ◇

Lieutenant T. W. Gerald Johnson, 5th Connaught Rangers, second son of Professor and Mrs. T. Johnson, 13 Palmerston Park, has been awarded the Military Cross for conspicuous bravery in Gallipoli, where, entering a Turkish trench, he bayonetted six and shot two Turks. Lieutenant Johnson is in his 23rd year, and entered Trinity College, Dublin, from Archbishop Holcate's School, Yorks, as a medical student. In November, 1914, he resigned his position as acting-house surgeon in Sir Patrick Dun's Hospital to join the 5th Batt. Connaught Rangers. Mr. Johnson is a prominent footballer, and played for Ireland against England in the Amateur International Association match. He is also a keen golfer, was Captain of the Dublin University Golf Club, and has twice won the Moncrieff Cup and Gold Medal of the Royal Dublin Golf Club at Dollymount.

◇ ◇ ◇

Captain Samuel Barbour Duffin, 2nd Batt. Royal Inniskilling Fusiliers, has had the Cross of the Legion of Honour conferred on him by the President of the French Republic for distinguished service in the field. Capt. Duffin is a son of the late Mr. Charles and Mrs. Duffin, Danesfort, Malone-road, Belfast.

◇ ◇ ◇

Captain Cecil Edward Walker, Royal Artillery, upon whom has been conferred by the French Government the Cross of the Legion of Honour, is the youngest son of the late Sir Samuel Walker, Bart., formerly Lord Chancellor of Ireland, and only son of Eleanor Lady Walker, Leeson Park. He is a nephew of Lieutenant-General Sir Mark Walker, K.C.B., who was one of the early recipients of the V.C., having obtained this distinction at the Battle of Inkerman. Captain Walker was educated at Rugby and joined the 102nd Battery, R.F.A., in 1901. In 1908 he was posted to D Battery, R.H.A., in which he served six years, and took over the Adjutancy of the Ayrshire R.H.A. in 1914. He received his Captaincy in the following autumn and has been at the front since May last.

◇ ◇ ◇

Captain R. L. Palmer, Royal Horse Artillery, was mentioned in first despatches October, 1914, for gallantry in action in France, and has been in all engagements from 20th August, 1914, to the present time. He is a son of Surgeon I. Mansergh Palmer, of Armagh.

◇ ◇ ◇

Lieutenant Bernard Score Browne, M.B., R.A.M.C., has been awarded the Military Cross for conspicuous gallantry and devotion to duty near Vermelles on the night of 2nd October, in searching for and carrying back wounded who were lying between our own and the enemy's lines, which were only 200 yards apart. At one time he tended the wounded within 15 yards of the enemy's trenches, though under fire all the time. Lieutenant Browne is a son of Lieutenant-Colonel A. W. Browne, R.A.M.C., of St. Kilda, Clooney, Londonderry, and was educated at Exeter College and Edinburgh University. He went to China as medical missionary in 1909, and in 1911 rendered invaluable services in the suppression of plague, for which he received the thanks of the Chinese Government and the British Minister at Peking, and received the insignia of the 1st class of 3rd division of the Order of the Double Dragon. On the outbreak of the war he returned home to volunteer his services and has since been at the front with the 2nd Batt. Cheshire Regiment.

◇ ◇ ◇

Captain M. W. Hawkes, 2nd Royal Munster Fusiliers, has been awarded the Military Cross and been mentioned in despatches twice. He was very severely wounded in action on May 9th, having received 16 wounds, one of which was caused by a bullet passing through his mouth and out under the jaw. Captain Hawkes is the eldest son of Mr. and Mrs. Hawkes, Barony's Hall, Timoleague, County Cork, and before he went to the front in December last was on General Hill's Staff.

◇ ◇ ◇

Lieutenant John Bell Hollwey, 52nd Brigade, Royal Field Artillery, has been awarded the Military Cross for conspicuous gallantry and devotion to duty on many occasions, notably on 25th September, 1915, when, as observing officer, he accompanied the infantry attack on Hohenzollern redoubt and laid a telephone wire under fire. Lieutenant Hollwey is a son of Mr. John Hollwey, Ardfallen, Dalkey. He was educated at St. Andrew's College, Dublin.

1. LIEUT. I. M. PALMER, Royal Navy. Distinguished Service Cross.
2. CAPT. F. P. FREEMAN, R.A.M.C. Military Cross.
3. LIEUT. T. W. G. JOHNSON, 5th Batt. Connaught Rangers. Military Cross.
4. CAPT. S. B. DUFFIN, 2nd Royal Inniskilling Fusiliers. Cross of the Legion of Honour.
5. CAPT. C. E. WALKER, R.A. Cross of the Legion of Honour.
6. CAPT. R. L. PALMER, Royal Horse Artillery. Mentioned in Despatches.
7. LIEUT. B. SCORE BROWNE, R.A.M.C. Military Cross.
8. CAPT. M. W. HAWKES, 2nd Royal Munster Fusiliers. Military Cross.
9. LIEUT. J. BELL HOLLWEY, R.F.A. Military Cross.

OUR HEROES.

Lieutenant Percy J. Jordan, 3rd Batt. Inniskilling Fusiliers, attached to the 1st Batt., killed in action at the Dardanelles on 21st August, 1915, was the only son of the late Rev. Dr. Jordan, Rector of Magherafelt. He was educated at St. Columba's College and Trinity College, Dublin. He offered himself for Army service on the outbreak of the war and received his commission just a year ago.

◊ ◊ ◊

Captain C. Palliser Wheeler, 1st Royal Berks Regiment, was the only son of Colonel and Mrs. Wheeler, The Rocks, Kilkenny, and nephew to the late Sir Chas. D. Wheeler Cuffe, Bart., Co. Kilkenny. He was educated at Haileybury and Sandhurst, obtained his commission in the 1st Royal Berks in 1910, and became Captain in May, 1915. He was in the retreat from Mons, was wounded in the battle of the Aisne, and was killed instantaneously by a burst of shrapnel on the morning of September 26th last.

◊ ◊ ◊

Lieutenant Francis Joseph Wisely, R.A.M.C., died of wounds received in action in the Dardanelles on September 1st last. He was the second son of the late Mr. James Wisely and Mrs. Wisely, Ravenhill Road, Belfast, and was educated at Clongowes Wood College, Royal University and Queen's College, Belfast. He had a brilliant Intermediate and University career, taking his degree in Medicine and Arts and securing a valuable scholarship for Botany and Zoology. He was for a short time Resident Surgeon at the Mater Hospital, Belfast and afterwards Resident Surgeon in Worcester County Asylum.

◊ ◊ ◊

Captain John Clarke, R.A.M.C., died of wounds received in action at the Dardanelles. He was the third son of Mr. William Clarke, Ballymena, and brother of Mr. James Clarke, solicitor, Ballymena. Captain Clarke was 32 years of age and was educated at Ballymena Academy, Edinburgh University and Queen's College, Belfast, where he took his degree in medicine. He subsequently practised at Aberbargoed, Cardiff, but when war broke out he offered his services and obtained his commission in the R.A.M.C. He was promoted Captain shortly after landing at the Dardanelles.

◊ ◊ ◊

Major Frederick Thomas Cecil Hill, 6th York and Lancaster Regiment, was the third surviving son of Arthur Manley (late 5th Fusiliers) and Mrs. Hill, Goodameavy House, Yelverton, S. Devon, and grandson of the late General J. T. Hill, 32nd Light Infantry, and of James Arthur Browne, Browne Hall, County Mayo. He joined the Army from Sandhurst in 1895, was promoted Lieutenant in December, 1897, and received his Captaincy in the Middlesex Regiment in 1901. From 1902 until 1911, when he retired, he was employed with the Army Pay Department. On the outbreak of the war he volunteered his services and was appointed Captain in the 6th Service Batt. York and Lancaster Regiment, and was created Major in December, 1914. He left with his Battalion for the Dardanelles in July last and fell whilst gallantly leading his Company in attacking a hill. He was 41 years of age and had married in 1900 Elizabeth, only child of the Comte de Foresta, and leaves one son.

◊ ◊ ◊

Captain James Anson Otho Brooke, V.C., 2nd Batt. Gordon Highlanders, who has been killed in action, was a son of Captain and Mrs. Harry Brooke, Fairley, Aberdeenshire, and grandson of Sir Arthur Brinsley Brooke, Bart., M.P., of Colebrooke, Co. Fermanagh, where the Brooke family have lived since 1658. Captain Brooke was mentioned in despatches and awarded the Victoria Cross for his coolness and gallantry in reforming the line and taking a most important trench at a critical moment, thus saving the situation, but the gallant Captain was shortly afterwards killed.

◊ ◊ ◊

Second Lieutenant Irvine J. Smyth, 6th Batt. Royal Inniskilling Fusiliers, was killed in action at Gallipoli on September 3rd last. He was a son of the Rev. W. H. Smyth, Methodist Minister, of 2 Wellesley Terrace, Wellington Road, Cork, and had been in the Civil Service until the war broke out, when he at once volunteered from T.C.D. into the 6th Black Watch and was appointed to a commission in the 6th Inniskillings. Lieut. Smyth was edcuated at Belfast Academy, Methodist College, Belfast, and Wesley and Trinity Colleges, Dublin.

◊ ◊ ◊

Captain Craig Nelson, 3rd Brahmas, attached 69th Punjabis, was killed in action in France on September 26th last. Captain Nelson was a son of Surgeon-Major Nelson, The Hill, Downpatrick, and was educated at Armagh Royal School and in Germany. He went through the South African campaign with the 2nd Royal Irish Rifles, and afterwards joined the Indian Army. On the outbreak of the war he went to Egypt, where he was appointed Staff Officer and was about to be re-appointed Staff Officer in Flanders when he fell in action. Captain Nelson married some years ago Miss Irene Sawyer, daughter of Colonel Sawyer, Indian Army, and leaves two boys.

◊ ◊ ◊

Second Lieutenant R. A. McCall, 9th Cheshire Regiment, who was killed in action in France, was the younger son of Mr. C. H. McCall, J.P., Duneda, Banbridge, County Down. He was educated at Weymouth College. He was the first volunteer from Banbridge to offer his services on the outbreak of the war. He went with his Battalion to the front in July last.

1. LIEUT. P. J. JORDAN.
3rd Batt. Inniskilling Fusiliers.

2. CAPT. C. PALLISER WHEELER,
1st Royal Berks Regiment.

3. LIEUT. F. J. WISELY,
R.A.M.C.

4. CAPT. J. CLARKE,
R.A.M.C.

5. MAJOR F. T. HILL,
6th York and Lancs. Regiment.

6. CAPT. J. A. O. BROOKE, V.C.,
2nd Batt. Gordon Highlanders.

7. LIEUT. I. J. SMYTH,
6th Royal Inniskilling Fusiliers.

8. CAPTAIN C. NELSON,
3rd Brahmas.

9. LIEUT. R. A. McCALL,
9th Cheshire Regiment.

OUR HEROES.

Lieutenant Charles E. S. Irvine, C.E., Northern Rhodesian Rifles, was killed in action at Mwenengambe, on the Myasaland border. He was the fourth son of the late Colonel Irvine, D.L., of Killedeas, Co. Fermanagh. He was educated at Trinity College, where he took his Engineering degree, and was subsequently engaged on railway work in Rhodesia. He joined a volunteer corps during the South African War, and on the outbreak of the present war he was given a commission in the Northern Rhodesian Rifles.

◇ ◇ ◇

Lieut.-Surgeon P. J. Walsh, R.A.M.C., killed in action in France in September last, was the eldest son of Mr. Patrick Walsh, Midleton, and a very talented medical officer. He was educated at the University College, Cork. He subsequently obtained a high place in the Indian Medical Service, and was appointed to an important Government position in India, but on the outbreak of hostilities he accompanied the Indian troops to France as a R.A.M.C. subaltern.

◇ ◇ ◇

Lieutenant H. A. H. Warnock, 4th Batt. Royal Irish Fusiliers, was killed in action on August 16th, at Bapaume. He was officially reported wounded and missing on August 12th. Lieutenant Warnock was the eldest son of the late Dr. Hugh Warnock and Mrs. Warnock, of Clogher, County Tyrone. He was educated at St. Columba's College and Trinity College, Dublin, gaining his commission from the O.T.C. in August, 1914, and was promoted in May of the following year. He was sent to France in June, 1915.

◇ ◇ ◇

Captain James Seymour Strachan Mowbray, Black Watch, of Killeany, Mountrath, was killed in action in France early in September last. He was the eldest son of the late Mr. Seymour Mowbray, of Killeany, and was educated at Leamington. He adopted the profession of Engineering and entered the L.N.W.Rly. Co.'s Works at Crewe, where he was a member of the Volunteer (Railway) Battalion of the Royal Engineers. He was in the service of the Land Commission at the outbreak of the war, but volunteered for active service and obtained a commission in the Black Watch, with which regiment his family had been honourably associated. Captain Mowbray was the fourth of his family killed in action in the present war, and leaves a widow and daughter to mourn his loss. He was well known as a keen rider to hounds in King's and Queen's Counties and Kilkenny. He had been at the front since April.

◇ ◇ ◇

Major W. H. Nichols, 8th Batt. Somerset Light Infantry, of Kilbrack, Doneraile, Co. Cork, was wounded in the attack on Hill 70 on September 26th, and died of his wounds on October 15th, at Munich. He was born in Dunedin, New Zealand, and educated at Christ's College, Christchurch, New Zealand, and Jesus College, Cambridge, where he played in the College Rugby team and rowed in the College 1st boat and won his oar. He went to South Africa with the North Cork Militia. He was secretary to the Duhallow Hounds before the outbreak of the present war, but immediately offered his services and was gazetted to the 8th Somerset Light Infantry.

◇ ◇ ◇

Captain A. J. W. Blake, 5th Connaught Rangers, was killed in action at the Dardanelles on August 21st. Captain Blake served in the South African War and obtained three medals. He had travelled extensively in Canada, and on the outbreak of the war he joined the South Irish Horse, subsequently receiving a commission in the 5th Connaught Rangers and being promoted Captain prior to his departure for the Dardanelles.

◇ ◇ ◇

Lieutenant Robert Carlyle Baile, Royal Engineers, who was killed in action at Loos about the 24th October, was the eldest son of the Rev. G. W. Baile, LL.B., Consular Chaplain, Pernambuco, Brazil, and grandson of the late Robert Baile, M.A., Head Master of Ranelagh School, Athlone. He was educated at Ranelagh School and Trinity College, Dublin, where he graduated in Arts and Engineering. He was Resident Engineer to the Great Western Brazil Railway, but on the outbreak of war resigned and returned to England, where he enlisted in the Royal Naval Division, subsequently obtaining a commission in the Royal Engineers.

◇ ◇ ◇

Second Lieut. Melbourne Ross, 4th Batt. Royal Irish Rifles, who has been killed in action, was a son of Mr. George Ross, Cultra, of the well-known firm of William Ross and Sons, Ltd., Belfast. Immediately war broke out Lieut. Melbourne Ross and his brother, Lieut. Kenneth Ross, patriotically volunteered and on the 15th of August, 1914, were gazetted to the 4th Batt. Royal Irish Rifles. They went to the front and were attached to the 2nd Batt. They had only been a short time at the front when Lieut. Melbourne Ross was killed and Lieut. Kenneth Ross was wounded and is reported missing.

◇ ◇ ◇

Lieutenant Vesey A. Davoren, 7th Suffolk Regiment, was wounded in the action on the Hohenzollern Redoubt on October 13th, but continued to lead his Company until killed by a shot from a machine gun. He was educated at St. Paul's School, London, and Trinity College, Dublin, where both his grandfather, Colonel Vesey Davoren, J.P., and his father, Major Vesey Davoren, were educated. He had just taken his degree when the war broke out and immediately volunteered, obtaining his commission in the 7th Suffolk Regiment.

1. LT. C. E. S. IRVINE, Northern Rhodesian Rifles.
2. LT.-SURGEON P. J. WALSH, R.A.M.C.
3. LT. H. A. H. WARNOCK, 4th Batt. Royal Irish Fusiliers.
4. CAPT. J. S. MOWBRAY, 8th Black Watch.
5. MAJOR W. H. NICHOLS, 8th Batt. Somerset Light Infantry.
6. CAPT. A. J. W BLAKE, 5th Batt. Connaught Rangers.
7. LT. R. C. BAILE, Royal Engineers.
8. LT. M. ROSS, 2nd Batt. Royal Irish Rifles.
9. LT. V. A. DAVOREN, 7th Suffolk Regiment.

OUR HEROES.

Lieutenant J. J. L. Morgan, 2nd Batt. Royal Inniskilling Fusiliers, died of wounds sustained in action in France on May 16th last. Lieutenant Morgan was a younger brother of Lieutenant S. V. Morgan, Adjutant, 3rd Batt. Royal Irish Rifles, Portobello Barracks, Dublin. He was born in Newtownards and joined the Royal Irish Rifles about 14 years ago. He served for five years with the 1st Battalion in India and returned to England with his Battalion shortly after the outbreak of war. He was posted to the Royal Inniskilling Fusiliers in November, 1914.

◇ ◇ ◇

Andrew John Viscount Stuart was killed near Haines, France, during a German counter-attack, after leading his men in the storming of the Hohenzollern Redoubt on September 25, 1915. The late Viscount, who was educated at Shrewsbury and Corpus Christi College, Oxford, was in his thirty-fourth year when he was killed. Viscount Stuart was a great lover of literature and art, and was the author of some verses, entitled, "Sailor, what of the Debt we Owe You?" which appeared in the "Times," September 16th, 1914. He was loved by all classes.

◇ ◇ ◇

Lieutenant T. C. Campbell, R.E., was the eldest son of the Rev. Wm. Howard Campbell, M.D., B.D., Missionary in Cuddapah, Madras, South India, and of Mrs. Campbell, of Edinburgh. He was born in India in 1887. He was educated at Foyle College, Derry, and afterwards at Queen's College, Galway, and had a brilliant University career. On the outbreak of war he gave up a good position in Toronto, and came to England. He left with the 11th Division for the Dardanelles on July 5th, and on October 5th was wounded in action and died three days later.

◇ ◇ ◇

Captain the Hon. Maurice Henry Dermot Browne, Coldstream Guards, second son of the Earl of Kenmare, has been killed in action in France. He was gazetted in January, 1914, and received his Lieutenancy on November 15th in the same year. Captain Browne was only 21 years of age, and is believed to have been the youngest Captain in the Army.

◇ ◇ ◇

Lieut.-Colonel Bertram Perceval Lefroy, D.S.O., 2nd Batt. Royal Warwickshire Regiment, who died on September 27th, from wounds received when leading his men into action, on the 25th, was born in May, 1878. He was the second son of Thomas Charles Perceval Lefroy, of 11 Ashburn Place, London, and Isabella Napier, daughter of the late Alexander Hastie, of Carnock, N.B. He served in the South African War, and received the D.S.O. for gallantry at the defence of Forts Prospect and Itala, where he was severely wounded. He held the Queen's Medal, with five clasps. At the beginning of August, 1914, he went out on the staff of the 1st Division, and remained seven months. He then served on the staff of the 26th Division in England until the beginning of July, when he returned to the Front to command the 2nd Batt. Royal Warwickshires. He was three times mentioned in despatches, and received the Legion of Honour. Lieut.-Colonel Lefroy was a grandson of the late Very Rev. Jeffry Lefroy, Dean of Dromore.

◇ ◇ ◇

Major J. W. Considine, 2nd Royal Munster Fusiliers, was killed in action in France on September 25th last. Major Considine passed through Sandhurst and was gazetted to the Munster Fusiliers in April, 1902, and had served with his Regiment in Gibraltar and India, where he took part in the North-West Frontier Expedition in 1907, for which he received the King's Medal and clasp. He had also served with the 1st Batt. in Burma, and altogether had $13\frac{1}{2}$ years' service. He had been in France since April last, and in command of the 2nd Batt. for $4\frac{1}{2}$ months. Major Considine married in 1912 Kathleen N., second daughter of William B. Law, 20 Royal Terrace, Kingstown.

◇ ◇ ◇

Lieutenant Richard Newman Somerville, 94th Field Company, Royal Engineers, was killed in action in France on Saturday, 9th October. Lieutenant Somerville was the eldest son of Mr. R. N. Somerville, of Osborne Park, Belfast, who for many years was County Surveyor of Cavan, and a grandson of the late Rev. J. D. Martin, of Tullyallen, County Armagh. He was educated at the Royal School, Cavan, and was a graduate of Trinity College, Dublin, and a member of the Officers' Training Corps.

◇ ◇ ◇

Lieutenant Henry Joseph Burke, 1st Batt. South Staffordshire Regiment, was killed whilst leading his Company in an attack on the German trenches on September 25th last, in his 21st year. He was the younger son of the late Captain Edward Plunkett Burke, King's Own Regiment, and grandson of the late Sir Bernard Burke, C.B., Ulster King of Arms. Lieutenant Burke was educated at Stonyhurst College and Sandhurst, and in July, 1914, was gazetted to the South Staffordshire Regiment.

◇ ◇ ◇

Lieutenant James A. Ronayne, 5th Batt. Royal Munster Fusiliers (attached 2nd Batt.), was killed in action on September 25th, in France, in his 25th year. He was the only son of Mr. James Uniacke Ronayne, of Summerfield House, Youghal, County Cork, and was gazetted on August 15th, 1914, to the 5th Batt. Royal Munster Fusiliers, and in July last joined the 2nd Batt. at the Front. He was educated at Midleton College and Trinity College, Dublin.

OUR HEROES

1. LT. J. J. L. MORGAN,
2nd Batt. Royal Inniskilling Fusiliers.

2. LT. VISCOUNT STUART,
6th Royal Scots Fusiliers.

3. LT. T. C. CAMPBELL,
Royal Engineers.

4. CAPT. THE HON. M. H. D. BROWNE,
Coldstream Guards.

5. LT.-COL. B. P. LEFROY, D.S.O.,
2nd Batt. Royal Warwickshire Regiment.

6. MAJOR J. W. CONSIDINE,
2nd Batt. Royal Munster Fusiliers.

7. LT. R. N. SOMERVILLE,
Royal Engineers.

8. LT. H. J. BURKE,
1st Batt. Sth. Staffordshire Regiment.

9. LT. J. A. RONAYNE,
5th Batt. Royal Munster Fusiliers.

OUR HEROES.

Second Lieutenant George G. Fowler, 2nd Batt. King's Royal Rifle Corps, died in hospital at La Pagnoy, from wounds received in action near Loos, on September 25th last, in his 19th year. He was the second son of Captain and Mrs. R. H. Fowler, Rahinstown, Co. Meath. He was educated at Eton and Sandhurst, and joined the King's Rifle Corps in November, 1914. He went to the front with his Regiment about the end of January, 1915.

◇ ◇ ◇

Second Lieut. Basil Montgomery Coates, 10th Rifle Brigade, was the only son of the late W. Montgomery Coates, M.A. and double gold medallist of Trinity College, Dublin, and Fellow and Bursar of Queen's College, Cambridge, and of Mrs. W. Montgomery Coates, of Sheringham, Norfolk. Born at Cambridge on September 16, 1893, he was educated at the Perse School, Cambridge, Oundle School (at both schools he served in the O.T.C.), and Queen's College, Cambridge. On the outbreak of war he was given a commission in the Rifle Brigade, and was killed in France on September 7, 1915.

◇ ◇ ◇

Lieutenant J. W. Bennett, 3rd Batt. Royal Munster Fusiliers (attached 2nd Batt.), was killed in action near Loos in France, on October 13th, aged 25 years. He was the only son of Mr. and Mrs. John H. Bennett, Charleston, Ballinacurra, Co. Cork, and was educated at Mostyn House School, Cheshire, and Shrewsbury School. He applied for a commission shortly after the outbreak of war and joined the 3rd Batt. Royal Munster Fusiliers in November, 1914. He went to France in August.

◇ ◇ ◇

Captain Harold E. Large, 10th Rifle Brigade, is the third son of Mr. and Mrs. Robert Emmott Large, of Surbiton, to fall in the present war. Major Philip Martin Large, 3rd Middlesex Regiment, was killed on April 23rd, and Captain Herbert Edward Large, also of the 3rd Middlesex Regiment, was killed on February 15th. Captain Harold Emmott Large, who was the fifth and youngest son, was killed in action in France on October 9th last. He was educated at Sherborne, and was formerly in the Militia, but on the outbreak of war obtained his Captaincy in the 10th Rifle Brigade. He lived at Plodstown, Mullingar, and was a well-known follower of the Westmeath Hunt.

◇ ◇ ◇

Major Harold B. Galloway, 7th Seaforth Highlanders, of Annestown, Waterford, was killed in action in Flanders on September 25th last. He was a keen follower of the Waterford Hunt, and his death is a loss to the Irish Hunting Field. Major Galloway was the only surviving son of Mr. Charles Galloway, Thorneyholme, Knutsford. He joined the 2nd Batt. Seaforth Highlanders in 1888, and served in the Hazara Expedition in 1891 (medal and clasps), the Relief of Chitral, 1895 (medal and clasps), and in the South African War, 1901-2, attached to Lovat's Scouts, for his services in which he received the medal and three clasps. At the outbreak of the war Major Galloway was in the Reserve of Officers, but joined the 7th Seaforth Highlanders and was promoted Major.

◇ ◇ ◇

Captain J. N. Armstrong, M.B., R.A.M.C., who was killed in action in Flanders on August 22nd last, in his 24th year, was the only son of Mr. J. N. Armstrong, J.P., of Dundalk. He was educated at Ipswich and Portora Schools and Trinity College, Dublin, where he obtained a Senior Moderatorship with gold medal. He also studied surgery in St. Mary's Hospital, Paddington, and at the outbreak of the war was employed as an assistant in the Wakefield Asylum. Volunteering immediately, he served for a time in base hospitals at Havre and Boulogne, and was appointed M.O. to the Durham Light Infantry (2nd Batt.), on 23rd December, 1914.

◇ ◇ ◇

Second Lieutenant Robert Stanton, 6th Royal Dublin Fusiliers, who had previously been reported wounded and missing, is now reported to have been killed in action at the Dardanelles on August 9th. He was the eldest son of Mr. John Stanton, Solicitor, Cork, and was educated at the Christian Brothers' College, Cork, and Trinity College, Dublin. He chose the profession of Solicitor and practised with his father until the outbreak of the war, when he obtained his commission in the 6th Royal Dublin Fusiliers.

◇ ◇ ◇

Lieutenant William C. Nesbitt, 6th Batt. Royal Dublin Fusiliers, of St. Mary's, Booterstown Avenue, Blackrock, was killed in action at the Dardanelles on August 16th last. He was educated at Blackrock College. He was a member of the Finance, Works, Library and Technical Committees of the Blackrock Council. Lieutenant Nesbitt was the only son of the late Mr. Wm. Nesbitt, Dove House, Blackrock. Immediately the war broke out he joined the 6th Dublin Fusiliers and went with his Regiment to the Dardanelles.

◇ ◇ ◇

Lieutenant B. G. MacDowel, 1st Batt. Connaught Rangers, who was killed in action in Flanders on September 22nd last, was the second son of Dr. and Mrs. MacDowel, The Mall House, Sligo. He was educated at Aravon, Bray, and Aldenham School, Herts, and was a young man of splendid physique, 6 feet 3 inches in height, a good golfer, football player, and a great all-round athlete. He was gazetted to the Connaught Rangers in October, 1914.

1. LT. G. G. FOWLER,
2nd Batt. King's Royal Rifle Corps.

2. 2nd LT. B. MONTGOMERY COATES,
10th Rifle Brigade.

3. LT. J. W. BENNETT,
3rd Batt. Royal Munster Fusiliers.

4. CAPT. H. E. LARGE,
10th Rifle Brigade.

5. MAJOR H. B. GALLOWAY,
7th Seaforth Highlanders.

6. CAPT. J. N. ARMSTRONG, M.B.,
R.A.M.C.

7. 2nd LT. R. STANTON,
6th Royal Dublin Fusiliers.

8. LT. W. C. NESBITT,
6th Royal Dublin Fusiliers.

9. LT. B. G. MacDOWEL,
1st Batt. Connaught Rangers.

OUR HEROES.

Second Lieutenant Walter Leslie Orr, 4th Batt. Royal Irish Rifles, who was killed in action in Flanders in his 25th year, was the youngest son of the late Mr. F. Harman Orr and Mrs. Orr, Crosthwaite Park, Kingstown. He was educated at Avoca School, Blackrock, and Trinity College. He subsequently went to Malay to join his brother in rubber planting, but was invalided home in March, 1914. On the outbreak of the war he immediately volunteered and received a commission in the Royal Irish Rifles. He left for the front in July last and was attached to the 2nd Batt. Royal Irish Rifles when he fell in action about September 25th.

◇ ◇ ◇

Capt. J. R. F. Lecky, 7th Batt. R. Fusiliers (Special Reserve), who was killed in action in the Persian Gulf operations, was the only son of Mrs. Rupert Lecky and the late Mr. J. Rupert Lecky, of Ballykealey, Tullow, Co. Carlow. He was educated at Elstree, Harrow, and was a member of the Middle Temple. Captain Lecky joined the 7th Battalion Royal Fusiliers in 1896, and on the outbreak of the war he went to the front, attached to the 4th Batt. Royal Fusiliers, in November, 1914. On December 14th he was wounded, and on the 16th obtained his Captaincy. At the beginning of May last he left for the Persian Gulf, was in the battle of Nasayral and was killed in action at the taking of Kutel Amara in September last. Captain Lecky was High Sheriff of Carlow in 1912, and is succeeded to the family estate by his uncle, Col. F. Beauchamp Lecky, D.S.O.

◇ ◇ ◇

Second Lieutenant James Gordon Caruth, 5th Batt. Royal Irish Rifles, was killed in action in France on September 26th last, in his 19th year. He was educated at Oakfield Preparatory School, Rugby, and Cheltenham College, where he played in the School Cricket 2nd XI. and Football in the 1st XV. He was champion gymnast of the School in March, 1914, and represented his school at Aldershot for the Public Schools Shield in April, 1914. On the outbreak of the war he was gazetted to the 5th Batt. Royal Irish Rifles and went to France, attached to the 2nd Batt. in July, 1915.

◇ ◇ ◇

Captain R. N. Pike, West African Frontier Force, who was killed in action at the taking of Mora, N. Cameroons, on September 8th last, was a son of Mr. and Mrs. Pike, Glenderary, Achill Sound, Co. Mayo. He served in the Irish Batt. Imperial Yeomanry during the Boer War. He afterwards joined the West African Frontier Force, and was later appointed Asst. Resident in West Africa, but when war broke out he again joined the West African Frontier Force and was promoted temporary Captain.

◇ ◇ ◇

Lieut.-Colonel Basil Edwin Phillips, 5th Royal Welsh Fusiliers, was killed in action on August 10th last. He was a brother of Mr. F. Phillips, of Gaulstown House, Coole, Westmeath, and a son of the late Captain E. W. Phillips and Mrs. Phillips, of Rhûaal, Flintshire. Colonel Phillips was closely associated with political work, and also took a great interest in educational and agricultural matters. He was gazetted to the command of the 5th Battalion Royal Welsh Fusiliers in July, 1912, and was extremely popular with all ranks, who held him in the highest respect. On the outbreak of war Colonel Phillips at once volunteered for foreign service, and had been only a few weeks at the front when he fell in action.

◇ ◇ ◇

Captain J. Percival Longfield, M.V.O., 1st Batt. Norfolk Regiment, who was killed in action in France on September 30th last, was the only son of Lt.-Colonel Longfield, of Waterloo, Mallow, County Cork. Captain Longfield retired from the Army in 1912, but immediately war broke out he rejoined his regiment. His death is a great loss to the Irish Hunting field, where he was well known as joint Master with Mr. R. G. Annesley of the Duhallow Hounds.

◇ ◇ ◇

Lieutenant George L'Estrange Cramer, 4th Batt. Royal Munster Fusiliers, attached to 2nd Batt., who has died of wounds received in action in Flanders, was the second son of the late Major J. T. Cramer, R.G.A., of Ballindinish, County Cork, who was for some time Asst. District Commissioner of the Sierra Leone Protectorate. Immediately the war broke out Lt. Cramer joined the 4th Munsters, and was only in his 19th year when he fell.

◇ ◇ ◇

Captain E. T. Milton, 13th Northumberland Fusiliers, was killed in action at Loos on September 26th, 1915, in his 28th year. He was educated at Belfast, and received his training as Marine Engineer with Messrs. Workman, Clark and Co., Belfast. He was serving as engineer in the Prince Line, Newcastle, when war was declared and immediately answered his country's call by enlisting in the Northumberland Fusiliers. He received his commission in September and was promoted Captain in the following November. He was a son of Mr. E. J. Milton, 27 West Avenue, Gosforth.

◇ ◇ ◇

Mr. George Lloyd, Winnipeg Light Infantry, who was reported missing after the charge at Langemarck, on April 22nd last, is now reported killed. At the outbreak of the war he held a position on the staff of the Hudson Bay Company, Winnipeg, but immediately joined the Canadian contingent. He was the youngest son of Mr. Thomas E. Lloyd, Heathfield, Co. Limerick.

1. LIEUT. W. L. ORR,
4th Batt. Royal Irish Rifles.

2. CAPT. J. R. F. LECKY,
7th Batt. Royal Fusiliers.

3. SECOND LT. J. G. CARUTH,
5th Batt. Royal Irish Rifles.

4. CAPT. R. N. PIKE,
West African Frontier Force.

5. COL. BASIL PHILLIPS,
5th Royal Welsh Fusiliers.

6. CAPT. J. P. LONGFIELD,
M.V.O.,
1st Batt. Norfolk Regiment.

7. LT. G. L'ESTRANGE CRAMER.
4th Batt. Royal Munster Fusiliers.

8. CAPT. E. T. MILTON,
13th Northumberland Fusiliers.

9. MR. GEORGE LLOYD,
Winnipeg Light Infantry.

OUR HEROES.

Lieutenant Francis Curley, Royal Engineers, who was killed in action in France on September 25th, was a son of the late Mr. Alex. Curley and Mrs. Curley, Mentmore, Lisburn Road, Belfast. He was educated at the Queen's University, Belfast, where he took his degree as Bachelor of Science in 1912. On the outbreak of war he obtained a commission in the Royal Engineers, and had been at the front since January last.

✧ ✧ ✧

Second Lieutenant the Rev. Dr. Everard Digges La Touche, 6th Reinforcements, 2nd Battalion, Australian Imperial Force, was killed in action between August 6th and 8th. He was the eldest son of Mrs. E. N. Digges La Touche and the late Major E. N. Digges La Touche, Bengal Infantry and Assam Commission. Educated at Bedford Grammar School he afterwards entered Trinity College, Dublin. He was a brilliant Scholar and Gold Medallist of his University. In 1910 he was appointed Donnellan Lecturer, and at the same time he published "Christian Certitude," for which he received the hon. degree of Litt.D. from his University. In 1912, being in delicate health, he went to Australia and worked there, principally in Sydney, as Diocesan Missioner, where he became well known. On the outbreak of the war he immediately volunteered for the front and came with the Reinforcements to Egypt, arriving on July the 18th. He fell in his first battle at Suvla Bay.

✧ ✧ ✧

Lieut. Averell Digges La Touche, 5th Royal Irish Rifles, was killed in action on September 25th last in France. He was the youngest and only surviving son of Mrs. E. N. Digges La Touche and the late Major E. N. Digges La Touche, Bengal Infantry and Assam Commission. He was educated at Bedford Grammar School, and afterwards entered the College of Science, Dublin. When the war broke out he immediately volunteered and got a commission in the 5th Royal Irish Rifles, and left for the front on June 21st. He was attached to the 2nd Royal Irish Rifles.

✧ ✧ ✧

Captain Vere Dawson Shortt, 7th Northamptonshire Regiment, who was killed in action in France on the 27th September, was the only son of the late James Fitzmaurice Shortt, of Moorfield, Mountrath, and grand nephew of the late Vere Shortt, of Larch Hill, Queen's County. He was in the Cape Mounted Rifles from 1890-1895 and served through the Pondoland campaign with them.

✧ ✧ ✧

Major John Noble Jephson, who died August 29th, 1915, of wounds received in action in Gallipoli, was the second son of the late Deputy Inspector-General Wm. Holmes Jephson, M.D., and nephew of the late Robert Holmes Jephson, Lansdowne Road, Dublin, and was born at Bangalore in 1864. He was gazetted from Sandhurst to the Manchester Regiment in 1885, joining the 5th Bengal Infantry in 1889. He retired from the Indian Army in 1905, through malaria. On the outbreak of the war he at once offered his services and was appointed 2nd in command of the 6th Batt. Royal Munster Fusiliers. He took part in the recent landing of that regiment in Suvla Bay, and the subsequent fighting from the 6th to the 29th of August, on which date he fell, shot through the head, while leading his men.

✧ ✧ ✧

Captain J. E. Lynch, who was killed in action at Loos in France on September 25th, was the second son of Mr. M. E. Lynch, Barrister-at-Law, of 4 Clifton Terrace, Monkstown, Co. Dublin, and formerly of Balrobin, Dundalk. Captain Lynch was educated at Clongowes Wood College and at Trinity College, Dublin, from which he entered the Army in 1905, joining the 2nd Batt. Royal Irish Fusiliers, then stationed in India. He subsequently retired, but on the outbreak of the war he offered his services, and was appointed in September, 1914, to the 10th Batt. Yorkshire Regiment.

✧ ✧ ✧

Lieutenant James MacLaughlin, 4th Batt. Royal Dublin Fusiliers, fell in action at the battle of Ypres, while gallantly defending a dangerous position, on the 25th May, 1915. He was the elder son of the late Mr. P. J. MacLaughlin and Mrs. MacLaughlin, Brackloon, Rathgar Road, Dublin. Previous to joining the Army he was a brilliant student of Belvidere College and the National University, and at the outbreak of war resigned a lucrative post in Chili, to rejoin his regiment.

✧ ✧ ✧

Second Lieutenant Llewellyn Charles Nash, 2nd Batt. King's Royal Rifle Corps, was educated at Eton. He went to Sandhurst in August, 1914, and was gazetted to the King's Royal Rifle Corps in November of the same year. He went to the front in January last, and was posted to the 2nd Battalion of his regiment. He was gazetted temporary Captain in July, 1915. He died in hospital on September 28th of wounds received in action on September 25th, aged 20.

✧ ✧ ✧

Lieutenant W. C. F. Darling, attached 1st Batt. Royal Irish Rifles, was killed in action in France on October 15th last. He was the eldest son of the late Rev. Oliver W. Darling, Rector of All Saints, Duncannon, Co. Wexford, and was educated at Braidlea, Stoke Bishop, and Haileybury College, Herts, where he was a member of the Officers' Training Corps. At the outbreak of the war he volunteered for service and was gazetted to the 14th Batt. Royal Irish Rifles, being subsequently transferred to the 3rd Batt.

1. LT. F. CURLEY, Royal Engineers.

2. 2nd LT. THE REV. DR. DIGGES LA TOUCHE, 2nd Batt. Australian Imperial Force.

3. LT. A. DIGGES LA TOUCHE, 5th Royal Irish Rifles.

4. CAPT. V. D. SHORTT, 7th Northamptonshire Regiment.

5. MAJOR J. NOBLE JEPHSON, 6th Batt. Royal Munster Fusiliers.

6. CAPT. J. E. LYNCH, 10th Batt. Yorkshire Regiment.

7. LT. J. MacLAUGHLIN, 4th Batt. Royal Dublin Fusiliers.

8. LT. L. C. NASH, 2nd Batt. King's Royal Rifles.

9. LT. W. C. F. DARLING, 1st Batt. Royal Irish Rifles.

OUR HEROES.

Second Lieutenant Sydney Vernon Young, Royal Engineers, was killed in action in Flanders on September 25th last. He was the elder son of Professor Sydney Young, F.R.S., Trinity College, and Mrs. Young, Raglan-road, Dublin. Lieutenant Young was educated at Charterhouse and passed into Woolwich in 1913. He was gazetted to the Royal Engineers in November last and after seven months at Chatham was sent to France, where he fell in action in his 19th year.

◇ ◇ ◇

Captain Anketell Moutray Read, Northamptonshire Regiment, was killed in action in France on September 25th. He was the youngest son of the late Colonel John Moutray Read and Mrs. Read, Wentworth, Wicklow. Captain Read was educated at Westward Ho College, from whence he passed direct to Sandhurst, was gazetted to the 20th Gloucester Regiment and served with them for three years in India. He went with the first Expeditionary Force to France on August 11th, 1914, was at Maubege and Mons and the retreat to the Marne. He was attached as Captain to the 9th Lancers, and while with them was severely wounded during the fighting on the Aisne. For his devotion to duty and bravery on the day of his death his name has been submitted for the Victoria Cross. He was previously noted for the D.S.O. for duties gallantly performed under heavy fire about the 29th August.

(The V.C. has since been awarded.)

◇ ◇ ◇

Second Lieutenant Wm. A. Birmingham, 6th Royal Irish Fusiliers, was killed in action in the Dardanelles on August 10th last. He was a member of an old Co. Galway family, his grandfather being the late Mr. Blake Birmingham, of Dalgan. Lieut. Birmingham obtained his commission in January last, and after three hard days' fighting he was badly wounded on the morning of August 10th, but gallantly held on until he was killed.

◇ ◇ ◇

Captain Francis John Brodigan, 1st Gloucester Regiment, who was killed in action on May 9th last, was the only son of the late Colonel Brodigan, of Piltown House, Drogheda, and was in his 31st year. He joined the Gloucester Regiment from the Militia as 2nd Lieutenant in 1902, and obtained his Captaincy in 1912. Captain Brodigan's father had been in the same regiment and served with distinction in the Crimean War.

◇ ◇ ◇

Major the Hon. Cyril Myles Ponsonby, M.V.O., Grenadier Guards, who was killed in France on September 28th, was the second son of the Earl and Countess of Bessborough. Born in 1881, he was educated at Harrow and Sandhurst, and joined the Grenadier Guards in 1900. He served in the South African War, 1902, taking part in the later operations in Cape Colony, and was A.D.C. to the Duke of Connaught from 1907 to 1909. He received his last promotion in May of this year. Major Ponsonby, who lived at 44 Gloucester Square, married, in 1911, Rita Narcissa, eldest daughter of Lieutenant-Colonel M. P. C. Longfield, of Castle Mary, Co. Cork, and leaves one son, born in 1912, Arthur M. L. Ponsonby.

◇ ◇ ◇

Captain Ernest C. Deane, R.A.M.C., was killed in action in France on September 25th last. He was the third son of Mr. T. S. Deane, Bank House, Rathkeale, Co. Limerick. Captain Deane was a well-known International Rugby player, and was formerly captain of the Monkstown and Adelaide Hospital fifteens. Ten days before his death he was awarded the Military Cross for a special act of gallantry. He had been a year at the front when he fell. His three brothers are also serving in India, England and the Cameroons.

◇ ◇ ◇

Lieutenant Richard P. W. Gethin, 2nd Battalion Royal Munster Fusiliers, was the only son and child of Mrs. Henry Gethin, 1 Carbury Place, Blackrock, and was educated at Stoneyhurst College. His father, Captain Henry R. Gethin, was killed in action in 1900 in South Africa leading his men into action, and now his son has also met a soldier's death on September 25-26.

◇ ◇ ◇

Second Lieutenant George R. Bennett, 5th Connaught Rangers, was the only son of the late Mr. George W. Bennett, of Miltown-Bruff, Co. Limerick. He was educated at Aravon and at Shrewsbury. He joined the O.T.C., Shrewsbury School Contingent, and trained for three years. At the beginning of the war he enlisted in the King's Shropshire Light Infantry and got his commission in the 6th Connaught Rangers in November, 1914. He was then sent to the 5th Battalion at the Curragh and afterwards to Basingstoke, where he finished his training before going to the Dardanelles, where he fell in action on August 21st.

◇ ◇ ◇

Lieutenant John Errol Burke, 5th Battalion Connaught Rangers, was killed in action at the Dardanelles on August 21st last. He was the youngest son of the late Mr. Dominick F. Burke, R.I.C., and Mrs. Burke, 5 Royal Terrace, Kingstown, and was a member of an old Co. Galway family. Lieutenant Burke resigned his position in the Royal Bank of Ireland in order to respond to his country's call. He was a keen sportsman and was a member of the Dublin Bay Sailing Club, the Water Wag Club and the Lansdowne Football Club.

Supplement to Irish Life, November 26th, 1915.

OUR HEROES

1. 2nd LT. S. V. YOUNG,
Royal Engineers.

2. CAPT. A. MOUTRAY READ, V.C.,
Northamptonshire Regiment.

3. LT. W. A. BIRMINGHAM,
6th Royal Irish Fusiliers.

4. CAPT. F. J. BRODIGAN,
1st Gloucester Regiment.

5. MAJOR THE HON. MYLES PONSONBY, M.V.O.,
Grenadier Guards.

6. CAPTAIN E. C. DEANE,
R.A.M.C.

7. LT. R. P. W. GETHIN,
2nd Royal Munster Fusiliers.

8. LT. G. R. BENNETT,
5th Batt. Connaught Rangers.

9. LT. J. E. BURKE,
5th Batt. Connaught Rangers.

OUR HEROES.

Second Lieut. Robert Townsend Vaughton Dymock, 3rd King's Shropshire Light Infantry, who has died from wounds received in action in Flanders, was the only son of Mr. R. G. V. Dymock, Shrewsbury, and a grandson of the late Rev. T. Townsend, Aghada, Cork. Lieutenant Dymock was educated at Clifton College and Oriel College, Oxford. On the outbreak of the war he was gazetted to the 3rd King's Shropshire Light Infantry, and went to the Front attached to the 1st Battalion in June last.

✧ ✧ ✧

Major A. S. V. Hume, Scottish Horse, who died of wounds received in action, was closely related to the well-known County Antrim family of Macartney, of Lissanoure Castle, Loughguile. His father, the late Sir Gustavus Hume, was the grandson of the Rev. Travers Hume, who married, in 1875, the niece and heiress of the distinguished Ulsterman, Indian Administrator and Ambassador, Earl Macartney, of Lissanoure, Antrim, through whom the Humes succeeded to Lissanoure Castle.

✧ ✧ ✧

Second Lieutenant Owen F. Goodbody, R.E., was the eldest son of Mr. and Mrs. Jonathan Goodbody, Pembroke House, Blackrock, Co. Dublin. He was educated at Bootham School, York, and afterwards passed through the Engineering School, Trinity College, Dublin. Lieutenant Goodbody obtained a commission in the Royal Engineers on November 17th, 1914, and sailed with the 13th Division last June to the Dardanelles, where he contracted enteric, of which he died at Alexandria, on October 20th, 1915.

✧ ✧ ✧

Captain Montagu Vernon Gore-Langton, Irish Guards, third son of Mr. and Mrs. W. F. Gore-Langton, of Padbury Lodge, Buckingham, was born in 1887, and first joined the Irish Guards in 1907, but retired with the rank of Lieutenant in 1910. On the outbreak of war he rejoined, and being wounded at Ypres was sent home in November, 1914, but rejoined at Warley in January, 1915, and went out again in May, with the rank of Captain. He was awarded the Military Cross for " conspicuous gallantry on the night of August 10th, 1915, when with an orderly and one bomber he carried out a successful and daring reconnaissance. Captain M. V. Gore-Langton was shot by a sniper while on duty in the trenches on October 10th.

✧ ✧ ✧

Lieutenant-Colonel Herbert Stoney Smith, D.S.O., 1st Leicestershire Regiment, was the only son of the late Arthur Smith of Hampstead, and of Mrs. Arthur Smith, and the eldest grandson of the late Major-General George Butler Stoney, of Waterloo Road, Dublin. He was gazetted Second Lieutenant in the King's Own Yorkshire Light Infantry in 1888, and in 1891 was appointed to the 1st Battalion Leicestershire Regiment, then in Bermuda. He obtained his Majority in 1908, and went out to France as Second in Command on September 8th, 1914. He had served previously in Canada, West Indies, South Africa, Natal and Egypt. In June last he was mentioned in Sir John French's Despatch, and was awarded the D.S.O. In October, 1914, he took an active part in a desperate engagement at Rue du Bris, near Armentieres, when he personally, on a critical occasion, carried ammunition up to the firing line. He was killed in action on October 22nd.

✧ ✧ ✧

Captain E. Gerald J. Moyna, 7th Battalion Royal Scots Fusiliers, was killed in action at Hill 70 in France, on September 26th, having returned to duty after being wounded while leading his Company to the attack, on 25th September. He was the only son of the late Edward Moyna of Valparaiso, Chile, and of Mrs. Moyna, Sandymount, Dundalk, and husband of Hilda Moyna, 93 Elm Park Gardens, London, S.W. He was educated at Rugby and Oxford. He enlisted in the London Scottish in August last year, and after rising to the rank of sergeant he was appointed temporary Captain in the 7th (Service) Battalion Royal Scots Fusiliers on January 15th this year.

✧ ✧ ✧

Second Lieutenant John Donald Forbes, 10th Lancashire Fusiliers, who died at No. 10 Casualty Clearing Station, Aveele, on September 27th, of wounds received the same day, was the youngest son of Mr. and Mrs. John Forbes, 72 Eglantine Avenue, Belfast. He was nineteen years old. He was educated at the Royal Academical Institution, Belfast, and on December 28th last he obtained his commission through the Queen's University O.T.C.

✧ ✧ ✧

Lieutenant A. Leslie Hamilton Jacob, 18th Batt. " London Irish Rifles," who was killed in action in France, September 25th, was the only surviving son of Mr. and Mrs. Arthur Jacob, Hatch End, Middlesex, and grandson of the late Dr. Archibald H. Jacob, M.D., F.R.C.S.I. Lieutenant Jacob was born in Dublin, 17th June, 1896, and was educated at Bowden House, Seaford, and at Felstead, Essex.

✧ ✧ ✧

Lieutenant Robert Martin O'Dwyer, Royal Field Artillery, Guards' Division, died of wounds received in action in France on October 18th last. He was the fourth son of Mr. W. W. O'Dwyer, J.P., Springhouse, Ballylanders, Co. Limerick. On the outbreak of the war he joined the Cadet Corps at Fermoy, and obtained his commission in the Royal Field Artillery, and shortly afterwards left for France.

OUR HEROES

1. LT. R. T. V. DYMOCK,
3rd King's Shropshire Light Infantry.

2. MAJOR A. S. V. HUME,
Scottish Horse.

3. LT. O. F. GOODBODY,
Royal Engineers.

4. CAPT. M. V. GORE-LANGTON,
Irish Guards.

5. LT.-COL. H. STONEY SMITH, D.S.O.,
1st Leicestershire Regiment.

6. CAPT. E. G. J. MOYNA,
7th Scots Fusiliers.

7. LT. J. D. FORBES,
10th Lancashire Fusiliers.

8. LT. A. L. H. JACOB,
18th London Irish Rifles.

9. LT. R. M. O'DWYER,
Royal Field Artillery.

OUR HEROES.

Second Lieutenant Thomas Pakenham Law, 2nd Batt. Irish Guards, was the third son of the late T. Pakenham Law, K.C., and Mrs. Pakenham Law, Elsinore, Howth. He was educated at Monkton Coombe School and took his degree in Trinity College, Dublin. He was called to the English Bar in 1900, but on the outbreak of the war volunteered his services and obtained his commission in the Irish Guards in June last. He fell in action near Loos on September 27th, 1915.

◇ ◇ ◇

Rev. John Gwynn, S.J., Chaplain to the Irish Guards, died on October 12th last. He had been wounded in January last, and though very much weakened as a result of his wounds and the exposure to which he was subjected whilst performing his duties as Chaplain, he returned to his regiment. Father Gwynn was highly esteemed by all for his fearlessness and devotion. He never thought of himself, but exposed himself under heavy fire time and again to bring comfort and succour to the wounded. Father Gwynn received part of his education at Tullabeg College and entered the Jesuits in 1884. He studied in Louvain and Austria and was a professor in Clongowes and a member of the Governing Body of University College, Dublin.

◇ ◇ ◇

Second Lieut. James Graves St. J. Ellis, Royal Engineers, was the son of Mr. W. E. Ellis, LL.B., 41 Waterloo Road. Lieutenant Ellis graduated B.A. and B.A.I. in Trinity College, Dublin, obtaining a special certificate in practical Engineering. He afterwards went as assistant Engineer on the Canadian Pacific Railway system in Nova Scotia, where he had been for four years. On the outbreak of war he immediately answered his country's call and went to the Dardanelles, where he received serious wounds in action, from the effects of which he died.

◇ ◇ ◇

Captain H. W. Wilson, 2nd East Yorkshire Regiment, fell whilst gallantly leading a charge against the Germans. Captain Wilson was a cousin of Mr. Alexander Donaghy, Railway View, Ballymoney, and had a distinguished military career. He had been through the Boer War, receiving the King's and Queen's medals with four clasps, also the D.C.M., and was three times mentioned in despatches. In South Africa he fought with the Mounted Infantry. He had received his Captaincy a short time before he fell in action between the 2nd and 4th of October last.

◇ ◇ ◇

Lieutenant=Commander H. T. Tipping, R.N., served his first commission in *Euryalus,* and was a midshipman on board her at the battle of Kigishima, when her captain and commander were killed on August 11, 1863. His next commission was in the *Doris* at the time of the St. Thomas hurricane, then in the Royal yacht, then as lieutenant in command of the *Dapper,* tender to the *Britannia,* at the time his present Majesty and his brother were cadets; then in H.M.S. *Ganges,* training ship in Falmouth. At the age of sixty-six he offered his services to the nation, and was killed off the Belgian coast in command of his ship, September 25, 1915. Lieut.-Commander H. T. Gartside Tipping was the eldest son of G. Gartside Tipping, of Rossferry, County Fermanagh.

◇ ◇ ◇

Lieutenant Maurice E. Nolan, Royal Engineers, was killed in action while constructing a road near Loos on September 24th, 1915. Lieutenant Nolan was a brilliant student of the College of Science, Dublin, where he completed his Engineering course before he was 20 years of age. He was a most promising and capable officer.

◇ ◇ ◇

Second Lieutenant R. H. Andrews, Royal Irish Rifles, was killed in action in France on 25th September last. He was the younger son of Mr. David Andrews, Fern Hill, Annaghlone, Banbridge, and was an engineer by profession. On the outbreak of the war he resigned an appointment in the West of Ireland under the Congested Districts Board, and joined the North Irish Horse as a trooper. He accompanied his regiment to France in September, 1914, and was subsequently gazetted to the 1st Royal Irish Rifles.

◇ ◇ ◇

Second Lieutenant W. H. Good, 7th Batt. Royal Munster Fusiliers, was the eldest son of the late Mr. Thomas Good, of Hunting Hill, Carrignavar, Co. Cork. He was educated at St. Luke's School, Cork, and graduated at Trinity College, Dublin. On the outbreak of the war he obtained his commission in the 7th Munsters and went with them to the Dardanelles, where on August 18th last he fell in action.

◇ ◇ ◇

Captain L. H. B. McCombie, Uganda Volunteer Reserve, son of Captain McCombie, Laurel Bank, Monkstown, Co. Dublin, was educated at Blackrock College and at King's College, London. He adopted a seafaring life and on his first voyage he and the crew of the vessel were cast away on the Meldivas Islands in the Indian Ocean for three months. On the outbreak of the Boer War he volunteered and served with distinction in the South African Constabulary. About five years ago he was appointed Assistant Commissioner in East Africa, and on the outbreak of the present war he volunteered for active service in the Uganda Volunteer Reserve, and took a very prominent part in crushing the German forces in East Africa; but unfortunately his brilliant career was brought to an end by a stray bullet from a delirious native policeman.

1. 2nd LT. T. PAKENHAM LAW, 2nd Batt. Irish Guards.
2. REV. J. GWYNN, S.J., Chaplain to the Irish Guards.
3. 2nd LT. J. G. ST. J. ELLIS, Royal Engineers.
4. CAPT. H. W. WILSON, 2nd East Yorkshire Regiment.
5. LT.-COM. GARTSIDE-TIPPING, Royal Navy.
6. LT. M. E. NOLAN, Royal Engineers.
7. 2nd LT. R. H. ANDREWS, Royal Irish Rifles.
8. 2nd LT. W. H. GOOD, 7th Batt. Royal Munster Fusiliers.
9. CAPT. L. H. B. McCOMBIE, Uganda Volunteer Reserve.

OUR HEROES.

Second Lieutenant H. R. S. Hackett, 1st Batt. Royal Irish Fusiliers, who was killed in action in the Dardanelles on November 2nd last, was the youngest son of the Very Rev. H. M. M. Hackett, lately Dean of Waterford, but now Vicar of St. Peter's, Belsize Park, Hampshire.

⬥ ⬥ ⬥

Second Lieutenant Samuel Spedding John, B.L., 9th Batt. Cheshire Regiment, has been awarded the Military Cross for conspicuous gallantry near Festubert on 25th September last. After a retirement to the trenches had been ordered Lieutenant John crawled out under heavy fire and assisted to bring in in succession a wounded officer and about twenty men of another regiment. He continued his heroic work until utterly exhausted. Lieut. John is the son of Mr. A. S. John, Roseville House, Bray, and was called to the Bar in June, 1914.

⬥ ⬥ ⬥

Corporal Ernest Yule Gaze, Despatch Rider, Royal Engineers, has had the Medal of St. George, 2nd class, conferred upon him by His Imperial Majesty the Emperor of Russia, for distinguished service in the field. Corporal Gaze is a son of Mrs. Gaze, 22 Elm Grove, Ranelagh, and in a letter to his mother he relates how, having got through safely with his despatches, he returned to relieve a wounded comrade when a shell burst right beside them, inflicting severe injuries on Corporal Gaze and killing his comrade. Corporal Gaze had no fewer than 25 shrapnel wounds. He is at present at home recovering, but has again volunteered for active service in Serbia.

⬥ ⬥ ⬥

Captain James A. Smithwick, 4th Batt. Royal Irish Regiment, has died in London from consumption due to injuries received on October 20th, 1914, at Le Pelly whilst gallantly leading his men, when he was seriously wounded and lay for several hours unconscious until picked up by a German ambulance party. He was removed to the German internment camp at Crefeld, where he was detained for nearly ten months before he was exchanged. His recovery from his wounds was very slow, and consumption directly traceable to his injuries set in which prevented any hope of his recovery. On his arrival in London he was visited in hospital by His Majesty King George, who complimented him on his great gallantry. Capt. Smithwick was the elder surviving son of the late Mr. J. F. Smithwick, J.P., who represented the City of Kilkenny in Parliament from 1880 to 1885, and a member of a well-known Kilkenny family.

⬥ ⬥ ⬥

Brigadier=General A. C. Lewin, D.S.O., of Roseanna, Kilroot, Co. Antrim, recently commanding the 3rd Battalion Connaught Rangers, has been promoted and is now in command of a Brigade in the Near East. He is a brother of Mr. T. Lewin, well known in hunting and sporting circles in Connaught.

Captain Herbert Maddick, 5th Royal Irish Lancers, died in St. Thomas's Hospital, London, one hour after his arrival from the Dardanelles, of typhoid contracted whilst on active service there. He joined the Welsh Fusiliers in 1898 and served in the Boer War. In 1903 he became A.D.C. to Sir Augustus Hemming, Governor of Jamaica, and was later on gazetted to the 14th Hussars and served in India. On the outbreak of the present war he took part in the actions of Le Cateau, Mons, Marne and Aisne. He was invalided home in October, 1914, and in July last was appointed Deputy Assistant Quartermaster-General to the British Mediterranean Force. He was the elder son of Mr. George J. Maddick, of Surbiton, Surrey.

⬥ ⬥ ⬥

Captain Robert William Sutton, 2nd Batt. Royal Dublin Fusiliers, who was killed in action in France on October 16th last, was the third son of Mr. Nathaniel Sutton, Richfordstown, Clonakilty, Co. Cork. Captain Sutton had 17 years' service and had been through the South African War, in which he obtained the Queen's Medal with six clasps and the King's Medal with two clasps, and was mentioned several times in despatches. He was transport sergeant, musketry instructor and company sergeant-major in turn of the 2nd Batt. Royal Dublin Fusiliers, and was promoted regimental sergeant-major of the 4th Batt. immediately after the war broke out. He obtained his commission on May 21st and was shortly afterwards promoted Captain.

⬥ ⬥ ⬥

Captain J. H. A. Ryan, 1st Batt. King's Liverpool Regiment, was the younger son of Dr. and Mrs. Ryan, of Roade, Northamptonshire, and a nephew of Mr. H. J. Ryan, of Scarteen, Knocklong, Co. Limerick, whose son Lieut. J. J. Ryan, 16th Lancers, is now a prisoner of war in Germany. Captain Ryan was educated at Downside School and Sandhurst. He joined the King's Liverpool Regiment in 1912 and went to France with the Expeditionary Force in August, 1914, serving at Mons, Marne, the Aisne, and Ypres. He was mentioned in despatches and was one of the earliest recipients of the Military Cross. After the first battle of Ypres he was the only unwounded officer in his battalion who went out with the Expeditionary Force in August, 1914. Capt. Ryan was a keen cricket and football player, and had played for Sandhurst and also played cricket for Northamptonshire and the Aldershot Command. He also won the Officers' Half-mile at the Army Athletic Meeting in 1913.

⬥ ⬥ ⬥

Warrant=Officer T. Tierney, H.M.S. *Juno*, has been awarded the Distinguished Service Cross for services during landing operations in the Persian Gulf. He is a son of Mrs. Tierney, Merchants'-road, Galway.

1. LIEUT. H. R. S. HACKETT,
1st Batt. Royal Irish Fusiliers.

2. LIEUT. S. S. JOHN,
9th Batt. Cheshire Regiment.
Military Cross.

3. CORPORAL ERNEST GAZE,
Despatch Rider, R.E.
Russian Medal of St. George.

4. CAPT. J. A. SMITHWICK,
4th Batt. Royal Irish Regiment.

5. BRIG.-GENERAL A. C. LEWIN, D.S.O.,
3rd Batt. Connaught Rangers.

6. CAPT. H. MADDICK,
5th Royal Irish Lancers.

7. CAPT. R. W. SUTTON,
2nd Batt. Royal Dublin Fusiliers.

8. CAPT. J. H. A. RYAN,
1st Batt. King's Liverpool Regiment.

9. WT.-OFFICER T. TIERNEY,
Royal Navy.
Distinguished Service Cross.

OUR HEROES.

"D" COMPANY, 7th ROYAL DUBLIN FUSILIERS.

Private Thomas E. Timoney was a son of Mr. P. Timoney, Crown and Peace Office, Sligo, and on the outbreak of the war he joined the " Pals " Battalion, and was with them at Suvla Bay and through many subsequent engagements until on October 20th last he died of dysentery in hospital at Alexandria, in his 19th year. His brother is also serving his country in France.

◇ ◇ ◇

Private William F. A. Matthews, who was killed in action at the Dardanelles on September 13th last, was a son of Mr. and Mrs. Matthews, Northern Bank House, Grafton St., Dublin, and was educated at St. Andrew's College, Dublin. He stroked Junior Crew for Neptune Rowing Club in 1913 and 1914, was a member of Wanderers' Football Club, and one of the under 15 team that won the Schools' Cup for St. Andrew's College. On the outbreak of the war he with many of his friends joined the " Pals " Battalion, and gave his life for his country.

◇ ◇ ◇

Private Victor Jefferson was the youngest son of Mr. and Mrs. Jefferson, 44 Grosvenor Road, Rathgar, and has been killed in action at the Dardanelles in his 22nd year. He was educated at Wesley College and was a member of the Old Wesley Football Club and the Leinster Cricket Club. On the outbreak of the war he joined the " Pals " Battalion, and was with them at Suvla Bay. A letter of his published in the Press describing the landing and the subsequent fighting attracted a good deal of attention at the time. A fortnight later, on August 23rd last, he was killed in action.

◇ ◇ ◇

Mr. Charles Frederick James Bell was the younger son of the late Mr. James Bell, of Armagh. He was educated at the Royal School, Armagh, and then entered the Civil Service. He was for some years on the staff of the Irish Land Commission, and latterly Junior Examiner under the National Health Insurance Commission. On the outbreak of war he joined " D " Company, 7th (Pals) Batt. Royal Dublin Fusiliers, with whom he went to the Dardanelles, taking part in the landing at Suvla Bay and subsequent fighting, and fell in action on August 16th, within a few weeks of his 31st birthday.

◇ ◇ ◇

Mr. Arthur C. Crookshank, who has been missing since August 15th in the Dardanelles, has been recommended for the D.C.M. for gallantry in action at the Dardanelles. He is a son of Mr. Charles H. Crookshank, B.L., Dublin, and grandson of the late Mr. Robert Crookshank, Glenmanus House, Portrush. At the outbreak of the war Mr. Crookshank was serving his apprenticeship in the Dublin office of Messrs. Crookshank, Leech and Davies, Solicitors, but immediately volunteered and joined the " Pals " Battalion, with whom he went to the Dardanelles. His brother, Lieutenant Henry Crookshank, was wounded in Gallipoli on August 27th, and is at present at home recovering from his wounds.

◇ ◇ ◇

Private C. F. Ball, who died of wounds received in action at the Dardanelles on September 13, was one of the best known botanists and horticulturists in Ireland, and held the position of Assistant Keeper to Sir F. W. Moore at the Royal Botanical Gardens, Glasnevin, and a short time before his death he enriched the collection of the Royal Botanical Gardens with a consignment of plants which he sent from the Dardanelles to Sir F. W. Moore. He was a popular member of the Finglas Golf Club, and was the third son of Mrs. Mary Bowley Ball, Loughborough, Leicestershire. On the outbreak of the war he joined the " Pals " Battalion.

◇ ◇ ◇

Lance=Corporal J. W. Little was the younger son of Mr. and Mrs. Little, Castlegarren, Sligo. He was educated at Wesley College, Dublin, and on the outbreak of the war was an official in the Registry of Deeds, but joined the " Pals '" Battalion and went with them to the Dardanelles, where he died on September 17th last from wounds received in action on August 24th.

◇ ◇ ◇

Private Cecil Keller was officially reported " missing " at Suvla Bay on August 16th. He has since been reported killed on that day, shot in a bayonet charge. He was the only son of Mr. and Mrs. J. J. Keller, of 9 Conquer Hill, Dollymount. Though only just 18 years of age at the time of his death, he had already seen much of the world, as an apprentice in the merchant service, his voyages having included a prior visit to the Dardanelles. Private Keller was an old Castleknock College boy.

◇ ◇ ◇

Corporal James Kelly was a son of Mr. and Mrs. Kelly, 9 Tower Avenue, Rathgar, and was educated at the High School, Dublin. At the outbreak of the war he was in the Engineering Department of Messrs. Guinness, Son and Co., but at once offered his services and joined the " Pals " Battalion. He was prominent in the formation of the 1st City of Dublin Cadets, in which he was Colour Sergeant, and was selected as one of the Cadet Guard of Honour at the Coronation of King George V. He was attached to the signalling section of the " Pals " Battalion, and was present at the memorable landing at Suvla Bay on August 6th. He was killed on September 20th last.

"D" COMPANY, 7th ROYAL DUBLIN FUSILIERS.

1. PRIVATE T. E. TIMONEY.	2. PTE. W. F. A. MATTHEWS.	3. PRIVATE VICTOR JEFFERSON.
4. PRIVATE C. F. J. BELL.	5. MR. A. C. CROOKSHANK, Recommended for D.C.M.	6. PRIVATE C. F. BALL.
7. LANCE-CORPL. J. W. LITTLE.	8. PRIVATE C. KELLER.	9. CORPORAL J. KELLY.

Our Heroes

OUR HEROES.

Captain W. Foot, M.B., attached 2nd Batt. Coldstream Guards, who has been mentioned in Sir John French's despatches and awarded the Military Cross, is the only son of Mr. A. Revell Foot, 57 Northumberland Road, Dublin. He was educated at Shrewsbury and Trinity College, and at the outbreak of the war at once offered his services. Capt. Foot is a keen sportsman and was an International Hockey player.

✧ ✧ ✧

Major Arthur Wallace, D.A.A.G., Q.M.G., 1st Durham Light Infantry, is the eldest son of the late Sir Arthur Wallace, C.B., D.L., Chief Secretary's Office, Dublin Castle, and Ardnamona, Lough Eske, Co. Donegal. He was educated at Shrewsbury and Trinity College, Dublin. Major Wallace has served a good deal abroad. In the present war he has been on active service since an early date, and has been mentioned in Sir John French's despatches.

✧ ✧ ✧

Captain R. S. Rait Kerr, 1st Indian Field Squadron, Royal Engineers, was mentioned in Sir John French's despatches for gallant and distinguished service in the field. Capt. Rait Kerr is a son of Mr. and Mrs. Rait Kerr, Rathmoyle, Edenderry, two of whose sons have been killed in the present war, one of them having gained the D.S.O. Capt. Rait Kerr came home from India on war being declared. He was wounded at Neuve Chapelle on October 28th, 1914. From February to June, 1915, he was A.D.C. to Major General Lawson, C.B., who holds the Northern command.

✧ ✧ ✧

Captain Quentin Wallace, R.A.M.C., is the youngest son of the late Sir Arthur Wallace, C.B., D.L., Chief Secretary's Office, Dublin Castle, and Ardnamona, Lough Eske, County Donegal. He was educated at Shrewsbury and Trinity College, Dublin, where he passed through the Medical School in an incredibly short time. At the outbreak of the war he volunteered, and has rendered excellent service, being mentioned in despatches, and now, when only 23 years of age, being awarded the Military Cross.

✧ ✧ ✧

Major Arthur Edward Newland, D.S.O., R.F.A., only surviving son of the late Rev. Canon Edward Newland, M.A., Rector of Buncrana, Canon of Derry Cathedral, by his second wife Mary, daughter of Rev. Mitchell Smyth, Ballintemple, Garvagh. Major Newland was through the South African War, for his services in which he was mentioned in Sir John Gough's despatches and received two medals. In the present war he has been twice mentioned in Sir John French's despatches and awarded the D.S.O. He was wounded in January, 1915. Major Newland married in September, 1911, Alice, daughter of Mr. Richard Burke, M.F.H., of Grove, Fethard.

✧ ✧ ✧

Captain Edward Sherlock, R.F.A., is the youngest son of Mr. David Sherlock, D.L., Rahan, King's Co. Captain Sherlock was in the Reserve of Officers, having belonged to the Wicklow Artillery. He left some years ago for the East, where he was appointed engineer on a rubber plantation in Lower Perak. As soon as the war broke out he volunteered for active service and returned at his own expense. He was very soon sent to France and put in charge of an ammunition train, where he did very good work. He was afterwards attached to the Field Artillery, and was through the action at Loos, being mentioned in Sir John French's despatches and awarded the Military Cross for distinguished service.

✧ ✧ ✧

Lieutenant Francis Cecil Law, who has been awarded the Distinguished Service Cross for service in Gallipoli, is the third and youngest son of Michael Law of Beaumond, Drogheda. He was born in August, 1895, educated at Monrue Grange, Kilkeel and Haileybury College. Joined the Royal Marines in 1913, served in Antwerp in October, 1914, and in Gallipoli from February to December, 1915. He took part in an early landing on March 4th in the Asiatic side. In the general landing of the morning of the 25th April he also took part at Y Beach, and after twenty-four hours' fighting he was wounded. After a lapse of three weeks, recovering from wound, he rejoined. He was invalided home after enteric fever on December 5th. His two elder brothers are both serving their country, Capt. Robert Law, Royal Dublin Fusiliers, and Lieut. M. T. N. Law, Royal Scots Fusiliers.

✧ ✧ ✧

Lieutenant H. G. O. Downing, 2nd Batt. Royal Irish Regiment, who has been mentioned in Sir John French's despatches, is a son of Lieut.-Colonel Downing, D.S.O., 8th Royal Inniskilling Fusiliers. Lieut. Downing was taken prisoner after the action at Le Pilly in October, 1914, and has been at Crefeld ever since.

✧ ✧ ✧

Lieutenant William Plato Oulton, 3rd Batt. Royal Dublin Fusiliers, has been awarded the Military Cross for conspicuous courage at "Dublin Castle" on the Gallipoli Peninsula on the night of October 2nd, 1915, when in charge of a covering party, who were being bombed. By his coolness and courage he kept those nearest him well in hand and rallied the others. He organised a rescue party and successfully brought in some wounded men.

1. CAPT. W. FOOT, M.B.,
2nd Batt. Coldstream Guards.
(Military Cross.)

2. MAJOR A. WALLACE,
D.A.A.G., Q.M.G.,
Durham Light Infantry.

3. CAPT. R. S. RAIT KERR,
Indian Field Squadron.

4. CAPT. Q. WALLACE,
R.A.M.C.
(Military Cross.)

5. MAJOR A. E. NEWLAND,
R.F.A.
(D.S.O.).

6. CAPT. E. SHERLOCK,
R.F.A.
(Military Cross.)

7. LIEUT. F. C. LAW,
Royal Marines.
(D. S. Cross.)

8. LIEUT. H. G. O. DOWNING,
2nd Royal Irish Regiment.

9. LIEUT. W. P. OULTON,
3rd Royal Dublin Fusiliers.
(Military Cross.)

OUR HEROES.

Lieutenant Hugo Graham de Burgh, R.F.A., is the eldest son of the late Mr. Hugo H. de Burgh, who was killed in the South African War. Lieut. de Burgh was wounded at Ypres on May 15th, and has been mentioned in despatches and awarded the Military Cross for gallantry in the field.

Captain J. Cecil A. Dowse, M.B., eldest son of Canon Dowse, of Monkstown, was educated at Trent College, Derbyshire, and Trinity College, Dublin, where he graduated in Arts and Medicine in 1914. On the outbreak of the war he joined the R.A.M.C., and went to France early in May, 1915. He was mentioned in Viscount French's despatches and awarded the Military Cross. During his college days he played Rugby football with Monkstown Club, and represented Ireland in 1913 and 1914. His brother, Charles E. Dowse, 7th Batt. Dublin Fusiliers, was killed in the Dardanelles on August 16th, 1915.

Lieutenant A. B. L. Vincent, 3rd Dragoon Guards, has been mentioned in Sir John French's despatches for gallant and distinguished conduct in the field. He is the only son of Colonel Vincent, Summer Hill House, Castleconnell, by his marriage with Miss Baxendale, only child of the late Mr. Birley Baxendale, of Blackmore End, Welwyn, Herts. Lieut. Vincent was educated at Cheltenham College and passed from there into Sandhurst. He obtained his commission in 1914 and has been at the front since October of that year. In May, 1915, he held a trench for eleven hours until relief came, and was in command of his squadron, all the other officers having been killed or wounded. Lieut. Vincent is in his 20th year.

Captain J. T. C. Moore-Brabazon, who has been mentioned in despatches, was born in 1884 and educated at Harrow and Trinity College, Cambridge. He was one of the pioneers of motoring, and the first Irishman and Britisher to fly in England, thus winning the *Daily Mail* £1,000 prize for the first Britisher to fly a mile.

✧ ✧ ✧

Major Ernest Brabazon Booth, M.D., Royal Army Medical Corps, who has been appointed a Companion of the Distinguished Service Order, is the younger son of the late Dr. Brabazon Shiels Booth, who was medical officer of the Newry General Hospital from 1874 to 1894. One of his sisters is the wife of Mr. W. H. B. Moorhead, J.P., Carnmeen, Newry, head of the firm of Henry Thomson and Co., Newry, a director of the Great Northern Railway Company (Ireland), and one of the commandants of the Newry companies of the Ulster Volunteer Force.

✧ ✧ ✧

Captain Hamilton-Stubber, who has been mentioned in despatches for gallant and distinguished service in the field, joined the 1st Life Guards in October, 1899, and served in the South African War, 1900-1902, with the Imperial Yeomanry, and for special service he received the medal with five clasps. He retired from the 1st Life Guards in 1912 with the rank of Captain. He then joined the South Irish Horse, with which regiment he served until October, 1914, when he was attached to the 1st Life Guards and went to the front, and has served with that regiment ever since.

✧ ✧ ✧

Private James Donaghey, 1st Batt. Royal Inniskilling Fusiliers, has been awarded the D.C.M. for distinguished conduct while serving with the Anglo-Indian Force in Mesopotamia. He took part in the advance on Bagdad and the subsequent retreat to Kut-el-Amara. He is a son of Mr. P. Donaghey, 44 Walker's-place, Londonderry.

✧ ✧ ✧

Lieutenant J. S. Drennan, R.F.A., who has been mentioned in Sir John French's despatches, is a son of Mr. Alexander Drennan, Dunalwiga, Helensburgh, and a nephew of Mr. John W. Drennan, Carse Hall, Limavady, whose son, Lieutenant James W. Drennan, is serving in France with the 10th Batt. Royal Munster Fusiliers. Lieut. J. S. Drennan was educated at Fetlis College, Edinburgh, and entered the Army from Woolwich. He went to India with his regiment, but was recalled to France in the winter of 1914, and has been on active service ever since.

✧ ✧ ✧

Sergeant E. F. Eager, Royal Irish Regiment, who has been mentioned in Sir John French's despatches, is the son of Mrs. M. Eager, Lahard Cottage, Killarney. He joined the Royal Irish Regiment in 1908, and in 1911 was promoted sergeant. He went to France in August, 1914, and was in several severe engagements, including Le Pelly, where his regiment suffered so severely. He has been recommended for conspicuous bravery and distinguished conduct in the field. His two brothers are also serving, one being at present a prisoner in Limburg.

1. LIEUT. H. G. DE BURGH, R.F.A. (Military Cross.)	2. CAPT. J. C. A. DOWSE, M.B., R.A.M.C. (Military Cross.)	3. LIEUT. A. B. L. VINCENT, 3rd Dragoon Guards.
4. CAPT. J. T. C. MOORE BRABAZON. R.F.C.	5. MAJOR E. B. BOOTH, M.D., R.A.M.C. (D.S.O.).	6. CAPT. HAMILTON-STUBBER, 1st Life Guards.
7. PRIVATE J. DONAGHEY. 1st Royal Inniskilling Fusiliers. (D.C.M.).	8. LIEUT. J. S. DRENNAN, R.F.A.	9. SERGT. E. F. EAGER, Royal Irish Regiment.

OUR HEROES.

Second Lieutenant R. W. McGonigal, Royal Garrison Artillery, elder son of the late Mr. David McGonigal, one of the best known solicitors in Belfast, and Mrs. McGonigal, The Laurels, Strandtown, has been awarded the Military Cross for conspicuous gallantry while serving on the Western front, when he lifted a live bomb which had been thrown into a British trench by the enemy and hurled it over the parapet, at imminent risk of being killed by the explosion. Lieut. McGonigal was educated at Coleraine Academical Institution, the Belfast Academical Institution, and Trinity College, Dublin.

✧ ✧ ✧

Capt. Sir John Keane, Bart., R.F.A., Cappoquin, Co. Waterford, has just been awarded the D.S.O. for distinguished service in the field. He was for some months Captain of the 29th Battery, R.F.A., in Flanders, and since June, 1915, has been Commandant of the French Howitzer School of the 2nd Army. Sir John Keane was A.D.C. to the Lord Lieutenant of Ireland in 1896. He served in the South African War, and was mentioned in despatches.

✧ ✧ ✧

Second Lieutenant Norman J. Patterson, Royal Field Artillery, who has been mentioned in Sir John French's despatches for gallantry and distinguished conduct, is the only son of Dr. R. D. Patterson, Cranogue House, Caledon, Co. Tyrone. He was educated at Armagh Royal School and Edinburgh School of Medicine, where he was a member of the O.T.C. Soon after the outbreak of war he offered his services and received his commission in the Royal Field Artillery. He left for France shortly afterwards, where he was attached to the 29th Battery, 3rd Division. Lieutenant Patterson went through the severe fighting at Hill 60, Neuve Chapelle and Ypres, and was severely wounded at Hooge in August last.

✧ ✧ ✧

Captain John Arnott, eldest son of Sir John Arnott, 12 Merrion Square, has been twice mentioned in Sir John French's despatches for distinguished service. He was educated at Eton, and Trinity, Cambridge. At the commencement of the war he acted as A.D.C. and Camp Commandant to General Allenby, and when the 15th Hussars were brigaded, Captain Arnott returned to his regiment as Adjutant.

✧ ✧ ✧

Lieutenant-Colonel Horace S. Sewell, D.S.O., 4th Royal Irish Dragoon Guards, brother of Miss Sewell, The Ivy House, Ballycastle, Co. Antrim, has been twice mentioned in Sir John French's despatches and awarded the D.S.O. Lieutenant-Colonel Sewell was born in 1881, and was educated at Harrow and Trinity College, Cambridge, from whence he obtained his commission at the time of the South African War, and subsequently served in Nigeria from 1907 to 1910. For his services in the present war Lieut.-Colonel Sewell has also received the Cross of the Legion of Honour.

✧ ✧ ✧

Captain B. J. Hackett, M.B., R.A.M.C., attached 7th Batt. Suffolk Regiment, has been mentioned in Sir John French's despatches and awarded the Military Cross for conspicuous gallantry and devotion to duty at Loos on October 2nd, 1915. Captain Hackett is the eldest son of the late Dr. John Byrne Hackett, Kilkenny, and was educated at Clongowes Wood College and the Royal University. He was house physician and surgeon at St. Vincent's Hospital from 1899 to 1900, and was captain of St. Vincent's Hospital Rugby team. He was assistant medical officer, Mountjoy Prison, on the outbreak of the war.

✧ ✧ ✧

Corporal R. M. Allison, 7th Batt. British Columbian Contingent (Canadian Force), has been mentioned in Sir John French's despatches for gallantry and distinguished conduct in the field. He is the son of Mr. R. M. Allison, Beulah House, Causeway-street, Portrush, and at the outbreak of the war was in the service of the Hudson Bay Company in Vancouver, but immediately enlisted and came to England with the 1st Canadian Contingent. He went to France in February, 1915, and took part in the engagements at Ypres, Festurbet and Loos.

✧ ✧ ✧

Captain H. Leslie McCarthy, R.A.M.C., recipient of the Military Cross, awarded for gallantry during the great retreat from Mons, is the eldest son of the late Mr. R. Hillgrove McCarthy, J.P., of Woodford House, Listowel, Co. Kerry, one of the old Cork family of McCarthy-Mores. Capt. McCarthy graduated at T.C.D., and took up an appointment and practice in London as a nerve specialist, which position he temporarily resigned to join the Irish Guards when the war began. His two younger brothers are now serving with the British Mediterranean Force in the "Pals'" Battalion of the R.D.F.

✧ ✧ ✧

Lieut. J. K. M. Greer, Irish Guards, has been mentioned in Sir John French's despatches and awarded the Military Cross for gallantry and distinguished conduct in the field. He is the son of Mr. and Mrs. Greer, Westoncrofts, Ballymoney, Co. Antrim, and enlisted in the North Irish Horse on August 17th, 1914, and a few days afterwards left for France, where he took part in the retreat from St. Quentin and the subsequent advance to the Aisne. In December, 1914, he received a commission in the 3rd Dragoon Guards, and served with them until April, 1915, being subsequently transferred to the Special Reserve, Irish Guards (3rd Batt.),

OUR HEROES

1. LIEUT. R. W. McGONIGAL, Royal Garrison Artillery. (Military Cross.)	2. CAPT. SIR JOHN KEANE, Royal Field Artillery. (D.S.O.)	3. LIEUT. N. J. PATTERSON, Royal Field Artillery.
4. CAPT. J. ARNOTT, 15th Hussars.	5. LIEUT.-COLONEL SEWELL, 4th Royal Irish Dragoon Guards. (D.S.O.)	6. CAPT. B. J. HACKETT, M.B., R.A.M.C. (Military Cross.)
7. CORPL. R. M. ALLISON, 7th Batt. British Columbian Regiment.	8. CAPT. H. L. McCARTHY, M.D., R.A.M.C. (Military Cross.)	9. LIEUT. J. K. GREER, Irish Guards. (Military Cross.)

OUR HEROES.

Second Lieutenant J. H. de la Maziere Harpur, 15th Batt. Royal Irish Rifles, who has been awarded the Military Cross for gallantry in carrying in a wounded man under very heavy shrapnel and machine-gun fire, is the youngest son of the Rev. Henry S. de la M. Harpur, The Rectory, Killeshandra, Co. Cavan. Immediately after the outbreak of the war he enlisted in the 13th Batt. Royal Irish Rifles. In January, 1915, he was given his commission in the 17th Batt. R.I.R., and was subsequently transferred to the 15th Battalion.

✧ ✧ ✧

Captain James Auchenleck Dane, R.F.A., who has been mentioned in Sir John French's despatches for distinguished conduct in the field, is a member of an old Fermanagh family, being the only son of His Honor the late Richard Martin Dane, K.C., County Court Judge of Co. Mayo, and M.P. for North Fermanagh from 1892 to 1898. He was gazetted to the Royal Garrison Artillery in 1902, but subsequently exchanged into the Royal Field Artillery. He received his promotion as Captain in the Special Reserve of the R.F.A. in December, 1912, and on the outbreak of the war he rejoined the R.F.A., and has served continuously in France since the British Expeditionary Force landed there.

✧ ✧ ✧

Captain Charles Joseph O'Reilly, M.B., R.A.M.C., has been awarded the Military Cross for conspicuous gallantry and devotion to duty near Hulloch from 25th to 28th September, 1915, in attending the wounded under heavy shell-fire. Captain O'Reilly is in his 24th year, and is the fifth son of Mr. Joseph R. O'Reilly, D.L., Sans Souci, Booterstown. At the outbreak of war he was house surgeon at Sir Patrick Dun's Hospital, but volunteered for active service, and was appointed to the 21st Field Ambulance, receiving his Captaincy in August, 1915.

✧ ✧ ✧

Captain John Grey Porter, D.S.O., 9th (Queen's Royal) Lancers, eldest son of Mr. John Porter-Porter, D.L., Belleisle, Co. Fermanagh, has been through the war since its commencement, and was twice wounded. He was awarded the Distinguished Service Order in recognition of his gallantry and devotion to duty on May 10th, 1915, when a very heavy attack was made on the front line near Hooge. Captain Porter went up to the infantry line and brought back very valuable information as to the situation, and on May 13th he rendered the greatest possible assistance in taking messages to various parts of the line under terrific shell-fire.

✧ ✧ ✧

Colonel Cecil Allanson, Gurkha Rifles, who has been awarded the Distinguished Service Order, and who has also appeared amongst the New Year Honours as the recipient of a C.T.E., is a son of Mrs. Allanson, 40 Pulteney Street, Bath, and a nephew of Mr. W. H. Lyons, D.L., Strandtown, Belfast. He joined the Royal Artillery in 1897 and acted as A.D.C. to the Lieutenant-Governor of Bengal from 1899 to 1901. He subsequently served in many important capacities in India, until July, 1915, when he rejoined his regiment on active service in the Dardanelles.

✧ ✧ ✧

Captain Clifford Humphrey Lloyd, Royal Field Artillery, is the son of Brigadier-General F. C. Lloyd, Bryntirion, Bersham, Wrexham, who has returned home from the Dardanelles severely wounded. Captain Lloyd has been twice mentioned in despatches and awarded the Military Cross. He obtained his commission in the R.F.A. in 1911; he went out with the 4th Division to France in August, 1914, and in the autumn of that year was awarded the French decoration, "Croix de Chevalier, Legion d'Honneur." He was wounded in November of that year, and subsequently went with the 29th Division to the Dardanelles. Captain Lloyd is a nephew of Mr. Clifford B. Lloyd, Lossett, Co. Cavan.

✧ ✧ ✧

Lieutenant R. B. Fitzgerald, Durham Light Infantry, who has been decorated with the Order of Chevalier of the French Legion of Honour, and has been twice mentioned in despatches, is the second son of Mr. and Mrs. R. Fitzgerald, Ballyard House, Tralee, Co. Kerry, and at the commencement of the war was a partner in the well-known stockbroking firm of Basil Montgomery, Fitzgerald & Co. He is a nephew of Sir M. Fitzgerald, Bart., Knight of Kerry.

✧ ✧ ✧

Staff Surgeon A. F. Fleming, H.M.S. *Queen Elizabeth,* who has been mentioned in despatches from the Dardanelles, is a son of the late Mr. W. M. Fleming, Youghal. Surgeon Fleming was educated in Clongowes College, and has rendered valuable service since the outbreak of the war.

✧ ✧ ✧

Lieutenant Gervais de la Poer Beresford, Royal Engineers (late of the R.N.A.S.), only son of Lieutenant-Colonel K. Beresford (late of the Royal Irish Rifles), 25th Northumberland Fusiliers, has been mentioned in despatches and received the Distinguished Service Medal for distinguished conduct with the Armoured Car Section in Gallipoli in repulsing an attack of the enemy in force on June 11th last. The Commander-in-Chief of the Mediterranean Expeditionary Force reported that the failure of the attack was almost entirely due to the good look-out, presence of mind and efficiency in handling their guns displayed by Lieut. Beresford and Chief Petty Officer Trussell.

1. LT. J. H. DE LA M. HARPUR, 15th Batt. Royal Irish Rifles. (Military Cross.)
2. CAPT. JAS. A. DANE, Royal Field Artillery.
3. CAPT. C. J. O'REILLY, M.B., R.A.M.C. (Military Cross.)
4. CAPT. J. G. PORTER, 9th Lancers. (D.S.O.).
5. COL. C. ALLANSON, C.T.E., 1st Batt. 6th Gurkha Rifles. (D.S.O.).
6. CAPT. C. H. LLOYD, R.F.A. (Military Cross). (Croix de Chevalier Legion d'Honneur).
7. LIEUT. R. B. FITZGERALD, Intelligence Corps. (Chevalier Legion d'Honneur.)
8. STAFF-SURGEON A. F. FLEMING, H.M.S. "Queen Elizabeth."
9. LIEUT. G. DE LA POER BERESFORD. (Distinguished Service Medal.)

OUR HEROES.

Lieutenant James Mackay, 1st Batt. Gordon Highlanders, who has been killed in action, was a son of Mr. Wm. Mackay, 63 Castlereagh Street, Belfast. He was educated at the Royal Academical Institution, Belfast, where he had a distinguished career as a student. Last year he won the Carnegie Research Scholarship of £100. In November, 1914, he received his commission in the 3rd Gordon Highlanders, and on being sent to the front was attached to the 1st Battalion.

✧ ✧ ✧

The Rev. Francis C. Roche, C.F., Chaplain attached to the 10th (Irish) Division, died in hospital in Alexandria on November 14th, 1915, of enteric fever contracted while on active service in Gallipoli. He was the eldest son of the late Mr. George M. Roche and Mrs. Roche, Cambridge House, Montpelier Hill, Dublin; was ordained for the curacy of Ballymena in 1908, and in 1910 was appointed curate of Mortlake, London. On the outbreak of war he offered his services and after some time at the Curragh was attached to the 10th (Irish) Division.

✧ ✧ ✧

Lieutenant Vincent MacNamara, Royal Engineers, was killed by a gas explosion at Suvla Bay on November 29th, 1915. He was the son of Mr. P. J. MacNamara, Analore, Blackrock, Co. Cork, and was educated at the University College, Cork, where he passed through the Engineering course with distinction. He was also a prominent football player, and played in international matches. He had been six months in Gallipoli, and had been through many severe engagements, including Suvla Bay.

✧ ✧ ✧

Captain Cecil Domville Wynter, 2nd Batt. Irish Guards, who died on October 5th of wounds received in action in France on September 27th, was the second son of Colonel and Mrs. Walter Wynter, of Woodhouse Eaves, Leicestershire. He was in his 32nd year and was educated at Eton. He had served in the South African War with the Sussex Militia, and received the Queen's Medal and two clasps. On the outbreak of the present war he came home from the Argentine, where he had been for some years, and obtained a commission in the Irish Guards, and was promoted Captain in the 2nd Battalion.

✧ ✧ ✧

Lieutenant-Colonel Gerald H. C. Madden, 1st Batt. Irish Guards, was severely wounded in the fighting near Bethune on October 11th, 1915, from the effects of which he died in hospital in London. Colonel Madden was a brother of Lieutenant-Colonel J. C. W. Madden, D.L., Hilton Park, Clones, now commanding the 4th Batt. Royal Irish Fusiliers, and brother-in-law of Major the Marquis of Ailesbury, D.S.O. He married, in 1901, Mabel Lucy, daughter of the late Sir George McPherson Grant, Bart., of Ballindalloch. Colonel Madden, who was in his 43rd year, formerly served in the 3rd King's Own Hussars, and took part in the South African War with the 16th Lancers.

✧ ✧ ✧

Captain Robert J. O'Lone, 2nd Batt. Royal Irish Rifles, was killed in action in Flanders about the 12th November, 1915, whilst engaged in reconnoitring duty. He was the third son of Quartermaster-Sergeant John O'Lone, Victoria Barracks, Belfast, and Loughries, Newtownards. Captain O'Lone was born in Belfast and had spent fourteen years' service with the 2nd Batt. Royal Irish Rifles, with whom he left for the front in August, 1914.

✧ ✧ ✧

Second Lieutenant Claud Henry Whish Darling, 3rd Battalion (attached 2nd) Royal Irish Rifles, who was killed in action in France on December 12th, 1915, was the second son of the late Rev. Oliver W. Darling, Killesk Rectory, Duncannon, Co. Wexford, and a grandson of Dr. George Newman Dunn, of Duncarrig, Kinsale, Co. Cork. He was educated at Braidlea, Stoke Bishop, Bristol, at Monkton Coombe School, Bath, where he was a member of the O.T.C., and on H.M.S. "Worcester," training ship for the merchant service. On the outbreak of the war he applied for a commision and was gazetted to the 3rd Batt. of the Royal Irish Rifles in February, 1915, and left for France at the end of September.

✧ ✧ ✧

Captain Ambrose Langley Hunt, R.N.R., was in command of an Admiralty transport when attacked by an Austrian submarine in the Eastern Mediterranean, and while endeavouring to save her under heavy fire was killed by shrapnel. The majority of the ship's company were rescued from the damaged boats, the ship, riddled with shell, being torpedoed and sunk by the submarine, which was afterwards accounted for by H.M.S. "Chatham." Captain Hunt was the fourth son of the late Dr. Ambrose Hunt, M.D., of Dungarvan, Waterford, and husband of Mrs. Catherine M. Hunt, Old Mill House, Westerham, Kent.

✧ ✧ ✧

Lieutenant Vincent Fox, attached to the 8th Infantry Brigade, was killed in the retreat from Mons. Lieut. Fox was a native of Hackballs Cross, Dundalk, where his family reside. He received an appointment in India as assistant to Dr. Spooner Hart, V.S. to the Governor-General in India and the Calcutta Turf Club. After 18 months in India he returned home, and having passed his exams. was gazetted Lieutenant on August 15th and attached to the 8th Infantry Brigade, with whom he went to France on August 17th, 1914.

1. LIEUT J. MACKAY, 1st Batt. Gordon Highlanders.
2. REV. F. C. ROCHE, M.A., Chaplain attached to 10th Division.
3. LIEUT. V. McNAMARA, Royal Engineers.
4. CAPT. C. D. WYNTER, Irish Guards.
5. COLONEL G. H. C. MADDEN, 1st Batt. Irish Guards.
6. CAPT. R. J. O'LONE, 2nd Batt. Royal Irish Rifles.
7. LT. C. H. WHISH DARLING, 3rd Batt. Royal Irish Rifles.
8. CAPT. A. L. HUNT, Royal Naval Reserve.
9. LIEUT. V. FOX, 8th Infantry Brigade.

OUR HEROES.

Second Lieutenant James Clarke Stokoe, 14th Battalion Manchester Regiment, was killed in action at the Dardanelles on November 11th, 1915, in his 22nd year. He was the eldest son of the late Mr. James Clarke Stokoe, L.D.S., M.R.C.S., and of Mrs. Stokoe, Hillside Terrace, Newry, and was educated at Newry Model School and Manchester Grammar School, and subsequently entered Oxford, where he was a member of the O.T.C. He received his commission in March last, and in September left for the Dardanelles, being attached to the 11th Manchester Regiment.

◇ ◇ ◇

Second Lieutenant Eric Henry Scott Smith, Royal Engineers, who died of dysentery at Mudros Bay, Island of Lemnos, on 29th October last, aged 20, was the only son of the Hon. Mr. Justin and Mrs. H. Scott Smith, of Lahore, Punjab, India, and a grandson of the late Rev. Frank Smith, of Stratford-on-Avon, formerly of Londonderry, and a grand-nephew of Mr. H. G. Cooper, 9 Clare-street, Dublin. He was educated at Clifton College, from which he entered Woolwich.

◇ ◇ ◇

Lieutenant Eldred Pottinger Gordon, 104th Wellesley's Rifles, Indian Army, was killed in action in Mesopotamia about the 23rd or 24th November, 1915, in his 24th year. Lt. Gordon belonged to a very old and well-known Irish family. He was the sixth and youngest son of the late Mr. Alexander H. M. H. Gordon, D.L., of Delamont, Killyleigh and Florida Manor, Killinchy, Co. Down. Lieut. Gordon held an appointment under the Board of Works, India, but on the outbreak of war he volunteered for service and was appointed to the 104th Rifles.

◇ ◇ ◇

Captain Edward Graeme Ozanne, 7th Royal Fusiliers (City of London Regiment), was killed in action near Ypres on 14th February, 1915. He was the only son of Edward C. Ozanne, Bailiff and President of the States, Island of Guernsey, and grandson of Mr. J. K. Boyd, Cultra House, Holywood, County Down. He was educated at Queen Elizabeth College, Guernsey, and at Rugby. Captain Ozanne was gazetted to the 7th Royal Fusiliers, May, 1901. He had served through the South African War, for his services in which he received the Queen's Medal with 4 clasps.

◇ ◇ ◇

Lieut=Colonel Alexander William Abercrombie, commanding 2nd Batt. Connaught Rangers, died at Magdeburg, Germany, on November 5th, 1915, whilst a prisoner of war. He was the son of the late Alexander Abercrombie, Bengal Civil Service, and Mrs. Abercrombie, 34 Gloucester Terrace, Hyde Park, London. He obtained his commission in the 51st King's Own (Yorkshire Light Infantry) on May 9th, 1885, and saw service with them in Burma in 1886-7 when he was mentioned in despatches. He was gazetted Captain in the Connaught Rangers in December, 1892, and was posted to the 2nd Batt. He went to France with the Expeditionary Force in August, 1914, in command of the 2nd Battalion, and was taken prisoner about a fortnight later in the retreat on Paris. He was taken to Torgeau, where he remained for three months, and in December, 1914, was moved to Magdeburg, and was there until his death. Colonel Abercrombie married in 1893 Ethel, second daughter of Major and Mrs. Lawrence Gordon, of Crescent Lodge, Southsea.

◇ ◇ ◇

Captain John Broadwood Atkinson, 5th Batt. Royal Irish Fusiliers, died in hospital at Alexandria on December 24th, 1915, of enteric fever contracted on active service in Gallipoli. He had just attained his 21st birthday, and was a son of Mr. Joseph Atkinson, D.L., of Crowhill, Armagh. He was educated at Mourne Grange, Co. Down, and Dundle School, Northamptonshire. On the outbreak of the war he offered his services and was gazetted to the 5th Batt. Royal Irish Fusiliers in September, 1914, and took part in the landing at Suvla Bay, where he was wounded.

◇ ◇ ◇

Lieutenant James Augustus Stewart, 2nd Batt. Royal Munster Fusiliers, who was killed in action on May 9th, 1915, while gallantly leading his platoon in an attack at Rue du Bois, Richebourg, France, was the only son of the late Mr. James Augustus Stewart, Buncrana, County Donegal, and nephew of the ninth baronet of Fort Stewart, County Donegal. He was twenty years old and was gazetted from Sandhurst to the 2nd Batt. Royal Munster Fusiliers in August, 1914.

◇ ◇ ◇

Lieutenant W. J. E. Morton, 5th Batt. Royal Irish Rifles, was killed in action at Hooge on September 4th, 1915. He had assisted his father, Mr. Wm. Morton, Hollydene, Holywood, in his office in Belfast, but when war was declared he immediately volunteered and was gazetted to the 5th Royal Irish Rifles, and went to the front on May 1st, 1914, where he received his Lieutenancy. He had been serving in the trenches from May until September.

◇ ◇ ◇

Second Lieutenant Cedric P. Christie, Liverpool Regiment, died of wounds received in action in France on December 14th last. He was in his 23rd year, and was a son of Rev. E. B. Christie, of Middletown, County Armagh. He was educated at Trinity College, Dublin, and had been only a month in France when he received the injuries to which he succumbed in hospital at Boulogne. His brother, Second Lieut. Reginald B. Christie, is also on active service with the Northumberland Fusiliers.

1. LIEUT. J. C. STOKOE, 14th Manchester Regiment.
2. LIEUT. E. H. SCOTT SMITH. Royal Engineers.
3. LIEUT. E. P. GORDON, 104th Rifles, Indian Army.
4. CAPTAIN E. G. OZANNE, Royal Fusiliers.
5. LIEUTENANT-COLONEL A. W. ABERCROMBIE, Connaught Rangers.
6. CAPT. J. B. ATKINSON, 5th Batt. Royal Irish Fusiliers.
7. LIEUT. J. A. STEWART, Royal Munster Fusiliers.
8. LIEUT. W. J. E. MORTON, 5th Batt. Royal Irish Rifles.
9. LIEUT. C. P. CHRISTIE, Liverpool Regiment.

OUR HEROES.

Lieutenant Gerald Bradstreet, R.E., who was killed in action at Gallipoli, was the only son of Sir Edward Bradstreet, Bart., of Castella, Clontarf, and his death leaves the baronetcy of Bradstreet, which was created in 1759, without an heir. Lieutenant Bradstreet was educated at Portora Royal School and Trinity College, and early in the war received his commission in the Royal Engineers, and was six months on active service with the Mediterranean Expeditionary Force, and was wounded in an engagement some months ago. Lieutenant Bradstreet was a well-known Rugby player and a thorough sportsman.

◇ ◇ ◇

Captain J. C. B. Joy, 1st Devonshire Regiment, was killed in action in Mesopotamia on December 11th, 1915, whilst serving with the 2nd Dorset Regiment in the I.E.F. He was the eldest son of Mr. George W. Joy, of the Red Lodge, Palace Court, London, W., and belonged to an old Ulster family, being descended from Captain Thomas Joy, whose name was one of the first on the list in the settlement of Ulster. Captain Joy was educated at Oxford University, where he was a member of the O.T.C., and rowed in his college boat. He had been promoted Captain a few weeks before his death, in his 29th year.

◇ ◇ ◇

Lieutenant C. E. Taylor, West Yorks Regiment, who has been killed in action, was a son of Dr. M. H. Taylor, Richmond, Surrey, and a member of a well-known Co. Mayo family, of which Dr. C. H. Foley, Ardrahan, and Mr. F. J. Hughes, Kiltimagh, are the representatives. Lieutenant Taylor had been specially mentioned in despatches for bravery in the retreat from Mons.

◇ ◇ ◇

Lieutenant Arthur McLaughlin, 3rd Batt. Royal Irish Rifles (attached 1st Batt.), was a son of Mr. W. H. McLaughlin, D.L., Macedon, Whitehouse, Co. Antrim. He was educated at Monkton Combe School, Bath, and when he left the school about a year before his death he was head prefect, captain of the football team, and captain and "stroke" of the boat in the rowing club. When war broke out he immediately offered his services and obtained a commission in the 3rd R.I.R., in which battalion his brother, Major McLaughlin, was serving. He went to the front in March, 1915, and was killed on the 9th of May at Fromelles whilst leading his men against the German trenches. His last words were: "I'm all right; lead on, lead on." He died shortly afterwards.

◇ ◇ ◇

Major F. W. J. MacDonnell, 14th (Reserve) Batt., attached 9th Batt., West Yorkshire Regiment, who died in hospital at Malta from dysentery contracted at Gallipoli, formerly held the rank of Captain in the 3rd Batt. Royal Dublin Fusiliers, and was gazetted Captain in the Reserve of Officers. In November, 1914, he was posted to the 12th Batt. of the West Yorks, with the rank of Major, and in July he went to the 14th Batt., being subsequently attached to the 9th Batt. for service with the Mediterranean Expedition. Before the present war Major MacDonnell saw active service in South Africa (1901-2), taking part in operations in the Transvaal and Orange River Colony, for his services in which he received the Queen's Medal with four clasps. Major MacDonnell was the son of Mr. Francis MacDonnell, of Dunfirth, and a grandson of Sir Francis MacDonnell, of Dunfirth, Enfield, Co. Kildare, and married, in 1898, Teresa, daughter of Sir John Lawson, Brough Hall, Yorkshire.

◇ ◇ ◇

Captain H. K. Oakes, Canadian Rifles, who was killed in action in France, was a son of the late Lieutenant-Colonel F. A. Oakes and grandson of the late Rev. Q. S. Kellett, The Rectory, Ballyconnell. Captain Oakes had taken part in many engagements, and was about to return home for a short leave when he fell in action.

◇ ◇ ◇

Second Lieutenant Robert W. MacDermot, 8th Batt. Royal Irish Rifles, was killed in action on the Western front. He was the second son of Rev. Dr. MacDermot, Belmont, and was educated at Campbell College, Belmont, and the Queen's University, Belfast. He was within a few months of being called to the Bar when war broke out, and immediately volunteered for service.

◇ ◇ ◇

Captain Cyril Richmond Shannon, 101st Field Company, R.E., was killed in Flanders while putting finishing touches to some barbed wire entanglements in front of the trenches just taken from the Germans. He was a son of the late Mr. Robert Shannon, M.I.C.E., and Mrs. Shannon, and had spent a good many years in India, China and Japan, and was a remarkably keen linguist. Captain Shannon was educated at the High School, Dublin, and subsequently at Woolwich and Bath College. He went to France on August 7th, 1914, and received his Captaincy in October of the same year.

◇ ◇ ◇

Lieut. Kenneth G. Haslam Ford, 11th Cheshire Regiment, who was killed in action in Flanders in December last, was a son of the Ven. G. A. Ford, Rector of Babington, Rockferry, Cheshire, and a nephew of Rev. Canon Lockett Ford, M.A., Rector of Ardee, County Louth. In September, 1914, he was given a commission in the 11th Cheshires, and was subsequently selected to command the machine gun section. He went to France in September, 1915, and was shot while carrying out a dangerous reconnaissance.

1. LIEUT. R. W. MACDERMOT, 8th Batt. Royal Irish Rifles.
2. CAPT. J. C. B. JOY, 1st Devonshire Regiment.
3. LIEUT. C. E. TAYLOR, West Yorkshire Regiment.
4. CAPTAIN H. K. OAKES, 3rd Canadian Mounted Rifles.
5. MAJOR F. W. MACDONNELL, 14th Batt. West Yorkshire Regiment.
6. CAPT. C. R. SHANNON, Royal Engineers.
7. LIEUT. G. BRADSTREET, Royal Engineers.
8. LIEUT. A. M'LAUGHLIN, 3rd Batt. Royal Irish Rifles.
9. LIEUT. K. G. H. FORD, 11th Batt. Cheshire Regiment.

OUR HEROES.

Second Lieutenant Patrick Stan McMahon, 8th Royal Munster Fusiliers, was the son of Mr. John McMahon, Knocknagarm House, Newmarket-on-Fergus, Co. Clare. He enlisted in the Cadet Company, 7th Leinster Regiment, on the outbreak of the war, and from thence obtained his commission in the 8th Royal Munster Fusiliers. He died on December 29th in France, of wounds received in action on the night of December 24th.

✧ ✧ ✧

Second Lieutenant George Carlyon Armstrong, 1st Batt. Coldstream Guards, who was killed at Givenchy on January 20th, 1915, was the only son of Sir George Armstrong, Bart., Winloed, Pangbourne, Berks, and nephew of Mrs. G. E. Kirk, Thornfield Carrickfergus.

✧ ✧ ✧

Second Lieutenant F. Lyttelton Lloyd Rogers, R.F.A., aged 20, who was killed in action on the 7th January, was the eldest son of Mr. and Mrs. Lyttelton Rogers, 11 Merrion Square, Dublin. Before the war he was in the Engineering School, Trinity College, and the O.T.C. He volunteered for active service the day after war was declared, and went to France last August, and was in the advance last autumn at Loos. An officer writes: "He was at his post doing his duty and seeing his men were under cover." His great-great-grandfather (maternal) was Colonel Richard Lloyd, 84th Foot, who fell in action in France on the 10th December, 1813.

✧ ✧ ✧

Fleet Paymaster Augustus Elliot Tabateau, R.N., was killed on board H.M.S. *Natal* on December 30th, 1915. He was the youngest Fleet Paymaster in the Navy, having received six years special promotion for distinguished service performed while serving with the Naval Brigade in the relief of the Legation at Peking during the Boxer rising of 1900, and held the China Medal. He was the eldest son of the late Mr. Joseph Manly Tabateau, J.P., and Mrs. Tabateau, Kilmalogue House, Portarlington.

✧ ✧ ✧

Major W. J. Law, Lancashire Fusiliers, who was killed in action at the Dardanelles on the 20th December, 1915, was the only son of Mr. Thomas Law, Portadown, Ireland. He was a graduate of the late R.U.I., and a senior exhibitioner of T.C.D. He ultimately became one of His Majesty's Inspectors of Factories, and was for some years a junior inspector at Preston, Lancashire. He joined the 7th (Salford) Territorial Battalion of the Lancashire Fusiliers about nine years ago, and accompanied it to Egypt shortly after mobilisation in 1914. His division was subsequently sent to the Dardanelles. In June Major Law was slightly wounded, and was mentioned in despatches last September by Sir Ian Hamilton. Major Law was a sportsman as well as a scholar.

Captain Louis Corbally, R.F.A., third son of the late Mr. Mathew James Corbally, of Rathbeal Hall, Swords, Co. Dublin, died of wounds at Bailleul on May 6th, 1915. He was born in 1876, educated at Stonyhurst College and Trinity College, Dublin. He served through the Boer War in the Irish Yeomanry, and was taken prisoner at Lindley. He married, in 1906, Nancy, daughter of Mr. John F. Whyte, D.L., of Loughbrickland, Co. Down. He re-joined the Army when the war broke out and received a commission as Captain in the Royal Field Artillery. He was a keen sportsman, a good rider to hounds, a good shot, and a well-known writer on these subjects.

✧ ✧ ✧

Second Lieutenant Wm. Fraser, 1st Batt. Black Watch, who died on September 29, 1915, of shrapnel wounds received in action in France, was the only child of Mr. and Mrs. Fraser, 15 Willowbank Gardens, Belfast. He had been serving with the Black Watch (Territorials) and gained his commission for distinguished conduct on the field. He was subsequently transferred to the 1st Battalion, and had been with them about five weeks when he was fatally wounded whilst leading his platoon in an attack on an enemy trench. Lieutenant Fraser was a prominent figure in athletic circles in the North of Ireland.

✧ ✧ ✧

Lieut. Edmund John Macrory Robertson, 70th Battery, R.F.A., who fell in action at Festubert, France, on May 22, 1915, was the son of Dr. J. R. S. Robertson, of Hayling Island, Hants, grandson of Edmund Macrory, K.C., and great-grandson of Adam John Macrory, of Duncairn, Belfast. He was born on May 29, 1891, educated at Parkfield, Hayward's Heath, and Bradfield College, Berks, and entered the Royal Field Artillery in 1910. He went out with his battery in August, 1914, with the First Expeditionary Force, was wounded at Mons, and mentioned in Sir John French's first despatch. Lieutenant Robertson's father was a surgeon with the British Army in the Egyptian campaign and was with the Gordon Relief Expedition.

✧ ✧ ✧

Second Lieutenant William H. Sargaison, 5th Batt. Connaught Rangers, who was killed in action in Serbia on December 6th, 1915, in his 22nd year, was a son of Mr. and Mrs. Sargaison, Battery Road, Longford. He was educated at Mountjoy School, Dublin, and St. George's College, London. At the outbreak of the war he joined the "D" Company of the 7th Royal Dublin Fusiliers at its formation and took part in the engagement at Suvla Bay and in the subsequent fighting in Gallipoli. He was then promoted to a commission in the 5th Connaught Rangers and transferred to Salonika, where he was killed while fighting in the rearguard action.

1. LIEUT. P. S. McMAHON, 8th Royal Munster Fusiliers.
2. LIEUT. G. C. ARMSTRONG, 1st Coldstream Guards.
3. LIEUT. F. L. LLOYD ROGERS, R.F.A.
4. FLEET-PAYMASTER A. E. TABATEAU, R.N.
5. MAJOR W. J. LAW, Lancashire Fusiliers.
6. CAPT. L. CORBALLY, R.F.A.
7. LIEUT. W. FRASER, 1st Batt. Black Watch.
8. LIEUT. E. J. M. ROBERTSON, R.F.A.
9. LIEUT. W. H. SARGAISON, 5th Connaught Rangers.

OUR HEROES.

Lieutenant Cecil Barton Hudson-Kinahan, 4th King's African Rifles, who died on December 30 in hospital in British East Africa of fever contracted while on active service, was the youngest son of the late Sir E. H. Hudson-Kinahan, Bart. He was born in Dublin in 1883, was educated at Shrewsbury, and entered the 4th Royal Munster Fusiliers, in which he served for two years. He afterwards went to British East Africa and was engaged in rubber and cocoanut planting.

✧ ✧ ✧

Second Lieut. James Douglas Tomblin, Motor Machine Gun Service, was the elder son of Mr. and Mrs. James Tomblin, Killarney, Heath Drive, Hampstead, and a grandson of the late Mr. J. D. S. H. McQuillan, former managing editor of the *Morning* and *Evening Mail,* Dublin. In July, 1915, he was gazetted to the Motor Machine Gun Section, and in September, 1915, went to France, where he fell in action.

✧ ✧ ✧

Second Lieutenant Logan Kyle, elder son of Mr. W. Kyle, B.A., Inspector of Schools, was born in Co. Armagh on 27th February, 1892. He was educated at St. Luke's School, Cork, Foyle College, Londonderry, and Trinity College, Dublin, and after a distinguished career he graduated both in Arts and Engineering in October, 1914, being awarded the large gold medal in History and Political Science. After graduation he applied for and received a commission in the Royal Engineers, and in May, 1915, was sent to Flanders, where, only four days after his arrival, he was killed by a sniper.

✧ ✧ ✧

Lieutenant Noel Trevor Worthington, 6th Batt. King's Own Royal Lancashire Regiment, was a son of Mr. Robert Worthington, J.P., of Salmon Pool, Dublin, and great-grandson of Sir William Worthington, Lord Mayor of Dublin in 1795-6, and Dr. Samuel Ball Labatt, an eminent physician in the early part of the last century, and a descendant of a very old Huguenot family, as appears from Smile's *Life of the Huguenots*: "The Labatts were a branch of the very ancient Normandy family related to the Sabatiers and Chateaneufs, and long settled in Ireland. The first Labatt came over with William III., in whose army he was an officer. He was afterwards at the siege of Derry on board the *Mountjoy,* which burst the boom across the harbour mouth and led to the raising of the siege. He eventually settled in the King's County. The representative of the family is the Rev. Edward Labatt, M.A., Rector of Kilcar, Co. Donegal." Lieut. Worthington was reported wounded at Suvla Bay on August 6th last, subsequently reported missing, and is now believed to have been killed. He was in charge of the grenadier company of his regiment and fell while rallying his men when attacked by overwhelming numbers. His brother, Lieut. G. Errol Worthington, is now serving with the Army Service Corps.

Lieutenant-Colonel W. Moyle O'Connor, M.D., who was recently mentioned in Sir John French's despatches for gallant and distinguished service in the field, was a member of a well-known Dublin family, being a son of the late Mr. Patrick O'Connor, of Ryevale, Leixlip, and a brother of Mr. P. J. O'Connor, land and estate agent, of Queen-street, and Stramorne, Sydney Parade. In March last he was sent to France as Commanding Officer attached to the London Field Ambulance. Colonel O'Connor had recently been invalided home, his health and eyesight having been very seriously affected, and died on 23rd inst.

✧ ✧ ✧

Captain R. B. Burgess, R.E., only son of Mr. H. G. Burgess, Irish manager of the L. & N.W. Railway Co., has died of wounds received in action in France. He was educated at Portora School and Trinity College, Dublin, and was afterwards called to the Bar. Early in the war he volunteered and obtained a commission in the Army Service Corps, and was rapidly promoted to a Captaincy in the Royal Engineers. Captain Burgess was one of the best Rugby players in Ireland.

✧ ✧ ✧

Second Lieutenant A. M. Horsfall, 2nd Batt. Royal Munster Fusiliers, was the second son of Mr. and Mrs. Horsfall, Denholme, Weybridge, Surrey. When war broke out he at once enlisted in the Artists' Rifles, and was sent to France the following October, obtaining his commission in the 2nd Munsters in January, 1915. He was killed at Rue du Bois on May 9th, 1915, and was, with other officers of his battalion, mentioned in Sir John French's despatches.

✧ ✧ ✧

Second Lieutenant Richard Clive McBryde Broun, 6th Batt. Royal Dublin Fusiliers, was the second son of Captain W. L. Broun, Colstoun, Park Road, Beckenham, Kent. Lieut. Broun was three years on board H.M. training ship *Worcester,* and then went one year as cadet on board the training ship *Medway.* In 1911 he went to Ceylon and belonged to the Ceylon Mounted Rifles, and on the outbreak of war came to Egypt with the Ceylon Contingent, obtained his commission and was attached to the 3rd Australian Reinforcements. In September, 1915, he joined the 6th Royal Dublin Fusiliers at Salonika, and was reported missing and believed killed in action between 6th and 11th December last.

✧ ✧ ✧

Second Lieut. Robert Maxwell Maccabe, 8th Batt. London Regiment, was the son of Mr. Thomas Maccabe, 45 Avoca-street, Belfast. He had been five years in the Queen's University O.T.C., and had got a medal from Count Gleichen for excellent work. He was mortally wounded at Givenchy on April 23rd, 1915, and died shortly afterwards in Bethune hospital.

1. LIEUT. C. B. HUDSON-KINAHAN, 4th King's African Rifles.
2. LIEUT. J. D. TOMBLIN, R.N.A.S.
3. LIEUT. LOGAN KYLE, Royal Engineers.
4. LT. NOEL T. WORTHINGTON, 6th K.O.R. Lancs.
5. LIEUT.-COL. M. O'CONNOR, M.D. R.A.M.C.
6. CAPT. R. B. BURGESS, Royal Engineers.
7. LIEUT. A. M. HORSFALL, 2nd Royal Munster Fusiliers.
8. LT. R. C. McBRYDE BROUN, 6th Royal Dublin Fusiliers.
9. LIEUT. R. M. MacCABE, 8th London Regiment.

Our Heroes

OUR HEROES.

Second Lieutenant R. C. Davis, 3rd Batt. Manchester Regiment, was killed in action in Mesopotamia on March 8th, 1916. He was the elder son of Mr. and Mrs. James Davis, Harpur House, Drogheda, and was educated at Drogheda Grammar School and Wesley College, Dublin. He subsequently entered Trinity College, and was a member of the O.T.C. In December, 1914, he obtained his commission, and in May, 1915, was sent to France attached to the Lahore Division of the Indian Expeditionary Force. He was wounded in June, 1915. In December, 1915, after a short leave, he went to Mesopotamia and joined General Lake's relief column. Lieut. Davis was a well-known football player, and a good all-round athlete.

◆ ◆ ◆

Lance-Corporal Henry B. Hodge, 4th Canadian Mounted Rifles, formerly 74th Dublin Company Imperial Yeomanry, acting Chaplain to the 2nd Brigade, was born in Clontibret, Co. Monaghan, and went to Canada. He was a theological student of Wycliffe College, Toronto, and on the outbreak of the war came over with the Canadian contingent, and was killed in action in France in December last.

◆ ◆ ◆

Second Lieutenant Herbert Augustus Johnston, Royal Flying Corps, youngest son of Dr. H. M. Johnston, J.P., Stranorlar, was killed in action in France. Before joining the Air Service Lieut. Johnston had served for twelve months in Kitchener's Army. He had given up a very lucrative position on the outbreak of the war to join the colours. He was a very clever electrician, and had been sent all over the world in connection with the erection of wireless installations. He was educated at Trinity College, Dublin, and was a rifle shot of exceptional skill.

◆ ◆ ◆

Major Lord Desmond Fitzgerald, 1st Batt. Irish Guards, heir-presumptive to the Duke of Leinster, was accidentally killed on duty in France. He was born in 1888, and was educated at Eton and Sandhurst, passing into the Irish Guards in February, 1909. He obtained his Captaincy in 1913, and in July last received his Majority. He had been twice wounded in action, had been mentioned in Sir John French's despatches, and awarded the Military Cross.

Surgeon-Colonel Arthur H. Moorhead, A.D.M.S., I.M.S., has died from sickness contracted on active service in France. He was the third son of Brigadier-Surgeon George A. Moorhead, A.M.S., and uncle to Dr. George A. Moorhead, Tullamore, and Dr. Henry Moorhead, Moate. Educated at the University of Edinburgh, he passed into the Indian Medical Service, gaining second place. He served in the Chitral Expedition, the Naziri Expedition, and the Pekin Relief Expedition, and for each was awarded medal and clasp. He was selected to represent the Indian Empire at the International Medical Congress held in America some years ago on bubonic plague. At the outbreak of the war he accompanied the first contingent of Indian troops in the autumn of 1914 to France, and was in medical charge of the Meerut Division. He rendered such services in the reorganisation of the ambulance department, and such fearless aid to the wounded under fire, that his name was mentioned in despatches, and he was promoted to the position of Assistant Director of Medical Services.

◆ ◆ ◆

Captain Patrick Richard Butler, Brigade-Major on Sir Bryan Mahon's staff at Salonika, has been mentioned in despatches for distinguished service. He is a son of the late Lieut.-General Sir William Butler, G.C.B., and Lady Butler, Bansha, Co. Tipperary. He was gazetted to the Royal Irish Regiment in 1902, with whom he served in India. He was promoted Captain in 1909. On the outbreak of the war he was appointed A.D.C. to Sir Thompson Capper, commanding the 7th Division. He was wounded in November, 1914, but returned to France in the spring of 1915, and is at present in Salonika.

Private Robert S. Hodge, 4th Canadian Mounted Rifles, was born in Clontibret, Co. Monaghan. He went to Canada some time ago, and was employed by the Canadian Pacific Railway at Winnipeg, but on the outbreak of the war he enlisted and came over with the Canadian contingent. He was killed in action in France in December last.

Lieutenant W. S. Drury, 8th Battalion Royal Dublin Fusiliers, was killed on active service in France on January 29th last as the result of a bomb accident. He was a son of Mr. T. C. Drury, one of the Dublin Divisional Magistrates.

Corporal Edward Quinn, Royal Field Artillery, has been recommended for the D.C.M. for gallantry in action at Neuve Chapelle. His battery was under the enemy fire, and their communication wires had been broken by a German shell. All attempts to connect them had failed, when Quinn gallantly made good the breach, and thus saved the British infantry from the fire of their own guns. Corporal Quinn is a son of Mr. Charles Quinn, Ballyrashane, Coleraine. He enlisted in 1897, and came from India with the Indian Expeditionary Force.

1. LIEUT. R. C. DAVIS, 3rd Manchester Regiment.
2. LCE.-CPL. H. B. HODGE, 4th Canadian Mounted Rifles.
3. LIEUT. H. A. JOHNSTON, Royal Flying Corps.
4. MAJOR LORD DESMOND FITZGERALD, 1st Batt. Irish Guards.
5. SURGEON-COLONEL A. H. MOORHEAD, Indian Medical Service.
6. CAPT. P. R. BUTLER, Staff Brigade-Major.
7. PRIVATE S. HODGE, 4th Canadian Mounted Rifles.
8. LIEUT. W. S. DRURY, 8th Royal Dublin Fusiliers.
9. CORPORAL E. QUINN, Royal Field Artillery.

OUR HEROES.

Lieutenant Arthur Cecil Winser, 8th East Lancs. Regiment, who died in France on the 22nd inst: from wounds received in action on the 17th inst., was the third son of the late Frank Winser, of Dublin. He was educated at St. Andrew's College, Dublin. Prior to the war he was engaged in railway construction in Canada. He came over with the first contingent, and got a commission in the 8th East Lancs. Regiment, and was mentioned in despatches for distinguished service on the field.

Major George Julian Ryan, D.S.O., 2nd Batt. Royal Munster Fusiliers, was killed on January 23rd, 1915, in France by a sniper as he was returning from an inspection of the trenches. Major Ryan was born in 1878, and was a son of the late Lieut.-Col. G. Ryan, Army Medical Department, and Mrs. Ryan, Ashby Cottage, Ryde, I.W. In 1897 he joined the 1st Batt. R.M.F. Major Ryan had seen much service abroad, and was all through the South African War, for his services in which he received the Queen's Medal with five clasps and the D.S.O. He served seven years in Egypt, and for his services in the Soudan in 1905 he was again mentioned in despatches and received the Egyptian Medal and clasps, and in the present war was once more mentioned in despatches.

Second Lieutenant Rowan Shaw, 9th Cheshire Regiment, who was killed in France on February 23rd, was the elder son of the late Judge Shaw, Recorder of Belfast. He was educated at St. Columba's College and Dublin University, and served through the South African War with the Imperial Yeomanry, for which he held the South African medal with three clasps. He was called to the Irish Bar, and subsequently went to the Federated Malay States. On the outbreak of this war he volunteered for service, and received a commission in the 9th Battalion Cheshire Regiment last April.

Captain O. G. de Courcy Baldwin, 8th Royal Munster Fusiliers, who was killed in action in France on January 26th, 1916. He was the second son of the Rev. W. H. de C. Baldwin, Rector, of Holtby, Yorkshire, and of Mrs. Baldwin, Charleville, Co. Cork. He joined the 3rd West Yorkshire Regiment in 1907, and in 1910 resigned his commission on passing into the Royal Irish Constabulary. He was D.I. at Ballinamore, Co. Leitrim, and subsequently at Charleville, Co. Cork. When war broke out he volunteered for active service, and was gazetted Captain in the 8th Royal Munsters.

Temporary Lieutenant-Colonel Charles Elrington Duncan Davidson-Houston, D.S.O., 58th Rifles, Indian Army, who was returned as "wounded and missing" on the 25th September last, and is now unofficially reported "killed in action" on that date, was the youngest son of the late Rev. P. C. Davidson-Houston, M.A., Vicar of St. John's, Sandymount, Ireland, and Chaplain to the Lord Lieutenant, was born on the 21st January, 1873, and married Constance Isabel Barton, daughter of the late Professor Robert Caeser Childers in 1907. He was educated in England and Germany, and entered the Indian Army in 1893, being promoted Captain in 1902, Major in 1911, and Temporary Lieutenant-Colonel in 1914. During this period he saw much active service. He succeeded to the command of his regiment, the 58th Rifles, Frontier Force, after the death in action on the 31st October, 1914, of the then Commanding Officer, Lieutenant-Colonel W. E. Venour. Lieutenant-Colonel Davidson-Houston had commanded his regiment ever since with conspicuous ability, and taking part in several actions. At Givenchy in December, 1914, he gained the D.S.O.

Captain Valentine Charles Joseph Blake, 1st Irish Guards, was the second son of the late Valentine Joseph Blake, of Towerhill, Co. Mayo, and Mary Blake, only daughter of Charles, third Baron de Freyne. He was born at Castlemore, Co. Mayo, and educated at Stonyhurst and Trinity College, Dublin. He joined the Royal Irish Constabulary in 1908, and was commanding No. 4 Company at their depot in Phoenix Park when war was declared. He volunteered and received a Captaincy in the Irish Guards in October, 1914, and went to France in May, 1915, where he was killed on January 29th.

Lieutenant Edward Workman, 5th Royal Irish Rifles, died in hospital in France on Jan. 26th, 1916, of wounds received in action on the 19th, for his valuable services in which he was awarded the Military Cross, having previously been mentioned in despatches for gallantry at Hooge. He was the only son of Mr. and Mrs. Frank Workman, The Moat, Strandtown, Co. Down, and had been a member of the firm of Workman, Clark and Co., Ltd., Belfast, but on the outbreak of the war obtained a commission in the 5th R.I.R. He went to the front on May 1st, 1915.

Lieutenant James Bohill, 2nd Batt. Royal Irish Rifles, was killed in action in France on November 19th, 1915. He was the youngest son of the late Mr. Thomas Bohill, Belturbet, and was educated at Trinity College, Dublin. On the outbreak of the war he enlisted, and on April 27th, 1915, was given a commission. He went to France in July, 1915.

Lieutenant C. B. Joy, 3rd Welsh Regiment, was the second son of Mr. George W. Joy, the Red Lodge, Palace Court, London, W.; was severely wounded on May 21st, 1915, whilst serving with the 1st Highland Light Infantry. He has since been reported missing, and is believed to have been killed. His brother was also killed in action in France.

1. LIEUT. A. C. WINSER, 8th East Lancs. Regiment.
2. MAJOR G. J. RYAN, D.S.O., 2nd Royal Munster Fusiliers.
3. LIEUT. ROWAN SHAW, 9th Cheshire Regiment.
4. CAPT. O. G. DE COURCY BALDWIN, 8th Royal Munster Fusiliers.
5. LIEUT.-COL. DAVIDSON-HOUSTON, D.S.O., 58th Rifles, Indian Army.
6. CAPT. V. C. J. BLAKE, 1st Irish Guards.
7. LIEUT. E. WORKMAN, 5th Royal Irish Rifles. Military Cross.
8. LIEUT. J. BOHILL, 2nd Royal Irish Rifles.
9. LIEUT. C. B. JOY, 3rd Welsh Regiment.

OUR HEROES.

Company Sergeant-Major James Daly, 2nd Royal Inniskilling Fusiliers, who has been awarded the D.C.M., is a son of Mr. Thomas Daly, Annahilla, Augher, Co. Tyrone. He has been at the front in France since August, 1914. He is over 13 years in the Army, and has seen a good deal of foreign service in South Africa, Egypt, and Crete.

Captain Henry Bowler Sherlock, R.A.M.C., L.R.C.S., P.I., who has been mentioned in despatches and awarded the Military Cross, is the second son of Mr. Henry Gregg Sherlock, F.R.C.S.I., of Carisfort, Glenageary. He was educated at the Royal College of Surgeons, Dublin, and shortly after the outbreak of the war offered his services, and has been "somewhere in France" ever since.

Lieutenant R. C. Byrne, 6th Royal Dublin Fusiliers, was mentioned in Sir Ian Hamilton's despatches, and has been awarded the Military Cross. He took part in the landing of the 10th Division at Suvla Bay, and in consequence of his services to his battalion during their stay in Gallipoli he has been referred to in many letters sent home as the "King of Quartermasters." After leaving Gallipoli he accompanied the 10th Division to Salonika, where he is still serving. Lieut. Byrne has been 22 years in the Army, serving all this time with the Dublin Fusiliers, in which regiment he has four brothers, two of whom have been wounded in Gallipoli. Before the present war he saw active service in South Africa, for which he received the Queen's Medal with six clasps. He is the eldest son of Mrs. Byrne, The Demesne, Lucan, Co. Dublin.

Captain Charles Edmund Ryan, R.F.A., is the fourth son of the late Major C. Ryan, R.A., and of Mrs. Lambert. He was educated at Stonyhurst, and passed from there into Woolwich. On leaving Woolwich he joined the R.F.A. in India, returning with his battery when war broke out, and saw service at St. Elois and Ypres. In May, 1915, he was attached to the Royal Flying Corps, and was wounded in November, 1915. He has been mentioned in despatches and awarded the Military Cross. Another brother, Lieut. K. V. Ryan, is serving with the 4th Royal Dublin Fusiliers, and has been wounded.

Major William S. Traill, Royal Engineers, has received the D.S.O. for distinguished services rendered in connection with military operations. He is the eldest son of the late Dr. Anthony Traill, Provost of Trinity College, and husband of Mrs. Traill, Ballylough House, Bushmills, Co. Antrim.

Captain Denis George Jocelyn Ryan, who has been awarded the D.S.O., is the second son of the late Major C. Ryan, Royal Artillery, and of Mrs. Lambert, and nephew of Mr. George Ryan, of Inch, Thurles. Educated at Stonyhurst and Wimbledon, he joined the Royal Sussex Regiment, transferring to the Indian Army three years later, and has been on active service with his regiment in Egypt and the Dardanelles. He has been twice mentioned in despatches.

Corporal George Bothwell, 16th Batt. King's Royal Rifles, has been awarded the D.C.M. for gallantry and devotion to duty in France. Corporal Bothwell is the third son of Mrs. Bothwell, Bath street, Portrush. He joined the Army in September, 1914, and has been at the front about three months. Soon after joining he distinguished himself as a crack rifle shot, and became a first-class Instructor at the Hythe School of Musketry.

Captain Ernest Hamilton, 10th Dublin Fusiliers, a son of Mrs. Hamilton, the White House, Portrush, enlisted as a private in the 7th Royal Dublin Fusiliers shortly after the outbreak of the war. He was quickly raised to the rank of Lieutenant, and went with his battalion to the Dardanelles, where he was wounded and afterwards invalided home. For distinguished conduct in the battle of Chocolate Hill he received his Captaincy in the 10th Dublin Fusiliers.

Sergeant-Major Henry Hamilton, 16th King's Royal Rifles, elder son of Mrs. Hamilton, The White House, Portrush, has been awarded the D.C.M. for gallantry in attempting to rescue two comrades who had been sent out to make a reconnaissance. He found them within five yards of the German trenches, the one killed and the other seriously wounded. As Sergeant-Major Hamilton was endeavouring to bring the latter to safety a machine gun was turned on them, killing the wounded man and severely wounding Sergeant-Major Hamilton, who is now recovering from his wounds.

Supplement to Irish Life, March 31st, 1916. 185

1. SERGT.-MAJOR J. DALY, 2nd Royal Inniskilling Fusiliers. D.C.M.	2. CAPTAIN H. B. SHERLOCK, R.A.M.C. Military Cross.	3. LIEUT. R. C. BYRNE, 6th Royal Dublin Fusiliers. Military Cross.
4. CAPT. C. E. RYAN, Royal Field Artillery. Military Cross.	5. MAJOR W. S. TRAILL, Royal Engineers. D.S.O.	6. CAPT. D. G. J. RYAN, 6th Gurkha Rifles. D.S.O.
7. CORPL. GEORGE BOTHWELL, 16th King's Royal Rifles. D.C.M.	8. CAPT. E. HAMILTON, 10th Royal Dublin Fusiliers.	9. SERGT.-MAJOR H. HAMILTON, 16th King's Royal Rifles. D.C.M.

OUR HEROES.

Lieutenant Kiggell, 3rd Field Squadron, Royal Engineers, who has been mentioned in despatches for distinguished service, is a son of Lieut.-General L. E. Kiggell, C.B., and a grandson of the late Major Kiggell, Cahara, Glin, Co. Limerick. Lieutenant Kiggell passed fourth out of Woolwich in December, 1913, and in September, 1914, was posted to the 3rd Field Squadron, Royal Engineers. He went to the front in October, 1914, and on January 18th, 1916, was gazetted A.D.C. to the Chief of the General Staff.

◇ ◇ ◇

Rev. F. S. Power, Australian Expeditionary Force, has been mentioned in despatches for distinguished service. He was educated at St. Vincent's College, Castleknock, and was first appointed to the English Mission, but was subsequently appointed Dean of Drumcondra Training College, and from thence called to Australia, where he was when war broke out, and immediately volunteered to accompany the first Australian Expeditionary Force, and was with them in the landing at Suvla Bay, where he remained until the retreat. He is a brother of Mr. Frank Power, Waterford.

◇ ◇ ◇

Second Lieutenant George E. B. Lyndon, who has been mentioned in Sir Ian Hamilton's despatch and awarded the Military Cross, is a younger son of the late Robert Lyndon and of Mrs. Lyndon, Mount Salus, Dalkey. He was educated in the Masonic Boys' School and St. Andrew's College. On the outbreak of war Lieutenant Lyndon joined the South Irish Horse as a trooper, but subsequently received a commission in the 6th Inniskilling Fusiliers, and took part in the Suvla Bay operations with the 10th Division.

◇ ◇ ◇

Captain George Montgomery Kidd, 5th Royal Irish Fusiliers, who has been awarded the Military Cross in recognition of his services in Gallipoli, is the son of Dr. Fred Wm. Kidd, 17 Lower Fitzwilliam-street. He was educated at the Abbey, Tipperary, and subsequently entered Trinity College, where he had a distinguished career, and took a prominent part in the social and athletic activities, and was Colour-sergeant in the O.T.C. He entered the Indian Civil Service, but on the outbreak of the war volunteered for service and received temporary leave from his post as Acting Assistant Commissioner. He was with his regiment in the Suvla Bay landing on August 8th

◇ ◇ ◇

Lieutenant-Colonel Frank Purcell Barnes, A.S.C., who has been recently made a Companion of the Distinguished Service Order, is the eldest son of Canon Barnes, of Ballycastle, Co. Antrim. He was educated at Bilton Grange Preparatory School, and at Tonbridge School, of which he was a House Scholar. Subsequently he obtained an exhibition at Magdalene College, Cambridge, and at the degree examination was placed on the "Classical Tripos" list. He obtained a commission in the Army Service Corps as a University candidate, and about a year later was sent out to South Africa. On his return to Aldershot he was selected for a special course of training in motor car structure, and having completed the course was appointed Instructor of Mechanical Transport, which post he held when the war broke out. He was sent to France at the outset of the war in charge of a detachment of Mechanical Transport.

◇ ◇ ◇

Captain James Lee Jackson, Royal Flying Corps, is a son of the Rev. Canon Jackson, M.A., The Rectory, Belmullet, Co. Mayo. He was gazetted to the Connaught Rangers in April, 1913, and in July, 1914, was promoted Lieutenant. Having already taken the Royal Aero Certificate at Messrs. Vickers' Flying School, Brooklands, he entered the Royal Flying Corps on the outbreak of hostilities, being subsequently promoted Captain, and in May, 1915, Flight Commander. He was wounded in the air reconnaissance at the battle of Festubert, and has been mentioned in Sir John French's despatches and awarded the Military Cross.

◇ ◇ ◇

Lieutenant J. G. Fitzmaurice, 7th Royal Munster Fusiliers, is a son of Mr. W. H. Fitzmaurice, National Bank House, Cahirciveen, Co. Kerry. He obtained his commission in the 7th Munsters in September, 1914, and was with his regiment in the landing at Suvla Bay, where he was wounded and invalided home. He is now serving with the 2nd Royal Munster Fusiliers in France, and has been mentioned in Sir Ian Hamilton's despatches.

◇ ◇ ◇

Dr. Patrick Cagney, who has been awarded the Military Cross for distinguished conduct in the field, is a son of Mr. M. Cagney, Gibbonsgrove, Charleville, and a graduate of University College, Cork, where he had a brilliant career, capturing the much-coveted Blaney Scholarship in his final exam. Dr. Cagney is a well-known Rugby football player. He has served in Flanders for over a year, attached to the Essex Regiment.

◇ ◇ ◇

Mr. E. Stuart White, of H.M.S. "Prince Rupert," who has been mentioned in despatches and awarded the D.S.M., is a son of Mr. Edmond Wolfe White, Coole House, Athea, Co. Limerick. He was educated at Chesterfield College, where he obtained his degree as Mechanical and Electrical Engineer. He subsequently joined the merchant service, and on the outbreak of the war volunteered for service in the Navy, and having passed his examinations with distinction was sent to the Clyde to supervise turrets and guns on monitors.

1. LIEUT. KIGGELL, Royal Engineers.	2. REV. F. S. POWER, Australian E. F.	3. LIEUT. G. E. B. LYNDON, 6th Inniskilling Fusiliers. Military Cross.
4. CAPT. G. M. KIDD, 5th Royal Irish Fusiliers. Military Cross.	5. LIEUT.-COL. F. P. BARNES, Army Service Corps. D.S.O.	6. CAPT. J. L. JACKSON, Royal Flying Corps. Military Cross.
7. LIEUT. J. G. FITZMAURICE, 7th Royal Munster Fusiliers.	8. DR. P. CAGNEY. Military Cross.	9. MR. E. S. WHITE, H.M.S. "Prince Rupert." D.S.M.

OUR HEROES.

Lieutenant Charles Gage Stuart, R.N., was awarded the Distinguished Service Cross "for meritorious service in connection with the sinking of the German cruiser Dresden, 14th March, 1915. Lieut. Stuart is a son of Mr. William Stuart, C.E., of Mount Earl, Ballymena, and a brother of Second-Lieutenant W. B. Stuart, of the 12th R.I.R. (Central Antrim Volunteers) and Second-Lieutenant L. I. Stuart, North Irish Horse. He is also a nephew of the late Rear-Admiral Leslie Stuart, C.M.G., and served with that officer on H.M.S. Vengeance on the China Station during the Russo-Japanese War. Lieut. Stuart's seniority dates from 1st April, 1909. When the war broke out he was serving in H.M.S. Glasgow on the South-East coast of South America. He was in the action with Von Spee's squadron off Coronel on 1st Nov., 1914, in which the Good Hope and Monmouth were sunk. Lieutenant Stuart had the satisfaction of taking part in the engagement off the Falklands on Dec. 8th, 1915, when the Glasgow assisted in sinking the German cruiser Leipzig.

◇ ◇ ◇

Captain J. H. Fletcher, R.A.M.C., eldest son of Mr. J. H. Fletcher, Killeshandra, was mentioned in Sir John French's despatches and awarded the Military Cross for conspicuous gallantry and devotion to duty at Loos in October, 1915. He was educated at Mountjoy School and Trinity College, and graduated in medicine, June, 1914. He received his commission on Sept. 4th, 1914, and went to France in April, 1915. His younger brother, J. Seabourne Fletcher, is also on active service with the M.T.A.S.C.

◇ ◇ ◇

Mr. R. H. Nixon, Superintending Clerk, Royal Engineers, has been mentioned in despatches and awarded the Military Cross. He is a son of Mr. John Nixon, Lurgandarragh, Enniskillen, and has been serving in France since the outbreak of the war. He joined the Royal Engineers in 1896, and served in the South African campaign, for which he obtained the Queen's Medal with three clasps, and the King's Medal with two clasps.

◇ ◇ ◇

Captain Robert Henry Walshe, Royal Horse Artillery, is the youngest son of the Archdeacon of Dublin. He was educated at Marlborough College. In 1904 he passed out of Woolwich R.M.A., and was gazetted to the R.F.A. In 1906 he went for service to India, where he remained until 1910, when he was gazetted Lieutenant, and returned to England. In 1914 he was promoted Staff Officer and Captain at Trinidad, but on his arrival found that war had been declared with Germany, and applied to be recalled and sent to the front. He was gazetted Lieutenant, R.H.A., 3rd Cavalry Division, and was sent to the relief of Antwerp, being subsequently promoted Captain. He has been at the front since October, 1914, and has been mentioned in despatches and awarded the Military Cross. His elder brother, Commander J. G. Walshe, is also on active service with H.M.S. Australia, 2nd flagship North Sea Fleet.

◇ ◇ ◇

Lieutenant=Colonel G. Downing, Commanding the 7th Service Battalion Royal Dublin Fusiliers, who has been mentioned in despatches for his services in the Dardanelles, is a son of Dr. Samuel Downing, formerly Professor of Engineering in Trinity College, Dublin, and a brother of Lieutenant-Colonel H. J. Downing, D.S.O., 8th Batt. Royal Inniskilling Fusiliers. Lieut.-Col. G. Downing was in the Reserve of Officers when the war began, and was appointed to the command of the 7th Dublins on the formation of the battalion in August, 1914. He was Adjutant of the 4th (Royal City of Dublin Militia) Battalion Royal Dublin Fusiliers during its services in the South African War (Queen's Medal with three clasps).

◇ ◇ ◇

Captain L. S. Norman Palmer, Royal Dublin Fusiliers, 7th Battalion, was mentioned in General Sir Ian Hamilton's despatches for gallantry at the Dardanelles. He took part in the Suvla Bay landing. After fourteen days' severe fighting he was wounded and invalided home. Captain Palmer served in the South African War, and was awarded the Queen's Medal with three clasps. When war was proclaimed in 1914 he again volunteered for active service. He is the eldest son of the late T. R. Palmer, physician and surgeon, Limerick.

◇ ◇ ◇

Sergt. Charles L. Taylor, South Irish Horse, has been mentioned in despatches for distinguished service. He was educated at St. Vincent's College, Castleknock, Dublin, and afterwards took up mechanical engineering. He joined the South Irish Horse some years ago, and when war broke out he volunteered for active service, and landed in France on 19th August, 1914. He fought all through the retreat from Mons, and is still on active service in France.

◇ ◇ ◇

Captain H. S. C. Panton, 5th Royal Irish Fusiliers, whose name was mentioned in Sir Ian Hamilton's despatches, and who has also received the Military Cross in recognition of his services at the Suvla Bay landing, is the son of the late Dr. A. W. Panton, F.T.C.D., Greenmount, Clontarf. He joined the Irish Fusiliers in September, 1914.

◇ ◇ ◇

Lance=Corporal A. Laughlin, Royal Irish Rifles, has been mentioned in despatches for distinguished conduct at Suvla Bay on August 16th, 1915, when all the officers and non-commissioned officers of his regiment having been either wounded or killed, he was left with three comrades, but held out until wounded and reinforcements arrived. Lance-Corporal Laughlin is a native of Belfast.

1. LIEUT. C. G. STUART, R.N. D.S.C.
2. CAPT. J. H. FLETCHER, R.A.M.C. Military Cross.
3. MR. R. H. NIXON, Royal Engineers. Military Cross.
4. CAPT. R. H. WALSHE, Royal Horse Artillery. Military Cross.
5. LIEUT.-COL. G. DOWNING, 7th Royal Dublin Fusiliers.
6. CAPT. L. S. N. PALMER, 7th Royal Dublin Fusiliers.
7. SERGT. C. L. TAYLOR, South Irish Horse.
8. CAPT. H. S. C. PANTON. 5th Royal Irish Fusiliers.
9. LCE.-CPL. A. LAUGHLIN, 5th Royal Irish Rifles.

OUR HEROES.

Lieutenant Charles G. Barton, 6th Batt. Royal Inniskilling Fusiliers, has received the Military Cross for services rendered in Gallipoli. Lieut. Barton is the sixth son of the late Colonel Baptist J. B. Barton, D.L., of Greenfort and Portsalon, Co. Donegal, and a brother of Major Baptist Barton, of the Duke of Wellington's Regiment, who received the D.S.O. for distinguished services on the Western front.

◇ ◇ ◇

Major C. B. Hoey, 7th Royal Dublin Fusiliers, has been mentioned in Sir Ian Hamilton's despatches for services rendered in the operations in Gallipoli. Major Hoey is the only son of Mr. Frederick Hoey, Belfast, and grandson of the late Mr. Robert Hoey, Kilmacud House, Stillorgan. He was educated at Sandhurst, joined the 1st Batt. Royal Dublin Fusiliers in 1902, and received his Captaincy in 1912. Major Hoey served in the South African War, and obtained the Queen's Medal with four clasps. On the outbreak of the present war he was posted to the 7th Batt. R.D.F. as Adjutant to Col. G. Downing, and proceeded with his battalion to the Dardanelles, where he took part in the landing at Suvla Bay, and subsequent Balkan operations.

◇ ◇ ◇

Lieutenant Beresford Herbert Wallis, M.C., was educated at Aravon School, and passed out of Sandhurst in 1908. After joining the Royal Irish Regiment in India, for a time he was gazetted to the 107th Pioneers, and was on duty at the great Delhi Durbar. When war broke out he returned with his regiment to France, was wounded at Festubert, and later mentioned twice by Sir John French in despatches. In January last he was given the Military Cross for his services in France, and is now serving in Mesopotamia. He is the only son of the late Beresford Graham Wallis, Supt. Engineer, P.W.D., India.

◇ ◇ ◇

Captain R. M. F. Patrick, 42nd Deoli Regiment, Indian Army, who has been mentioned in despatches and awarded the Military Cross, has been at the front since November, 1914, as mortar trench officer. Capt. Patrick served through the South African War, when he was twice mentioned in despatches, and received the King's and Queen's Medals with six clasps. He subsequently entered the Indian Army, and in 1914 came over to France in charge of reinforcements, and has been through many engagements, including Neuve Chapelle. He is one of three who survive out of his brigade, and was some time ago severely wounded. Capt. Patrick is the son of the Rev. Chancellor Patrick, M.A., Mocollup Rectory, Ballyduff, Co. Waterford.

◇ ◇ ◇

Lieutenant-Colonel G. A. Moore, M.D., R.A.M.C., has been mentioned in despatches and awarded the C.M.G. He is son of the late William Moore, of Moore Lodge, Co. Antrim. Col. Moore was educated at Charterhouse and Trinity College, Dublin. He was in the Indian Frontier War of 1898, and obtained the Tirah Medal and two clasps; also in the South African War, for which he received the Queen's Medal and four clasps, and the King's Medal and two clasps. Lieut.-Col. Moore took a prominent part in the formation of the ambulance train service in this war, and lately was appointed to the charge of a general hospital.

◇ ◇ ◇

Captain John de la Hay Gordon, 6th Jat Light Infantry, Indian Army, who has been mentioned in despatches and awarded the Military Cross, is the third son of the late Mr. A. H. Gordon, D.L., of Florida Manor and Delamount, Co. Down, and of Mrs. Gordon, Bidna, North Devon. Capt. Gordon was educated at Sandhurst, and gazetted to the 1st Royal Irish Regiment. He subsequently entered the Indian Army, and was appointed to the 67th Punjabis. He was on leave when the war broke out, and applied for service at the front. He was sent to France, attached to the 6th Jats, and has seen eleven months' service in France, three in Egypt, and recently went to Mesopotamia.

◇ ◇ ◇

Captain A. W. Gates, an old H.M.S. Worcester boy in the P. and O. service at the beginning of the war, in H.M. hospital ship China. In January, 1915, he received a commission in the 3rd Batt. the South Lancashire Regiment, and in April was attached to the 2nd Batt. in France. He has been wounded three times, and has been mentioned in despatches. He received the Military Cross for conspicuous gallantry on the morning of 25th September, 1915, near Hooge.

◇ ◇ ◇

Captain C. J. Newport, 1st Royal Irish Rifles, has been mentioned in despatches for conspicuous gallantry in the battle of May 9th last in the advance trenches, when, being the senior surviving officer of his regiment, he resisted all efforts of the enemy to dislodge him, though heavily pressed and attacked on both flanks, until his command was reduced to twenty or thirty men, whom he managed to withdraw safely, being himself dangerously wounded. Captain Newport is the eldest son of Mrs. Edith Newport, Ballygallon, Inistioge, Co. Kilkenny.

◇ ◇ ◇

Corporal Robert McNicol, 1st Batt. Royal Dublin Fusiliers, second son of Mr. Daniel McNicol, Killycurragh, enlisted as a youth in the Royal Garrison Artillery. After two years in Falmouth his regiment was ordered to Hong Kong, China, where he remained four years. On his return to England he joined the 1st Batt. Royal Dublin Fusiliers, and served with distinction in the Dardanelles, being recommended for the Distinguished Conduct Medal for gallantry in carrying off wounded soldiers under heavy shrapnel fire.

OUR HEROES

1. LIEUT. C. G. BARTON,
6th Royal Inniskilling Fusiliers.
Military Cross.

2. MAJOR C. B. HOEY,
7th Royal Dublin Fusiliers.

3. LIEUT. B. H. WALLIS,
107th Pioneers.
Military Cross.

4. CAPT. R. M. F. PATRICK,
42nd Deoli Regiment.
Military Cross.

5. LT.-COL. G. A. MOORE, M.D.,
R.A.M.C.
C.M.G.

6. CAPT. J. DE LA HAY GORDON,
6th Jat Light Infantry.
Military Cross.

7. CAPT. A. W. GATES,
3rd Batt. South Lancs. Regiment.
Military Cross.

8. CAPT. C. J. NEWPORT,
1st Royal Irish Rifles.

9. CORPL. R. McNICOL,
1st Royal Dublin Fusiliers.

OUR HEROES.

Lieutenant Alfred Lennox, 2nd Royal Irish Rifles, who has been killed in action in France, was the only son of Mr. W. J. Lennox, Market street, Armagh. He was educated at the Royal School, Armagh, and on the outbreak of the war he at once volunteered and joined the 6th Black Watch, and in December, 1915, received a commission in the Royal Irish Rifles. Lieut. Lennox had been wounded in action previous to the engagement in which he was killed.

✧ ✧ ✧

Captain Charles Palmer, 5th Shropshire Light Infantry, died in hospital in London as a result of wounds received in action about three months ago. Capt. Palmer was a son of the late Mr. Joseph W. Palmer, of Waterford, and a nephew of Miss Palmer, Mowbray Cottage, Tramore. He was educated at Waterpark College, and subsequently at Liverpool College. He was subsequently appointed manager of important engineering works in China, but on the outbreak of the war he returned home to join the colours. He obtained his commission in the 5th King's Shropshire Light Infantry, and was promoted Captain in December last.

✧ ✧ ✧

Lieutenant Douglas Herbert Lewin Fergusson, 79th Queen's Own Cameron Highlanders, who died at 17 Park Lane, London, W., on 2nd February, of wounds received in action in France, was the only son of Colonel Herbert Fergusson, C.M.G., Highland Light Infantry, and of Mrs. Fergusson, of 152 Cromwell Road, London, S.W., and grandson of F. T. Lewin, Esq., D.L., of Castlegrove, Co. Galway, and Cloghane, Co. Mayo. He was born on 17th September, 1894, and was educated at Eton College. He served in the Eton College O.T.C., and was stroke oar of the House Boat; entered Sandhurst 1914; was gazetted to the 1st Battalion Queen's Own Cameron Highlanders the following October, and joined his battalion in Flanders.

✧ ✧ ✧

Captain C. Morton Horne, 7th Batt. King's Own Scottish Borderers, was a son of Mr. A. G. Horne, R.M., 16 Palmerston Park, and met his death whilst rushing from his dug-out with two comrades to save a wounded soldier. Whilst lifting the wounded man a shell exploded, killing Capt. Horne and Lieut. Miller and severely wounding Lieut. Penfield, who died next day. Captain Horne had great musical and dramatic talent, and when the war broke out he was in the midst of a brilliant career on the American stage, and had written an opera which was well received, but he abandoned a lucrative position to answer his country's call, and was a gallant soldier, highly spoken of by all his comrades. He was promoted Captain in October, 1915, and was killed on January 27th, 1916.

✧ ✧ ✧

Lieutenant-Colonel E. W. Grimshaw, who is reported to have been killed in action on the Tigris, was the eldest son of the late Dr. T. W. Grimshaw, who was Registrar-General for Ireland, a member of a well-known Co. Antrim family. Col. Grimshaw first joined the Dublin Fusiliers, afterwards transferring to the Indian Army.

✧ ✧ ✧

Captain W. H. Barker, Royal Garrison Artillery, was a son of the late Rev. Canon William Chichester Barker, M.A., Incumbent of Kilbroney Parish, Rostrevor, and of Mrs. Barker, Rosina, Rostrevor. He was born in 1881, educated at Aldenham, Herts, and obtained his commission as 2nd Lieutenant R.A. 19th December, 1900, and was promoted Captain in December, 1913. He served in Gibraltar, Malta, Aden Hinterland, and in India from 1905 to 1910. He was appointed Adjutant of the Lancashire and Cheshire R.G.A. (T.F.) in 1911. He volunteered for active service on the outbreak of war, and proceeded to the Dardanelles in July, 1915. He was fatally wounded on November 4, and died in First Australian Clearing Station, Anzac, November 5, 1915.

✧ ✧ ✧

Second Lieutenant A. T. Bantock died from wounds accidentally received at the Dardanelles, November 23rd, 1915, in his 22nd year. He was elder son of Mr. and Mrs. A. D. Bantock, Walsall, and grandson of Mr. T. Bantock, Merridale House, Wolverhampton, and nephew of Alderman W. A. Murray, Waterford. He was educated at St. George's College, Weybridge, Surrey; also at Paris and Lausanne. In 1910 he proceeded to Ceylon to take up tea and rubber planting. Being eager to take his part at the front, he got attached to the 2nd Royal Fusiliers, and proceeded to the Dardanelles.

✧ ✧ ✧

Captain George Herbert Hastings, 1st Batt. Middlesex Regiment, died of wounds on Feb. 5th, 1915. He was the third son of the late Rev. S. Hastings, Rector of Halton, Lancaster, and Mrs. Hastings, St. Wilfrid's House, Halton, and grandson of John Hastings, Esq., of Downpatrick. He was educated at Aldenham School, Herts. He went to France with his regiment in August, 1914, and was in all the fighting in the retreat from Mons. Captain Hastings was mentioned in despatches published on February 18, 1915.

✧ ✧ ✧

Second Lieutenant Denis Harrison Donaldson (killed in action on September 25) was the elder son of Dr. T. C. Donaldson, of Harlington, Middlesex, and grandson of the late Mr. Samuel Donaldson, J.P., Glenafton, Welchtown, Co. Donegal. After being educated at Epsom College, he entered the City and Guilds Engineering College. When war broke out he enlisted in the 7th London Regiment, and went to the front with his battalion in March.

1. LIEUT. A. LENNOX, 2nd Royal Irish Rifles.	2. CAPT. C. PALMER, 5th Shropshire Light Infantry.	3. LIEUT. D. FERGUSSON, 79th Queen's Own Cameron Highlanders.
4. CAPT. C. MORTON HORNE, 7th Batt. K.O.S.B.	5. LT.-COL. E. W. GRIMSHAW, Royal Dublin Fusiliers.	6. CAPT. W. H. BARKER, Royal Garrison Artillery.
7. LIEUT. A. T. BANTOCK, 13th Royal Fusiliers.	8. CAPT. G. H. HASTINGS, 1st Batt. Middlesex Regiment.	9. LIEUT. D. H. DONALDSON, 7th London Regiment.

OUR HEROES.

Second Lieutenant Ronald Fitzmaurice Geary, 21st County of London Regiment (1st Surrey Rifles), was killed by a German sniper in France on January 15th, 1916. Lieutenant Geary joined the Artists' Rifles on the outbreak of the war, and was gazetted to the 1st Surrey Rifles in September, 1914. He went to France in July, 1915, and was appointed bombing officer to his battalion. Lieutenant Geary was the son of Mr. J. A. Geary, 43 Crockerton-road, Wandsworth Common, London, and came of an Irish family. He was a nephew of Mr. Richard Geary, of Cork. His Colonel states that had Lieutenant Geary survived his name would have been included in the list of honours for Military Cross.

✧ ✧ ✧

Lieutenant T. J. Carson Murdoch, 24th Service Batt., Manchester Regiment, the only son of Mr. Thomas Murdoch, Beechhurst, Mosside, Dunmurry, was killed in action in Flanders on February 6th, 1916. He was educated at the Queen's University, Belfast, and at the outbreak of the war was studying marine engineering in the firm of Messrs. Workman, Clark and Co., Ltd. On the outbreak of the war he at once offered his services and obtained his commission in December, 1914.

✧ ✧ ✧

Second Lieut. Robert Andrew Ferguson Smyly King was the eldest son of Canon and Mrs. King, of the Rectory, Limavady, and grandson of the Rev. Robert King, the Irish Church historian, and of the Very Rev. A. F. Smyly, Dean of Derry. He was born in Dublin in 1895, and was educated at Monkstown Park, Dublin; St. Bees, Cumberland, and Sandhurst. He was gazetted 2nd Lieutenant and posted to the 2nd Batt. Royal Dublin Fusiliers on November 11th, 1914. He was mortally wounded by a shell, which blew in the dug-out in which he was, on May 10th, and died at Boulogne on May 23rd, 1915.

✧ ✧ ✧

Captain Bernard Digby Johns, 10th Royal Welsh Fusiliers, who has been killed in action in France, was the only son of the late Mr. A. C. Johns, of Carrickfergus, and Mrs. French, and a step-son of Mr. J. A. French, of St. Ann's, Donnybrook. Captain Johns was educated at Hatfield Grange, Repton, and Oriel College, Oxford. In September, 1914, he obtained a commission in the Royal Welsh Fusiliers, and in July, 1915, was promoted Captain. He went to France in September last, and had just returned to the front after a week's leave when he fell.

✧ ✧ ✧

Major Godfrey M. Wheeler, V.C., was killed in action at Shaiba, Mesopotamia, on 13th April, 1915, while serving with the Indian Expeditionary Force, for his conspicuous gallantry, in which action the V.C. was conferred upon him. On the preceding day Major Wheeler had asked permission to take out his squadron and attempt to capture the enemy's flag, which was the centre point who were firing on our pickets. On the following day he led his squadron to the attack on the "North Mound," and was killed on the Mound, having ridden far ahead of his men, straight for the enemy's standards. He was the youngest and last surviving son of the late Lieutenant-General George Wheeler, Bengal Staff Corps, and Mrs. Wheeler, who was the eldest daughter of Mr. John Massy, Kingswell House, Tipperary.

✧ ✧ ✧

Captain Seymour Stritch, J.P., 6th Batt. Connaught Rangers, was killed in action in France on 7th February last. Capt. Stritch was educated at Armagh Royal School, Trinity College, and the Royal College of Surgeons, Ireland, and at the outbreak of the war was a medical practitioner at 3 Gardiner's Place, Dublin, but immediately volunteered and was gazetted to the 17th Durham Light Infantry, and was subsequently transferred to the Connaught Rangers.

✧ ✧ ✧

Lieut. Bertram Chiene Letts, R.A.M.C., was the only child of Edmund A. Letts, D.Sc. (Hon.), F.R.S.E. & C., Professor of Chemistry in the Queen's University, Belfast. He was educated at Rossall Preparatory School and Fettes College, Edinburgh; graduated M.B., B.Ch. at Queen's University, Belfast, 1913, and in that year was appointed Junior House Surgeon at the Infirmary, Warrington. On the outbreak of the war he felt it his duty to give his services to his country, and was gazetted Lieutenant in the R.A.M.C. on August 11th, 1915, and was engaged at a clearing station, where he contracted dysentery and died in Alexandria on October 21.

✧ ✧ ✧

Second Lieutenant J. Seymour Pressley, 1/5 King's Own Yorkshire Light Infantry, was killed in action in Flanders. He was the youngest son of Mr. D. L. Pressley, Holgate House, York. Lieutenant Pressley was born in Londonderry, and was educated in Aberdeen, at King Edward VI. School, Norwich, and Monk Bridge School, York. He was in Canada when war broke out, but returned to join the Army, and had seen a good deal of service at the front before he was killed on November 15th, 1915.

✧ ✧ ✧

Lieutenant John Barclay Clibborn, of Edmonton, Alberta, was killed on active service in Belgium on the 27th November, 1915. He was an officer in the 3rd Canadian Mounted Rifles, was 28 years of age, and the only son of Alfred E. and Mrs. Clibborn, of Crawford Bay, B.C.—formerly of Ury, Clara, King's Co., and husband of Catherine L. Clibborn, and a nephew of Miss Clibborn, 14 Carlisle-avenue, Donnybrook.

Supplement to Irish Life, March 31st, 1916.

1. LIEUT. R. F. GEARY, 1st Surrey Rifles.
2. LIEUT. T. J. C. MURDOCH, 24th Batt. Manchester Regiment.
3. LIEUT. R. A. F. S. KING, 2nd Royal Dublin Fusiliers.
4. CAPT. B. D. JOHNS, 10th Royal Welsh Fusiliers.
5. MAJOR G. M. WHEELER, V.C., Indian Expeditionary Force.
6. CAPT. S. STRITCH, 6th Connaught Rangers.
7. LIEUT. B. C. LETTS, R.A.M.C.
8. LIEUT. J. S. PRESSLEY, 1/5 King's Own Yorkshire L. I.
9. LIEUT. J. B. CLIBBORN, 3rd Canadian Mounted Rifles.

OUR HEROES.

Captain Shirley E. Apthorp, 96th Berar Infantry, Indian Army, has received the D.S.O. for conspicuous gallantry at Dilwar, Persian Gulf. During a retirement, when it was found that two wounded men had been left behind, he immediately volunteered with a private to return some 300 yards to their rescue, in face of a heavy fire from the rapidly advancing enemy. Captain Apthorp is the eldest son of the late Colonel F. E. Apthorp, 2nd Batt. Inniskilling Fusiliers, and grandson of the late Major-General Apthorp, C.B., K.S.F. He was educated at Portora Royal School. He served with the Imperial Yeomanry during the South African War, receiving a medal with two clasps. He subsequently obtained a commission and was gazetted to the Royal Irish Regiment, exchanging afterwards into the Indian Army. Capt. Apthorp was on active service since January, 1915, at the Persian Gulf, and is now invalided home.

✧ ✧ ✧

Major David Sherlock, Royal Artillery, is the eldest son of Mr. David Sherlock, D.L., Rahan, King's County. He has seen a good deal of service in the Royal Artillery, having been through the South African War. In the present war he served for a time in the French Artillery, was invalided home, but soon returned to the campaign in France, since which time he has been back in England on Staff work. Major Sherlock has been mentioned in despatches for distinguished services, and has been sent on several special missions.

✧ ✧ ✧

Captain J. N. MacLaughlin, R.A.M.C., has been mentioned in Sir John French's despatches for distinguished service in the field. At the outbreak of the war he was a Captain in the Special Reserve of Officers, but joined the 15th Field Ambulance and proceeded to France with that unit in August, 1914, taking part in the retreat from Mons, the advance to the Aisne, and was at La Bassee and Ypres. Captain MacLaughlin is the husband of Mrs. MacLaughlin, 13 Queen-street, Londonderry.

✧ ✧ ✧

Major F. C. Sampson, R.A.M.C., M.B., B.S., Royal University, Ireland, who has been twice mentioned in Sir John French's despatches (October 8th, 1914, and 15th October, 1915), has now been awarded the D.S.O. in recognition of his distinguished conduct and devotion to duty during the war. He is the son of Dr. F. C. Sampson, J.P., Moynoe House, Scariff, Co. Clare; was educated at Clongowes Wood College, and took out his degrees at the Catholic University, Dublin.

✧ ✧ ✧

Major=General Robert Wanless O'Gowan, formerly lived at Clonard, Dundrum, was first gazetted to the 2nd Battalion of the Scottish Rifles, and went through the South African War, where he was seriously wounded at the battle of Spion Kop. Later he was given command of the East Lancs., and on retiring from that was appointed Assistant Quarter-Master-General at the War Office. On the outbreak of the war he was promoted to Brigadier-General and sent to the front. He directed operations at the taking of Hill 60, and soon after was made Major-General and given a C.B. He has also received the Russian Order of St. Vladimir, 4th class.

✧ ✧ ✧

Major D. L. Harding, F.R.C.S.I., R.A.M.C., has been twice mentioned in despatches for distinguished services, and has now been awarded the D.S.O. He is the third son of the late Falkiner Harding and Mrs. Harding, 27 Wellington-place, Clyde-road, Dublin, and a nephew of Canon Harding, Belfast. Before the war he was on the medical staff of Victoria Barracks.

✧ ✧ ✧

Captain William J. Austin Lalor, 1st Canadian Infantry Brigade, is a nephew of Mrs. Rebecca Ardill, of Knockarley, Birr, King's County; has received the Cross of the Legion of Honour from the French Government; he has also gained the Military Cross. He has been in the trenches since February, 1915, being in charge of the machine guns in some of the heaviest battles. Captain Lalor was born in Muskoko, where his parents were amongst the pioneer settlers some 40 years ago, and where he holds a large tract of the lumber region in the Lake District, where his mother still lives.

✧ ✧ ✧

Major M. J. Mahony, M.D., R.A.M.C., attached 9th King's Liverpool Regiment, has been mentioned in despatches for distinguished services. Major Mahony took out his degrees in the Royal University of Ireland and practised in Liverpool. He served in the South African campaign in the Volunteers' Unit of the 1st King's Liverpool Regiment. He went to France at the outbreak of the present war as a member of the R.A.M.C., and is still on active service in France.

✧ ✧ ✧

Company Sergeant=Major W. J. Holmes, of the Irish Guards, has been awarded the D.C.M. for gallantry in going within a few yards of the enemy's lines and bringing back information which led to the destruction of a German trench. He also brought in a wounded comrade. He is a son of Mr. Thos. Holmes, Low-road, Lisburn. One of his brothers, Private J. Holmes, Royal Marines, was killed while serving on H.M.S. *London* early in the war, and another brother is at present serving with the Irish Guards.

1. CAPT. S. E. APTHORP, 96th Berar Infantry. D.S.O.	2. MAJOR D. SHERLOCK, Royal Artillery.	3. CAPT. J. N. MacLAUGHLIN, R.A.M.C.
4. MAJOR F. C. SAMPSON, R.A.M.C. D.S.O.	5. MAJOR-GEN. R. O'GOWAN, 2nd Batt. Scottish Rifles.	6. MAJOR D. L. HARDING, F.R.C.S.I. R.A.M.C. D.S.O.
7. CAPT. W. J. A. LALOR, 1st Canadian Infantry Brigade. Cross of the Legion of Honour. Military Cross.	8. MAJOR M. J. MAHONY, M.D., R.A.M.C.	9. SGT.-MAJOR W. J. HOLMES, Irish Guards. D.C.M.

OUR HEROES.

Lieutenant Arthur Hill Neale, 1st Brahmans, was the younger son of the late Dr. William Neale, Mountmellick, Queen's Co., and of Mrs. Neale, of 25 Ormond-road, Dublin. Lieutenant Neale was educated at St. Columba's College, Rathfarnham, Co. Dublin. He entered Trinity College, Dublin, in June, 1906, and in October, 1911, passed his final military examination, obtaining one of the two commissions in the Indian Army annually offered to the University. He was gazetted to the Indian Army, unattached list, in February, 1912, and after one year's service he was gazetted Second Lieutenant in the 1st Brahmans. After about five months' service in France his regiment was transferred to Egypt, and in December, 1915, was attached to the 6th Jats, and was killed in action in Mesopotamia on January 21, 1916.

✧ ✧ ✧

Lieutenant John Hammond Edgar, M.A., LL.B., Barrister-at-Law, Newcastle-on-Tyne, was killed in action on February 25th last whilst serving with the 9th Batt. Durham Light Infantry. He was the only son of the late Mr. R. S. Edgar, Dromore, Co. Down, and Mrs. Edgar, 15 Cliftonville-avenue, Belfast. He was educated at Queen's College, Belfast, and the Royal University of Ireland, where he had a brilliant career. He was called to the Bar in 1904 and subsequently practised in Newcastle.

✧ ✧ ✧

Second Lieutenant Charles Henry Tisdall, 8th Royal West Kent Regiment, was killed in action on February 13th, 1916, whilst gallantly rescuing a soldier who had been entombed by the falling in of a trench which was heavily bombarded. He was a son of the late Mr. A. W. Tisdall, LL.B., Dublin, and Mrs. Tisdall, Ellesmere, Tuslay Lane, Godalming, and grandson of Major-General Tisdall. He was born in Dublin and educated at Aravon School, Bray, and Tonbridge School. He obtained a commission in the 8th Royal West Kent Regiment as soon as he was eighteen, and went to the front in October, 1915.

✧ ✧ ✧

Major V. C. M. Reeves, Queen's Own Dorset Yeomanry, was killed in action in Egypt on February 26th, 1916. He was educated at Cheltenham and Magdalene College, Cambridge; joined the Yeomanry in 1906, and became Captain in 1913. When war broke out he went to Egypt with his regiment in charge of the machine guns of the Brigade, and in July, 1915, received his majority. He was then sent to Gallipoli, where he was wounded and sent back to Egypt, where he fell in action. He was the youngest son of Mrs. Reeves, Castle Kevin, Mallow.

✧ ✧ ✧

Lieutenant-Colonel M. H. Courtenay, Royal Garrison Artillery, who died of wounds received in action in Mesopotamia, was a son of the late Mr. William Courtenay, of Rathcoole, Co. Wicklow, and brother of Mrs. Gerald Moriarty, Ergenagh Rectory, Omagh, Co. Tyrone. He received his commission in the Royal Field Artillery in 1886, was promoted Captain in 1897 and Major in 1905. He was at one time Adjutant of the old Donegal Artillery in Letterkenny, after which he served in the R.G.A., and became Lieutenant-Colonel in 1914.

✧ ✧ ✧

Captain Bagot Blood, 4th Hussars and R. Flying Corps, was killed at Hounslow whilst flying. He was the eldest son of the late Captain Bagot Blood, of Rockforest and Gleninagh, Co. Clare. He had seen extensive service during the South African War and later at Burma, and was for some time at the Curragh. He went to Belgium with the 4th Hussars in August, 1914, and served with them continuously until last summer, when he joined the Royal Flying Corps.

✧ ✧ ✧

Lieutenant Guy R. Healy, 4th Royal Munster Fusiliers, was killed at Lateema Hill, East Africa, on March 11th, 1916. He was a son of the Ven. John Healy, B.D., Archdeacon of Meath. He was educated at Campbell College, Belfast, and Lycee Carnot, Paris. In 1900 he was gazetted Lieutenant in the Limerick Garrison Artillery (Militia), and afterwards joined the North of Ireland Yeomanry, with which he served during the Boer War. He was then appointed Ranger in the Transvaal Game Reserves, and resigned his commission. On the outbreak of the present war he volunteered for service and was gazetted to the 7th Cavalry Reserve. At the request of the War Office he was seconded to the King's East African Reserves, and subsequently exchanged into the Royal Munster Fusiliers, still continuing to serve in East Africa.

✧ ✧ ✧

Captain H. C. H. O'Brien, Royal Munster Fusiliers, was killed at Festubert on December 22nd, 1914, whilst bravely encouraging his men in the attack, though himself severely wounded at the time. He was a son of Lieut.-Colonel H. O'Brien, Whitepoint House, Queenstown, Co. Cork, and was gazetted to the Royal Munster Fusiliers in 1900. He served in the South African War, in the operations in Orange River Colony and Cape Colony, for which he received the Queen's Medal with five clasps. In 1902 he went with his regiment to India and took part in the N.W. Frontier operations, and received the medal with clasps.

✧ ✧ ✧

Lieutenant R. W. Proudfoot, 2nd Black Watch, who was killed in Mesopotamia, was the nephew of Mr. Alex Proudfoot, 127 Park-avenue, Belfast. He enlisted in 1900 and served in the South African War, subsequently going with his battalion to India. At the battle of Loos he received his commission as a reward of his services, an honour which he had twice previously refused.

1. LIEUT. C. H. TISDALL, 8th Royal West Kent Regiment.
2. LT. H. EDGAR, M.A., LL.B., 9th Durham Light Infantry.
3. LIEUT. A. H. NEALE, 1st Brahmans.
4. MAJOR V. C. M. REEVES, Queen's Own Dorset Yeomanry.
5. LT.-COL. M. H. COURTENAY, Royal Garrison Artillery.
6. CAPT. B. BLOOD, Royal Flying Corps.
7. LIEUT. G. R. HEALY, 4th Royal Munster Fusiliers.
8. CAPT. H. C. H. O'BRIEN, Royal Munster Fusiliers.
9. LIEUT. R. W. PROUDFOOT, 2nd Black Watch.

OUR HEROES.

Lieutenant-Colonel A. G. de V. Chichester, 28th Punjaubis, was severely wounded on January 21st in Mesopotamia, and is now in hospital in India. He was ordered to the front in November, 1915, to relieve General Aylmer's force, and after being severely wounded lay out for two days and nights without food, water, or medical attendance. Colonel Chichester is a member of an old Donegal family. He is a son of the late Rev. George Vaughan Chichester. He has 28 years' service in the Army, and took part in the Chitral and Momand expeditions. In 1914 he moved from Lahore to Ceylon with his regiment, and his courage and energy greatly contributed to the rapid suppression of the serious riots in Colombo.

Lieutenant-Colonel Charles Melville Macnaghten, C.M.G., Commanding 4th Battalion Australian Imperial Force, is the elder son of Sir Melville Macnaghten, C.B., and is a member of a well-known North Antrim family. He was educated at Eton and Trinity College, Cambridge. He subsequently went to New South Wales. At the commencement of the war he was appointed Major and Second in Command of the 4th Batt. A.I.F., in the formation of which he took a leading part. He received three wounds at the landing at Anzac in April last, and was again wounded at the taking of the Lonesome Pine trenches in August; has been mentioned in despatches, and appointed a Companion of the Order of St. Michael and St. George.

Lieutenant-Colonel Lewis Comyn, of Maretimo, Salthill, Galway, went to France as D.A.A. and Q.M.G., with rank of Captain, with the 14th Division in 1915. He got his Majority in August, and in October was appointed Assistant Adjutant and Q.M.G. to the 36th Ulster Division under General Oliver Nugent. He was shortly afterwards mentioned in despatches for distinguished service, and in January last received the D.S.O.

Lieutenant-Colonel H. F. N. Jourdain, 5th Service Battalion the Connaught Rangers, has been appointed to the most distinguished Order of St. Michael and St. George for service rendered in connection with military honours in the field. He has also been mentioned in despatches for service in the Dardanelles. Col. Jourdain also commanded this gallant 5th Battalion in the recent retreat in Servia with the 10th (Irish) Division, when the battalion added fresh laurels to their name. He served in the South African War with the 1st Battalion of his regiment, and was then awarded the Queen's Medal with five clasps, and the King's with two.

Lieutenant-Colonel W. D. Beatty, Royal Flying Corps, has been mentioned in despatches, and has had the Order of St. Anne, third class, conferred upon him by His Imperial Majesty the Emperor of Russia. Col. Beatty was on active service in France from the beginning of the war until the end of October, 1915.

Lieutenant-Colonel S. H. J. Thunder, 1st Northamptonshire Regiment, is a son of the late Captain M. H. D. Thunder, 58th Regiment, and grandson of the late Mr. Michael Thunder, J.P., D.L., of Lagore, Co. Meath. He was appointed Staff Captain in 1914, and in 1915 was appointed D.A.A. and Q.M.G. He was mentioned in despatches and awarded the Military Cross in June, 1915. He has recently been appointed to the 47th Division at Headquarters as A.A. and Q.M.G., with the rank of Lieutenant-Colonel, and is on active service in France.

Captain Herbert Victor Bayliss, 2nd Batt. East Surrey Regiment, is the second son of Captain J. W. Bayliss, late South Irish Horse, and Lovat's Scouts, who has 40 years' service to his credit, and is now attached to the Railway and Transport Service. Captain Bayliss joined the Royal Fusiliers in 1905, and in 1907 received his commission in the East Surrey Regiment, with whom he served in India as Captain and Adjutant. He has been mentioned in despatches for distinguished service in action, and has been recommended for the Military Cross.

Lieut.-Colonel P. J. Hanafin, R.A.M.C., who has been mentioned in Sir John French's despatches and awarded the D.S.O. for gallantry and distinguished service, is the eldest son of Dr. James Hanafin, Milltown, Co. Kerry. He is a past pupil of Clongowes Wood College, and had a distinguished career in the University School of Medicine, obtaining five medals.

Captain Charles E. R. Holroyd-Smyth, 3rd Dragoon Guards, has been mentioned in despatches and awarded the Military Cross for conspicuous gallantry in action. He is the second son of the late Colonel Holroyd-Smyth and Lady Harriette Holroyd-Smyth, of Ballynatray, Youghal. Captain Holroyd-Smyth served in the South African War. He is well known in Ireland as a fine rider, and has won many point-to-points.

Supplement to Irish Life, March 31st, 1916.

1. LIEUT.-COL. A. G. DE V. CHICHESTER,
28th Punjaubis.

2. LIEUT.-COLONEL C. M. MACNAGHTEN, C.M.G.,
4th Batt. Australian Imperial Force.

3. LIEUT.-COLONEL L. COMYN, A.A., Q.M.G.
D.S.O.

4. LT.-COL. H. F. N. JOURDAIN,
5th (S.) Batt. Connaught Rangers.
C.M.G.

5. LIEUT.-COL. W. D. BEATTY,
Royal Flying Corps.

6. LT.-COL. S. H. J. THUNDER,
A.A., Q.M.G.,
1st Northamptonshire Regiment.

7. CAPT. H. V. BAYLISS,
2nd East Surrey Regiment.

8. LIEUT.-COL. P. J. HANAFIN,
R.A.M.C.
D.S.O.

9. CAPT. C. E. HOLROYD-SMYTH,
3rd Dragoon Guards.
Military Cross.

OUR HEROES

OUR HEROES.

Lieutenant John Perry Lavery, Royal Garrison Artillery, who was recently wounded and is at present in hospital in London, has been awarded the Military Cross for conspicuous gallantry in the field. He was educated at Cookstown Academy and gained the Nutting Scholarship into Trinity College, where he graduated. On the outbreak of the war he volunteered and received his commission in the R.G.A. He went to France in August, 1915, where he was in charge of a Trench Mortar Battery. Lieutenant Lavery is in his 23rd year.

Lieutenant Daniel D. Hudson=Kinahan, of the Irish Guards, was the third son of the late Sir Edward Hudson-Kinahan, Bt., and of Lady Hudson-Kinahan, of The Manor, Glenville, Co. Cork. He was born in Dublin in 1877, and was educated at Cheam and Eton. During the South African War he served in the Irish Yeomanry, and at the outbreak of the present war joined the Scottish Horse, and was with them till he transferred to the Irish Guards, in August, 1915. On September 18th of that year he joined his battalion at the front.

Lieutenant Kenneth Moss Wallace, B.A., T.C.D., Royal Irish Fusiliers, has died from the effects of wounds received in action. He was the son of Mr. Hugh Wallace, Ard Brugh, Dalkey.

Second=Lieutenant Michael Richard Leader Armstrong, R.E., who fell in action on April 22nd, was the second son of Mr. Henry Bruce Armstrong, of Dean's Hill, Armagh. He was educated at Cheltenham College and Trinity College, Cambridge, where he took his Degree in the Mechanical Sciences Tripos in 1911. He was engaged for nearly three years at the Naval Base at Rosyth, which he left shortly after the outbreak of war to take a commission in the R.F.A., in which he served for about a year before being transferred to the 150th Field Company R.E., of the 36th Division. He had been recommended for promotion. His brothers, Captain W. F. Armstrong, R.G.A., and Second-Lieutenant J. R. B. Armstrong, 8th Hussars, are at present serving in France.

Major Edward Harvey Jarvis, 4th Batt. Royal Inniskilling Fusiliers, has been awarded the D.S.O. for gallant and distinguished service. Major Jarvis served through the South African War with the Imperial Yeomanry and for his services received the Queen's Medal with three clasps.

Second=Lieutenant W. F. Ellis, 8th Royal Inniskilling Fusiliers, has been awarded the Military Cross for conspicuous gallantry in endeavouring to rescue an N.C.O. who was mortally wounded whilst assisting Lieutenant Ellis in wiring in front of the trenches. Lieutenant Ellis made several attempts to rescue him, and only desisted when the man was again hit and killed. Lieutenant Ellis is the sixth son of Mr. James T. Ellis, Rathgar. Two other sons served through the Boer War.

Corporal Jack Byrne, Royal Flying Corps, has been awarded the D.C.M. for conspicuous gallantry in the management of an aeroplane during action. He is a son of the late Major Byrne, who served in the Indian Mutiny, and a brother of Mrs. Cowan, Nursery avenue, Coleraine. He was a talented member of the Belfast Amateur Company, and toured with Sir J. Forbes Robertson's and Mr. Esme Percy's companies, but on the outbreak of war he joined the Royal Flying Corps.

Lieutenant T. K. Walker, Irish Guards, was killed in action near Ypres on the night of April 24th, 1916. Lieutenant Walker was in his 20th year, and was the second son of the late Capt. T. J. Walker, 1st Royal Dragoons, and Master of the Co. Wexford Hounds for nine years, and of Mrs. Walker, Tykillen, Wexford. He passed through Sandhurst and was gazetted to the Irish Guards in July, 1915, and went to France in the following August, and had been through Loos and subsequent fighting.

Second=Lieutenant N. Cargin, The Prince of Wales' (North Staffordshire) Regiment, previously reported wounded, and now died of wounds, was a son of Mr. Hugh Cargin, Market street, Lurgan. He won his commission from the ranks of the 6th Battalion Royal Inniskilling Fusiliers, in which he was a sergeant. In civil life he was employed by Messrs. Lindsay Bros., Donegall Place, Belfast.

1. LIEUT. J. P. LAVERY, Royal Garrison Artillery. Military Cross.	2. LIEUT. D. HUDSON-KINAHAN, Irish Guards.	3. LIEUT. K. M. WALLACE, Royal Irish Fusiliers.
4. LIEUT. M. R. L. ARMSTRONG, Royal Engineers.	5. MAJOR E. H. JARVIS, Royal Inniskilling Fusiliers. D.S.O.	6. LIEUT. W. F. ELLIS, 8th Royal Inniskilling Fusiliers.
7. CORPORAL J. BYRNE, Royal Flying Corps. D.C.M.	8. LIEUT. T. K. WALKER, Irish Guards.	9. LIEUT. N. CARGIN, North Staffordshire Regiment.

OUR HEROES.

Sub-Lieutenant Herbert Rutter Simms was 24 years of age, and the son of Alderman and Mrs. D. R. Simms, of Chipping Norton, Oxfordshire, and a nephew of Mrs. R. H. Lamb, of Wheatfield, Portadown.

When quite a boy he took great delight and interest in attempting to fly, and made a flying machine of his own, and took short flights in his father's garden. As soon as possible he entered into the flying profession. He was appointed an instructor under the Greek Government, but shortly after the outbreak of war obtained his release and joined the Flying Corps of the British Navy. Being attached to the British section in Flanders he became very useful and shot down a hostile aeroplane on February 29th, 1916. After a period in hospital and a short visit home he again returned to Flanders and met his death, falling into the sea off Dunkirk.

✧ ✧ ✧

Captain R. J. Smith, Lancashire Fusiliers, elder son of Mr. and Mrs. Smith, Jigginstown, Naas, was killed in action on May 5th, 1916. Captain Smith was educated at Ranelagh School, Athlone, and Mountjoy School, Dublin, from which he entered Trinity College, where he had a distinguished University career. On the outbreak of the war he volunteered for service and obtained his Commission in the Lancashire Fusiliers in October, 1914, and was given his Captaincy in February, 1915. He went with his regiment to the front in August, 1915.

✧ ✧ ✧

Private Edward Willington Shelton, 2nd Battalion Columbian Contingent, second son of Mr. and Mrs. Deane Shelton, Rossmore, Limerick, was severely wounded in action in France on May 16th, 1915, as a result of which his right leg was amputated in hospital at Rouen, but unfortunately he succumbed on June 18th, 1915. Private Shelton was ranching in Western Canada when war broke out but at once joined the 30th Battalion 2nd British Columbian Contingent, with whom he went to France on April 30th, 1915.

✧ ✧ ✧

Second Lieutenant Charles L. Crockett, 12th Royal Inniskilling Fusiliers, was killed in action in Dublin. He was the eldest son of Mr. Andrew A. Crockett, Templemore Park, Londonderry, and was educated at Foyle College, Londonderry. Lieutenant Crockett was posted to the 12th Royal Inniskilling Fusiliers in April, 1915, and was stationed with his regiment at Enniskillen.

✧ ✧ ✧

Major W. T. R. Browne, A.S.C., has been mentioned in despatches for distinguished service. He is the second son of Major J. Browne, late Devonshire Regiment. He was gazetted to the service in 1900 and served through the Boer War. In August, 1914, he went to France with the Expeditionary Force, and is now on the Staff.

✧ ✧ ✧

Lieutenant R. L. Valentine, 7th Battalion Royal Dublin Fusiliers, who died on 30th April, 1916, from wounds received near Loos, was the youngest son of Mr. W. J. M. Valentine, of 51 Lower Beechwood avenue, Dublin. He received his earlier education at the High School, Dublin, and gained a scholarship in the Royal College of Science for Ireland, where he devoted himself especially to natural history and geology. He gained by competition the post of Geologist on the Geological Survey of Ireland, and completed the qualifying Civil Service examination while actually in military training.

✧ ✧ ✧

Second Lieutenant N. H. Collins, Inniskilling Fusiliers, who has been killed in action in France, was a son of Dr. Collins, Laghey. Lieut. Collins was a fine cricketer and had played in Dublin for the Leinster and Civil Service Clubs. He joined the Irish Guards, subsequently obtaining his Commission in the Inniskillings, and had been only a few days at the front when he fell in action.

✧ ✧ ✧

Lieutenant Francis Patrick Mapletoft Leonard, son of Francis Mapletoft Leonard, late Chief Clerk of H.M. Customs, Belfast, and grandson of the Rev. F. Burford Leonard, was born in the year 1889. He was educated in Belfast and at Ellesmere College, Shropshire. He served his apprenticeship as an engineer at Messrs. Combe Barbour's, Belfast, and during that time matriculated at London University. On the outbreak of the war he joined the University and Public Schoolboys' Battalion of the Royal Fusiliers, but immediately afterwards received a Commission in the Royal Inniskilling Fusiliers.

He accompanied his regiment to the front in February last, and died in action on April 29th.

✧ ✧ ✧

Lieutenant Louis Quinlan, 8th Battalion Royal Inniskilling Fusiliers, fell during a gas attack in France on April 27th, 1916. He was the fourth son of Mr. Michael Quinlan, Bandon, and was educated at Clongowes and Belvedere Colleges. Lieutenant Quinlan was an all-round athlete and played for Leinster in the Senior Schools Interprovincial Rugby Matches in 1914. In October, 1914, he joined the Cadet Company of the 7th Leinsters at Fermoy, and obtained his Commission in the Inniskillings in April, 1915. He went to the front in February, 1916, and a few days before his death was commended for good work, and was given command of a trench mortar battery.

1. SUB.-LIEUT. H. R. SIMMS, Royal Navy.
2. CAPT. R. J. SMITH, Lancashire Fusiliers.
3. PTE. E. W. SHELTON, 2nd Batt. Columbian Contingent.
4. LIEUT. C. L. CROCKETT, 12th Royal Inniskilling Fusiliers.
5. MAJOR W. T. R. BROWNE, A.S.C.
6. LIEUT. R. L. VALENTINE, Royal Dublin Fusiliers.
7. LIEUT. N. H. COLLINS, Royal Inniskilling Fusiliers.
8. LIEUT. F. P. M. LEONARD, Royal Inniskilling Fusiliers.
9. LIEUT. L. QUINLAN, 8th Royal Inniskilling Fusiliers.

OUR HEROES.

Captain Gilbert Nagle, 7th Batt. Royal Sussex Regiment, has been awarded the Military Cross for conspicuous courage in organising a skilful defence and repelling two attacks though wounded at the time. Captain Nagle received his promotion from Second Lieutenant on March 20th last. He is the only son of Mr. Garrett Nagle, R.M., Fortwilliam, Belfast, and was educated at the Oratory School, Birmingham; St. George's College, Weybridge; and Queen's University, Belfast; and prior to the war was an Engineering student at Bedford. He received his Commission in September, 1914.

◇ ◇ ◇

Lieutenant Jerome Lennie Walker, Royal Irish Rifles, was born in Cork and was educated at Campbell College, Belfast. At the outbreak of the war he was in business with his father, of the firm of Reilly and Walker, Courtrai, Belgium. The family escaped, but Lieutenant Walker remained behind and assisted the Red Cross with his motor car in conveying wounded to the hospitals. He had some very trying experiences at Ypres. He ultimately came to Belfast, and received his Commission in the Rifles in December, 1914. He went to France with his regiment and assisted on the staff till he met his death in action on May 5th, 1916. Lieutenant Walker's father resides at Wynard, Helen's Bay, Co. Down.

◇ ◇ ◇

Lieut. H. W. Cecil Weldon, Royal Irish Fusiliers, who was killed in action on April 28th last, was the second son of the late Mr. Henry Walter Weldon, Bantry, Co. Cork, and of Mrs. Weldon, Belmont avenue, Donnybrook. He was educated at the High School, Dublin, and subsequently entered the service of the Provincial Bank. On the outbreak of the war he returned from Persia, where he held an appointment, and received his Commission in the East Surrey Regiment, afterwards transferring to the Royal Irish Fusiliers. He went to the front in February, 1916, and had quite recently been promoted.

◇ ◇ ◇

Captain W. A. Colhoun, who has been awarded the Military Cross, is second son of the late Mr. Wm. Colhoun, proprietor of the Londonderry *Sentinel*, a former High Sheriff of Londonderry, and Chairman of the Ulster District of the Institute of Journalists. Captain Colhoun was educated at Foyle College, Londonderry, and passed into Trinity College, of the O.T.C. of which he was a member. He was in his second year as a medical student when he obtained a Commission in the Royal Irish Fusiliers. He has had many months' service in the Western front, and is now with his regiment at Salonika.

◇ ◇ ◇

Engineer Lieut.-Commander J. Mansergh Walker, R.N., who died on the 28th April, 1916, at the Royal Naval Hospital, Malta, from injuries received on the sinking of H.M.S. *Russell*, which was struck by a mine on the day previous somewhere in the Mediterranean, was the youngest son of the late Mr. Robert Walker, C.E., J.P., and Mrs. Walker, of 17 South Mall, Cork, and 1 Alta Terrace, Monkstown, Co. Cork.

He was born at Monkstown on the 9th August, 1879, and educated at Fawcett's Collegiate School, Cork. He gained a Cadetship in the Royal Naval Engineering College, Devonport, by competitive examination in the year 1896; he duly passed out of the College as a Probationary Assistant Engineer in the year 1901, when his naval career afloat commenced by service on H.M.S. *Diadem*. Served in H.M.S. *Ure*, 1911-1913, and was appointed to H.M.S. *Russell*, 1913, when he was promoted to the rank of Engineer Lieutenant-Commander.

◇ ◇ ◇

Captain Alfred Ernest Warmington was the only son of Mr. and Mrs. Warmington, of Naas, Co. Kildare. He served four years in the Cape Mounted Rifles. At the outbreak of the Boer War he volunteered for service in Thorneycroft's Mounted Infantry, was awarded the Queen's and King's Medals, with seven clasps. At the outbreak of the present war he was appointed Captain in the Royal Irish Regiment, and saw service in France. He returned to this country for special duty in the middle of April, was engaged in the suppression of the rebellion, and was killed in action at the South Dublin Union on the 24th (Easter Monday).

◇ ◇ ◇

Lieutenant Charles E. Newell, Royal Inniskilling Fusiliers, third son of the late Mr. A. C. Newell, R.M., Ballinasloe, and Mrs. Newell, 2 Crosthwaite Terrace, Kingstown, has been killed in action in his 19th year. He obtained his Commission in September, 1914, and went to the front with the 16th Division in January, 1916, shortly afterwards obtaining his promotion. He was a very promising officer, and was spoken of in the highest terms by his Commanding Officer.

◇ ◇ ◇

Lieutenant Alan L. Ramsay, Royal Irish Regiment, who was killed in action in Dublin on April 24th, 1916, was a son of Mr. Daniel L. Ramsay, The Nurseries, Ballsbridge, and was in his 25th year. He was educated at St. Andrew's College, and was gazetted to the Royal Irish Regiment from the O.T.C. of Trinity College in August, 1914. He had seen service in Flanders, and was wounded at Ypres in May, 1915.

◇ ◇ ◇

Second Lieut. Arthur Gorman Mitchell, Royal Irish Rifles, who was killed in action on May 14th, 1916, was a son of Mr. A. B. Mitchell, M.B., F.R.C.S.I., 18 University Square, Belfast. He was educated at Campbell College and Queen's University, Belfast. On the outbreak of the war he at once volunteered, and received his Commission in the 5th Batt. Royal Irish Rifles. He went to the front in March last and was only in his 19th year when he fell in action.

1. CAPT. G. NAGLE, 7th Batt. Royal Sussex Regiment.	2. LIEUT. J. L. WALKER, Royal Irish Rifles.	3. LIEUT. H. W. C. WELDON, Royal Irish Fusiliers.
4. CAPT. W. A. COLHOUN, Royal Irish Fusiliers.	5. LIEUT.-COMMANDER J. M. WALKER, H.M.S. "Russell."	6. CAPT. A. E. WARMINGTON, Royal Irish Regiment.
7. LIEUT. C. E. NEWELL, Royal Inniskilling Fusiliers.	8. LIEUT. A. L. RAMSAY, Royal Irish Regiment.	9. LIEUT. A. G. MITCHELL, Royal Irish Rifles.

OUR HEROES.

Lieutenant J. M. White, A.V.C., was the third son of Mrs. White, Tulla, Co. Clare, and nephew of James White, M.D., J.P., Kilkenny. He qualified at the Royal Veterinary College, Dublin, in 1910, and subsequently entered the service of the British South African Co., Rhodesia. On the outbreak of the war he returned at his own expense to join the colours. He contracted pneumonia while on active service in France and died on March 16th, 1916. Lieutenant White was a young man of splendid physique and a noted football and golf player.

◇ ◇ ◇

Second Lieutenant Cecil R. Booth, 1st Gordon Highlanders, who died on March 21st of wounds received in action in France on March 2nd, was the fourth son of Mr. and Mrs. John Booth, 14 Grosvenor-rd., Rathmines, Dublin. He was on the staff of the Royal Bank of Ireland, Dublin, and at the beginning of the war enlisted in the Black Watch, Territorials. He afterwards received his commission in the 1st Gordon Highlanders. He had been ten months at the front when he received the wounds which proved fatal.

◇ ◇ ◇

Lieutenant A. W. Lane-Joynt, Dorset Regiment, who was killed in action on February 26th, 1916, was the only son of Mrs. Glenleigh J. S. Taylor, 21 Ashbournham Mansions, Chelsea, London, S.W., and the late Albert Lane-Joynt, B.L., Dublin. Lieut. Lane-Joynt was educated at Elstree and Radley, where he was a member of the O.T.C. for five years. When war broke out he received a Commission in the Dorset Regiment, and got his second star two months later. In March, 1915, he was transferred to the Motor Machine Gun Service, and went to France in June, 1915.

◇ ◇ ◇

Captain William T. Lyons, 10th Battalion Royal Welsh Fusiliers, who was killed in action in France, was the eldest son of Mr. and Mrs. William Lyons, 21 Kersland Drive, Strandtown, Belfast. He was educated at the Methodist College, Belfast, and Royal School, Dungannon. On the outbreak of the war he applied for a Commission, and was gazetted to the 10th (Service) Battalion, Royal Welsh Fusiliers. He was later promoted Captain, and in September was appointed Adjutant of the Battalion.

◇ ◇ ◇

Major C. E. Luard, D.S.O., Norfolk Regiment, of Hollywood, Co. Down, who was reported missing, is now stated to have been killed in action on September 15th, 1914. Major Luard served in the expeditions in Central and West Africa, and was severely wounded in the operations in Ashanti; was mentioned in despatches, and awarded the D.S.O.

Captain Gordon James Rennie, 6th South African Regiment, was killed in action on February 12th, 1916, in British East Africa. He was a son of Mr. and Mrs. John Rennie, Ardlumcart Lodge, Aberdeenshire, and grandson of the late Mr. John Lloyd Blood, J.P., Monkstown. Captain Rennie was born at Durban, Natal, and was educated at the Durban High School, Ashampstead, Eastbourne, and Radley College, Abingdon. He served all through the German South-West African campaign as Captain in the Durban Light Infantry, and was subsequently given command of a Company of the 6th South African Regiment, in British East Africa, where he fell.

◇ ◇ ◇

Lieutenant R. W. McConnell, King's Own Royal Lancaster Regiment, was the second son of Rev. James McConnell, B.A., Megain Memorial Presbyterian Church, Belfast, and a nephew of Rev. F. C. Gibson, Ormond Quay Presbyterian Church, Dublin. He was educated at Campbell College and Queen's University, Belfast, where he had a distinguished career as a student, and at the annual meeting of the Literary and Scientific Society, of whose Council he was a member, in 1915, he was awarded the Dufferin Medal for Oratory. He received his commission in February, 1912. He served at Suvla Bay and took part in the evacuation of Gallipoli. He was afterwards attached to the Indian Expeditionary Force for the relief of General Townshend, and was slightly wounded on April 5th, 1916, but bravely remained on duty until the 9th.

◇ ◇ ◇

Second Lieutenant William Hamish Chalmers, 19th Punjabis, who was killed in action on April 13th, 1916, was the elder son of the late Mr. John Sheed Chalmers, Aberdeen, and Mrs. Chalmers, Uplands, Breldside, Aberdeenshire, and brother of Mrs. James Gray Kyd, St. Kevin's Park, Dublin. Lieut. Chalmers had been engaged on a frontier station between Baluchistan and Persia. Early in 1916 German influence was being brought to bear on some of the hill tribes and trouble arose on the frontier. On April 13th Lieutenant Chalmers' Company encountered a hostile force and drove them out of the villages which they had plundered, and on the same day Lieut. Chalmers fell at the head of his company.

◇ ◇ ◇

Sub-Lieutenant Samuel T. Smiley, who was killed when H.M.S. *Arabic* was torpedoed in the North Sea, was the third son of Captain and Mrs. Smiley, 18 Chichester Avenue, Belfast. Lieutenant Smiley was in the Lord Line (Messrs. Thomas Dixon and Sons), Belfast, for about eighteen years and resigned his position as chief officer of the Lord Dufferin in May, 1915, in order to offer his services to the Navy. After a period of training in Devonport he was appointed navigating lieutenant on H.M.S. *Arabic* at the beginning of December.

1. LIEUT. J. M. WHITE, A.V.C.
2. LIEUT. C. R. BOOTH, 1st Gordon Highlanders.
3. LIEUT. A. W. LANE-JOYNT, Dorset Regiment.
4. CAPT. W. T. LYONS, 10th Batt. Royal Welsh Fusiliers.
5. MAJOR C. E. LUARD, D.S.O., 1st Batt. Norfolk Regiment.
6. CAPT. G. J. RENNIE, 6th South African Regiment.
7. LIEUT. R. W. McCONNELL, Royal Lancaster Regiment.
8. LIEUT. W. H. CHALMERS, 79th Punjabis.
9. SUB-LIEUT. S. T. SMILEY, H.M.S. "Arabic."

OUR HEROES.

Private James Campbell, 17th Signal Company, Royal Engineers, has been mentioned in despatches for gallantry in action. He is a son of Mr. John Campbell, Minaduff, Gortin, Co. Tyrone. Previous to the war he was foreman in Messrs. Swan, Hunter and Wigam Richardson's Shipbuilding Yard, Wallsend-on-Tyne, but at once joined the colours on the outbreak of hostilities.

Lieutenant Leslie Charles Badham, only surviving son of the late Rev. F. J. Badham, D.D., Kilbixy, Co. Westmeath, and Mrs. Badham, West End, Hants, has been mentioned in Sir John French's despatches, and awarded the Military Cross for gallant and distinguished service. Lieut. Badham was educated at Armagh Royal School. He landed at Marseilles with the Indian Corps in September, 1914, and was seriously wounded in the second battle of Ypres, in April, 1915, unfortunately losing his right eye.

Lieutenant Hugh Campbell, 17th Signal Company, Royal Engineers, has been awarded the D.C.M. and promoted Lieutenant for conspicuous gallantry during operations when working day and night repairing telephone wires under heavy fire when, during the British attack at Ypres, he succeeded after several failures in making good the signal lines through the German curtain of fire. He is a son of Mr. John Campbell, Minaduff, Gortin, Co. Tyrone.

Captain Samuel William Howard, 1st Batt. Connaught Rangers, has been awarded the D.S.O. He is the second son of Major R. J. Howard and Mrs. Howard, Annaguinea House, Dungannon, and nephew of Mr. Samuel Howard, "Ardavon," Rathgar. Educated at the Royal School, Dungannon, he entered Sandhurst in 1909. After he received his Commission in the Connaughts, he proceeded to India with his regiment. Three years ago he was seconded to the Southern Nigeria Regiment and saw service in the Cameroons at the outbreak of the war, after which he was invalided home. A few months later he rejoined the Connaughts, and after a long spell of service in France he joined the relief force in Mesopotamia, where he was slightly wounded.

Lieutenant-Colonel Gilbert Steward Crawford, C.M.G., M.D., R.A.M.C., has served with distinction during the war, and for his services, which were mentioned in despatches, by Field-Marshal Viscount French, he was appointed a Companion of the Order of St. Michael and St. George. He was in command of the 14th Field Ambulance from mobilisation until August last, and was through some of the heaviest fighting on the western front, frequently carrying out his work under heavy shell fire. He is at present in command of the 18th Stationary Hospital, Mediterranean Expeditionary Force. Lieut.-Col. Crawford is the seventh son of the late Mr. S. Crawford, Clough, Co. Antrim, and brother of Mr. Robert Crawford, Ashville, Ballymena.

Lieutenant George William Panter, who has been mentioned in despatches for distinguished gallantry, is the second son of George William Panter, M.A., of The Bawn, Foxrock, Co. Dublin. He was educated at Sedbergh, Trinity College, Dublin, and Sandhurst, and was gazetted to the 1st Batt. Royal Irish Rifles in 1914. He has now joined the Royal Flying Corps.

Sergeant T. Corry, 1st Battalion Irish Guards, of Labasheeda, Co. Clare, has been decorated by the King with the D.C.M. for conspicuous gallantry. He has been twice mentioned in Sir John French's despatches. Sergeant Corry was wounded at the battle of Loos, previous to which he had been thirteen months in the firing line.

Lance-Corporal Henry S. Robinson, 5th Buffs, has been awarded the D.C.M. for conspicuous gallantry in going out to rescue a wounded comrade under fire. He is a son of the late Mr. St. G. C. W. Robinson, of Woodville, Sligo, and of Mrs. Robinson, Lumville House, Curragh, and a nephew of Sir Edward Carson. He was educated at Malvern College. His brother, Captain G. St. G. Robinson, was awarded the Military Cross early in the war, and another brother, Lieut. E. F. Robinson, was killed in action in France.

Trooper R. J. Dewar, Royal Scots Greys, was awarded the D.C.M. for gallant and distinguished conduct in France. He is a son of Mr. P. M. Dewar, The Original Hotel, Roslin, and a grandson of Mr. Dewar, Kilcoobin Cottage, Bush Mills, Co. Antrim. On the outbreak of the war he joined the Royal Scots Greys, and went to France in October, 1915.

1. PTE. J. CAMPBELL, Royal Engineers.	2. LIEUT. L. C. BADHAM, Indian Corps. Military Cross.	3. LIEUT. HUGH CAMPBELL, Royal Engineers. D.C.M.
4. CAPT. S. W. HOWARD, 1st Batt. Connaught Rangers. D.S.O.	5. LIEUT.-COL. G. S. CRAWFORD, M.D., R.A.M.C. C.M.G.	6. LIEUT. G. W. PANTER, Royal Flying Corps.
7. SERGT. T. CORRY, Irish Guards. D.C.M.	8. CORPL. H. S. ROBINSON, 5th Buffs. D.C.M.	9. TROOPER R. J. DEWAR, Royal Scots Greys. D.C.M.

OUR HEROES.

Second Lieutenant George Malcolm Steward McAlister, is the second son of Captain D. A. McAlister, Shropshire Royal Horse Artillery, and Mrs. McAlister, St. Mary's Court, Shrewsbury, and a grandson of the late Mr. Archibald McAlister, of Cushendall, Co. Antrim, who was for many years land agent to Mr. Mitchell Henry, Kylemore, Co. Galway, including the troubled time of the early eighties. He was educated for the Civil Service, and on the outbreak of the war applied for and obtained permission from the head of his department to enlist. He joined the Army Veterinary Corps, T.F., and after seven months' service was promoted to a Commission as Second Lieutenant in the 26th (Service) Battalion Northumberland Fusiliers (The 3rd Tyneside Irish). He accompanied his Battalion to France, and was mentioned in Routine Orders of the First Army last month for an "act of courage," for which he will most probably be awarded the "Albert Medal" in due course. His elder brother is also a Lieutenant in the 2nd Battalion Cheshire Regiment, to which he was promoted last July from Sergeant in the 11th (P.A.O.) Hussars for "service in the field."

✧ ✧ ✧

Captain F. Casement, R.A.M.C., has been awarded the French Legion of Honour for distinguished service on the field in France. He is a son of Mr. Roger Casement, D.L., Magherintemple, Ballycastle, and is at present home on leave.

✧ ✧ ✧

Lieutenant John Mitchell, Royal Field Artillery, gained the Military Cross at the battle of Shaik Said. Lieutenant Mitchell is a son of Mrs. Mitchell, Bath Street, Waterford, and has been in France since the outbreak of the war. He gained his Commission on the field. Lieut. Mitchell is a well-known Rugby player.

✧ ✧ ✧

Lieutenant-Commander J. L. Clark, R.N., son of Lieutenant-Colonel J. J. Clark, D.L., of Largantogher, Maghera, has been awarded the D.S.O. for gallant service with the destroyer flotilla during the evacuation of Gallipoli.

Major T. Crean, V.C., D.S.O., Royal Army Medical Corps, is a son of the late Mr. R. T. Crean, B.Sc., Irish Land Commission, and is at present on service in France where he went with the First Expeditionary Force. He was in the retreat from Mons, was mentioned in despatches, and awarded the D.S.O. Major Crean served through the South African War, where he was badly wounded, and gained the V.C.

✧ ✧ ✧

Captain Charles Jasper Martin, Army Service Corps, has been awarded the Military Cross and was mentioned in despatches. He entered the Army in 1912 and went to France with the Expeditionary Force. He is the only son of the late Charles Fox Martin, of Ross, Co. Galway.

✧ ✧ ✧

Private J. Henry, Irish Guards, of Swinford, Co. Mayo, has been awarded the D.C.M. for conspicuous bravery. He joined the Irish Guards on the outbreak of the war, was wounded at the battle of Loos, but continued to hurl bombs at the advancing enemy for twelve hours, thus preventing their attack being successful and saving the lives of many of his comrades. Private Henry is in his 27th year.

✧ ✧ ✧

Lieutenant Hugh Maxwell Pim, 24th Punjabis, is the youngest son of the Rev. John Pim, Christ Church, Kingstown. He was educated at Rossall and T.C.D., and got his Commission in the O.T.C. He was gazetted to the Indian Army in January, 1914, and served with his regiment, the 24th Punjabis, in Egypt and Mesopotamia, and gained the Military Cross for services in the Euphrates Expedition. His two brothers are also serving.

✧ ✧ ✧

Lieutenant R. J. Casement, 1st Canadians (Engineering Section), was awarded the D.C.M. last year for bravery. He is a son of Mr. Roger Casement, D.L., Magherintemple, Ballycastle, Co. Antrim, and on the outbreak of the war was in British Columbia where he enlisted in the Canadian Engineers. He went to the front in France in February, 1915, and obtained his Commission in March last.

1. LIEUT. G. M. S. McALISTER, Northumberland Fusiliers.
2. CAPT. F. CASEMENT, R.A.M.C. Legion of Honour.
3. LIEUT. J. MITCHELL, R.F.A. Military Cross.
4. LIEUT.-COMMANDER J. L. CLARK, Royal Navy. D.S.O.
5. MAJOR T. CREAN, V.C., R.A.M.C. D.S.O.
6. CAPTAIN C. J. MARTIN, A.S.C. Military Cross.
7. PTE. J. HENRY, Irish Guards. D.C.M.
8. LIEUT. H. M. PIM, 24th Punjabis. Military Cross.
9. LIEUT. R. J. CASEMENT, 1st Canadians. D.C.M.

OUR HEROES.

Lieutenant Gerald A. Neilan, who was killed in Dublin on Easter Monday, was a son of the late Mr. John Neilan, J.P., Ballygalda, Roscommon, and of Mrs. Neilan, Leinster Road, Dublin. He was educated at Clongowes Wood College, and receiving his Commission in the Northumberland Fusiliers in December, 1914, transferred to the 10th Batt. Royal Dublin Fusiliers in February last. He had seen previous service with the Sherwood Foresters through the South African War, where he was severely wounded in action. Lieutenant Neilan was a keen athlete.

◇ ◇

Captain Frank Heuston, Royal Montreal Regiment, who was killed in action on 7th April, 1916, was the only surviving son of the late Surgeon Francis T. Heuston, 15 St. Stephen's Green, his twin brother having been killed in action in Gallipoli in August, 1915. Captain Heuston went to Canada three years ago as an engineer and on the outbreak of the war obtained a Commission in the Royal Montreal Regiment. He came over with the 1st Contingent and had been at the front for nearly a year when he fell.

◇ ◇ ◇

Sec=Lieut. Frederick Gibson Heuston, 6th Royal Irish Fusiliers, was in the Medical School, Trinity College, and joined the Army at the commencement of the war. He went to the Dardanelles and was reported wounded and missing on August 16th, but later unofficially known to have been killed in action on that date. He was mentioned in despatches and was awarded the Military Cross. He was a son of the late Surgeon Francis T. Heuston, 15 St. Stephen's Green, and was in his 23rd year. His twin brother was also killed in action.

◇ ◇ ◇

The late **Lt. C. F. L. Bailey** was the only son of the late Mr. C. F. Bailey, Marksbury, Bath, and of Mrs. Bailey, Eastville, Dunmanway, Co. Cork. For six weeks prior to his death he had been operating trench mortar guns. On the 9th May he was struck by a piece of high explosive shell and killed instantaneously. He received a commission in the 8th R.D.F. in March, 1915, and went to France in December last with the 16th Division.

◇ ◇ ◇

Captain Ernest R. Cooke, Royal Irish Fusiliers, killed in action, was the elder son of Mr. and Mrs. R. E. Cooke, of Teignmouth. He was educated at Dunstable College and Birmingham University, where he took his diploma in chemistry. He was a member of the staff of Messrs. Guinness and Co., of Dublin. At the outbreak of the war he obtained his commission as lieutenant in the Royal Irish Fusiliers, and was promoted captain in January of this year.

Sec.=Lieutenant Noel Desmond Trimble, 8th Royal Inniskilling Fusiliers, who has been killed in action, was the youngest son of Mr. W. Copeland Trimble, J.P., Enniskillen. He was educated at Enniskillen Royal School, where he won several distinctions, and at Trinity College, Dublin, when on last Trinity Monday he became a (classical) Scholar of the House and therefore a Governor of the foundation, and had already given promise of a brilliant university career. He obtained his commission in the 12th (Reserve) Battalion Royal Inniskilling Fusiliers on the 23rd June, 1915, and was posted to the 8th on arrival at the base in France. The late Second-Lieutenant Trimble was one of the three brothers in the Junior Service, the others being Lieutenant R. S. Trimble, 6th Battalion Royal Irish Fusiliers, who was wounded at the Dardanelles in August last, and Second-Lieutenant A. E. C. Trimble, 7th Battalion Royal Inniskilling Fusiliers, who was recently commended by Major-General W. B. Hickie, C.B., for gallant conduct and devotion to duty in the field.

◇ ◇ ◇

Second=Lieutenant A. E. Carrette, 9th Battalion, Royal Dublin Fusiliers, was a son of Mr. E. W. Carrette, Postmaster, Bandon. He enlisted in December, 1914, and obtained his commission in March, 1915. He went to the front in December, 1915, and was in charge of the machine guns on the morning of April 27th when the German attack was so gallantly and successfully repelled.

◇ ◇ ◇

Lieutenant Cecil Stacpoole Kenney, King's Shropshire Light Infantry, was drowned at sea on active service on November 11th, 1915. He was the youngest son of Mr. Thomas Hugh Kenney, Indiaville, Limerick, and Louisa M. Stacpoole Kenney. Lieut. Stacpoole Kenney graduated in Trinity College in 1912 and was called to the Irish Bar in the same year. In August, 1915, he was gazetted to the King's Shropshire Light Infantry and was in his 25th year.

◇ ◇ ◇

Sec.=Lieutenant Archibald Frizelle, Royal Field Artillery, who was killed in action on May 4th, 1916, was in his 26th year, and was the youngest son of Mr. John H. Frizelle, Ballinglen, Ballycastle, Co. Mayo. He was educated at the Ranelagh School, Athlone, and subsequently at Mountjoy School, Dublin. When the war broke out he was in Canada on the engineering staff employed in constructing the railway from Le Pas to Hudson Bay, but immediately returned and applied for a commission, but without waiting for it enlisted in the Irish Guards, being shortly promoted Corporal and received his lieutenancy in six months. He had been only a month in France when he fell in action.

1. LIEUT. G. A. NEILAN, 10th Royal Dublin Fusiliers.
2. CAPT. F. HEUSTON, Royal Montreal Regiment.
3. LIEUT. A. E. CARRETTE, 9th Royal Dublin Fusiliers.
4. LIEUT. C. F. L. BAILEY, 8th Royal Dublin Fusiliers.
5. CAPT. E. R. COOKE, Royal Irish Fusiliers.
6. LIEUT. N. D. TRIMBLE, 8th Royal Inniskilling Fusiliers.
7. LT. C. STACPOOLE KENNEY, Shropshire Light Infantry.
8. LIEUT. A. FRIZELLE, R.F.A.
9. LIEUT. F. G. HEUSTON, 6th Royal Irish Fusiliers.

OUR HEROES.

Lieutenant George B. Keeling, Royal Indian Marine, drowned at sea while on active service, was the third son of Mr. John S. Keeling, Summerville, Millisle, Co. Down. On relinquishing the command of the ss. Lord Dufferin of the Lord Line, he obtained a Commission in the Royal Indian Marine, and had only been a short time in the East when he lost his life through the sinking of the steamer during the voyage between Bombay and Karachi, on March 19th, 1916.

◇ ◇ ◇

Second Lieutenant Noel J. Davies, Royal Dublin Fusiliers, was killed in action in France on April 27th, 1916, in his 25th year. He was the third son of the late James Taaffe Davies, D.I., R.I.C., and of Mrs. Davies, 46 Kenilworth Park, Rathgar, and grandson of the late Edward Ffrench Beytagh, Q.C. He was educated at the Presentation College, Cork, and later entered the service of the Munster and Leinster Bank, Dame Street. On the outbreak of the war he volunteered and received a Commission in the Dublin Fusiliers. He went to France early in the year, where his absolute fearlessness under fire and soldierly ability earned the praise of his officers.

◇ ◇ ◇

Lieutenant T. H. Bor, R.N.R., was drowned at sea whilst on active service, about March 11th, 1916. He was the eldest son of Mr. and Mrs. Bor, Bank of Ireland, Maryborough, and was educated at Kilkenny College. He entered the Mercantile Marine when 14 years of age and secured his captain's certificate at 22. On the outbreak of the war he offered his services and obtained a Commission in the Royal Naval Reserve.

◇ ◇ ◇

Captain Henry R. Cruise, 1st King's African Rifles, died of fever on April 22nd at Karonga, where he had been stationed since the outbreak of the war. He was the youngest son of the late Sir Francis Cruise, and commenced his career under Sir Gerald Strickland, then Governor of the Leeward Islands. He subsequently served in the Colonial service, and in 1912 was appointed Assistant Resident Commissioner at Cheradzulu, near Blantyre, which post he held until the outbreak of the war, when he was appointed Transport Officer to the 1st King's African Rifles, and later was promoted temporary Captain.

◇ ◇ ◇

Lieutenant-Colonel J. C. Browne, A.S.C., has been awarded the D.S.O. He is the eldest son of Major J. Browne (late) Devonshire Regiment, and has been on Headquarters Staff since the beginning of hostilities. He was gazetted to the service in 1899, and went through the Boer War, for his services in which he was mentioned in despatches.

Captain Edward Fleetwood Berry, 9th Gurkhas, was the only child of the Rev. J. F. Berry, Rector of Galway, and grandson of the late Mr. Abraham Chatterton, Clyde Road, Dublin. He was educated at Abingdon School, passing into the Royal Military College, Sandhurst, in 1906. He received his Commission in the Wiltshire Regiment in 1907, and two years later joined the 2/9th Gurkha Rifles. In 1913 he became A.D.C. to Lord Carmichael, Governor of Bengal. On the outbreak of the war he was home on leave, and was attached to the 9th King's Royal Rifles, until his regiment came from India, when he joined it in Flanders, and with it saw much strenuous service. He subsequently became Adjutant of his regiment, which went to Mesopotamia in December last, and had been through many severe engagements when he fell in action on April 17th, 1916.

◇ ◇ ◇

Lieutenant Francis Molyneux Badham, R.N.V.R., Collingwood Battalion, R.N.D., who was killed in action on June 4th, 1915, was a son of the late Rev. F. J. Badham, D.D., Kilbixy, Westmeath, and Mrs. Badham, West End, Hants. Lieutenant Badham came from Canada at the beginning of the war and joined the Royal Naval Division. He went to the Dardanelles with his battalion in May, 1915, and was wounded on June 4th, but continued to fight on until shot through the head.

◇ ◇ ◇

Captain Frederick J. Duggan, Royal Field Artillery, who has been killed in action, was a son of Mr. Creighton Duggan, Clones, Co. Monaghan, and was well known as a steeplechase rider. Before the war he was stationed with his battery at Woolwich, and went overseas in August, 1914, and had been almost continuously on service since the beginning of the war. He was Adjutant to the 29th Brigade.

◇ ◇ ◇

Lieutenant Ernest Dickinson Price, 3rd Battalion Royal Irish Regiment, was killed in action on 19th March, 1916, in his 22nd year. He was the second son of Major Ivon H. Price, County Inspector, Royal Irish Constabulary, and was educated at Mourne Grange School, then at St. Columba's College, and Trinity College, Dublin. He was a member of the Dublin University Officers' Training Corps, and joined the Special Reserve on the outbreak of the war. He was attached to the Royal Irish Rifles for the past six months at the Front. Two of his brothers are also in the Army, a third in the Dublin University O.T.C., and a fourth a Royal Naval Cadet at Osborne.

1. LIEUT. G. B. KEELING, Royal Indian Marine.
2. LIEUT. N. J. DAVIES, Royal Dublin Fusiliers.
3. LIEUT. T. H. BOR, R.N.R.
4. CAPT. H. R. CRUISE, 1st King's African Rifles.
5. LIEUT.-COL. J. C. BROWNE, Army Service Corps. D.S.O.
6. CAPT. E. F. BERRY, 9th Gurkhas
7. LIEUT. F. M. BADHAM, R.N.V.R.
8. CAPT. F. J. DUGGAN, Royal Field Artillery.
9. LIEUT. E. D. PRICE, 3rd Royal Irish Regiment.

THE LATE FIELD-MARSHAL EARL KITCHENER OF KHARTOUM AND OF BROOME, K.G., Etc.
Born, June 24, 1850.   Died, June 5, 1916.

Among Herculean deeds the miracle
That mass'd the labour of ten years in one
Shall be thy monument. Thy work is done
Ere we could thank thee; and the high sea swell
Surgeth unheeding where thy proud ship fell
By the lone Orkneys, ere the set of sun.
—Robert Bridges.

OUR HEROES.

Lieut. Alexander Douglas Peel Hamilton, Royal Marine Light Infantry, who was killed in action off Jutland on H.M.S. "Defence" on the 31st May, 1916, in his 20th year, was the only surviving son of Mr. W. A. Hamilton, Coxtown, Donegal. He was educated at "The Wick," Brighton, and Wellington College, and received his commission in August, 1914. He passed as a first-class rifle shot. In the naval engagement the aft guns of the "Defence" were put out of action, but she continued to fire her forward guns until blown out of the water, both magazines exploding, having previously, assisted by "Warspite," sunk two German cruisers.

Acting Sub-Lieutenant Desmond Frank Charles Tottenham, R.N., who was lost with H.M.S. "Invincible" in the great naval battle on May 31st, 1916, in his 19th year, was the second son of Captain C. G. Tottenham, Tudenham, Mullingar. He entered the Royal Navy in September, 1909, and had been serving in the North Sea since the outbreak of the war.

Midshipman Kildare Henry Borrowes, R.N., of H.M.S. "Queen Mary," who was killed in the naval action off Jutland on May 31st, 1916, was the only child of Mr. and Mrs. Eustace Borrowes, 18 Warwick Villas, Leeson Park, and was only in his 16th year. On January 1st, 1916, he was appointed to H.M.S. "Queen Mary" on leaving the Royal Naval College, Dartmouth.

Sub-Lieutenant Patrick H. G. I. Vance, of H.M.S. "Shark," which went down fighting gallantly in the forefront of the British destroyers against the German High Sea Fleet in the battle off the coast of Jutland. Lieut. Vance was the only son of Mr. J. G. Irving Vance, of Helen's Bay, Co. Down, High Sheriff of Co. Monaghan.

Major Gerald C. Rooney, R.M.L.I., H.M.S. "Queen Mary," was the second son of Colonel and Mrs. Rooney, of Monkstown, County Dublin. Born in 1876, he obtained his first commission in January, 1896, and in 1900 served in the China War, acting as Adjutant to the R.M. Batt. Major Rooney joined the "Queen Mary" in March, 1914, and was present on the occasion of the visit of the British Squadron to Kronstadt in June of that year. He took part in the battle of Heligoland Bight on August 28, 1914. He was a skilled officer in gunnery, and commanded the Marines on board the "Queen Mary," having control of the fore-turret guns. Major Rooney was an artist in water-colours, and a grandson of James Hogan, the celebrated Irish sculptor.

Sub-Lieutenant Humphrey F. Vernon, R.N., was the youngest son of Mr. Fane Vernon, D.L., Erne Hill, Belturbet, Co. Cavan, and 1 Wilton Place, Dublin. He was educated at Winton House, Winchester, and Royal Naval Colleges, Osborne and Dartmouth. He served on board H.M.S. "Cumberland," "Shannon," "Hibernia," "Commonwealth," and "Hampshire," and in the last named ship took part in the naval action off the coast of Jutland and was lost by the sinking of the ship off the west coast of the Orkney Islands on the 5th June, 1916, with Field-Marshal Lord Kitchener on board, only 11 survivors being washed on shore on a raft.

Midshipman J. H. G. Esmonde, of H.M.S. "Invincble," who was lost in the naval battle off Jutland, was a son of Sir Thos. Esmonde, the well-known member of Parliament for North Wexford. He obtained his seniority on August 2nd, 1914, and was a very promising young officer.

Engineer-Lieutenant Samuel Alan Adams, R.N., aged 34, was the second son of Mr. S. A. Adams, J.P., of Northlands, Carrickmacross, and great-grandson of the Very Rev. Samuel Adams, Dean of Cashel. He was educated at King's Hospital and entered the merchant service at 18, and becoming Commodore-chief at 27. He then obtained a commission in the Royal Navy, and was appointed to H.M.S. "Indefatigable," on which he remained until she was lost in the battle of Jutland, May 31st, 1916.

Surgeon George Bassett Moon, who was killed on board Admiral Beatty's flagship, the "Lion," by a shell during the Jutland fight, was the eldest son of Dr. George D. Moon, a native of Dungannon (Co. Tyrone), and grandson of the late Mr. George Moon, Castle Hill House, Dungannon, who was closely identified with the civic life of that town. The deceased officer was 6ft. 1in. in height, and was a noted athlete.

1. LIEUT. A. D. PEEL HAMILTON, H.M.S. "Defence."
2. LT. D. F. C. L. TOTTENHAM, H.M.S. "Invincible."
3. MIDSHIPMAN K. H. BORROWES, H.M.S. "Queen Mary."
4. SUB-LIEUT. P. H. G. I. VANCE, H.M.S. "Shark."
5. MAJOR G. C. ROONEY, H.M.S. "Queen Mary."
6. SUB-LIEUT. H. F. VERNON, H.M.S. "Hampshire."
7. MIDSHIPMAN ESMONDE, H.M.S. "Invincible."
8. ENG.-LIEUT. S. A. ADAMS, H.M.S. "Indefatigable."
9. SURGEON G. B. MOON, H.M.S. "Lion."

OUR HEROES.

Lieutenant Dacre W. Moore, Machine Gun Corps, elder son of the Bishop of Kilmore, was killed in action in France on June 11th, 1916, in his 23rd year. He was educated at Pocklington School, Yorks, and Trinity College, Dublin, where he was 1st Honours man in Mathematics, and was about to enter the Divinity School when war broke out, but at once offered his services and was gazetted to the 15th Batt. Royal Irish Rifles (Ulster Division). He went to the front in October, 1915, was subsequently transferred to the Machine Gun Corps, and was in charge of the machine guns in the front trench when he fell. His brother, Lieut. E. D. Moore, an engineering student of T.C.D., was dangerously wounded in Gallipoli in June, 1915, and is now serving in France with the Royal Engineers.

✧ ✧ ✧

Captain William D. Holmes, D.S.O., Canadian Light Infantry, who fell in action in the advance about the beginning of July, was a son of Mr. William Cuthbert Holmes, a retired Indian judge, and grandson of the late Dr. Charles Holmes, Dublin. On the outbreak of the war Captain Holmes was in Canada. He received his commission in the First Contingent from Canada, and saw a great deal of service in France, where he won the D.S.O. last year for conspicuous gallantry near Messines, having previously been mentioned for gallantry at Festurbet. Captain Holmes was a cousin of Mr. George McCurdy, Meenahoney, Castlefinn.

✧ ✧ ✧

Lieutenant I. W. Usher, Royal Irish Regiment, was killed whilst leading his platoon in a very dashing attack against a very strong German position, which was afterwards captured, and though wounded he refused to leave his men. Lieut. Usher was in his 20th year, and was a son of Dr. Isaac W. Usher, J.P., Dundrum. He was educated at St. Stephen's Green School and Trinity College, where he was a member of the O.T.C. He was nominated for the R.M.C., Sandhurst, in December, 1914, and was gazetted to the Royal Irish Regiment in June, 1915, obtaining his promotion in the following November, when he left for the front.

✧ ✧ ✧

Captain Cecil Frederick Kelso Ewart, Royal Irish Rifles, was killed in action on 1st July, aged 28. He was the second son of Mr. and Mrs. F. W. Ewart, Derryvolgie, Lisburn, and was educated at Winchester. On the outbreak of war, with his two brothers, he joined the New Army. He was given a commission in the Royal Irish Rifles, and was promoted Captain early in the present year.

✧ ✧ ✧

Lieutenant-Colonel R. J. W. Mawhinny, R.A.M.C., son of the late Thomas Mawhinny, M.D., Woodlawn, Mountnugent, Co. Cavan, served with the Isarzai Expedition of 1892 and in the operations in Natal. He also took part in the defence of Ladysmith, and was mentioned in despatches and awarded the Queen's medal with six clasps. He has been recently serving in Mesopotamia, and is included in the recent Indian Honours List as C.B. Colonel Mawhinny married Kathleen, eldest daughter of the late Mr. Alex. Knox M'Entire, B.L., who was Official Assignee, Court of Bankruptcy, Dublin.

✧ ✧ ✧

Captain J. F. Ruttledge, 2nd Batt. Prince of Wales' Own West Yorkshire Regiment, was the eldest son of Lieutenant-Colonel A. Ruttledge, of the Woodlands, Castleconnell. He was gazetted on the 24th February, 1914, to his father's old regiment, and had seen much service in France. He was awarded the Military Cross for great coolness and gallantry near Neuve Chapelle on December 19th, 1914, for rescuing under very heavy fire in daylight men lying in the open on "no man's land." He was killed in action on July 1st, 1916, whilst leading his men with great gallantry right up to the enemy's trench. His bravery and firm leading of his company under heavy shell fire was particularly noted by his Colonel.

✧ ✧ ✧

Lieutenant MacDonnell Campbell, Lancashire Fusiliers, who has been killed in action, was the second son of Mr. Robert M. Campbell, Dungiven. He was cashier in the Larne branch of the Northern Banking Co. previous to joining the Army. He served for some time in Egypt and was subsequently sent to France. His two brothers are also serving in the Army, one with the Australian Forces and the other in the North Irish Horse.

✧ ✧ ✧

Second Lieutenant E. W. G. Hind, Royal Irish Rifles, who has been killed in action, was the eldest son of Mr. W. E. Hind, The Cottage, Demesne Road, Hollywood. Lieut. Hind fell in the advance on July 1st whilst gallantly leading his men in an attack on the German trenches. On the outbreak of the war he was on the staff of Messrs. Graham and Co., accountants, Belfast, but at once offered his services and obtained his commission in the Royal Irish Rifles.

✧ ✧ ✧

Lieutenant Myles Henry O'Donovan, Royal Munster Fusiliers, attached 8th Battalion, was killed in action on June 21st, 1916. He was the second son of The O'Donovan, C.B., D.L., J.P., and Madam O'Donovan, of Liss Ard, Skibbereen. Lieut. O'Donovan was in his 20th year, and was educated at Bilton Grange, Rugby, and Marlborough College, Wilts. He had not been long gazetted to his regiment, but had already earned the highest tribute from his Colonel and officers for his fine soldierly qualities.

1. LIEUT. D. W. MOORE, Machine Gun Corps.	2. CAPT. W. D. HOLMES, Canadian Light Infantry. D.S.O.	3. LIEUT. I. W. USHER, Royal Irish Regiment.
4. CAPT. C. F. K. EWART, Royal Irish Rifles.	5 LT.-COL. R. J. W. MAWHINNEY, R.A.M.C. C.B.	6. CAPT. J. F. RUTTLEDGE, 2nd West York Regiment. Military Cross.
7. LT. MacDONNELL CAMPBELL, Lancashire Fusiliers.	8. LIEUT. E. W. G. HIND, Royal Irish Rifles.	9. LIEUT. M. H. O'DONOVAN, Royal Munster Fusiliers.

OUR HEROES.

Second Lieutenant Robert Warnock, 7th Battalion Royal Scots Fusiliers, who has been decorated by the King at Buckingham Palace with the Military Cross for gallant and distinguished service in the field, is the only son of Mr. S. Warnock, Lenzie, and a nephew of Mr. W. W. Warnock, of Lis-na-Tragh, Sutton.

✧ ✧ ✧

Captain N. L. Joynt, R.A.M.C., attached 255th Tunnelling Corps, Royal Engineers, has recently been awarded the Military Cross for gallantry and devotion to duty in the field. Captain Joynt is a son of Mr. A. E. Joynt, Manager of the National Bank, Doneraile, Co. Cork.

✧ ✧ ✧

Second Lieut. Ailwyn Egerton Copeland Trimble, who has received two distinctions for bravery during engagements on May 6 and 11, is the third son of Mr. W. Copeland Trimble, J.P., Enniskillen. He was wounded on 21st June when in the trenches with his battalion, the 7th Royal Inniskillings, in which at the time he was commanding his company. Mr. Trimble was a divinity student, and on the outbreak of war offered himself for a commission at the Regimental Depôt, and pending the reply joined with his friends, the Trinity lot, in the 7th Dublins, and when at the Curragh received orders to join his battalion at Fermoy. Mr. Trimble's elder brother, R. Stuart, is the signal officer of the 6th Royal Irish Fusiliers, and his younger brother, Noel, fell in action when warning his men of the 8th Inniskillings of the approaching poison gas on 22nd April.

✧ ✧ ✧

Temporary Lieutenant-Colonel Nixon, D.S.O., 1st King's Own Royal Lancaster Regiment, was educated at Willington College and Sandhurst. He served all through the South African war, set out to France with the original Expeditionary Force, and was severely wounded at Le Cateau. He afterwards commanded his regiment at the front, and was mentioned in despatches and received the D.S.O. He is the eldest son of Major-General A. J. Nixon, D.L., late R.A., of Clone, Ballyraggett, Co. Kilkenny.

✧ ✧ ✧

Lieutenant-Colonel Lord Crofton, 13th Northumberland Fusiliers, of Moate Park, Roscommon, was in the battle of Loos and Hill 70, and since then has been in the trenches in France. He has been mentioned in despatches of June 16th, 1916, for distinguished service. Lord Crofton was last year elected a representative Peer for Ireland. His son, the Hon. Edward Crofton, is also in the trenches with the 14th Northumberland Fusiliers.

✧ ✧ ✧

Temporary Captain F. C. Atkinson Fleming, M.B., R.A.M.C., attached 8th Batt. Royal Inniskilling Fusiliers, has been awarded the Military Cross "for conspicuous gallantry and devotion to duty when tending casualties during and subsequent to a hostile attack. He worked without ceasing under difficult and dangerous conditions." Captain F. C. Atkinson Fleming is the only son of Mr. Frederick Fleming, K.C., and Mrs. Fleming, of 69 Merrion Square, Dublin.

✧ ✧ ✧

Second Lieutenant S. J. Parr, attached 1st Royal Dragoons, son of Mr. and Mrs. R. W. Parr, Ballyboy, Athboy, has been awarded the Military Cross for bravery in the field at Loos. He was educated at St. Andrew's College and is well known in football circles, being a prominent Irish Rugby International forward and a member of Wanderers' Football Club. At the outbreak of the war he offered his services and has been through many engagements in France. His brother, Captain V. H. Parr, is serving with the Inniskillings.

✧ ✧ ✧

Captain E. J. Nixon, R.A., was educated at Cheltenham College and the R.M.A., Woolwich. He went to Mesopotamia in the 30th Native Mountain Battery of Artillery at the commencement of the war, and served through the various engagements in the advance up the Tigris, and then became A.D.C. to Sir John Nixon. He was mentioned three times in despatches and awarded the Military Cross. He is the second son of Major-General Nixon, late R.A., of Clone, Ballyraggett, Co. Kilkenny.

✧ ✧ ✧

Lieutenant H. Manifold Mitchell, Royal Munster Fusiliers, has been awarded the Military Cross "for conspicuous gallantry during a hostile attack. He rallied his men, reconstructed his trench and re-organized his defences under difficult circumstances. His personal courage and power of command helped much to avert a serious situation. Lieutenant Mitchell is the youngest son of the late Dr. A. G. Mitchell, and of Mrs. Mitchell, The Island, Kinnetty. His elder brother, Lieut. Courtland G. Mitchell, 6th Royal Irish Regiment, was dangerously wounded in France in May, 1916.

1. LIEUT. R. WARNOCK,
7th Royal Scots Fusiliers.
Military Cross.

2. CAPT. N. L. JOYNT,
R.A.M.C.
Military Cross.

3. LIEUT. A. E. C. TRIMBLE,
7th Royal Inniskilling Fusiliers.

4. LIEUT.-COL. NIXON,
1st King's Own Lancs. Regiment.
D.S.O.

5. LIEUT.-COL. LORD CROFTON,
13th Northumberland Fusiliers.

6. CAPT. F. C. A. FLEMING,
R.A.M.C.
Military Cross.

7. LIEUT. S. J. PARR,
1st Royal Dragoons.
Military Cross.

8. CAPT. E. J. NIXON,
Royal Artillery.
Military Cross.

9. LIEUT. H. M. MITCHELL,
Royal Munster Fusiliers.
Military Cross.

OUR HEROES.

Lieutenant J. Ernest Richey, Royal Engineers, has been awarded the Military Cross for gallant and distinguished services in the field. Lieut. Richey is the son of the Rev. J. Richey, M.A., of Ballymully, Tullahogue, Co. Tyrone. He was educated at St. Columba's College and Trinity College, Dublin. He was a Fellow of the Royal Geological Survey and was attached to the Geological Survey of Scotland.

⋄ ⋄ ⋄

Captain Dermott McCalmont, who has been mentioned in General Smuts' despatches of May 8th, 1916, for gallant and distinguished conduct in the field, is the well-known owner of The Tetrarch and other racehorses, and is a well-known sportsman. He has been through the campaign in East Africa with General Smuts as military secretary.

⋄ ⋄ ⋄

Second Lieutenant James Stapleton, Royal Field Artillery, has been awarded the Military Cross for conspicuous bravery at the battle of St. Eloi. Lieut. Stapleton was well known in Rugby and rowing circles, and before joining the colours was an officer of the Pembroke Municipal Council. He is a son of Mr. and Mrs. Stapleton, Partevine, Strand road, Merrion, and was educated at Blackrock College.

⋄ ⋄ ⋄

Major Warren J. Peacock, 9th Batt. Royal Inniskilling Fusiliers, has been awarded the D.S.O. for gallant and distinguished service in the field. Major Peacock has seen much active service during the war, and has been mentioned in despatches.

⋄ ⋄ ⋄

Colonel A. L. F. Bate, A.M.S., is a Dublin man, having obtained his qualifications through the Royal College of Surgeons, Ireland. He entered the Army in 1886, attaining the rank of Major in 1899, Lieut.-Colonel in 1906, and Colonel in 1916. He served in the Sikkim Expedition in 1888, and in India 13 years altogether. He also served in South Africa, 1899-1902, as S.M.O. in Zululand; took part in the operations in Natal (relief of Ladysmith); was secretary and registrar to the P.M.O. at Pietermaritzburg, and O.C. at Machadodorp. He holds the Queen's Medal and two clasps, also the King's Medal and two clasps, and has served throughout the present war, being mentioned in despatches by Sir John French and Sir Douglas Haig. The now famous sanatorium established by Col. Bate close behind the lines has done much for our armies, and on a recent visit of inspection Mr. Asquith was very enthusiastic in his praise of Colonel Bate for the excellence of the arrangements. Some idea of the splendid work of the institution may be gathered from the fact that since December last 13,000 patients have passed through its hospitable doors. Colonel Bate is a brother of Mr. A. L. Bate, Eden Park, Kingstown.

⋄ ⋄ ⋄

Captain J. Ritty, Inniskilling Fusiliers, who has been awarded the Military Cross for distinguished service in the field, had been twice previously mentioned in despatches for signal acts of bravery and devotion to duty. He is the eldest son of Lieutenant Ritty, R.M., Harbour View, Sligo.

⋄ ⋄ ⋄

Captain I. W. Corkey, M.B., R.A.M.C., has been awarded the Military Cross for distinguished service in the field. Capt. Corkey is the only son of the late Mr. I. Corkey, Warrenpoint, Co. Down, and of Mrs. Corkey, Ballsbridge, Dublin. On taking his degrees at Dublin University in June, 1915, he immediately obtained his commission, and has since seen considerable service with the 15th Battalion Royal Irish Rifles, and also when on leave in Dublin during Easter week was on duty for several days in the recent rebellion.

⋄ ⋄ ⋄

Second Lieutenant David M. Tidmarsh, 4th Batt. Royal Irish Regiment and Royal Flying Corps, was recently invested by the King with the Military Cross for conspicuous gallantry and skill in having wrecked three hostile aircraft. Lieut. Tidmarsh is the second son of Mr. and Mrs. Tidmarsh, Lota, Limerick.

⋄ ⋄ ⋄

Second Lieutenant Richard Turner, 6th Royal Dublin Fusiliers, was wounded in the fighting near Doirian and Ghevcheli, and was awarded the Military Cross for conspicuous gallantry in action. He is a son of Mr. David Turner, Mount Pleasant Square, Ranelagh.

1. LIEUT. J. E. RICHEY, Royal Engineers. Military Cross.	2. CAPT. DERMOTT McCALMONT.	3. LIEUT. J. STAPLETON, Military Cross.
4. MAJOR W. J. PEACOCK, 9th Royal Inniskilling Fusiliers. D.S.O.	5. COL. A. L. F. BATE, A.M.S., C.M.G.	6. CAPT. J. RITTY, Royal Inniskilling Fusiliers. Military Cross.
7. CAPT. J. W. CORKEY, R.A.M.C. Military Cross.	8. LIEUT. D. M. TIDMARSH, Royal Flying Corps. Military Cross.	9. LIEUT. R. TURNER, 6th Royal Dublin Fusiliers. Military Cross.

OUR HEROES.

Second Lieutenant Bernard Reid, 9th Batt. Royal Dublin Fusiliers, who was killed in action in France on June 28th, 1916, was a son of Mr. Michael Reid, Tower Hill, Dalkey. He was educated at St. Mary's College, Rathmines, and subsequently entered the National University, where he graduated and took a leading part in the activities of the college, being for some time editor of the *National Student,* the college magazine. He joined the Cadet Corps of the Leinster Regiment shortly after the outbreak of the war and was subsequently gazetted to the 8th Batt. Royal Dublin Fusiliers.

◇ ◇ ◇

Lieutenant Richard Brinsley Sheridan, 8th Batt. Royal Dublin Fusiliers, was killed on active service in France through the premature explosion of a bomb. He was Battalion Grenadier Officer, and as such had shown exceptional efficiency and initiative, and had been recommended for honours by his Commanding Officer. Lieut. Sheridan was in his 26th year, and was the elder son of Mr. and Mrs. John R. Sheridan, of Slievemore, Dugort, Achill Island.

◇ ◇ ◇

Lieutenant Charles E. P. Kelly was killed in action on July 2nd. He was the third son of the late Mr. T. P. Kelly and Mrs. Kelly, 63 Northumberland Road, Dublin, and was in his 27th year. He was educated at Woburn Park, Weybridge, Surrey, and Trinity College, Dublin, where he took his B.A. in December, 1913, and his M.B., B.A.O., B.Ch. in April, 1914. He went to Southport Infirmary as medical officer and later took over charge of the fever hospital at Fazakerley, near Liverpool. When released from command there, in August, 1915, he took a commission in the R.A.M.C. and proceeded to France with the 96th Field Ambulance.

◇ ◇ ◇

Captain Thomas Kevin O'Brien, 6th Batt. Connaught Rangers, who was killed in action on May 31st, 1916, in his 22nd year, was the eldest son of Dr. Thomas O'Brien, Ard-na Greine, Mitchelstown. On the outbreak of the war he was amongst the first to offer his services and obtained his commission in October, 1914, was gazetted Lieutenant on July 9th, 1915, and obtained his Captaincy on April 20, 1916.

◇ ◇ ◇

Colonel Herbert Clifford Bernard, who was killed on July 1, was the only surviving son of the late Robert Bernard, M.D., R.N., Deputy Inspector-General of Hospitals and Fleets and Honorary Surgeon to the Queen. Colonel Bernard, who was born in 1865, was educated at Llandovery School and at Derby Grammar School. He passed through Sandhurst as Queen's cadet, was gazetted to the 67th (Hampshire) Regiment in 1884, joined the Indian Army in 1885, and served in Burmah until 1905, when he joined Rattray's (45th Sikhs) as second in command. He commanded this regiment from 1909 to 1914. His war service included the Burmese Expedition (1885-89), Manipur Expedition (1891), Burmese War (1889-92), and the Chinuk Expedition (1901). On the outbreak of war he was given command of a battalion of the Royal Irish Rifles.

◇ ◇ ◇

Lieutenant Robert Bernard, younger son of the Archbishop of Dublin, and Maud his wife, was born in Dublin, 21st December, 1891; educated at Arnold House, Landulas, and at Marlborough College, where he was a member of the O.T.C.; entered Sandhurst, January, 1911; gazetted to the 1st Battalion Royal Dublin Fusiliers, March, 1912; promoted Lieutenant, November, 1913; served from October, 1912, to November, 1914, with his battalion in India; killed in action, 26th April, 1915, at Sedd-el-Bahr, the day after the Dublin Fusiliers effected a landing at the extreme point of the Gallipoli Peninsula whilst gallantly leading his men.

◇ ◇ ◇

Mr. Colin Biggs, 16th Canadian Scottish Regiment, who was killed in action about June 13th, was the third son of Lieutenant Thomas J. Biggs, R.E., and Mrs. Biggs, Dungarvan, and grandson of the Rev. John Bain, M.A., late Rector of Dungarvan, and of the Rev. Thomas Biggs, LL.D., late of Templemartin, Co. Cork. He went to Canada in 1912, but on the outbreak of the war joined the Canadian Scottish and had spent over ten months in the trenches when he fell in action in his 20th year.

◇ ◇ ◇

Captain Cecil Herbert Michael Furnell, R.G.A., who died of wounds on 30th April, 1916, at Abeele Hospital, was the fourth son of the late Mr. G. C. Furnell and of Mrs. Furnell, of Ballyclough, Co. Limerick. He was born on May 30th, 1882; was gazetted in 1902 to the R.G.A., having served in Bermuda and Egypt. He had fought with the Expeditionary Force since the commencement of the war, and commanded a heavy battery, when he was wounded by shell-fire.

◇ ◇ ◇

Lieutenant Fendall Powney Thompson, Hampshire Regiment, only son of Lieut.-Col. Powney Thompson, Indian Army, and grandson of Lieut.-General Clifford, C.B., Carn Cottage, Belturbet, was killed in action on July 2nd, 1916. When war broke out the doctors refused to pass him as fit for service owing to a slight stiffness of the left arm, the result of an accident in childhood, but being resolved to serve in some capacity he offered himself as a chauffeur, without pay, to St. John Ambulance Society, was accepted, and spent two months in France. On Colonel Thompson's return from India the facts were represented to Lord Kitchener's secretary, who said "a boy like that is worth having," and Lieutenant Thompson was eventually posted to the 3rd Batt. Hampshire Regiment, from which he joined the 1st Battalion.

1. LIEUT. B. REID, 9th Royal Dublin Fusiliers.
2. LIEUT. R. B. SHERIDAN, 8th Royal Dublin Fusiliers.
3. LIEUT. C. P. KELLY, R.A.M.C.
4. CAPT. T. K. O'BRIEN, 6th Connaught Rangers.
5. COLONEL H. C. BERNARD, Royal Irish Rifles.
6. LIEUT. R. BERNARD, 1st Royal Dublin Fusiliers.
7. MR. COLIN BIGGS, 16th Canadian Scottish.
8. CAPT. C. H. M. FURNELL, R.G.A.
9. LIEUT. F. P. THOMPSON, Hampshire Regiment.

OUR HEROES.

Lieutenant Thomas Greenwood Haughton, Royal Irish Rifles, was killed in action in France on July 1st, 1916. He was educated at Edgbaston Preparatory School, Birmingham, and St. Edmund's School, Oxford. When war broke out he at once offered his services and had been at the front since October, 1915. Lieut. Haughton was an able and enthusiastic officer and very popular with his brother-officers and men. He was a son of Mr. T. W. Haughton, J.P., Hillmount, Ballymena.

◇ ◇ ◇

Lieutenant Edward Lowry Tottenham, North Lancashire Regiment, was the eldest son of Mr. L. C. L. Tottenham, of The Grange, Moy, Co. Tyrone. He was educated at St. Bee's School, Cumberland, and entered the Royal Veterinary College, Edinburgh, in 1914. He belonged to both School and College O.T.C., and on the outbreak of the war he volunteered for service. He was joined to the Lowland Division at Stirling and was subsequently given a commission in the Loyal North Lancashires. He was transport officer for some time and then joined the 6th Batt. in Egypt. He served in the battles of 5th and 6th April when the 13th Division captured the Turkish positions in Mesopotamia, and at the repulse at Sanna-y-Hat on 9th April was reported missing and subsequently reported killed on that day.

◇ ◇ ◇

Second Lieut. Arthur Henry Tottenham, 8th Royal Inniskilling Fusiliers, was killed in action in France on June 27th last. He was educated at Mostyn House Preparatory School, Chester, and at St. Bee's School, Cumberland. When war broke out he volunteered and obtained his commission in the 8th Inniskillings. He subsequently entered and passed through Sandhurst, on leaving which he was attached to the 3rd Batt. He served in Dublin during the rebellion and was directly afterwards sent to the front.

◇ ◇ ◇

Captain Christopher James Hughes, Connaught Rangers, died from sunstroke on May 13th, 1916, while on active service in Mesopotamia. He was the only surviving son of the late Mr. Christopher Hughes, of Graigue, Co. Kilkenny, and was in his 33rd year. He joined the 3rd Connaught Rangers in 1901 and served through the South African war with the 3rd Highland Light Infantry, and was awarded the medal and clasps. He was subsequently transferred as Captain to the 4th Batt.

◇ ◇ ◇

Major Ernest Graham Hamilton, D.S.O., the Connaught Rangers, is now commanding the 1st Batt. of that regiment. He has been awarded the D.S.O. for services in Mesopotamia, where he was Brigade Major of the 9th Infantry Brigade. He went to France in August, 1914, and took part in the Retreat from Mons, and the battles of the Aisne, the Marne, Ypres, Neuve Chapelle and Festubert. He was awarded the Military Cross and has been three times mentioned in despatches.

◇ ◇ ◇

Captain Griffiths, 12th Batt. Royal Irish Rifles, was killed in action whilst leading his company in the battle of the Somme on July 1st. Capt. Griffiths was a graduate of the University of Wales, and on the outbreak of the war was Science Master in the Grammar School, Larne. He was a leading member of the Ulster Volunteers, and on entering the Army in January, 1915, joined the Ulster Division and obtained his commission in the 12th Royal Irish Rifles, where his soldiery ability gained him rapid promotion.

◇ ◇ ◇

Second Lieutenant Allan J. McClellan, 18th (attached 15th) Royal Irish Rifles, who has been killed in action, was a son of Mr. James McClellan, Ballyboley, Co. Antrim, and on the outbreak of the war was an assistant master at Larne Grammar School. He received his commission from the 16th Royal Irish Rifles, in which he was a Sergeant, being gazetted to the 18th (Reserve) Battalion. His eldest brother is second in command of a torpedo boat destroyer in the North Sea, and his youngest is serving with the 196th Western Universities Batt., Canada. Lieutenant McClellan had just passed his 21st birthday when he fell.

◇ ◇ ◇

Rev. Donald O'Sullivan, Roman Catholic Army Chaplain, was killed in action in France on July 5th, 1916, whilst courageously attending the wounded under heavy fire. He had been only two years ordained and a few months ago offered his services as an Army Chaplain. He was very popular amongst the soldiers, to whom he ministered with the utmost zeal and devotion and his early death is much regretted, especially in his native district of Killarney.

◇ ◇ ◇

Lieutenant Francis Bland Hewson, 4th Batt. York and Lancaster Regiment, who has been mentioned in Sir Douglas Haig's recent despatch for gallant and distinguished service, is the second son of Major Lionel Hewson, Direen, Kenmare. Lieut. Hewson joined the York and Lancaster Regiment in 1913 and was stationed at Sheffield until he went with his Battalion to France in the spring of 1915, and has been with them on active service ever since.

1. LIEUT. T. G. HAUGHTON, Royal Irish Rifles.	2. LIEUT. E. L. TOTTENHAM, 6th Batt. North Lancs. Regiment.	3. LIEUT. A. H. TOTTENHAM, 3rd Batt. Royal Inniskilling Fusiliers.
4. CAPT. C. J. HUGHES, 4th Batt. Connaught Rangers.	5. MAJOR E. G. HAMILTON, 1st Batt. Connaught Rangers. D.S.O.	6. CAPT. GRIFFITHS, 12th Batt. Royal Irish Rifles.
7. LIEUT. A. J. McCLELLAN, 15th Batt. Royal Irish Rifles.	8. REV. DONALD O'SULLIVAN, Army Chaplain.	9. LIEUT. F. B. HEWSON, 4th Batt. York & Lancaster Regiment.

OUR HEROES.

Second Lieutenant J. S. Kirker Hunter, Special Reserve of Officers, Royal Field Artillery, who was killed in action on June 30th, 1916, was the elder son of Mr. R. J. Hunter, B.L., of Dromore, Co. Down, and 142 Royal Avenue, Belfast. He was educated at the Academical Institution, Banbridge, where he was a very distinguished pupil, and in 1911 was appointed to the Irish Land Commission. In 1913 he was appointed, after examination, to the Chinese Imperial Customs Service and was stationed at Shanghai, but the climate not agreeing with him he returned home in 1914, and when war was declared was amongst the first to offer his services. In August, 1914, he joined the North Irish Horse, received his commission in the Special Reserve of Officers in October, 1915, and went to the front in February last. He was one of the officers selected for special training as an artillery observation officer in the R.F.C., and was about to proceed when he was ordered to return to his battery to take part in the offensive, and fell in action on June 30th.

⋄ ⋄ ⋄

Captain P. Cruickshank, Royal Inniskilling Fusiliers, who fell in action during the offensive on July 1st, was, prior to the outbreak of the war, editor of the "Tyrone Constitution," and a well-known and popular figure in Unionist circles in the North of Ireland. He was a journalist of much ability and a talented writer. On the outbreak of the war he at once volunteered. He served with the Tyrone battalion, and was soon promoted Captain. He went to the front in October, 1915, and had, previous to the action in which he fell, been twice wounded.

⋄ ⋄ ⋄

Lieutenant David Matthews, Connaught Rangers, who was killed in action, was the son of Mr. William Matthews, Hardwood, Aughrim, Co. Galway. On the formation of the 16th Division he joined its Cadet Corps and was afterwards gazetted to a commission in the Connaught Rangers. Previous to the outbreak of war he had been on the staff of Messrs. Shaw and Son, Mullingar, but at once offered his services.

⋄ ⋄ ⋄

Captain James Claude Beauchamp Proctor, M.A., LL.D. (Inniskillings), who has been killed in action, was the eldest son of the late Mr. James E. Proctor, solicitor, Limavady, and of Mrs. Proctor, Tullydoey House, Moy. He was educated at Reading School, Berks, and at Trinity College, Dublin. He practised as a solicitor and afterwards joined the North-West Circuit. He was Unionist in politics, a member of the Ulster Unionist Council, organiser and secretary of the Limavady Unionist Club, and also county organiser and secretary of the U.V.F. On the outbreak of war he obtained a commission in the Inniskillings.

Major H. Albert Uprichard, 13th Royal Irish Rifles, who was killed in action, was the second son of the late Mr. H. A. Uprichard, Elmfield, Gilford, Co. Down. He was educated at Leighton Park, Reading. Major Uprichard was a keen sportsman, having won many point-to-point races. He was a member of the Co. Down Staghounds, and in 1914 was elected Master of the Iveagh Harriers on the resignation of his brother, Mr. W. F. Uprichard. He received his majority in February last.

⋄ ⋄ ⋄

Second Lieutenant Kenneth K. Ross, 4th Royal Irish Rifles, who had been previously reported wounded and missing, is now reported killed in action on the British front in September last. He was a son of Mr. George H. Ross, of the firm of Messrs. William Ross and Sons, Belfast. His brother was also killed in action last year.

⋄ ⋄ ⋄

Lieutenant Alexander Percy McMullen, eldest son of Alexander Robert McMullen, Dixie, Ontario, formerly of Tullamore, King's County, was lost in the "Invincible" off Jutland. He joined the Navy through Osborne Naval College. He was promoted to Engineer Lieutenant in 1914, and was in the "Invincible" in the battle off the Falkland Islands. He was a very promising officer and very popular with his comrades. He was 24 years of age.

⋄ ⋄ ⋄

Second Lieutenant Myles Whitford, 7th Batt. Royal Irish Rifles, was killed during a gas attack by the Germans about the 30th April. He was a son of the late Mr. John Whitford, Templeshannon, Enniscorthy, and soon after the outbreak of the war he enlisted in the 7th Leinsters, subsequently obtaining his commission in the 7th Batt. Royal Irish Rifles. At the time of his death Lieutenant Whitford was attached for a few days to the Dublin Fusiliers. His Commanding Officer speaks in the highest terms of Lieutenant Whitford's efficiency as an officer and his zeal and devotion to duty.

⋄ ⋄ ⋄

Second Lieutenant T. R. H. Dorman, 2nd Battalion Munster Fusiliers, only son of the late Major T. Dorman, R.A.M.C., Kinsale, was severely wounded and taken prisoner by the Germans on February 23rd last. His relatives have been informed that he died the following day, never having recovered consciousness from the effects of his wounds. Lieut. Dorman was educated at the Royal School, Armagh, and previous to the outbreak of the war was a medical student of Trinity College, Dublin.

OUR HEROES

1. LIEUT. J. S. K. HUNTER, Royal Field Artillery.
2. CAPT. P. CRUICKSHANK, Royal Inniskilling Fusiliers.
3. LIEUT. D. MATTHEWS, Connaught Rangers.
4. CAPT. C. B. PROCTOR, Royal Inniskilling Fusiliers.
5. MAJOR H. A. UPRICHARD, 13th Royal Irish Rifles.
6. LIEUT. KENNETH ROSS, 4th Batt. Royal Irish Rifles.
7. LIEUT. A. P. McMULLEN, H.M.S. "Invincible."
8. LIEUT. M. WHITFORD, 7th Batt. Royal Irish Rifles.
9. LIEUT. T. R. H. DORMAN, 2nd Batt. Munster Fusiliers.

OUR HEROES.

Lieutenant John Frederick Healy, Royal Irish Rifles, killed in action in France on 2nd July, 1916, aged 19 years, was the elder son of Mr. and Mrs. George F. Healy, Peafield, Blackrock, Co. Dublin. He was educated at Avoca School, Blackrock, from whence he went to Elstow (Bedford County) School, where he remained about five years, being in his time both house and school captain. He also served while there in the School O.T.C. He then entered Trinity College, Dublin, and joined the 3rd Royal Irish Rifles before he was 18 years old. He served about 16 months in the army, including nearly four months at the front. He was attached to the West Belfast Regiment at the time of his death.

Captain James Samuel Davidson, Royal Irish Rifles, who has been killed in action, was the only surviving son of Mr. Samuel Cleland Davidson, Seacourt, Bangor, Co. Down, founder and managing director of the Sirocco Engineering Works, Belfast, of which Capt. Davidson was prior to the outbreak of the war a director and general manager. He was amongst the first to answer his country's call and received his commission in the County Down Battalion Royal Irish Rifles, and was quickly promoted Captain. Captain B. Spender, General Staff Headquarters, in writing to Mr. Davidson on the death of his son states: " I am told your son fell after gallantry which deserved the Victoria Cross. Though badly wounded he had insisted in carrying on, and was killed when his men had at last persuaded him to consent to letting them carry him back."

Lieutenant John Malby Hanly, R.N., who was killed in the naval action in the North Sea on May 31st, 1916, was the younger son of Lieutenant-Colonel and Mrs. Edward Hanly, of 57 Eaton place, London, S.W., and Avonmore House, Co. Wicklow, and was in his 28th year. Lieut. Hanly was on board H.M.S. Queen Mary, and was a most promising young officer.

Captain Charles Moore Johnston, youngest and only surviving son of Charles Johnston, Esq., J.P., Portadown, Co. Armagh, born 1886, was killed at the battle of the Somme, July 1916. He was educated at Lurgan and Campbell Colleges, and Royal School of Mines, London, and was member of the R.S.M. rowing eight and Rugby XV. 1904-05. Before enlisting in the Royal Irish Fusiliers he was a company commander in the U.V.F.

Major A. P. Jenkins, Royal Irish Rifles, who has been killed in action, was the eldest son of the late Mr. W. J. Jenkins, formerly of Windsor Avenue, Belfast, who died recently in Dublin. Major Jenkins was a prominent member of the Ulster Volunteers and was very popular in Lisburn, where he resided.

Captain E. W. Barrett, Royal Flying Corps, who has been killed in action, was a son of Mr. James H. Barrett, Bangor, Co. Down. He was educated at Campbell College, Belfast; Royal School, Armagh; and Queen's University, Belfast. He was a noted athlete and a well-known cricketer and football player, as well as a keen golfer. Captain Barrett was killed on May 29th when on patrol duty, in an attack on two German machines, having the previous day attacked and skilfully outmanœuvred a Fokker.

Second Lieutenant J. W. Salter, 11th Batt. Royal Irish Rifles, who has been killed in action, was the elder son of Mr. and Mrs. Salter, Skibbereen. He was educated at Kilkenny College, and subsequently entered the Civil Service Rifles. He belonged to the Civil Service Rifles and was well-known in Rugby circles. He obtained his commission in the 18th Batt. Royal Irish Rifles in March, 1915, and was later gazetted to the 11th Battalion. He went to France in February, 1916, and was killed during the offensive on July 1st.

Mr. John Creagh, S.A.M.R., eldest son of the late Francis Creagh, The Castle, Listowel, Co. Kerry, and of Mrs. Creagh, Dalkey, Co. Dublin, was educated at Portora Royal School, Enniskillen. Joined B.P.'s army from Cape Police, and fought all through the Boer war, where he got the medals and had a commission. He was in the siege of Kimberley, and afterwards at the relief of Mafeking, and was one of the three first to enter, and was severely wounded by a splinter from a shell which killed his horse under him. He joined the present war for active service, was through the successful campaign in German West Africa. He died on June 15th of gastritis, contracted while on active service.

Second Lieutenant Victor M. Giles, 7th Royal Irish Rifles, was killed in action on June 28th, 1916. He was the eldest son of Mr. and Mrs. Marshall Giles, Navan, Co. Meath, and was educated at Preston College, Navan, and King's College. He joined the Cadet Corps, 7th Leinsters, in May, 1915, and was gazetted to the 7th R.I.R. in October of the same year. He had been on active service with his regiment for the past six months and was a very capable and courageous officer

1. LIEUT. J. F. HEALY, Royal Irish Rifles.	2. CAPT. J. S. DAVIDSON, Royal Irish Rifles.	3. LIEUT. J. M. B. HANLY, Royal Navy.
4. CAPT. C. M. JOHNSTON, Royal Irish Fusiliers.	5. MAJOR A. P. JENKINS, Royal Irish Rifles.	6. CAPT. E. W. BARRETT, Royal Flying Corps.
7. LIEUT. J. W. SALTER, 11th Batt. Royal Irish Rifles.	8. MR. JOHN CREAGH, S.A.M.R.	9. LIEUT. V. M. GILES, 7th Batt. Royal Irish Rifles.

OUR HEROES.

Second Lieutenant Claud A. L. Walker was killed in action on July 11, 1916. He joined the Public Schools' Corps in September, 1914, and shortly afterwards was nominated to a cadetship in the Royal Military College, Sandhurst. He received his commission in the 2nd Batt. Royal Inniskilling Fusiliers in May, 1915, and two months afterwards, on July 12, left to join his battalion in France. He was 21 years of age, and was the second son of the Rev. Dr. Walker, Rector of St. Matthew's, Shankill, Belfast.

◇ ◇ ◇

Lieutenant Finlay Kerr, Royal Irish Regiment, who was killed in action on July 4th, whilst gallantly leading his platoon against a very strong German position, was the only son of Mr. Finlay Kerr, M.R.C.V.S., Clarinda Park, West, Kingstown. He was educated at Carrig School, Kingstown, and St. Bee's, Cumberland, and was a student in Engineering at the Royal College of Science, Dublin.

◇ ◇ ◇

Lieutenant W. A. D. Goodwin, York and Lancaster Regiment, was the only son of Mr. Singleton Goodwin and Mrs. Goodwin, Ballyroe, Tralee, Co. Kerry. Lieut. Goodwin was educated at Burnsgrove School and was a scholar and undergraduate of Corpus Christi College, Oxford. He obtained a commission in November, 1914, and was gazetted to the York and Lancaster Regiment in January, 1915. He went to the front in April, 1916, and was acting as signalling officer to his battalion at the time he was killed in action on July 1st, 1916, in his 23rd year.

◇ ◇ ◇

Lieutenant William C. McConnell, Royal Irish Rifles, who was killed in action on July 8th, was the youngest son of Sir Robert McConnell, Bart., D.L., Glen Dhu, Strandtown, Belfast. He was gazetted to the Royal Irish Rifles in October, 1914, and was attached to a battalion of the regiment as machine-gun officer in September, 1915. He was educated at Shibbington House, Fareham, and on the outbreak of war was a partner in the firm of McConnell and Bailey, engineers, London.

◇ ◇ ◇

Lt.=Colonel the Hon. Anthony Morton Henley, 5th Royal Irish Lancers, who was awarded the D.S.O. on June 3rd, 1916, served in the South African War with the Imperial Yeomanry, and took part in the operations in the Transvaal, including actions in Johannesburg and Pretoria, also in the operations on the Zululand frontier and in Cape Colony, for which he was awarded the Queen's Medal with three clasps, and the King's Medal with two clasps.

◇ ◇ ◇

Second Lieutenant Thomas H. Clesham, Manchester Regiment, who was killed in action in the offensive on July 1st, was the eldest son of the late Rev. T. Clesham, M.A., Rector of Aasleigh, and Mrs. Clesham, Caherduff, Cong. He graduated at Trinity College, Dublin, and subsequently went to South Africa to take up an important post in the mining fields. On the outbreak of the war he joined the forces of General Botha and took his full share in the campaign, on the termination of which he hurried home to take his part in the Western field. He was gazetted to a lieutenancy in the Manchester Regiment and joined the Flying Corps until he became a fully qualified aviator. Lieut. Clesham was a splendid type of officer and beloved by his comrades. He fell just as he led his men over the parapet and was killed instantly.

◇ ◇ ◇

Second Lieutenant J. L. Hay, killed in action on the 3rd July, was the only son of Mr. W. L. Hay, Clonbrock and Grange, Co. Galway. He was educated at the Grammar School, Galway, from which he passed into the college as a student of engineering. He was in his second year when the war broke out and was among the first to volunteer for the new army. He received a commission in the 15th Batt. Northumberland Fusiliers, but was subsequently transferred to the 12th, and sent to France in October last. Since then he has been in active service, with the exception of a few days' leave. In the words of the Captain of his company: " He met his death gloriously, leading his platoon in an attack on a wood which was finally captured."

◇ ◇ ◇

Lieutenant W. T. Richardson, Ulster Division, youngest son of Mrs. Richardson, St. Dolough's, Co. Dublin, killed in action on 1st July, was a well-known athlete, and for a number of years was a prominent member of the Old Wesley Rugby Football Club. Early in March, 1915, he obtained his commission in the 12th Batt. Royal Irish Rifles, and having completed his training left for the front with his regiment some ten months ago, but was attached to the Infantry Brigade (Ulster Division) at the time of his death. From reports to hand we learn he was one of the first to leave his trench on the opening day of the " big advance," but had only reached the parapet when he was shot through the head. Lieut. Richardson was a popular official of the Midland Great Western Railway, Broadstone.

◇ ◇ ◇

Second Lieutenant Geoffrey R. Bible, Royal Sussex Regiment, who was killed in action during the great offensive whilst gallantly leading his section forward, was the only surviving son of Mr. H. Bible, 50 Grosvenor Road, Dublin. Lieut. Bible was attached to the machine gun company of the Royal Sussex Regiment, and the gallant conduct of the machine gun corps earned a special tribute of admiration from the Brigadier-General.

1. LIEUT. C. A. L. WALKER, 2nd Batt. Royal Inniskilling Fusiliers.	2. LIEUT. FINLAY KERR, Royal Irish Regiment.	3. LIEUT. W. A. D. GOODWIN, York & Lancs. Regiment.
4. LIEUT. W. C. McCONNELL, Royal Irish Rifles.	5. LIEUT.-COL. A. M. HENLEY, 5th Lancers. D.S.O.	6. LIEUT. T. H. CLESHAM, Manchester Regiment.
7. LIEUT. J. L. HAY, 12th Batt. Northumberland Fusiliers.	8. LIEUT. W. T. RICHARDSON, 12th Batt. Royal Irish Rifles.	9. LIEUT. G. R. BIBLE, Royal Sussex Regiment.

OUR HEROES.

Lieut. Leonard William Hugh Stevenson, younger son of Mr. Isaac Stevenson, Hampstead Hall, Londonderry, and nephew of Mr. J. M. MacCaw, M.P., was educated at Sherbourne, where he was in the O.T.C. He entered Trinity College, Dublin, June, 1914, and passed his Junior Fresh whilst awaiting his commission. He received his commission in the 9th Royal Inniskilling Fusiliers (Tyrones) in October, 1914, and went to France with the regiment in October, 1915. He was awarded the Military Cross in May, 1916, for conspicuous gallantry and promptness during a successful raid on the enemy's trenches. His quickness at a critical moment saved two minutes, and the enemy were actually issuing from their dug-outs as his party entered their trenches. Later he organised a party, and brought in a wounded man under fire. He was killed, in his 20th year, whilst leading his men in the famous charge of the Ulster Division on July 1st.

◇ ◇ ◇

Second Lieutenant A. M. Rose-Cleland, Royal Dublin Fusiliers, was killed in action in France on July 1st. He was the only child of Mr. H. S. Rose-Cleland, Redford House, Moy, and was educated at Dungannon Royal School and St. Columba's College, Rathfarnham. At the outbreak of the war he was in the employment of the well-known firm of M'Laughlin and Harvey, Ltd., Belfast, but at once enlisted in the Royal Inniskilling Fusiliers, and was gazetted Second Lieutenant in February, 1915.

◇ ◇ ◇

Second Lieut. Francis T. G. Corscadden, Royal Irish Rifles, who has died of wounds, was the youngest son of Mr. T. Corscadden, Hollymount, Manorhamilton, Co. Leitrim. He was educated at Portora Royal School, Enniskillen, and Trinity College, Dublin, and before the war was on the staff of the Ocean Accident and Guarantee Corporation (Limited), Belfast. He joined the Royal Irish Rifles as a private at the beginning of the war and was promoted to a commission in January, 1915. He was sent to France in September, 1915, and was home on his first leave just one month before his death.

◇ ◇ ◇

Captain Randolph Noel Murray, Royal Inniskilling Fusiliers, the official report of whose death in a German field hospital, at the age of 21, has reached the War Office through the American Embassy, was the only son of Mr. George M. P. Murray, F.R.C.S.I., of Dublin. Educated at Monkstown Park School and Bromsgrove, he entered Trinity College, Dublin, in 1912, where he studied in the Medical School for two years. In September, 1914, he obtained his commission in the newly-formed 7th Battalion of the Inniskillings, and was gazetted Lieutenant in November of the same year and Captain in last April. He was reported missing on April 27th.

Lieut.-Colonel Arthur Maxwell, who has been mentioned in despatches and awarded brevet promotion for gallant and distinguished service in the field, was born in Dublin and belonged to a well-known County Down family. He received his commission in the Post Office Rifles in 1900. He went to France in March, 1915, and since October last was in command of his battalion. Colonel Maxwell was wounded in May, 1916.

◇ ◇ ◇

Captain William Tillie Dickson, 6th Inniskilling Fusiliers, was severely wounded while leading his company in the attack on the German trenches on July 1st, and succumbed to his wounds on the 9th. He was the eldest son of Mr. and Mrs. James Dickson, Miltown House, Dungannon. He was educated at Uppingham and was married a few years ago to a daughter of Mr. Edward Coey, D.L., of Merville, Whitehouse. On the outbreak of the war he obtained his commission in the 6th Inniskilling Fusiliers, with whom he served at Gallipoli. He was subsequently invalided home and was attached to the 1st Battalion, with which he went to France.

◇ ◇ ◇

Second Lieutenant C. H. Kinsman, 16th Batt. King's Liverpool Regiment, was killed in action in the battle of St. Eloi on March 28th, 1916. He was a son of Mr. Henry Kinsman, Ashgrove Villas, Glenburn Park, Belfast. Lieut. Kinsman was on the surveying staff of the Congested Districts Board, but when the call of his country came he enlisted in the 5th Batt. Connaught Rangers, and subsequently, on receiving a commission, was transferred to the 16th Batt. Liverpool Regiment. He went to the front in the summer of 1915, where he served with the 10th Liverpool Scottish and was transferred to the 1st Cheshire Field Co. Royal Engineers a few days before he fell in action.

◇ ◇ ◇

Second Lieutenant Hubert P. Fisher, 3rd Shropshire Light Infantry, attached Gloucester Regiment, was killed in action in France on July 9th, 1916, whilst leading his platoon to the first German trenches. Lieut. Fisher was in his 20th year, and was educated at the High School, Waterford, and Chesterfield College, Birr. He obtained his commission in May, 1915.

◇ ◇ ◇

Second Lieutenant Robert Taylor Montgomery, 9th Royal Irish Fusiliers, who was killed in action, was the second surviving son of Mr. T. J. Montgomery, High Street, Portadown. At the outbreak of the war he was commandant of the local medical corps of the U.V.F., and was amongst the first to volunteer for active service. He enlisted in the 9th Royal Irish Fusiliers and received his commission in May, 1915. Lieut. Montgomery was an enthusiastic athlete and had won several medals in competitions.

1. LIEUT. W. H. STEVENSON, 9th Royal Inniskilling Fusiliers.
2. LIEUT. A. M. ROSE-CLELAND, Royal Dublin Fusiliers.
3. LIEUT. F. T. CORSCADDEN, Royal Irish Rifles.
4. CAPT. R. N. MURRAY, 7th Royal Inniskilling Fusiliers.
5. LIEUT.-COL. A. MAXWELL,
6. CAPT. W. T. DICKSON, 6th Inniskilling Fusiliers.
7. LIEUT. C. H. KINSMAN, 16th Batt. King's Liverpool Regiment.
8. LIEUT. H. D. FISHER, 3rd Shropshire Light Infantry.
9. LIEUT. R. T. MONTGOMERY, 9th Royal Irish Fusiliers.

OUR HEROES.

Lieutenant James Dermot Neill, Machine Gun Corps, 108th Brigade Ulster Division. Killed on the 1st July in the splendid attack made by this Division in the battle of the Somme. He was 29 years of age. Educated at Royal Academical Institution, Belfast, and Alderham School, Herts, on the outbreak of war he was among the first to join the 13th Batt. Royal Irish Rifles (the Down Regiment), afterwards joining the Machine Gun Company of his Brigade. He was on the Committee of the Royal North of Ireland Yacht Club and a member of Holywood Golf Club, in both of which sports he was an enthusiast. Mr. Neill was the eldest son of Mr. Sharman D. Neill, Donegall Place, Belfast, and Cultra, Co. Down.

✧ ✧ ✧

Second Lieutenant Thomas White, Loyal North Lancashire Regiment, who was killed in action in France on the 8th July, 1916, was the younger son of W. J. White, of Winston Gardens, Knock, Belfast. He was educated at the Royal Belfast Academical Institution, and served his apprenticeship with Messrs. Thomas McMullan & Co., Belfast. He afterwards went to London, where he became Secretary to the firm of Harker, Stagg & Morgan, Ltd., of which his uncle, Mr. Thomas White, is a director. Deceased joined the Inns of Court Training Corps in April, 1915, and was given a commission in the Loyal North Lancashire Regiment in the following August.

✧ ✧ ✧

Second Lieutenant Douglas Gunning, Royal Inniskilling Fusiliers, who was killed in action during the recent offensive, was a son of the late Mr. Sinclair Gunning and Mrs. Gunning, Willoughby Place, Enniskillen. He had fought as a private with the " Pals' " Battalion, Royal Dublin Fusiliers, through the Dardanelles campaign. From there he was invalided home, and in December, 1915, received his commission in the Inniskillings.

✧ ✧ ✧

Second Lieutenant Hugh Alexander Small, 20th King's (Liverpool) Regiment, who was killed in action on 11th July, was the only son of Mr. Alexr. Small, Keady, Co. Armagh, and former student of McCrea-M'Gee College, Londonderry. He was awarded the Military Cross for conspicuous gallantry during a heavy bombardment by the enemy on 9th May. He displayed great coolness, helped to dress the wounded, and after being himself covered with earth by the explosion of a shell, continued to work till all the wounded had been removed.

✧ ✧ ✧

Lieut.-Colonel Carroll Charles Macnamara, Royal Irish Rifles, who was fatally wounded in action on July 1st, 1916, while commanding his regiment, was the elder son of Mr. Charles Nottidge Macnamara, F.R.C.S., of Chorley Wood, Herts. He was educated at Winchester and received his commission in 1896. While with his regiment in South Africa he was appointed A.D.C. to Lord Milner. He had seen much service in India and China, and in 1908 was seconded with the Egyptian Army and held the rank of Kaimakam Commanding the Equatorial Battalion, which he commanded on active service, and received the Order of the Nile. He resigned his command in Egypt to serve in Gallipoli. He was Staff Major to General Lord Hampden, and was wounded. He afterwards served as Brigade Major at Bedford, and in May last rejoined the Royal Irish Rifles at the front.

✧ ✧ ✧

Lieutenant George Guy Finlay, who has been killed in action, was the second and only surviving son of Colonel Henry T. Finlay, D.L., of Corkagh, Clondalkin, Co. Dublin. He was 26 years of age. Lieutenant Finlay volunteered for active service from the Malay States at the outbreak of the war, and arrived in Ireland in December, 1914. He obtained a commission in the Royal Irish Regiment in January, 1915, and in May of the same year he was attached to a battalion of that regiment, with which he served up to the time of his death.

✧ ✧ ✧

Lieutenant Arthur Samuel Montgomery, 5th Batt. Royal Inniskilling Fusiliers, died from dysentry, contracted whilst on active service, at the 5th Canadian General Hospital, on June 21st, 1916. He was the only son of Mr. T. B. Montgomery and Mrs. Montgomery, Annerville, Clonmel, and was educated at Cheltenham, Glenalmond College, Perth, and Trinity College, Dublin. On the outbreak of the war he served for six months in the Remount Department and subsequently obtained his commission in the 5th Royal Inniskilling Fusiliers, with whom he sailed for Salonika in October last.

✧ ✧ ✧

Second Lieutenant Robert Victor Hamilton, 9th Batt. Royal Irish Rifles, who was killed in action on July 1st, 1916, was a son of Mr. James Hamilton, 2 Glendarra, Charnwood Avenue, Belfast. He was educated at the Royal Academic Institution, Belfast. At the outbreak of the war he held an appointment in the Treasury Department, Dublin Castle. He joined the Army as a cadet in March, 1915, and after training was gazetted to the 9th R.I.R. in September, 1915, and in March, 1916, went to the front.

✧ ✧ ✧

Lieutenant G. M. Rogers, 13th Royal Irish Rifles (1st County Down Volunteers), killed in action 1st July, was the only son of Mr. G. M. Rogers, Hazelbank, Banbridge, who is a prominent figure in the flax trade. Lieut. Rogers, who had been prominently identified with the Down Volunteers, was in Courtrai in charge of his father's business when the war broke out, but succeeded in getting away before the German invasion. On returning he joined the Ulster Division, and received his commission as Second Lieutenant on the 12th November, 1914.

1. LIEUT. J. D. NEILL,
13th Royal Irish Rifles.

2. LIEUT. T. WHITE,
North Lancs. Regiment.

3. LIEUT. D. GUNNING,
Royal Inniskilling Fusiliers.

4. LIEUT. H. A. SMALL,
20th King's Liverpool Regiment.

5. LIEUT.-COLONEL C. C. MacNAMARA,
Royal Irish Rifles.

6. LIEUT. G. G. FINLAY,
Royal Irish Regiment.

7. LIEUT. A. S. MONTGOMERY,
5th Royal Inniskilling Fusiliers.

8. LIEUT R. V. HAMILTON,
9th Royal Irish Rifles.

9. LIEUT. G. M. ROGERS,
13th Royal Irish Rifles.

CORRECTIONS AND ADDITIONS.

Page 6—LIEUT. H. V. GERRARD should be Capt. H. V. Gerrard.

,, 50—LIEUT. GERARD RIBTON GORE.—Regiment should be 1st Royal Welsh Fusiliers.

,, 57/138—CAPT. J. A. BROOKE, V.C., should be Capt. J. A. O. Brooke, V.C.

,, 162—CAPT. W. FOOT, M.C. and bar, should be R.A.M.C., attached Coldstream Guards.

,, 166—CORPORAL B. J. ALLISON—Initials should be R. M.

,, 198—MAJOR V. C. M. REEVES.—Since our notice appeared Major Reeves has been mentioned in Sir John Maxwell's despatches for gallant and distinguished service in the field.